The Redivision of Labor

SUNY Series in the Anthropology of Work
JUNE NASH, EDITOR

LAUREL HERBENAR BOSSEN

Department of Anthropology

University of Pittsburgh

The Redivision of Labor

WOMEN AND ECONOMIC CHOICE IN FOUR GUATEMALAN COMMUNITIES

State University of New York Press

ALBANY

Dedicated to: Ingrid, Helen, And Frank

HD
6105
.B67
1984

Published by State University of New York Press, Albany

© 1984 State University of New York

All rights reserved

Printed in the United States of America

For information, address State University of New York Press, State University Plaza, Albany, N.Y., 12246

Library of Congress Cataloging in Publication Data

Bossen, Laurel, 1945–
   The redivision of labor.

   (SUNY series in the anthropology of work)
   Includes bibliographical references.
   1. Women—Employment—Guatemala—Case studies. 2. Women—Guatemala—Economic conditions—Case studies. 3. Women—Guatemala—Social conditions—Case studies. 4. Sex discrimination in employment—Guatemala—Case studies. 5. Work groups—Guatemala—Case studies. I. Title. II. Series.
   HD6105.B67   1983   305.4'2'097281   83–426
   ISBN 0-87395-740-7
   ISBN 0-87395-741-5 (pbk.)

10   9   8   7   6   5   4   3

Contents

v

CONTENTS

Illustrations

Acknowledgments

In writing this book, I have benefited from the encouragement and assistance of many individuals and institutions. My interest in Guatemala was first stimulated by Robert Carmack of the State University of New York at Albany whose solid scholarship and commitment to Maya studies would be hard to match. His consistent support, encouragement, and advice have been very valuable. Moreover, the enthusiastic environment for Mesoamerican studies and the many-faceted collaboration among faculty and students at SUNYA enriched my perspectives on Guatemala. The summer field schools of 1972 and 1973 in Guatemala were of great help to my subsequent research design addressing the issues of the sexual division of labor and the changing character of sexual inequality in different segments of Guatemalan society.

The major portion of my fieldwork in 1974–1975 was made possible by a research fellowship from the Organization of American States (PRA 42831) and by financial assistance from the Department of Anthropology of the State University of New York State at Albany. The final stages of writing were completed with the aid of a Faculty Grant from the University of Pittsburgh (1982).

In presenting the Guatemalan communities that form the basis for my research, I have used pseudonyms to protect the privacy of the many people who shared personal information. Thus the names of the four communities and the individuals discussed are fictitious. Nonetheless, I wish to thank the municipal officials and plantation authorities who gave me permission to conduct local research and to use their records. The plantation owners of "El Cañaveral" generously provided hospitality and access to facilities and information.

In Guatemala I received assistance from a variety of institutions and individuals with an interest in social science research. I am grateful to José Castañeda Medinilla, Director of the Instituto Indigenista Nacional, Luís Luján Muñoz, Director of the Instituto de Antropología e Historia, and Carlos Herrera, Census Chief of the Dirección General de Estadistica, for their assistance. Personnel at the Instituto de Investigaciones Económicas y Sociales of the University of San Carlos and individuals from the Movimiento Nacional de Pobladores generously shared data and resources that contributed to the urban phase of my study. Peace Corps worker Mary Cavanaugh shared valuable information on her field experiences, and Joy Hairs made available the late Susan Miles' unpublished ethnographic notes. The Centro de Investigaciones Regionales de Mesoamerica in Antigua generously made available research facilities on a return visit in 1978.

I want to thank many other friends and colleages who provided helpful advice, criticism, and encouragement to finish this book. Although I cannot hope to name them all, they include: June Nash, Billie Jean Isbell, Peter Furst, Bette Denich, Richard Salisbury, Julio C. Cambranes, Jude Pansini, Gloria Rudolf, Arthur Tuden, Barbara Tedlock, and Norman Schwartz.

My greatest thanks go to the people of Guatemala, and above all to the women who are the subject of this study. They helped me to understand their work, their lives, and their communities. I hope that I have done them justice and that this book will call attention to their needs. To those many Guatemalans who have shared their personal experiences, their homes and hospitality, and who taught me about their country's problems, I cannot adequately express my appreciation and my hopes, in this time of turmoil, for an end to the bloodshed and poverty that afflicts their nation.

xi

CHAPTER ONE

Introduction:
Women and Development

What is the impact of economic change on women in developing countries? Despite brief bursts of scholarly attention during periods of female militancy in Western nations, the effects of economic development on women are still rarely the subject of concerted academic study or deliberate, explicit national planning. Do women take part in the changes that are transforming their societies, or do they merely witness them? Do women, who are usually presumed to start from second place, benefit and "catch up" to men as development accelerates, or are they cast aside in the development race? Do women enjoy a "free ride" as their society becomes more urbanized, more industrialized? Or are there costs to economic change that fall disproportionately upon women? And finally, can "women" be accurately studied as a homogeneous social category, or do their experiences vary too greatly according to their social class, and their ethnic and regional backgrounds?

Questions such as these gave rise to my research on the experience of women in Guatemala. This small Central American nation, with its diverse Maya and Latin cultural traditions and its extreme disparities in wealth and industrial development, represents much of the variety and complexity found in Latin American and other underdeveloped countries. The experience of women in such contexts is not uniform, yet it is nearly always distinct from the experience of men. These distinctions are rarely appreciated since women have been rendered almost invisible by methods of most research on developing nations.

LAUREL HERBENAR BOSSEN

Direct inquiry is needed to discover what happens to women and to what extent general developments or specific conditions shape women's new roles.

This book represents an effort to show how women fit into the changing economic and social structure of Guatemala. Based on fieldwork in four Guatemalan communities, it analyzes the local variations in women's work and social activities, presenting variations in male socioeconomic roles in counterpoint to those of women. The research sites may be briefly described as: (1) a remote Maya farming village; (2) a modernizing sugarcane plantation; (3) a crowded urban shantytown; and (4) a sleek urban middle-class neighborhood. Each of these sites represents different options to women and a different way of organizing sex roles. Yet each community also represents an important segment of the national society with links to the modern world economy.

My overall view is that the expansion of capitalism encourages sexual stratification (1) through implantation of the structural arrangements of capitalist production, and (2) through cultural diffusion of ideology and social organization conforming to a "pretested" sexual division of labor found in advanced capitalist countries. This is not a uniform process. Although social scientists often use the concept of "cultural lag" to describe the retention of conservative ideologies that no longer correspond to changing political-economic conditions, I suggest that changes in the sexual division of labor can be prepared for or instituted with a "cultural lead." That is, missionaries, consumer advertising, development agents, educators, and legislators can channel and prepare populations ideologically and organizationally for a new sexual division of labor for which the material conditions have not yet been fully implanted. The structural arrangements of capitalism institutionalize both an unequal accumulation of capital by selected groups at the expense of others, and a gender division of the labor force into two labor markets. Men are channeled into the market for higher-paying formal occupations, while women are constrained to straddle capitalist and noncapitalist sectors, becoming dependent on male incomes at home, and denied the higher-paying, more secure jobs in the capitalist sector. They shuttle back and forth between one kind of economy and the other, according to the dynamics of capitalist growth; but their conditions of work present minimal opportunities for class organization and mobilization.

Three areas of social science inquiry, each with a distinctive theoretical orientation, contribute to this study: economic development, women's studies, and Mesoamerican culture. First, the literature on

2

development, which discusses the impact of capitalist economies on the Third World, provides a general background for interpreting Guatemalan socioeconomic change. Second, women's studies, particularly the recent research on women and development, advances our understanding of the theoretical issues and scope of contemporary changes in female-male relations. Third, Mesoamerican social anthropology, with its ethnographic tradition of analysing cultural microsystems, contributes a rich documentary record of the variety of local adaptations and their internal dynamics. In this chapter, I will briefly outline the influence that each of these theoretical areas has had on the problem focus and methods of the present study. I will note as well some of the contributions of my material to these fields.

Perspectives on Development

Economic and social changes experienced by Guatemalans in different sectors and regions are linked to a single much larger process: the growth of the modern world economy. Because this modern economy is so far-reaching, it is important to study the imprint that it leaves upon the individuals, communities, and subcultures that are pulled into its orbit. Despite the variety of local adaptations to specific ecological and historical conditions, there are nevertheless general similarities in the way women and men of different communities are affected. Comparison of the changing patterns of economic opportunities in farming areas and in urban milieux can indicate the extent to which the larger economic system is becoming a factor that contributes to sexual equality or inequality. Also, an understanding of the changes in female and male roles in a Guatemalan peasant community, to take one example, can be instructive for the study of other Third World peasant communities that are encountering the modern economy on similar terms.

To clarify the way the expanding world capitalist economy impinges upon the communities, I refer to two characteristics of capitalist development that are emphasized in much of the literature on the Third World. One is the dependent nature of capitalist development in countries such as Guatemala, also described as the "development of underdevelopment" (Frank 1967). The second is the corresponding development of the class structure. Awareness of both of these characteristics is basic to an understanding of the dynamic relation between Guatemalan women and men.

3

LAUREL HERBENAR BOSSEN

Dependency in a World Capitalist System

Dependent capitalism is a label that has been widely adopted to draw attention to the fact that underdevelopment and poverty in the Third World are not products of isolation, but of a dependent relationship with the developed capitalist economies.[1] This concept emphasizes that countries such as Guatemala are not encountering the achievements of Western Civilization for the first time in the 20th Century, as we witness their efforts to "catch up" to the standards set by the developed nations. Rather, it suggests that the underdeveloped countries of Latin America have been funding world capitalist development, centered in Europe and later the United States, ever since the Spanish Conquest.

While pulled into the orbit of capitalist development, the way in which such Third World countries have developed has not mirrored the past and present processes of development in the political and economic centers of the world economy. Instead of fueling local development, the fruits of Third World resources and labor are, through plunder or purchase, transformed into capital that is accumulated in other nations and regions: the metropolises of the world system. By no means a peaceful process, historically this transformation and capital transfer has been accomplished through recurrent military defeat of popular resistance, rebellions, anticolonial and revolutionary movements against the different political and economic elites that have assumed the role of supervising international capital accumulation.

The dependent aspect of this process of capitalist integration resides in the way economic and political decisions are made in peripheral areas: They are continually distorted by the need for dependent capitalist elites to appease outside interests and powers at pain of losing their mandate to govern the hinterlands. This ongoing pressure to conform to the imperatives of the most powerful (financial, political, and military) institutions of international capitalism thwarts efforts to employ resources and labor for the benefit of peripheral regions and populations. In dependent capitalism, the growth and capital accumulation that does take place is generally more fitful and discontinuous than in the fully developed centers of capitalism, which offer a safer climate for accumulation. At the periphery, harsh measures are often necessary to maintain the system. The nature of dependent capitalism is such that it is based more on successful dealings with external economic and political configurations than on popular support.

This model emphasizes two features: 1) The political and economic links between the developed and underdeveloped countries are of long standing; and 2) the uneven, centralized accumulation of capital in the

4

developed nations has been based on a worldwide system of incorporating labor and resources that leaves many areas impoverished and burdened with political and economic structures designed to continue the process. This dependency—the unequal bargaining power of the world's partners in capitalist development—now means that most Third World countries like Guatemala are considered "debtors" to the developed countries that control world finance and political power.

This external power relationship is bound to have an impact on internal developments. In Guatemala, the concentration on agricultural exports, the perpetuation of a landed oligarchy with a vast impoverished labor force, the persistence of peripheral peasant producers, and the military response to popular dissent may all be seen as aspects of dependent capitalism which constrict the possibilities for economic growth (Jonas and Tobis 1974). The relationships between working women and men—which may at first seem far removed and merely tradition-bound—can be included among those internal features that are transformed by dependent capitalism and world economic integration.

How do these economic changes relate to the condition of women at the community level? Studies of dependent capitalism rarely trace its impact down to the local level or to the smaller units of social organization (J. Nash 1976). They tend to concentrate on the unequal relations between nations, or on how disparities between center and periphery are recreated in regional (urban-rural) and class (capitalist-proletarian) divisions that mimic external power relationships. In this context, the inequalities of gender are hardly mentioned.

In Guatemala, the growth of dependent capitalism, the condition of export dependency, and the history of economic, political, and military interventions and influence by foreign powers (primarily the United States and Germany in this century) have received considerable scholarly attention.[2] Questions that are not addressed in this literature, but which interest us here are: How does this chain of influence and dependency reach women and men within regional and class divisions? How does the capitalist transformation affect what women and men are doing in their households and communities? And more generally, how is gender used in the reorganization of the labor force under dependent capitalism?

Knowledge of the changing status of women in the Third World has been held back by some of the same biases that earlier resulted in a myopic view of underdevelopment. Just as peasants once were viewed as unchanging within their "isolated" and "closed" communities, women were dealt with as unchanging behind the closed doors of the

5

household. It was assumed that custom kept women indoors in domestic roles where they were not exposed to the innovations and the liberating effects of the market economy. But if the rural workforce began to change with production for a world market, would this change not also apply to women? The static approach (or nonapproach) to women who have not yet joined the urban industrial workforce is now being challenged in many quarters as more complete studies of nonwestern and rural women are being published.

My research in Guatemala suggests that women's changing status can be fruitfully studied by extending our awareness of dependency from the macrolevel into microlevel discussions of underdevelopment. (This is not because the status of women represents a microlevel problem, but in large part because national and macroeconomic data collection on women in noncapitalist economies or economic sectors has generally been neglected or negated by data collection conventions. Detailed, microlevel data are needed to show why these conventions and macrolevel theories are inappropriate and often wrong for a good half of the population.) The modern structure of sex roles develops unevenly in a way that is comparable to the relationship between a capitalist metropolis and a dependent satellite, or between central and peripheral nations. Gender categories, like national categories, become instrumental in defining hierarchical positions in the division of labor and rewards. One sex (usually male) acquires more bargaining power than the other (usually female), which is then constrained to accommodate the former.

Abandoning the notion that women's "traditional" roles have been untouched by the expanding world economy and capitalist wage labor relations, I hold that the content of the "traditional" role is often a rather recent product (Bossen 1975); women's domestic dependency may be magnified, if not introduced as well, by discriminatory practices and unequal integration into the market economy.[3] This approach draws attention to the pressures that induce dominated or peripheral groups to specialize rather than diversify their position in the market economy, and emphasizes the unequal access to resources such as financial capital, education, and technological expertise.

Extending these ideas a little further, it can be argued that the thesis that nonwage workers in the Third World have been funding the accumulation of capital in Western nations strongly applies especially to women.

Thus the non-exchanged, noncapitalist production indirectly contributes to the capitalist process of capitalist accumulation . . . . But—extending this argument to its logical conclusion—the most widespread and important incidence of capitalist accumulation of capital . . . through "noncapitalist" relations of production is the unrequited production and reproduction (literally) by the wife and mother within the bourgeois and working class family. (Frank 1977:92)

Just as subsistence farming is seen to supply cheap labor for capitalist growth, so does the subsistence production and reproduction performed by women of various classes fund capitalist development, suggests Frank. Leacock similarly holds that "development in capitalist terms relies on the exploitation of women both in public production and in the private domain of reproduction" and that the "human cost of industrialization" has been "not only the enslavement of labor and looting of resources around the world but the severe exploitation of women and children" (1981:479). If true, this implies that the relationship between the poverty of the Guatemalan Indian woman and the North American standard of living is much stronger than we are conventionally prepared to believe.

A complete investigation of the multitude and magnitude of specific mechanisms by which outside interests have affected the internal development of sexual stratification in Guatemala would be an enormous undertaking.[4] The effects of dependent capitalism cannot be confined to structural economic features alone; cultural components of advanced capitalism may penetrate as unevenly as capital itself. In this book, I do not attempt to trace these massive influences that so differently affect women and men. Rather, I present the general features of participation in a world capitalist system as the context for differential economic development and analyse the data from specific communities and strata that contribute to the larger system. In the course of my exposition, varied external as well as internal forces are considered. Yet even when the international links are not always as obvious as Coke bottles in a country store, McDonald's hamburgers in the city, or U.S. military equipment in the hands of the army (features that are hard for the most casual tourist to miss), I maintain that the influence of both economic and cultural imperialism in Guatemala is long-standing and pervasive, affecting its communities in many unforeseen ways.

Class Stratification: Where Do Women Fit In?

The growth of the world economy not only affects the people of Guatemala by linking them to a competitive system of exchange where they are at a disadvantage, but it also restructures their productive relations internally and promotes the development of a capitalist class structure. The people discussed in this study share with populations around the world the experience of joining the wage labor force, of coming to depend on the sale of their labor, and of losing control over the means of production to a small capitalist class that owns most of the wealth. How are women affected?

Analyses of class stratification commonly commit one of two errors regarding women and class: (1) they assume that women are a homogeneous category whose domestic roles exempt them from the class divisions of the market economy, or (2) they assume that women merely reflect the class position of their husbands. In either case, these assumptions imply that it is pointless to examine directly women's class position. Women either have none, or it is uninteresting. Critical research of the last decade, rejecting these assumptions, shows that women are not immune to the development of the class structure. Class differences develop among women, and between women and men (Nash and Safa 1976; Kuhn and Wolpe 1978; Young 1978; Leacock 1981).

Accordingly, when Guatemalans are incorporated into the capitalist system as wage laborers or as owners of capital, we find that women and men tend to be treated differently. They do not enter the labor force in the same rhythms; they are channeled into different economic niches; their patterns of internal migration differ; their access to capital is unequal; their rates of employment are distinct. These obvious facts have been masked by the tendency to view women's class position as inseparable from that of their household, where the "class" of the household has been defined by its male "head." Yet in Marxist terms (if not in Marxist theory) it is often evident that women and men of the same household are engaged in different modes and relations of production: capitalist and noncapitalist.

Class analysis in underdeveloped areas is complicated by the coexistence of different modes of production. While capitalism emanating from the developed centers may dominate the economy, subordinate noncapitalist forms of household production for subsistence may be preserved, or even promoted, by the capitalist sector as a partially self-sustaining reservoir of cheap labor. For instance, Guatemalan peasant farmers who engage in seasonal wage work are only partially dependent on capitalist wage labor, yet often they cannot survive without several months of it. This leads to confusion and debate over attempts to assign class labels to these fluid populations. While the problem is generally discussed in terms of the male worker, we may suppose that the problem of class membership may be still more ambiguous for women who often have a less secure position as wage laborers or property

8

owners and hence whose membership in a given class may be even more partial and fragmented than men's. Despite this confusion, the simplistic notion that class status is defined for men by their work, and for women by their men, must be abandoned. There is ample evidence that differential access to capital or skills acquired through family relations contribute—for both men and women—to different sets of occupational choices and different sexual divisions of labor. There is little reason to assume, moreover, that access to capital, skills, or family resources are evenly distributed *within* families or that familial-marital bonds are necessarily strong or stable determinants of class position for individuals.

The fact that so little attention has yet been directed to the process by which half of the population adapts to economic change and class formation may account for some of the problems with our models of economic change. Even if the changes that affect men *appear* to be more dynamic, this is often an artifact of where we cast our glance. Women are part of the same economic system, affected directly and indirectly by changes that affect men, and vice versa.

The class interests and conflicts perceived by men may not, however, correspond to the perceptions of class held by women, precisely because the conditions of their work tend to be quite different—women's work typically including the care of children (Safa 1976; Young 1978). Women's class affiliations need to be determined by looking directly at women's economic situation, in its entirety, not simply at men's as a proxy. The class divisions between capitalists, wage laborers, and peasants have been useful for analysing inequalities among men, and can similarly be useful in understanding women's oppression. But it is deceptive to treat these divisions as if they have equal or unvarying sex ratios.

Women and Development

On Sexual Apartheid in Research

Studies of women's economic and social conditions still form only a small part of all social science research. As women have become increasingly educated and conscious of their places in society, there has been a rising demand for research that explains cross-cultural differences and historical changes in women's status. Unfortunately, research that is identified as concentrating on women is most typically written and read by women. There is a lingering notion that the study of women in society is somehow more specialized and limited than the study of men in society, or of men *as* society. Ironically, it could be argued that "women's studies" are misnamed since in general they explicitly acknowledge the existence of men and male social roles, while outside of women's studies there has been a strong tendency to study only one of the two sexes: men (often misleadingly called "man"). In this "mainstream" research, the female presence in society is invisible, or the female experience is given short shrift as deviant or intractable data. This has been particularly true of studies of development. The present work contributes to the study of women in that it places women at center stage and explicitly seeks to analyse and explain what happens to them. Yet it also includes comparative data on men. It is, in this sense, a general contribution to our understanding of the basic economic and social structure of Guatemala as an underdeveloped nation.

Non-Western women have become subjects of growing research for a variety of reasons. Such research can: (1) provide alternate models of female-male interaction which loosen the grip of conventional thinking about women and help us perceive how gender is shaped by differing socioeconomic conditons; (2) provide insights into the evolution and history of female oppression, especially as they relate to the contemporary transformations produced by modern agriculture and industry (Leacock 1981); (3) reveal whether female oppression is systematically expanding or withering away with the spread of world capitalism; and (4) improve development planning. On this last point, there is a growing opinion that development programs, typically aimed at men and presumed male "heads" of families, have faltered because they failed to anticipate and plan for women and family members (Jacobs 1982; Papanek 1977; Dixon 1978).

How Does Development Affect Women?

Recent research has shown that a variety of economic factors operate to change the status of women relative to men in developing areas. Some studies have emphasized the discriminatory introduction of new technology and development of intensive forms of agriculture favoring men as significant factors contributing to female subordination (Boserup 1970; Chaney and Schmink 1976; Dauber and Cane 1981). The emergence of a dichotomy between cash crops (especially export crops) and subsistence farming, often superimposed upon a sexual division of labor, also can handicap women in (and outside of) the market economy. Changes in land tenure, and the introduction of wage labor and migrant labor systems have also been shown to disfavor women (Brain 1979; Remy 1975). Still others point to the growth and preservation of the informal economy of self-employed street vendors and domestic servants as a catchall for displaced and unemployed women (Arizpe 1977; Safa 1976; Nelson 1980). Finally, a number of recent studies emphasize that while capitalist growth does not have a uniform impact upon women in different regions and classes it does tend to seize upon gender divisions as a basis for hierarchically defining different categories of labor; women are loaded with the double burdens of unpaid reproduction and underpaid production (Deere and Leon de Leal 1981; Schmink 1977; Leacock 1981; J. Nash 1981a).

One of the major concerns of this book, reflected in recent research on women in many parts of the world, is that women seem to be short-changed and devalued by the overall social and economic transformations occurring in the Third World. Rather than achieving "emancipation" involving greater public participation and more equal economic rewards, it is feared that women are being left behind, with increasingly heavy burdens and a decreasing share of the benefits. Indeed, the report of the 1980 United Nations conference on women asserts this (Leacock 1981).

Why should this be so? Is it merely an impersonal force called "capitalism" working according to inexorable laws? Is the maternal function of women the crucial factor? Or is there a worldwide cultural movement promoting "creeping misogyny"? I have explored some of these questions within the Guatemalan context by comparing the work, the choices, and the rewards open to women, to see how these match up against those of men. While the description of the experience of these Guatemalan women cannot be transferred uncritically to other cultural contexts, general similarities in the way agro-industrial capitalism conducts business throughout the world, as well as similarities in the function of repressive governments, make the Guatemalan case relevant to other underdeveloped nations.

Mesoamerican Anthropology

Mesoamerica has been the locus of a great deal of anthropological research, particularly the regions of Mexico and Guatemala that retain high concentrations of indigenous populations. Inspired by the independent evolution of civilization in Mesoamerica and seeking to complement the archeological and historical records, early anthropologists focussed on the nature of cultural differences between Maya and Ladino populations. With the goal of discovering and reconstructing aboriginal cultures, many anthropologists deliberately sought the most isolated communities and villages for study, and attempted to filter out of their descriptions and analyses any intrusive features from modern Western culture.

Isolation, self-sufficiency, and cultural continuity were stressed, contributing to a trend in which they Maya were presented as members of egalitarian, closed corporate communities that were viewed as the repositories of stable Indian traditions and values.[5] Explanations for the continuity of Maya culture were to be found essentially within the Maya community and its peculiar institutions such as the fiesta system. Although it was recognized that the Maya were conquered and subordinated by the Spanish, it was felt that culturally they had managed to maintain a defensive cohesion that was still resistant to Western values. While the holistic community study was in vogue, examination of the manifold links between village, nation, and world economy was generally deemed less crucial, if not offtrack. At present, many scholars believe attention to the larger historical and regional context would have demonstrated that the colorful but impoverished Maya communities (and their distinctive male-female role patterns) were not simply self-regulating survivals of a different path of cultural evolution but were and are greatly affected and reshaped by their condition of subordination to the Western political and economic system (Carmack 1981; W. Smith 1977; Wasserstrom 1975).

Despite these deficiencies from a theoretical perspective, the attraction and strength of the traditional anthropological approach was that it provided a close-up view of the way people were living and interacting in Mesoamerican communities.[6] First-hand knowledge and experience of the way other people live, the "emic" approach of listening to the way people of other cultures interpret their situation, are extremely valuable as means of overcoming the limitations and biases of our own cultural traditions of scientific distance and statistical reduction. Although the isolationist approach is no longer tenable, community-level research using anthropological methods of participation and observation remains valuable (Dixon 1978; J. Nash 1981b).

If on-the-spot first-hand observations are the strength of the anthropologist, one would expect fuller coverage of the female population in the communities studied, particularly since women often become the core of community life when men work away from home. This expectation is, alas, but very weakly fulfilled at the descriptive level and even less so at the analytical level of Mesoamerican research. Often ethnographies which purport to describe the richness and variety of the Maya cultural heritage, to examine ethnic relations, stratification, acculturation, or modernization have been and continue to be negligent in describing the status of women under these rubrics.[7] Moreover, the subjects of economics, politics, and religion have been largely conceived and defined as areas of masculine concern and participation, while women are generally granted scholarly attention only for their role in the life-cycle events such as birth and marriage. Even in the area of anthropological life histories, the male biography predominates (Moore 1973; Schwartz 1977; Sexton 1981). Taken together, the corpus of information on Guatemalan women is thin; the search for information leads to data that are fragmented, incomplete, and frequently laced with generalizations for which supporting evidence is not provided.

Despite these criticisms, a small number of anthropologists have been explicitly concerned with women. Maynard's research (1963, 1974) compared the cultural roles of Ladinas and indigenous women in Palin, while the Pauls (Paul 1974; Paul and Paul 1975) have provided several brief reports on the cultural roles of Maya women. Exceptional for its data on women as economic agents in an indigenous community is Tax's early study of "penny capitalism" in Panajachel (1953), while Reina's study of Chinautla (1966) briefly describes women's economic roles as potters and some of their religious functions. Information on women as economic and cultural agents can also be culled from various accounts of Guatemalan arts and crafts, such as weaving and ceramics, that tend to be female occupations (see, for example O'Neale's study of Guatemalan textile production, 1965). To date, there has been very little investigation of the plantation or urban sectors of Guatemala, although some very interesting data on women is embedded in recent studies (Pansini 1980; Roberts 1973). (The neglect of these sectors is related to the concentration of anthropologists overall on the questions posed by the persistence of traditional indigenous culture.)

Only recently have researchers shown an interest in the changes in women's role produced by Guatemala's increasing integration into the world economy. Chinchilla (1977), using national statistics, has discussed the relationship between increasing occupational segregation by sex and the process of capitalist industrialization. Ehlers (1980) describes and analyzes changes in women's participation in cottage industries in the western highlands, and Irías and Alfaro (1977) examine an unsuccessful attempt at labor union organizing among Guatemalan women factory workers. Some of my own previous work explores the range of economic options for women and the implications of mod-

13

ernization in an indigenous municipality (1975), as well as problems surrounding women's work as domestic servants and on plantations (1976, 1980, 1982). All of these studies point out the obstacles women face in gaining entry to the modern economy and labor force.

My primary objective here is to provide more complete data on the variations in women's position in Guatemala and the ways they are interconnected, and to examine the nature and causes of sexual inequality under conditons of dependent capitalism. By beginning to document the full range of women's activities in Guatemala, these findings can eventually be integrated with the relatively abundant but one-sided research on men. Only with a more balanced approach to the study of women and men will we be able to understand the full implications of Guatemalan socioeconomic change.

Methodological Issues

The comparison of four communities is undertaken at two levels: (1) comparison of women and men *within* each community, and (2) comparison of the degree of sexual stratification *among* the four communities, each representing important socioeconomic segments of Guatemalan society. Application of similar standards and methods of comparison to each community serves to show how sex roles can be more systematically understood within the larger context of a complex nation.

Efforts to compare women and men, and degrees of sexual stratification inevitably raise many questions. Abstractly, sexual stratification may be defined as a condition in which the sexes are systematically channeled into hierarchical relationships where one sex is subordinate and consistently finds its power, choices, and autonomy limited by the opposite sex (see Schlegel 1977). Conversely, a condition of sexual equality is one in which both sexes enjoy equal autonomy or freedom from control, or in which the sexes exercise a balance of power with each other—with power simply defined as the ability to control the actions of others.

While the concepts appear straightforward, they are not easy to place upon a single definitive scale. They involve evaluation of a wide variety of factors operating differently in different contexts. Moreover, fieldwork conditions (described in detail in Appendix Two) differ in each community environment. Qualitative judgements inevitably come into play. Yet consistency and clarity regarding the nature of the data collected can counteract subjective leanings, by permitting others to consider the data from a different perspective. In comparing sex roles in the four communities, I concentrated on a set of economic and social variables as measures of sexual stratification in different dimensions. These need some clarification.

Economic Measures of Sexual Stratification

Three main economic variables are considered in each community: (1) the division of labor by sex; (2) the distribution of rewards; and (3) the control of strategic resources. The division of labor by sex refers to the productive and reproductive activities of each sex, irrespective of their conventional designations as "economically active" members of the labor force or as unpaid family members who are implicitly economically passive and "outside" the labor force. That is, it refers to work contributions both within the cash economy and within the subsistence economy. In the subsistence economy, production refers not just to peasant farming seen as field labor, but to the entire complex of household chores that are inseparable from production.[8] Related aspects include (a) the extent to which each sex works in public activities requiring a complex organization of labor as opposed to private tasks that isolate and disperse individuals; (b) the degree of sexual segregation in various types of work; and (c) the overall range of economic options open to each sex. In general, work options that are public, flexible, and wide-ranging are deemed signs of greater power and autonomy.

The distribution of rewards refers primarily to the material rewards for different contributions to the production process. These rewards may vary in quantity, form (cash income or subsistence goods), and immediacy (short- or long-term rewards). Even though quantitative comparisons are not always feasible, it is worthwhile to consider the different advantages and risks implied by a cash income that is easily converted into a wide variety of goods, and income in kind which may have greater value in direct consumption than in exchange. Similarly, the relative income from work for wages, an immediate and determinate reward, can be weighed against child-raising, which is sometimes a long-term and indeterminate investment in social security in the form of future family labor and retirement support. Another dimension of the reward structure is the relative security and regularity of some types of income versus the high risk or irregularity of others. While quantification may prove impossible for some types of rewards, we nonetheless may appreciate the distinct advantages and disadvantages they represent in a changing economic system, as well as their implications for sexual stratification.

The control of strategic resources involves different kinds of control and a variety of resources when applied to different socioeconomic contexts. Control may range from the unencumbered right to own and dispose of private property backed by juridicopolitical institutions to restricted moral claims on the labor of one's children or one's spouse. The variety of strategic resources may include land ownership, rights to labor and reproductive capacity, a secure job, liquid capital, a house, and many other assets which can have varying strategic value depending on the context. For instance, a low but steady cash income may not have high strategic value in a complex society divided into capitalist and working classes, but within the context of a working class population where unemployment is high, a steady cash income may become a strategic resource, and one which confers power within the class and particularly the household. As capitalist relations of production increasingly predominate, two important variables are the extent to which each sex can claim: (1) an individual cash income, and (2) steady formal employment that provides job security and regular income outside the home. If one sex systematically lacks access to either, its members become susceptible to dominance by the other.

My analysis of women's position distinguishes between three general types of economic participation that are found in complex, capitalist societies:

1. Formal employment for cash
2. Informal employment for cash
3. Subsistence production.

Formal employment implies permanent wage-labor or salaried employment in large nonfamilial enterprises where duties and remuneration are standardized or regulated by contract. In contrast, informal employment is variable, irregular, and/or unspecialized; hours of work, tasks, and rewards are not governed by formal contract. Informal employment includes irregular wage-work, self-employed trades, family employment, and personal services. It is typically performed in small domestic establishments, workshops, or impermanent quarters in markets or on the streets, with few people combining to form a work unit. Subsistence production is work that occurs altogether outside the cash economy, unregulated by contract, and performed for direct use by the individual and family members rather than for regular exchange beyond the household. Such work is frequently described as noncapitalist, or as characterized by noncapitalist relations of production even when it occurs within a capitalist system.

Some analyses of economic change have compared communities by categorizing them as noncapitalist or capitalist according to the percentage of the population engaged in wage labor.[9] My distinction between formal and informal occupations focuses on the scale and stability of enterprises within the cash economy. I maintain that those workers with access to wages in formal jobs are generally associated with large capitalist institutions more directly than are those who have informal employment, whether it provides wages or not. This proximity, I argue, is akin to proximity to capitalist centers in my larger framework. Those who are on the perimeter, in informal occupations or in subsistence occupations, would have a weaker bargaining position. Recent economic history and technological change, as well as the level of integration into the modern market economy, condition the types of economic participation that are open to women and men in each of the four communities studied.

Social Measures of Sexual Stratification

The examination of the social roles of women considers three major categories of social structure:
1. Formal public organizations
2. Informal public networks
3. The domestic sphere

A social classification based on dichotomies between formal and informal roles cross-cutting public and private (domestic) spheres was used by Chiñas (1973) to conceptualize sex roles in different social systems.[10] Again, within each of these categories, the relative power and autonomy of the sexes may differ along qualitative and quantitative axes.

Formal organizations are defined as those social groups which have publicly recognized status, identifiable membership, a specified sphere of interest, and specialized leadership roles. Organizations are considered public if their membership extends beyond the family or household. As a rule, formal public organizations encompass the recognized political, religious, and educational institutions of the social system from village to national levels. Informal public networks include the diffuse ties and irregular contacts that occur between neighbors, kin, and friends. These are often conceived of as social resources which can be dormant or activated for diverse purposes. The domestic sphere generally refers to the private social activity centered on the family, the structure of the household group, marriage and family relationships, and the social organization of reproduction.

These categories are not perfectly distinct in reality, but it is generally easy to assign behavior to one of them. Also, their relative importance may vary between and within social systems. In some cases, formal organizations may be poorly developed or so externally controlled that they consume very little time or energy in the community under consideration. In others, domestic organization may predominate not only as the unit of reproduction, but also as the most cohesive social unit of economic and political action.[11] Alternately, the domestic sphere may have a much attentuated social function. It is important to consider not only the proportions of women participating in each sphere of social organization, but also the extent to which the various spheres represent power in society.

The relative inclusion of women and men in formal public organizations is an important indication of their respective power in society, but it must be considered carefully, for exclusive male participation may amount to little more than local rubber stamping, albeit a function that might give an edge to the men involved (Rothstein 1979; Reiter 1975; Young 1980). Increasing attention is being given to the formal/informal division of social organization as a means of discovering the sexual distribution of power in society. Various studies suggest that where women are denied access to formal public organizations, they tend to develop alternate channels and indirect methods to increase their power and autonomy.[12] They may exercise covert or surreptitious power which men are hardly aware of, or men may recognize and defer to the informal roles of women.

As Chiñas (1973) observes, informal roles are more difficult to document than formal roles because they are not standardized and therefore require a more intimate knowledge of the social system than many researchers are able to acquire during fieldwork. Further, if women are primarily active in informal social organization, male researchers may have little access to this area of social maneuver.

The difficulty of directly measuring informal social power suggests that indirect methods can be of use. One approach is to evaluate the *potential* for women to exercise informal power, for if no avenues can be discovered, the probability that women exercise power or autonomy in informal organization is low. For example, if women enjoy a high degree of physical mobility and have numerous informal meeting places, it is likely they will be able to use these to further their social objectives. If, however, they are confined to the home and permitted to interact only with immediate kin, their influence is probably minimal. I endeavor to show the extent to which informal channels of public social activity are open and legitimately used by women in the four Guatemalan communities. This information, when integrated with an analysis of formal institutional roles, yields a fuller understanding of the relative power and influence exercised by each sex.

In the domestic sphere, I assume that if marriages are arranged and indissoluble, and if women (but not men) are restricted in their sexual behavior and penalized for premarital sex relations, illegitimate children, or adultery, then women have less domestic power and autonomy than men. But as in other spheres, women's status is not established simply by noting the presence or absence of restrictions. Any restrictions must be evaluated against the restrictions on the domestic or private activities of men of the same social group and age. For instance, a girl of fifteen whose first marriage is arranged must not be compared to the man of thirty who perhaps may choose his own mate, but to the boy of fifteen. If it turns out that the fifteen-year-old boy is also subject to a marriage arranged by his parents, or that he is denied the option of marrying young because he is first required to work for his parents for a number of years, then it is not clear that females experience greater subordination. The power and autonomy of senior males in the household must not be compared to that of junior females, but to that of senior females. Only then can we determine the extent to which power imbalances in the domestic spheres are a function of sex and not age or other variables.[13]

Data Collection

Four communities were selected for this study with two major considerations in mind: (a) that they represent the major sociocultural and economic divisions within Guatemalan society, and (b) that, if possible, they be located in areas where earlier studies are available to provide greater background material and supplementary data. This latter condition, although imperfectly fulfilled, made it possible to devote greater attention to the specific problem of determining women's position and less time to collecting the essential "base-line data" from which comparisons of sex roles can be launched.

The communities were intensively studied during one full year of field research (1974–75), divided into discrete periods of residence in each area. Fortunately, this year of fieldwork was preceded by two summers of research experience in Guatemala, which meant that I had already acquired general familiarity with some of the areas and problems to be studied. Moreover, I maintained informal contact with people in each community following the interval of direct research, thus acquiring a somewhat longer view of the data I had already obtained and finding opportunities to pursue leads that had been overlooked.

The data collected derive from quantitative and qualitative research techniques (for details, see Appendix Two). They include "extensive" survey samples taken within each community. These centered on relatively straightforward socioeconomic data, designed to serve as a standard basis for quantitative comparisons between the sexes within each community and within the nation. Yet in a complex society characterized by ethnic pluralism, class divisions, uneven economic development, and sexual stratification—as is Guatemala—I learned it is hazardous to assume that a given statistical index would have the same implications across these divisions. Quantitative methods are no guarantee against ethnocentric assumptions or other forms of collective bias; they only protect against random or individual variation. Some areas of social behavior are not amenable to easy quantification without butchering the data. This is particularly true of subsistence economies and informal sectors where women are often concentrated. Comprehending these limitations, quantitative data can still be effective for careful cross-community comparisons within the nation.

My research also employed the traditional anthropological techniques of participant observation and open-ended interviewing with a subset of individuals who, based on both subjective and objective criteria, seemed to represent major variations in the social system. These sources of information provided greater depth than I could obtain by formal interviewing alone. For example, through informal interaction I could discover that the woman who claims she does not "work" because she is busy with "domestic duties" is in many cases earning money for the family by taking in laundry or selling foodstuffs.

The recording of individual case histories was a technique used to reveal the range of variables that affect women's status. I sought such "intensive" data from a number of informants in each community. These life histories were not collected strictly for the purpose of illustrating the "typical" relationship between the sexes in each area, or the life of the "typical woman." Rather they serve to demonstrate the range of alternatives which women experience in each community, the potential and limitations of changing relationships where many variables come into play. Such individualistic sources of information must be accepted with caution as a basis for generalizations about sex roles and stratification within the community and in complex society. But they describe some of the specific mechanisms by which sociocultural and economic variables affect women's life choices. This type of data forms a vital complement to my statistical information. Statistical methods could not possibly cover the same range of variables without massive investments of time, personnel, and money (which no doubt would thoroughly transform any community under study). This combination of extensive and intensive data-gathering techniques makes possible a relatively complete description of sex stratification in each community, and lays the groundwork for comparative analysis of sexual stratification across communities and within the nation.

The effort to apply a unified body of research questions using a similar approach to communities that are not located within a single region, yet are integrated into a single national system, is relatively unique in the anthropology of Mesoamerica, and specifically Guatemala.[14] This investigation strives to combine the intimacy of community-level data with the broad issues of national-level issues of development and change.

CHAPTER TWO

The National Setting and the Four Communities

Of the seven nations that comprise Central America, Guatemala is the largest and richest, located at Mexico's southern doorstep. Its population in 1981 has surpassed 7 million people. Physically, Guatemala's environment is highly varied between cool highlands and mountain ranges studded with volcanic peaks, and warm lowland plains that descend to the coasts. The population is also heterogeneous, combining a large proportion of Maya-speaking inhabitants with a Ladino, or Spanish-speaking, population that dominates national affairs. The Maya, cultural heirs of a great pre-Hispanic civilization that flourished prior to the conquest by the Spanish four and a half centuries ago, are a colorful but largely impoverished agricultural population. Ladinos are the heirs of the Hispanic and Latin American cultural traditions, and heirs to a power structure based on the continued subordination of the Maya. Environmental and cultural diversity are compounded by the extreme contrasts in standard of living and internal levels of economic development which typify Third World countries. The modern central metropolis, Guatemala City, displaying the wealth of the capitalist sector and its ties to the advanced industrial economies, stands out incongruously against the vast regions of rural and urban poverty which contain the majority of the population, both Maya and Ladino.

In this chapter, the complexity of Guatemalan society is briefly outlined in terms of regional differentiation, the economic divisions between rural and urban sectors, the class structure, and ethnicity. These variables form the background for an introductory description of each of the four communities of this study: T'oj Nam, El Cañaveral, San Lorenzo, and Villa Rosa. Their socioeconomic background is an essential prelude to this inquiry into the division of labor between Guatemalan men and women, but a familiarity with the historical background and political conditions is also necessary to appreciate more fully the dynamic of recent Guatemalan development problems and Guatemala's uncertain future. Since the changing status of women is intimately bound up with the historical and contemporary struggles that characterize Guatemala, a postscript will review the major features of Guatemala's socioeconomic history and political clashes that have always affected the ways men and women interact, joining or dividing against shared or separate foes. The reader who wishes to understand this dimension of the Guatemalan condition as a more complete background to the case studies is directed to that section (Appendix One).

Regional Representation

Guatemala can be divided into five major developmental zones (Adams 1970): the western highlands; the eastern highlands; the northeast and northern lowlands; the south coast; and metropolitan Guatemala. The western highlands are an area of dense indigenous population and small-scale agricultural production for subsistence and local markets (See Map 2–1).[1] Ladinos are present mainly in the towns and act as commercial and cultural intermediaries between the Maya peasants and national institutions. The eastern highlands differ in that they are an area of predominantly Ladino culture and the scale of agricultural production is more mixed between small, medium, and large-sized farms. Both regions are characterized by impoverishment and emigration of small-scale subsistence farmers. The northern regions are relatively underpopulated and undeveloped for either commercial or subsistence farming. Recently they have begun to receive significant immigration from landless peasants and are currently the focus of major national development projects.[2]

The south coast, along with the coffee piedmont, is Guatemala's area of commercial export agriculture *par excellence*. A growing population of landless wage laborers who have migrated from the highlands, particularly from the eastern region, have been settling there. Between the south coastal plain and the highlands is an intermediate zone, the coffee piedmont, which is also involved in export agriculture.

The metropolitan area centers on Guatemala City itself, along with its expanding residential and industrial suburbs. As the principal city

23

of Guatemala, the capital directs the dominant political, economic and cultural activities of the nation. It is the financial, commercial, and industrial capital which dominates the internal regions and coordinates the foreign trade and economic relations of Guatemala within the national arena. It is also the home of a growing urban labor force.

This study looks intimately at communities drawn from three of these five major regions of Guatemala: T'oj Nam in the western highlands; El Cañaveral on the south coast, San Lorenzo and Villa Rosa in the metropolis. These regions, taken together, contain approximately 71 percent of Guatemala's population.[3] While I certainly would not claim that these communities "typify" the economies or the configu-

MAP 2-1. Guatemalan Regional Divisions.

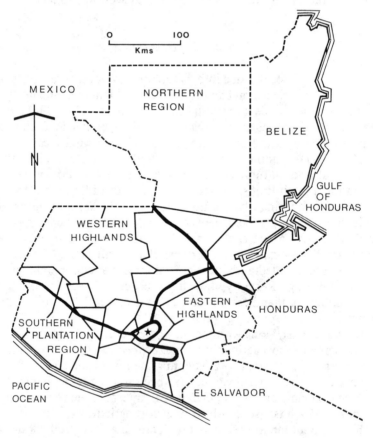

* Metropolitan Area: Guatemala City.

rations of male-female relations for any region as a whole, they do underscore some of the major regional differences and highlight the ways that local patterns evolve.

The National Economic Structure

The Rural Sector: Uneven Development

As in most underdeveloped nations, Guatemala's population remains predominantly rural, with approximately 64 percent living in rural areas and 57 percent of the labor force working in agriculture (Guatemala 1977; Petras and Morley 1981:72).[4] At the same time, agricultural production accounted for only 25 percent of the Gross Domestic Product in 1980, continuing its decline from 32.5 percent in 1950 (IDB 1981:257; Monteforte 1972). The agricultural sector itself is sharply divided between two interdependent systems of production: small-scale peasant subsistence agriculture and large-scale commercial agriculture. Subsistence farming is losing ground as commercial production expands. In 1976, crops for internal consumption, such as corn, beans, potatoes, and other vegetables, accounted for only 31 percent of all agricultural production, declining from 39 percent in 1950 (see Table 2-1).

Table 2-1 shows that the proportional decline in subsistence agriculture was due to growth first in export crops such as coffee, cotton, and bananas, and later in intermediary commercial crops such as sugarcane, wheat, rice, and tobacco destined for industrial processing prior to export or domestic consumption.

Table 2-1. Sectoral Distribution of Guatemalan Agricultural Crops, 1950–1976

Sector	Year			
	1950 (%)	1956 (%)	1966 (%)	1976 (%)
Export crops	49.8	50.6	54.3	48.8
Domestic consumption crops	39.2	38.6	35.7	31.4
Intermediate products	10.8	10.9	10.0	19.8
Total agricultural crops	99.8%	100.1%	100.0%	100.0%

Sources: Fletcher et al. 1970:40; Guatemala 1977.

The division between subsistence and commercial production corresponds to a very unequal distribution of landholdings between very large farms (*latifundios*) and tiny farms (*minifundios*). The last (1964) agricultural census showed that 87 percent of Guatemala's farms were classified as microfamily and subfamily farms of less than seven hectares. By definition, most of these minifundios are too small to meet family subsistence needs, but they are still essential for food production. Controlling only 19 percent of the total farm land, they produced 62 percent of the staple food—corn—grown in Guatemala, with 94 percent of them using only human energy for production (Fletcher et al. 1970: 60, 78, 86, 74). Many such farms are best described as "sub-subsistence" farms; intensively cultivated, crowded on mountainous and eroding lands, they feed the rural poor.

Farms or plantations with more than 45 hectares comprise about 2.1 percent of all farms, but control about 62 percent of the farm land.[5] These plantations are capitalist enterprises, concentrated in the fertile coastal plains, where 4 percent of the farms control 80 percent of the land (Fletcher et al. 1970:60). The larger plantations specialize in the production of export crops such as coffee, cotton, sugarcane, and bananas. They are much more likely than small farms to utilize mechanical power, but even among the 388 largest farms in 1964, as many as 50 percent relied solely on human labor in production (Fletcher et al. 1970:74). Intensity of land use is inversely related to farm size: On small farms in the subsistence sector, 91 percent of the land is cultivated, in sharp contrast to 15 percent for farms in the largest of five farm size categories (calculated from Fletcher et al. 1970:68–70).

Maya farmers. The distinction between subsistence farms and commercial plantations is related to the cultural division of the population into native Maya and Ladino populations, a legacy of colonialism. Despite earlier indications that the Maya proportion of the population was declining, Early (1983:75) estimates that the Maya were still 47.3 percent of the Guatemalan population in 1980.[6] The majority of the Maya continue to live in the western highlands where minifundios and traditional subsistence agriculture predominate. Eight of Guatemala's 22 departments are over 60 percent Maya, accounting for 72 percent of the nation's indigenous population (Guatemala 1973), and seven of these eight departments are in the western highlands,[7] the area most associated with traditional subsistence agriculture. (See Map 2-2.)

In 1964, 81 percent of the Maya who were economically active were employed in the agricultural sector, in contrast to only 53 percent of the economically active Ladinos (Monteforte 1972:60). The disadvantaged position of the Maya farmer also stands out in the distribution

MAP 2-2. Guatemalan Maya Regions

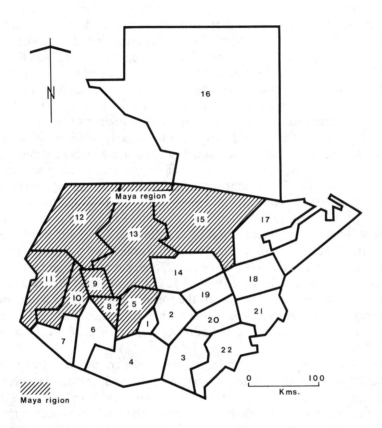

Departments
1. Sacatepequez. 2. Guatemala (Capital). 3. Santa Rosa. 4. Escuintla. 5. Chimaltenango.
6. Suchitepéquez. 7. Retalhuleu. 8. Sololá. 9. Totonicapán. 10. Quetzaltenango. 11.
San Marcos. 12. Huehuetenango. 13. Quiché. 14. Baja Verapaz. 15. Alta Verapaz. 16.
Petén. 17. Izabal. 18. Zacapa. 19. Progreso. 20. Jalapa. 21. Chiquimula. 22. Jutiapa.

of landholdings by ethnic group. The Maya comprised 62 percent of
the agricultural landowners, but their holdings were only 25 percent of
the nation's total cultivated land (Guzman et al. 1971).[8] The continued
dependence of the Maya on subsistence farming is suggested by the fact
that in 1973, 75 percent still lived in rural areas, significantly higher
than the national average of 64 percent. Although the last decades have
undoubtedly brought some shifts in employment and landholding, current economic and political conditions do not suggest dramatic improvements in the Maya position as landowners.

Migrant labor. Unequal control over land is basic to the success of the large commercial plantations that employ seasonal wage labor to harvest their crops.[9] As land appropriation, highland erosion, soil depletion, population growth, and land fragmentation leave more and more peasants with inadequate subsistence plots, they are impelled to migrate from the highlands to work as wage laborers or to rent lands in the more fertile coastal regions. Inadequate lands in the peripheral highland peasant regions, including communities such as T'oj Nam (and eastern Ladino regions), ensure a cheap labor supply for commercial agriculture on the lowland plantations. In 1965–66, it was estimated that between 300,000 and 400,000 seasonal laborers migrated to work in Guatemala's cotton, coffee, and sugarcane plantations (Schmid 1973). More recent estimates suggest that this figure is now closer to 600,000 to 650,000 workers (Pansini 1980; Richards 1981 citing *El Grafico;* CGS 1981). According to 1977 U.S. Agency for International Development report by Gordon Brown, a conservative estimate of the number of seasonal migrant workers and their dependents is approximately 1,500,000 or nearly 25 percent of the country's total population (cited in Pansini 1980). A large proportion of these seasonal migrant workers are Mayas from the western highlands, although migrants come from nearly all departments of Guatemala and include significant numbers of eastern Ladinos (Schmid 1973: 26, 112; Pansini 1980).

This seasonal labor migration occurs in the context of a free labor market system based on unequal control over land, and unequal access to alternative occupations. In itself, it is strong evidence that even the indigenous peasant population does not stand outside the modern market economy, but is much affected by national conditions of supply and demand for land and labor, by national minimum wage legislation (however weakly enforced), and by the economic power of the capitalist export sector. Historically, Guatemala's plantations relied upon forced labor from the peasant sector; the free market in labor was permitted to develop only when supply and demand conditions favored the commercial sector. As Adams observed:

> Until approximately 30 years ago, the Guatemalan campesino would have had an advantage in a free labor market. . . . The market was not allowed to become free until the rural population had grown equal to or beyond the national needs in export agriculture. As a result campesinos, primarily Indians, today need the work available on the fincas and plantations more than the plantations need them. . . . This labor-market situation is important, since it places the campesino in a position where he cannot use a

labor shortage as a means of pressure to better his circumstances. (1970:425–426)

There is little doubt that growing dependence on migratory labor reflects the progressive impoverishment and proletarianization of the peasant sector. From the perspective of the plantation owners, this cheap, seasonal supply of labor which returns to the subsistence sector between periods of peak plantation demand is highly advantageous. Indeed, the "complementarity" between the periods of slack work on subsistence farms and intense work in coastal plantations (which varies in timing and duration for different cash crops) means that subsistence farmers often need supplementary work just when plantations need additional labor. This tends to keep wages low for migrant workers despite the fact that demand for labor should theoretically be at its seasonal high.

Even with the appearance of free labor market conditions, however, inherent instability in this arrangement leads to coercive measures to keep it in place. With low wages in agriculture, better earnings in any competing sector—from petty commerce or commodity production to construction—would tend to tempt peasants away from plantation labor. For instance, construction wages rose after the earthquake that left 75,000 homeless in 1976. Moreover, in the face of inflation, plantation managers struggle to keep their labor costs down by holding wages constant. With declining real wages in the 1970s, agricultural unrest and strikes increased, while the government and the landed oligarchy increasingly resorted to repressive measures to maintain the status quo. Guatemala's military budget and international reputation for human rights violations is bleak testimony to the political costs of maintaining a cheap labor force in agriculture.

The important role of commercial agriculture in the national economy is indicated by the fact that this sector accounted for 80 percent of all exports in 1980 (IDB 1981). In the pattern of most underdeveloped countries, Guatemala depends heavily on the export of a small number of agricultural crops, although their relative contributions are constantly shifting with rising and falling world market prices.

Sugar is particularly important here because it is the principal crop produced in the plantation community case study, El Cañaveral. Sugar exports have only become important since 1962, and have grown rather steadily, with about half going to the United States (Gonzalez 1970:117). Coffee, the most important export, is also a second-order crop at El Cañaveral (see Chapter Four).

29

Table 2-2. Contributions of Four Major Export Crops to Total Guatemalan Merchandise Exports, 1966–1975/1979

Crop	1966 %	1975–1979 %
Coffee	44.3	38.5
Cotton	19.7	12.9
Sugar	2.7	8.5
Bananas	2.0	2.3
Total	68.7%	62.2%

Source: OECEI (Oficina de Estudios para la Colaboración Económica Internacional), Mercado Común Centroamericano, Síntesis económica y financiera núm. 2, Buenos Aires: La Técnica Impresora, 1968, cited in Monteforte (1972:231); IDB (1981:447).

The permanent workers. The commercial plantations also depend on a permanent workforce for part of their labor needs. These resident workers are largely Ladino in ethnic composition, since indigenes who remain away from their home villages tend to lose their distinctive traits (Hoyt 1955; Whetton 1961).[10] The permanent workers include landless workers and *colonos* (tenant farmers) who reside on plantations and receive houses and plots for food crops, as well as wages for regular labor on the plantations.

It is difficult to estimate accurately the number of permanent agricultural workers on the plantations today. In 1964, there were nearly 103,000 resident colonos on farms, but only 48 percent of them actually had land (Fletcher et al. 1970). An estimated 70 percent of these colonos were employed on coffee plantations, and less than 5 percent on cotton plantations. There are no estimates of the numbers working specifically in sugar plantations, but Schmid found that there are relatively more permanent workers on sugar and coffee plantations than in cotton plantations (1973:271).

In the early 1970s, Guatemala had 175,000 landless rural families, and another 98,000 with less than 0.7 hectares (1.7 acres) each. Together these two groups comprise 41.3 percent of the farm families (Torres-Rivas 1980a, SIECA 1975). While it is clear that subsistence farming does not support these families, it is not known how many are colonos or permanent plantation workers, how many are permanently floating from one agricultural job to the next—a pattern identified among eastern farm workers (Pansini 1980), and how many support themselves primarily through rural commerce and cottage industries, an important alternative for rural Maya in some "core" departments such as Totonicapan (C. Smith 1981). Despite evidence that the numbers of colonos are declining as plantations switch to cheaper migrant or day labor, Fletcher et al. (1970) found that the coastal plantation region was "the fastest growing area of economic significance" in Guatemala, with a 4 percent average annual rate of population increase, matched only by the capital city and the underpopulationed northern regions.

Women in agriculture. The role of women in the agricultural sector of Guatemala is equally difficult to determine using national statistics. In 1973, women were reported as 14 percent of the nation's labor force, with a participation rate of 8.4 percent compared to 52.1 percent for males. Yet only 7.2 percent of these working women were reported to be in the agricultural sector, forming a tiny 1.7 percent of the total agricultural labor force (see Table 2-3).

In a nation where agriculture remains the single most important category of economic activity, the census data anomolously imply that rural and indigenous women work less than urban women or Ladinos.[11] If true, this would directly contradict the pattern of higher participation rates reported for rural and indigenous males (and run counter to ethnographic observation as well). These peculiar census findings prompted the comment by Monteforte that:

> This does not at all mean that, in general, the rural woman works less than the city woman. What happens is that the participation of women in domestic labor, very closely linked to the activity of the men in agriculture, is not calculated as remunerated according to census criteria and so they do not figure in the labor force (translated, 1972:178).

Failure to count women is a common problem with labor force statistics in agrarian economies where a large part of the population continues to produce for the household subsistence economy. Modern convention dictates that men be considered economically active if they

Table 2-3. Economically Active Work Force in Guatemala by Economic Sector and Sex

Sector	Male (%)	Female (%)	Total	
			(%)	(Number)
Agricultural	98	2	100	885,989
Nonagricultural	69	31	100	659,669
Total	86	14	100	1,545,658

Sources: Guatemala 1976; Chinchilla 1977:48.

farm, regardless of the extent to which their farming may be considered subsistence or commercial production. The bias of this convention is that farm women are "inactive" regardless of the magnitude of their contributions to diverse agricultural, artisan, and domestic activities essential to agricultural production.[12] Men are taken to represent the units of labor in family farms that are based on the "participation of all members of the family—including the children" (Monteforte 1972:183). Conventions of census statistics and modern economics conceal the actual size and disposition of the female labor force in agriculture, and tend to inflate the statistics on national labor force growth when women move from an "invisible" rural work force to an urban context where more of their activities are counted. Hence, a recent report that estimates that the growth from 1975–1980 in labor force participation by Guatemalan women (at 3.7 percent per annum) exceeds that for men (at 2.7 percent per annum) may reflect urbanization more than real growth in the labor force (IDB 1981). Numerous researchers, noting the particular distortions of census data regarding women in the agricultural sector, prefer to use labor force data for males only, or for nonagricultural occupations only (C. Smith 1978, Arizpe 1977, Boserup 1970, IDB 1981).

The time which women or men in peasant areas commit to informal subsistence or cash activities depends on a wide range of factors (family size, sex ratio, the types of crops, landholdings, crafts, and changing market opportunities) that can vary temporally and spatially. With superficial and incomplete national-level data, it is not known where or when women form the backbone of rural subsistence production (especially if males migrate) or whether growing female urban migration may hamper food production. Ethnographic data on the division of labor, such as that presented in Chapter Three regarding the peasant village, T'oj Nam, can aid in the recognition of women's diverse contributions to the agricultural sector, and in more accurate analyses of labor force changes.

While the informal nature of subsistence work eludes quantification, one would expect better records on women's participation rates among rural workers contracted to work seasonally on plantations. Yet despite wide recognition that women and children participate in seasonal wage labor migrations and work in the harvesting of certain crops, national studies surveying the extent of female participation are still lacking. Schmid (1973:215, 199) in his study of migrant workers, estimates that 130,000 wives and 60,000 children or even higher numbers may have accompanied migrant workers (presumed male) to plantations in

1965–66.[13] He also observed that labor contractors sometimes make contracts directly with women, for among 90 migrants he found 17 percent were accompanied by other family members with contracts, including wives.[14] Apart from data which merely affirm women's participation, the extent to which women work as contracted members and as family assistants in the migrant labor stream remains largely a matter of speculation.

Among the permanent plantation labor force, it is less likely that female agricultural workers would be overlooked, but comprehensive data on this sector are lacking as well. It is clear from some reports (Pansini 1980) that resident women work in plantation agriculture, but their opportunities seem more often to be temporary and limited. Perhaps the most revealing data available are simply demographic. Throughout the coastal plantation areas of Guatemala, one observes a marked tendency toward an excess of males relative to females. High indices of masculinity (males per 100 females) are most common in rural areas of the nation, and reach their highest levels in plantation as opposed to subsistence farming regions, where sex ratios tend to be more balanced.[15] (See Map 2–3.) This simple fact suggests that regular employment opportunities are relatively scarce for women on plantations, a problem evident at El Cañaveral.

The Urban Sector

In 1973, 36 percent of Guatemala's population was classified as urban, with nearly 50 percent of the total urban population concentrated in the Department of Guatemala. Guatemala City alone reached 700,538, with a concentration of 37 percent of the nation's total urban population. Guatemala City has grown rapidly since 1950, at a rate of about 5.13 percent per annum in 1950–1964, and a lower rate averaging 2.25 percent per annum from 1964 to 1973. Growth most likely accelerated again after the 1976 earthquake, when thousands whose homes in the countryside had been destroyed established squatter colonies on the city's perimeter. During the period of most rapid population growth, 40 percent of the population increase was due to migration, according to a study by Deanne Termini (cited in Roberts 1973:28). Urbanization in Guatemala is closely associated with Ladinization, since the indigenous population in cities falls much below their percentage in the population as a whole. In Guatemala City, only 7 percent of the population is classified as indigenous (Guatemala 1974c).

MAP 2-3. Guatemalan Regions with Male Surplus

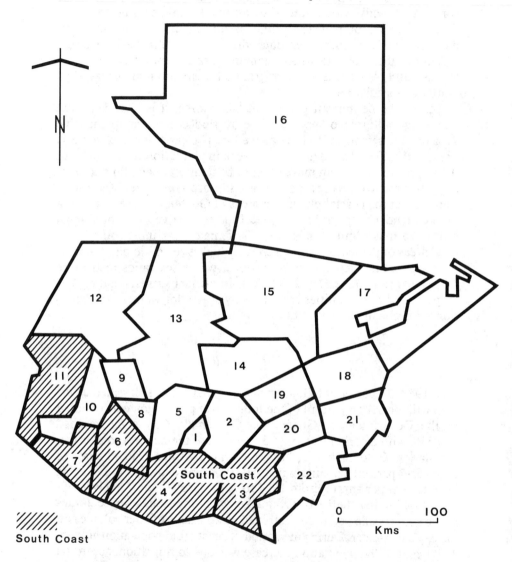

Departments with Index of Masculinity—male/female ratio—greater than 1.05:

Departments
1. Sacatepequez. 2. Guatemala (Capital). 3. Santa Rosa. 4. Escuintla. 5. Chimaltenango. 6. Suchitepéquez. 7. Retalhuleu. 8. Sololá. 9. Totonicapán. 10. Quetzaltenango. 11. San Marcos. 12. Huehuetenango. 13. Quiché. 14. Baja Verapaz. 15. Alta Verapaz. 16. Petén. 17. Izabal. 18. Zacapa. 19. Progreso. 20. Jalapa. 21. Chiquimula. 22. Jutiapa.

As the national capital and largest city in the nation, Guatemala City is not only the center of government administration and services, but also the nucleus of modern commercial activity and industrial production. Table 2–4 shows the contrasting distribution of the labor force by economic sector for the Department of Guatemala and for the nation. The importance of agriculture in the remainder of the country is reversed, with tertiary and secondary sectors employing 82 percent of the population in the department containing the nation's capital. Although the secondary sector accounted for only 31 percent of the department's economically active population in 1966, 66 percent of the nation's manufacturing and 65 percent of all those employed in manufacturing were located in Guatemala City.[16] In 1978, the predominance of Guatemala City and its environs as the center of industry remained unchallenged: The city alone held 52 percent of the nation's 2,357 industrial establishments, and the Department of Guatemala accounted for 64 percent of the nation's total (Guatemala 1979).

Since 1950, industrial production in Guatemala has increased both absolutely and relatively until it now accounts for nearly 17 percent of Gross Domestic Production (IDB 1981). While agricultural employment decreased steadily between 1950 and 1964, employment in the secondary sector of the economy (manufacturing and construction) did

Table 2-4: Proportion of the Economically Active Population in Guatemala, 1964 and 1973, and in Guatemala City, 1974, by Economic Sector

Sector	Nation 1964 (%)	Nation 1973 (%)	Guatemala City 1974 (%)
Primary (agriculture and mining)	66	57	3
Secondary manufacturing, construction, and utilities)	14	18	34
Tertiary (commerce, transportation, communications, and services)	19	22	60
Unknown	1	2	3
Total	100	99	100

Sources: Adapted from Deanne Termini, "Socio-economic and Demographic Characteristics of the Population of Guatemala City with Special Reference to Migrant–Non-Migrant Differences." Master's thesis, University of Texas at Austin, cited in Roberts (1973:30); Guatemala, Censo de la Poblacion, 1964, cited in Fletcher et al. (1970:12–13).

not keep pace or serve as a reliable outlet for underemployed farm labor (Fletcher et al. 1970:9). The changes in the structure of the labor force in the Department of Guatemala (shown in Table 2–5) suggest that displaced agricultural labor disappears into the service, commercial, and "unclassified" categories.

The expansion of industry in Guatemala appears to be capital-intensive rather than labor-intensive, despite the availability of a large urban work force. Chinchilla asserts that recent industrial strategy in Guatemala has favored

> capital-intensive, multinational giants which consolidate or eliminate existing industries, replace old job categories which some new ones, and create little overall employment. . . . While there are no available statistics on the capital-labor ratio for industry alone, a United States AID study reported that U.S. investment in Guatemala accounts for 11% of the total direct investment but only 1% of the labor force. (1977:47)[17]

The concentration of 51 percent of the economically active population of the Department of Guatemala in the tertiary sector of the economy indicates that this sector absorbs at least some of the surplus labor force and jobless urban migrants. The 1973 census showed that 56 percent of the total national labor force in the tertiary sector resided in the Department of Guatemala. Services alone contributed 31 percent

Table 2–5. Proportion of the Economically Active Population in Department of Guatemala by Economic Sector, 1950, 1964, 1973

Sector	1950 (%)	1950 (%)	1964 (%)	1964 (%)	1973 (%)	1973 (%)
Primary		23		14		12
Agriculture	23		14		12	
Secondary		32		31		31
Industry	24		24		23	
Construction	8		7		8	
Tertiary		45		52		51
Transportation and communications	5		5		5	
Commerce	12		14		15	
Services	28		33		31	
Unclassified		1		3		5
Total		100%		100%		99%

Source: Guatemala, Censos de la Población, 1950, 1964, cited in Fletcher et al. 1970; Guatemala 1975.

of all employment in the Department of Guatemala (see Table 2-5). Urban growth is thus not so much a response to economic opportunities in industry as a response to insufficient alternatives in the rural subsistence sector. As in Latin America generally, the capital city is the mecca of the unemployed and landless.

Since neither commercial agriculture nor modern industry has required a large stable labor force, those squeezed out of subsistence farming enter the urban tertiary sector. There, high levels of unemployment and underemployment are disguised by the proliferation of informal, irregular jobs and self-employment in marginal services, petty vending, and domestic craft production (Arizpe 1977).[18] The shortage of low-income urban housing and the growth of "marginal zones" such as the urban squatter settlement of San Lorenzo (discussed in Chapter Five) are associated with the economic factors that push a growing labor force into the urban sector. In Amaro's interpretation:

> The growing presence of marginal zones that surround the capital, whether in the gulleys or periphery, signifies that the process of industrial growth is very slow and is not sufficient to absorb the labor power existing in these areas. . . . As a consequence of the increase of these marginal zones, there is an increase in the people occupied in the tertiary sector, since lacking work in industry and unable to carry out agricultural tasks in the urban area, they tend to work in activities with very low productivity, as shoe shiners, ticket sellers, artisans, etc. These are practically equivalent to what the economists call "disguised unemployment." (translated, 1970:150)

The development of capitalist industry and agriculture in Guatemala entails competition with the traditional peasant farmer and the household system of handicraft production, both of which are labor-intensive forms of production. As small-scale producers are forced out of production by the more lucrative use of land for large-scale commercial agriculture and by the cheapness of mass-produced industrial products, they become increasingly dependent upon wage labor in large capitalist enterprises, or lacking such opportunities, they turn to marginal sources of employment where capitalist relations of production have not yet penetrated. Many recent observers have found that the net effect of these changes is increasing economic inequality (Fletcher et al. 1970:23; Adams 1970:393; Chinchilla 1977:56; Jonas and Tobis 1974). These changes are consistent with the features of dependent capitalism.

Guatemala City plays a central role in the hierarchal structure of the nation. In the economy as a whole, a small minority wields tremendous power, based on its economic interests in both the rural and urban sectors of the nation. It is composed of large property owners and top-level personnel in the corporate sector: "administrators, executives, and managers," as well as "professionals and technicians." In 1964, this elite was only 4.2 percent of the nation's economically active population, but accounted for 11.6 percent of the active population in the Department of Guatemala (Guatemala 1964). The concentration in the capital is further revealed by the fact that nationally 48 percent of those in the administrative category and 59 percent of those in the professional category resided in the Department of Guatemala. Appropriately, Adams reports that 85 percent of all lawyers are concentrated in the metropolis (1970:165). These groups form the middle- and upper-income levels of Guatemalan society and reside in the capital's exclusive areas, ranging from neighborhoods of fortress-like mansions to the more modest but well-to-do suburban-style developments such as modern Villa Rosa. In general, big capital and its professional staff concentrate in the capital city.

Women in nonfarm employment. The available data on the sex composition of the nation's nonagricultural labor force hint at the way dependent capitalism incorporates women. With women as 31 percent of the nonagricultural labor force, Chinchilla points out that the 1973 census figures show a decline from the 1921 census when "women made up more than half (58 percent) of the nonagricultural labor force." (1977:41). Between 1950 and 1973, the percentage of all economically active women in the tertiary sector increased from 57 percent to 68 percent, while that for working men increased less dramatically to 15 percent starting from only 11 percent in 1950. In contrast, in the secondary sector the proportion of all employed women decreased from 28 percent to 22 percent while that of men increased from 12 percent to 18 percent in this same period.

In manufacturing, the percentage of active females had declined from 22 percent in 1946 to 18 percent by 1965, with a much lower proportion of women working for wages than men. Just 32.4 percent of the women compared to 57.6 percent of the men worked for wages or salaries. The corresponding self-employment figures, 57 percent for women and 35 percent for men, show that women more often must generate their own jobs in manufacturing. These figures suggest that men are preferred in formal wage work in the larger capitalist enterprises of the secondary sector. In manufacturing, Chinchilla notes, new occupational specialties have "created a demand for new labor which men have filled in much greater proportion than women, even in industries such as textiles and tobacco, that have traditionally hired women" (1977:48).

In the tertiary sector, male workers are more evenly distributed between commerce, transportation, and communication, as well as services, while 64 percent of the women are concentrated in domestic service (Chinchilla 1977:49–50). More strikingly, 54 percent of all economically active women in Guatemala City work as domestic employees (Jonas and Tobis 1974:9). The thesis that dependent capitalism tends to generate urban growth that is absorbed by tertiary sector employment has special significance for women. As in Latin America generally, Guatemalan urban populations show a preponderance of women. This has been attributed to the existence of female employment opportunities in the cities, while male employment opportunities tend to be concentrated in the countryside, particularly the centers of commercial agriculture (Adams 1970:135; Dombrowski et al. 1970:75). Guatemala City itself shows a large surplus of women; in the 1973 census the index of masculinity was but 88.48, indicating a surplus of 42,816 women in a population of 700,538. Since migration accounts for a large percentage of the population growth, women evidently predominate among the migrants to the city. Roberts (1973:29) cites Deanne Termini's study of migration to Guatemala City, which shows that among economically active women migrants, the proportion of service workers is particularly high—64 percent—compared to 28 percent for nonmigrant women. This contrasts with the findings for migrant and nonmigrant male workers, who show low levels of economic activity in services and much higher participation in artisan occupations (see Table 2–6).

These figures strongly suggest that new forms of sex segregation are developing in urban employment. Women are disproportionately found in informal employment in both the secondary and tertiary sectors of the urban economy. Migrant women are the most critically affected by the lack of economic alternatives and must either find work as domes-

Table 2-6. Some Types of Economic Activity among Migrants and Non-Migrants of Each Sex in Guatemala City

Type	Men		Women	
	Non-Migrant (%)	Migrant (%)	Non-Migrant (%)	Migrant (%)
Services	1.9	10.7	28.3	63.7
Crafts	46.2	33.2	NA	NA

Source: Deanne Termini, "Socio-Economic and Demographic Characteristics of the Population of Guatemala City with Special Reference to Migrant–Non-Migrant Differences, Master's thesis, University of Texas at Austin, cited in Roberts (1973:29).
NA: Information not available.

tic employees or turn to self-employment in petty commerce or craft activities. The hypertrophy of tertiary economic activities that affects both sexes under a system of dependent capitalist development appears in Guatemala to apply with much greater severity to women.

Women's limited access to formal employment in higher occupational categories is also revealed by the census. Table 2–7 shows the degree of occupational segregation in nonagricultural employment by sex for three census years covering the period 1950 to 1973.

Higher-level positions such as the professions and particularly management have become increasingly male dominated over the last twenty years, while women increased their proportions in the lower categories of office workers and to a lesser extent sales. In the professional category, women are predominately teachers (three-fourths of all women professionals) at lower-level institutions, while as clerical workers women are concentrated in secreterial positions (Chinchilla 1977). Among the nation's total population of public and private school teachers (nearly 26,000 in 1974), the male/female ratio ranges from a very low 0.08 for preprimary teachers, to 0.62 for primary school teachers, up to a high 1.97 for middle-level teachers—showing a marked male predominance at the upper levels (Guatemala 1974a:214). The data suggest that the distribution of formal positions in the modern economy follows the patterns of sex segregation that have become entrenched in industrially developed societies.

By categorizing certain occupations as "middle and upper strata" (primarily professional, managerial, clerical, and sales), Amaro found that a higher proportion of working women (26 percent) than of work-

Table 2-7. Ratio of Male to Female Workers in Nonagricultural Occupations, Guatemala, 1950, 1964, 1973

Category	1950	1965	1973
Professional	1.34	1.55	1.47
Managerial	1.76	2.56	4.32
Office work	3.96	2.49	1.94
Sales	2.30	2.46	1.86
Mines	89.50	—	160.00
Transportation	109.50	255.10	211.90
Artisan, operative	2.87	4.36	4.70
Unskilled	7.14	12.30	12.90
Service	.55	.47	.66
Total nonagricultural	1.93	2.24	2.29

Source: Calculated from Guatemala, Censos de la Poblacion, 1950, 1964, 1973, as cited in Chinchilla (1977:55).

ing men (12 percent) belong to these strata, which comprise 14 percent of the nation's economically active population. He also found that "58 percent of the women who belong to the upper and middle strata are concentrated in the capital" (1970:156), suggesting that women of the urban middle classes are more likely to be economically active than women of the lower classes—a finding congruent with Safa's thesis that in Latin America primarily middle- and upper-class women benefit from the (initial) expansion of formal employment in the urban tertiary sector (1977). Yet this does not mean that upper strata women are more highly motivated to "work" than others. Just as when low-paid primary school teachers are lumped with high-income doctors as professionals, we should be wary of crude assumptions regarding class, keeping in mind that (a) the allegedly higher "sales" category includes many informal and marginal women vendors, and (b) census data tend to underreport informal employment of women, which is how poor women generally earn a living. Of some 800 urban households belonging to the "popular classes" studied in 1948 and 1951, Monteforte (1959) found that women form an important part of the urban labor force, albeit in a form not enumerated by most census takers. The sample showed that in addition to the work of the "head" (man) of the household, 90 percent of the wives work—two-thirds in piece-work within the home, and one-third in work outside the home—with the remaining 10 percent performing domestic duties only (1959:282–284). This strongly suggests that in the city as well as in peasant areas, censuses do not report domestic piece work for cash income as "economic activity." This discrepancy between census data and fieldwork recurs at the community level.

The National Social Structure: Class Divisions

The social structure of Guatemala is often described in terms of class relations compounded by the ethnic division between Mayas and Ladinos. In general, in areas where both cultural groups are present, Ladinos still dominate Maya groups through greater control over the socioeconomic resources of a capitalist society. Some writers interpret the overall relationship between the two ethnic groups as a "class" relation of Ladino dominance (Herbert 1970). Class relations are further complicated by the degrees to which various sectors of Guatemalan society are integrated into a capitalist market economy (Carmack 1976). Both the rural and urban sectors are characterized by segments of the population that stand outside the conventional division of capitalist society into capitalists and wageworkers.

Guzman et al. (1971) proposed a general framework of Guatemalan class structure.[19] In the rural sector, 40 percent of the population are peasants or semiproletarians who remain at least partly dependent on a "precapitalist" or domestic mode of production. These peasants are an extremely poor, predominantly Maya population that resorts to low-paying seasonal wage labor to supplement a peasant livelihood. Another stratum, the rural-urban subproletariat also remains largely excluded from capitalist relations of production but has lost its connection to the land. Estimated to include 7 percent of the population, it depends on informal sources of income, self-employment, and personal services, that are generally considered "marginal" to the capitalist economic system. While both the peasantry and subproletariat are often seen as "marginal" to the capitalist economy, they act as an elastic labor reserve responsive to major swings in demand for labor, both seasonally and regionally.

More completely integrated into capitalist production is the proletariat, which has been estimated to include around 20 percent of the population (Guzman et al. 1971). Roughly three-fourths are agricultural workers, while the rest are urban workers in industrial enterprises. An estimated two-thirds of the agricultural proletariat are Ladinos. This class is defined by its lack of control over productive capital and its complete dependence upon regular wage labor. An additional quasi-proletarian stratum (7 percent of the population) consists of tenant farmers. Since these tenants are granted the use of small plots belonging to large landowners, they gain some control over the production process, but ultimately they depend upon the landowner as their employer. Taken together, the peasant and proletarian classes comprise as much as 76 percent of the nation's population.

The dominant classes in Guatemala are the bourgeoisie and the petty bourgeoisie—distinguished in part by the quantity of capital they work with. The petty bourgeoisie include around 20 percent of the population, of whom roughly three-fourths are rural residents. Mainly Ladinos (around three-fourths), these are small business owners, shopkeepers, owners of family artisan workshops or farms, truck owners, and lower-level bureaucrats. In rural towns, this class may form the local elite, although its power to dominate is limited by the scale of its resources.

The bourgeoisie, or large capitalists, by definition control the means of production on a large scale: landed property (the agro-export latifundios), and commercial and industrial capital. This class can be further divided into a tiny stratum (0.3 percent of the population) with agricultural and export interests: large landowners, industrialists, major importers and exporters, managers of foreign interests, bankers, and major stockholders in diverse businesses and services. The remainder of the bourgeoisie has been described as a "dependent" bourgeoisie which serves as the instrument of capitalist domination. This group encompasses public and private bureaucrats at executive levels; medium sized merchants, industrialists, owners of agricultural and artisan enterprises; owners of the communications media; professionals, intellectuals, and politicians. In my own view, it should also include the military elite who are the dominant "politicians," with substantial control over economic resources as well.

Although the nature and implications of the class structure of Guatemala is a subject of debate (as in most Latin American nations), there is general agreement that at least three-fourths of the population belong to low-income groups and own little or no property, while a tiny minority of the remaining population controls most of the nation's wealth. There is also general agreement that a significant part of the elite is "dependent," serving as functionaries or intermediaries for an international capitalist class (Cf. Monteforte 1959, 1972; Amaro 1970; Guzman et al. 1971; Flores Alvarado 1971; Stavenhagen 1975).

How do women fit into Guatemala's class structure? This question has received far less attention in Guatemala than ethnicity in relation to class. Rather, as mentioned earlier, women disappear within designations of class by household, where men are defined as representatives of the household. If class is occupationally defined, then we encounter anomalies where women's class designation and their occupation do not agree. If class is defined according to control over capital, landed or otherwise, published studies are lacking. Some writers point out that "certain social strata, such as bureaucrats, the armed forces, students, domestic servants, and the lumpenproletariat, cannot be classified as 'classes' (Bath and James 1976:15). If so, then most Guatemalan urban working women, among whom more than half are domestic servants, are "classless" in their own right. The failure to analytically confront the problem of women and class is related to the general uncertainty over the implications of maternity, and the ways it is enlisted into the system of class reproduction. Curiously, it is much easier to discover the number of children per woman, married (4.8) or single (0.86) (Guatemala 1974a:30) than it is to discover the proportions of women that are landless. Even where women do have land rights, they tend to be poorly defined and defended by notions that empower (male) heads of households with managerial rights. Just as the conventional tallying of "economic activity" may undercount women, class analyses may overcount women as members of classes when in certain circumstances they may be merely servicing those classes. Research that draws attention to these issues will help to advance our understanding of the relationship of women to the class structure. The present research features the major components of Guatemalan class structure: Maya peasants, rural and urban proletarians, urban subproletarians, petty bourgeois, and dependent bourgeois. Relations between gender and class are explored in each case.

Ethnicity

Ethnicity in Guatemala has already been linked to regional, economic, and class divisions. Here I simply outline general cultural characteristics that distinguish the Maya and Ladino populations of Guatemala. We have seen that the Mayas are largely concentrated in the western highlands where most are rural peasants, partly dependent on subsistence production, supplemented by wage work and cottage industries. Ladinos are found in all regions of Guatemala and represent the full spectrum of the socioeconomic class structure within the nation. Where the two cultural groups are in intimate contact, as in the towns of the western highlands, the Ladinos generally have been able to monopolize the dominant positions as urbanized commercial, cultural, and political intermediaries between the Maya-speaking peasants and the national society. There is a vast literature analysing the manifold general and local variations between Maya and Ladino cultures and their interaction in Guatemala. The interaction has been variously described as one of "caste" stratification, cultural pluralism, and outright racism.[20] Undisputably, by virtue of their shared language and cultural orientation, Ladinos have an advantage operating in a capitalist system encrusted with a European heritage.

Guatemala's indigenous population is generally identified by the ability to speak one of twenty-two Maya languages, and by the use of distinctive styles of clothing which differ from European standards because they are handmade, colorful, and conform to local styles of decoration. Ladinos use the Spanish language, and dress in Euro-American clothing styles that identify them with a worldwide cultural mainstream. Language and clothing are the most obvious cultural differences between the two ethnic groups. In addition, Maya religious beliefs and practices are commonly cited as major areas of cultural difference from the Ladino traditions of Catholicism. Many Maya com-

44

munities continue to combine pre-Hispanic religious elements with veneers of Christianity, although these pre-Conquest aspects have been eroding rapidly in the last forty years. These elements include the maintenance of pre-Hispanic calendric systems, rituals and deities, ceremonial dances, and possibly some aspects of the cargo system for filling community religious and political offices (Carmack 1981; Tedlock 1982). As Carmack has shown, the surviving fragments of Maya culture are "highly provincial and distorted elements of that ancient culture" (1981:355). Certain other cultural differences such as high illiteracy, rural residence patterns, and other aspects of the cargo system (e.g., unpaid labor for municipal duties) seem to be related more to the subordinate socioeconomic status of the Maya relative to the Ladino than to cultural difference per se.

Gender and Ethnicity

Guatemalan gender roles have been the subject of intriguing observations and speculation but relatively little detailed study regarding cultural differences. Paradoxically, using the standard cultural criteria to define indigenous groups, women are generally more "indigenous" than men throughout the nation. It is consistently found that women are more likely than men to be monolingual Maya-speakers, and to maintain distinctive indigenous clothing styles (See Adams 1956; Applebaum 1967:12; Dombrowski et al. 1970; Herbert 1970; Hinshaw 1975; Tax 1952). Further, Maya women are less literate than men, and generally have less complete knowledge and experience of the national society. This is because Maya men are more completely integrated into Ladino culture; they are significantly affected by it in their behavior and undoubtedly influenced in their beliefs about gender. I suggest that this occurs not because traditional Maya gender roles make men more receptive to foreign influence, but because the culture that accompanies capitalist growth differentiates by gender.

Various comparisons of gender roles among Ladinos and indigenous groups have stressed the high value placed on machismo (male dominance) by Ladino men (Wolf 1959; Colby and van den Berghe 1969).[21] Male-female relations within indigenous cultures are described as more egalitarian although still characterized by a degree of male dominance. More specifically, indigenous men have been described as more committed to their families, with "strong paternal dyads," in contrast to Ladino families where male commitments are weaker (Wolf 1966; Adams 1960; Maynard 1974). Maynard has characterized the sex roles of

45

the indigenous and Ladino cultures in the village of Palin as two forms of patriarchy: "responsible patriarchy" among the Pokomam-Maya indigenous groups and "irresponsible patriarchy" among the Ladinos. Men are seen as dominant in both cultural groups in this village, but indigenous men were more likely to provide regular economic support for their families while Ladino men were less reliable. An implicit paradox in these findings is that Ladino males, who are generally conceded to enjoy real economic advantages relative to indigenous males, are more likely to neglect their families economically, and be preoccupied with demonstrating male dominance through sexual promiscuity. Both Wolf (1959, 1966) and Maynard (1963, 1974) interpret these behavioral differences largely in terms of different systems of cultural values held by the two ethnic groups. Wolf claims that in indigenous culture the male role has greater "prestige," and that men "play significant roles in the social and ceremonial life" which support a strong husband-father role even where their economic role is weak (1966:64).

Neither Wolf nor Maynard examine the possibility that the different relations between men's and women's economic roles in each ethnic group may have a bearing on male behavior and masculine values. Recent work by Ehlers (1980) on Maya women in cottage industries parallels my own efforts to understand the economic bases for the development of male chauvinism among the Maya. In the community of T'oj Nam, consideration of gender divisions among the Maya and local Ladino minority can shed some light on the problem of machismo, particularly when compared to the urban and plantation communities where Ladino culture predominates.

Introducing the Four Communities

The selection of four research sites was guided by the desire to compare sexual economics and stratification across class, ethnic, and rural-urban divisions. My interest was to discover whether the agrarian Maya populations did represent a substantially different sexual order than the more capitalistic Ladinos. I also believed that capitalist plantation agriculture would be associated with strong male dominance, deriving not only from Latin cultural tradition, but also from the large-scale organization of a male work force. The choice of two urban communities was prompted by questions regarding the impact of urbanism on male-female work and social relations. The condition of poverty in shantytowns, I suspected, would not support great male domination, although it would be affected by male supremacist ideals emanating both from traditional Hispanic and modern Western cultures. In the middle class, I expected a mixture of model Latin domesticity for women combined with higher education and some professionalism, tinged with feminism given that the feminist movement was in full swing in capitalist centers throughout the Western world.

T'oj Nam: A Rural Maya Village

Located in Guatemala's western highlands, T'oj Nam has a predominantly Maya population and a small but influential Ladino minority. The local economy is based on domestic subsistence production which, due to insufficient landholdings, must be supplemented by seasonal wage labor and other sources of cash income. The community is part of a regional marketing system, yet remains relatively cut off from urban commerce and industry.

Most people of T'oj Nam are proletarianized peasants.[22] Surplus leaves the community not so much in the form of goods produced within the peasant community as in the form of migrant wage labor to be consumed by other sectors of the economy. With meagre minifundios, the vast majority of peasant households lack enough land for subsistence and are economically compelled to send seasonal wage laborers to commercial plantations. In addition, peasants migrate to lowland regions to rent land on which to grow subsistence crops.

By virtue of their seasonal wage labor, T'oj Nam migrants might be regarded as semi-proletarian (Guzman et al. 1971). Monteforte, however, points out that "the semi-proletarian indigene is a landholder and unites more of the characteristics of the traditional peasant than of the agricultural worker" (translated 1972:83). Although T'oj Nam contributes an important part of its labor force to Guatemala's massive annual migrations of seasonal workers, I focus on its inhabitants as peasants residing in their home community where they are occupied with household subsistence production.

Culturally, T'oj Nam shares a fragmentary Maya heritage which in the distinct communities of the highlands has been transformed and distorted to varius degrees by Spanish colonial and Guatemalan national influences. The people of T'oj Nam are Mam-speakers, one of the largest of Guatemala's twenty-two Maya language groups. Selected for study because it appears to be one of the more "traditional" communities, T'oj Nam is distinguished by the vigor of its native language, the use of colorful handmade clothing by both sexes, as well as the production of Maya staple foods. Traditional Maya religious practices can also be found there, although Christianity has had a great deal of influence. While other Maya communities have different features derived from Maya traditions, the particular patterns of T'oj Nam suggest that both sexes have been relatively cut off from the mainstream of national culture. Nonetheless, given the dependence on seasonal wage labor migration and regional marketing found in T'oj Nam, labeling it "traditional" should not be taken to mean that this is an "unchanged" indigenous community or an example of "pure" Maya culture. In Guatemala there are no virgin villages.

Apart from its Maya features, T'oj Nam was a desirable research site because earlier anthropological studies had been conducted in this area (Stadelman, 1940; Wagley 1941, 1949; Oakes 1951a, 1951b).

El Cañaveral: A Sugar Plantation

El Cañaveral is a large sugarcane plantation located in Guatemala's south coast plantation belt. It has a resident worker's comunity on its land which became the focus of my research. El Cañaveral belongs to the agro-export sector of the economy and in many respects fits the classic image of the "factory in the field." As a commercial enterprise, the economic base of El Cañaveral is capital-intensive production of the sugar crop destined for sale both within Guatemala and abroad. For the worker's community, the economic base is their wage labor.

The permanent plantation workers are rural proletarians. Unlike peasants, they lack land or even housing of their own and depend entirely upon their employment as wage laborers. The fact that they are awarded various prestations such as housing, food rations, and the use of small plots of land, in addition to wages, does not substantially alter their position as rural workers dependent upon cash wages. The permanent workers and their families form a relatively homogeneous Ladino-mestizo[23] community with little or no cultural identification with Maya populations. Both culturally and as a class, the resident workers' community can be distinguished from the cosmopolitain elite which owns and administers the plantation and from the seasonal wage laborers, the semi-proletarians, who migrate from Maya and Ladino peasant communities.

El Cañaveral is intimately tied to the world market economy through its exports. It enjoys efficient transportation links to provincial cities, the port, and to the national capital. But its local economy, like a company town, is almost entirely dependent upon the cash incomes earned by those with formal plantation employment.

Large plantation communities such as El Cañaveral have been little studied in Guatemala. Much of the data available focuses on the condition of the migrant labor force rather than the stable plantation community (see Schmid 1973; Hoyt 1955; and for an exception, Pansini 1977).

San Lorenzo: An Urban Squatter Settlement

This community is part of a large urban squatter settlement or shantytown located in Guatemala City. As an urban community, it is not distinguished by shared ethnic origins or by shared economic activities. Its boundaries are marked off by the slopes of the ravine where the makeshift houses of the urban poor crowd in upon each other. That is, it is most easily defined by its precarious location and visibly poor standard of living. Lacking economic alternatives, San Lorenzans built their homes and their community on marginal land without the security of ownership titles or the benefit of basic urban services.

The squatter settlement includes both city-born residents and a high proportion of migrants from provinces throughout the country, both Ladinos and Mayas.[24] It is a kind of urban melting pot for the nation's low-income groups. With an economic infrastructure that is diversified and relatively unstable, low incomes are a common denominator.

As a fully urban district within the nation's capital city, San Lorenzo is integrated into the market economy and completely dependent upon cash incomes that are earned and spent in the diverse zones of the city. Yet few of the residents are integrated into the *formal* sectors of the economy. The class composition includes petty bourgeois elements and proletarians, but many people in informal pursuits lack a clearly defined class status. Variously described as the "marginalized mass," the "informal labor sector" (Arizpe 1977), the "reserve labor supply," or "sub-proletariat" (Guzman et al. 1971), squatter populations such as those of Guatemala City are held to be part of capitalist society, yet not fully or stably integrated into the capitalist productive processes and labor relations. When demand for their labor in the capitalist sector is inadequate, they survive by performing varied services and other economic activities which remain outside the scope of the industrial capitalist form of production.

San Lorenzo was selected as a research site because an important study of the neighborhood was conducted by Roberts (1973), and various other studies and government surveys have dealt with the subject of squatter settlements and "marginal areas" within the city. Although squatter settlements are just one type of low-income housing in Guatemala City, Robert's comparative study has shown that the socioeconomic differences between a planned and legally settled urban neighborhood, Planificada, and San Lorenzo are not very great.

Villa Rosa: An Urban "Middle-Class" Neighborhood

This community is an urban middle-income housing development located within Guatemala City. I describe it as "middle-class" on the basis of its standard of living and consumption patterns. In these terms, it ranks below the most powerful and wealthy segments of the bourgeoisie residing in more exclusive and luxurious neighborhoods, but well above the vast majority of the urban population in terms of comforts and conveniences, and largely conforms to what is known as a middle-class lifestyle in North America.

Like San Lorenzo, the population of Villa Rosa is heterogeneous in its origins and socioeconomic activities, with spheres of interest that are in no way confined to the residential community. Culturally, the population is cosmopolitan, well-educated, and nationalistic. Links with North American and European culture are esteemed, and contemporary Maya cultures are disdained.

Highly integrated into the national socioeconomic system, the economic underpinnings for Villa Rosa are found in formal, salaried employment in modern capitalist enterprises or in the civil and military bureaucracies. The class composition can be described as the "dependent bourgeoisie." At the extremes, the community also includes a few families that belong to the agricultural-export bourgeoisie and to the higher levels of the petty bourgeoisie.

Although Villa Rosa represents a social sector whose lifestyles, socioeconomic concerns, and cultural values receive wide exposure in the public media, this type of community has been largely ignored as a subject of anthropological research in Guatemala, so that I was unable to build on previous community-based data. Still, the population of Villa Rosa is highly articulate and conscious of its role in national society. This tends to compensate for, as well as explain, the lack of initiative by social scientists in studying such communities. However, community-level research can yield greater understanding of the role of women in the population.

Summary

In this chapter I have outlined the general characteristics of Guatemala as a complex society, and of the four communities as subunits within the nation. Clearly, each community is conditioned by the nature of its interaction with the larger socioeconomic system. An understanding of this interaction makes it possible to study women's roles without losing a larger perspective, even as we focus on community-level data. The following exposition of the role of women in each community undertakes a more detailed description and analysis for each area. I intend to show how the position of women is conditioned not just by local relationships to work, men, family, and the community, but also by the national socioeconomic structure.

CHAPTER THREE

T'oj Nam: A Maya Peasant Village

The Setting: Isolation, Contact, and Change

T'oj Nam is a *municipio* of the northwest highlands of Guatemala, a region characterized by the persistence of Maya peasant communities with a network of small, urban market and administrative centers serving a predominantly rural population. As a municipio, T'oj Nam is both an administrative unit somewhat comparable to a U.S. county, and a cultural subunit of one of the major Maya linguistic and cultural groups (Tax 1937). Most of the people are indigenous Mam-speakers who share distinctive features of dialect and dress that set them apart from neighboring Mam municipios as well as from Ladinos. Compared with other Maya areas such as the more densely populated central highlands to the southeast, T'oj Nam and its Mam neighbors may be characterized as "peripheral" (W. Smith 1977, C. Smith 1978).[1] (Fieldwork in T'oj Nam is described in Appendix Two.)

With a population close to 11,000, T'oj Nam has a strong Mam majority making up 92 percent of the population, while the remaining 8 percent are Ladinos. As in similar isolated Maya communities, the Ladino minority appears to have relatively recent origins, the first known permanent settlers arriving in the latter half of the nineteenth century with the capitalist expansion of coffee production (Colby and van den Berghe 1969; Oakes 1951a; Wasserstrom 1975).[2] Only 11 percent of the municipal population is classified as "urban"—those living in the town center. Nearly all the Ladinos are town residents, holding a central economic position despite their small numbers in the municipio as a whole. The municipal sex ratio, unlike the ethnic and urban variables, shows an exceedingly balanced division: 50.005 percent are males. Family size in both rural and town areas averages close to five persons per family (Anonymous 1973). The population is young and poorly educated, with 53 percent under age eighteen and only 11 percent literate.

T'oj Nam is a mountainous area of about 320 square kilometers (124 square miles). The town center is situated in a picturesque valley at an altitude of nearly 2,500 meters (over 8,000 feet). A small river descends through the valley and flows beside the town. The single road suited for automobiles bisects the town as it passes from the departmental capital on to one of the *aldeas* (hamlets). As link to the nation, the town center contains the municipal buildings, the marketplace, the large Catholic church, a primary school, and a small medical clinic. The few major stores and large homes are also located in the center. Some are two-story stucco buildings with glass windows and decorative features that give them an alpine appearance suited to the mountainous terrain. Houses in town are usually painted white and enjoy the prestige of having several rooms, wooden or tile floors, and tile or corrugated metal roofs. Those along the main street usually have electricity, and sometimes running water. In contrast, the rural population lives in small, isolated homesteads or hamlets scattered among the hillsides and high plateaus, or further along the valley. Rural homes are generally one-room adobe structures with dirt floors and roofs of thatch or of wooden shingles. The poorer ones may be constructed of wattle and daub, with plastic sheets to keep out the wind, while the costlier ones may sport whitewashed walls and new tile or metal roofs. Since nighttime temperatures frequently drop to freezing at this high altitude, most families have their cooking fires within their one-room houses. Rural homes lack electricity or running water.

In the valley, maize is the dominant crop and the staff of life to the Mam population. Maize is planted in nearly 85 percent of the cultivated fields and it surrounds the village. The fields at higher altitudes are too cold for maize, but are used for potato cultivation and sheep herding. Potato crops use about 10 percent of the total cultivated land, and around 19,000 sheep and 2,000 goats graze the high meadows (Anonymous 1973). The higher altitudes also contain valuable tree cover, the source of firewood for cooking and heating homes in the chilly climate. Visually, the lack of trees near the town is a bleak testimony to the constant search for firewood, while the spacing of rural houses and the patchwork appearance of small cornfields on the hillsides suggests a scarcity of arable land. As already noted, land scarcity is an acute problem throughout the highlands, and one which critically affects the people of T'oj Nam.

Isolated by mountain ranges, T'oj Nam has limited transportation facilities linking it to the rest of the nation. The nearest major city, the departmental capital, is located about forty-eight kilometers away via a rough dirt road passable only to sturdy vehicles. Road and bus service have just been opened during the last decade. The bus ride to the national capital requires another four to five hours. Two buses enter and leave the town daily, loaded with migrants, market vendors, retailers, and their goods. Few residents own vehicles and these are infrequently used. Beyond this, there is only an irregular traffic of trucks that transport migrant workers to the coast, and occasional tourist cars.

Compounding its physical isolation, T'oj Nam has poor communication services. There is postal service and a telegraph, but no telephone. Newspapers arrive by bus for subscribers only, of which there are only one or two. Although the town has electricity, until recently the power source was a local diesel motor which operated only a few hours each evening. Since the period of fieldwork, this has been replaced by a connection to a national hydroelectric power source. While only two homes have televisions, transistor radios have become fairly commonplace, bringing news and marimba music from afar.

Urban services are haphazard. They include a health center staffed with a nurse's aid and secretary, with periodic visits from a doctor. Lacking a pharmacy, local stores and individuals supply and administer a variety of drugs. There is no professional dental care (but there are experienced tooth pullers).

Religious services are offered by a Catholic priest, a part-time resident. Occasionally a group of nuns visit to present lectures. The only other nationally organized religion present in T'oj Nam is Evangelism which has a local temple and has sponsored a visiting American missionary couple.

Since representatives of the national police are not stationed in the municipio, policing is handled by local officials under the authority of the *alcalde* (mayor). In criminal cases, investigators from the departmental capital are called in. The educational system consists of ten primary schools: one in the town center that goes through sixth grade, and nine in the aldeas that teach only the first three or four grades. There are no private schools, and no local high school.

Commercially, the town center has a few general stores with a moderate supply of modern goods, but none sell modern appliances (radios are bought in larger towns or cities). There are no banks, industrial enterprises, nor even a cinema. Yet as an area of mild tourist interest, the town has two *pensiones* (guest houses) and three *comedores* (kitchen-restaurants) that open daily.

Despite its limited forms of modern transportation and communication with the outside world, the isolation of T'oj Nam should not be overemphasized. Although information on the intensity of direct contact in T'oj Nam during the colonial period is not available, the permanent settlement of Ladino labor contractors and intermediaries established roughly a century of regular contact with an alien culture. Apart from encounters with the dominant Ladino culture, there is a long history of regular contact and trade between T'oj Nam and other Maya municipios via mule trails and foot paths, while the rotating markets of Maya communities have roots in an ancient system of regional trade.

In recent times, modern national and international culture has penetrated with increasingly frequent visits by missionaries, teachers, anthropologists, linguists, Peace Corps workers, development agents, and hardy tourists.[3]

In the other direction, outmigration to seek work, land, goods, and services in other parts of Guatemala has grown rapidly and involves a large percentage of the population. Poverty and population pressure on a limited land base are obviously "push" factors, but the desire for cash and a growing awareness of modern goods and of educational and economic alternatives outside the municipio add to the outflow. On returning to T'oj Nam, the migrant workers, students, and entrepreneurs inevitably transmit new goods, ideas, and values to the community, as do the foreign visitors. These culture-brokers are not the *causes* of change in T'oj Nam as much as messengers who disseminate notions of appropriate cultural behavior. While the population of T'oj Nam is too tiny to leave its particular cultural stamp on the national culture, its mass-produced goods, and its major political and economic institutions, the two-way traffic between T'oj Nam and the rest of the nation is accelerating as the capitalist economy expands.

Economic Organization

The nature of the local economy is suggested by the degree of contact between T'oj Nam and the outside world. A high degree of economic self-sufficiency is no longer possible, while complete dependence on the external market economy is still impossible. Inhabitants achieve a measure of self-sufficiency through small-scale peasant farming, but all households require some cash income to purchase supplementary food and supplies. T'oj Nam demonstrates its dependence within a larger economic system by its need to generate cash income from external sources. A large percentage of its population must regularly migrate to find seasonal employment on the coastal plantations. From the national perspective, T'oj Nam is a labor reserve for the plantation economy.

Insulated by mountains and poor roads from the full impact of industrial capitalism, T'oj Nam operates with relatively little cash and a low level of economic specialization. It is a poor community. The level of demand is so low that few people with special skills can support themselves as full-time specialists. There are no industrial concerns or business enterprises that offer regular paid employment to as many as ten local people. The largest local employer is the civil bureaucracy which employs the school teachers, but even they are supervised by a head office located in the departmental capital. Locally, most work is organized by family units. The household is the most important unit of production and consumption.

Class Structure

The local population can be divided into two socioeconomic classes: a proletarianized peasantry, and the petty bourgeoisie. The peasantry[4] are the vast majority of the rural population who farm small plots of land, while the petty bourgeoisie, less than 10 percent of the population, is the small group of town residents composed mainly of shopkeepers, artisans, and low-level civil servants. The differences in standard of living between these two classes are not vast; both contain wealthy and poor households. It is apparent that the petty bourgeoisie tends to enjoy more urban advantages and more wealth, but this is not sufficient to place the wealthiest of them above the middle-income bracket on a national standard of comparison. A few rich peasant households may match the wealthier petty bourgeois households in terms of the total value of their assets, but their wealth is usually less conspicuous in their standard of living.

Among the peasant population, differences in wealth are closely related to the amount of land owned by a household. "Rich" peasants are those who own enough land to meet their family's needs for food and also to produce a surplus for sale. Poor peasants are those who must migrate to work on plantations or to rent farmland in other municipios. For the most part, T'oj Nam is an area of family-owned *minifundios,* or micro-farms. Few households lack land altogether, but the majority possess only small, fragmented plots whose output falls well below subsistence needs.

Statistics on local landholdings are not available, but there are several good indications of the severity of the problem. According to estimates by Stadelman's informants in the late 1930s, only about 3 percent of the households in this area did not need to supplement their farming income by renting lands outside the municipio (1940). Since that time, the population has doubled, so that the pressure to migrate is unquestionably much greater. Stadelman also estimated that the average household of five must have at least 30 *cuerdas* (1.08 acres) of land to meet its needs for corn, roughly 3,650 pounds per year. Municipal statistics for 1973 reported 20,000 cuerdas seeded with corn and an estimated yield of 10,000 *quintales* (1 quintal = 100 pounds). If these figures are roughly correct, then the average amount of land currently planted in maize per household is only 10 cuerdas, or only one-third the amount needed to sustain a family. In fact, the situation may be much worse, since municipal statistics also estimate the yield at 50 pounds a cuerda, where Stadelman estimated it at well over 100 pounds (Stadelman 1940; Anonymous 1973).[5] While renting lands ouside the municipio for subsistence farming is part of the current response to the problem of an inadequate land base in T'oj Nam, the acute local land shortage mandates an annual stint of plantation labor for large numbers of the population.[6] These marginal peasant-proletarians of T'oj Nam have their counterparts in many highland rural communities and comprise the most exploited sector of the national economy (Herbert 1970, W. Smith 1977).

T'oj Nam lacks its own aristocratic landowners, or a fully developed bourgeoisie that controls the local means of production through the control of capital. Members of such classes are not attracted by the isolation and lack of conveniences that characterize living in T'oj Nam. Nor do the poor quality of the land and difficult communication and transportation links recommend the municipio for strong capital investment. Nonetheless, T'oj Nam is strongly affected by the dominance of aristocratic landowning and capitalist classes within the national economy. The heavy dependence on plantation wage labor for cash income demonstrates this. As migrant laborers, the peasants of T'oj Nam periodically join the national proletariat. At home, they constitute a growing market for cheap industrial products. Increasingly, the labor-intensive products of peasant artisans are being displaced by mass-produced commodities that augment the need for cash.

The rural peasantry upholds the most traditional features of indigenous culture, including the Mam language, distinctive T'oj Nam clothing styles, and syncretic Maya-Christian religious customs. The petty bourgeoisie is identified with the urban Ladino culture, although a small minority of urbanized, bicultural Mam have joined this group by undertaking petty bourgeois and service occupations. The Mam-speaking petty bourgeois are generally bilingual, somewhat literate, and have begun to abandon traditional clothing and religion. Ethnically, they seem ambivalent as to whether they should embrace the national Hispanic code of behavior, or defend their Mam traditions. Often they continue to be part-time corn farmers.

The local Ladino minority of T'oj Nam is a distinctly urban element identifying with the national culture in their use of the Spanish language, their Catholicism, and their modern clothing. The Ladinos tend to be literate and better educated, and generally have social contacts and kinship ties outside the municipio. Lacking landed interests or deep historical roots within the municipio, they are nonetheless economically dominant due to their business interests and commercial skills, their ability to provide urban goods and services and to perform as intermediaries between the local and national cultures. To maintain their privileged position, they are careful to avoid any signs of identification with the local Mam population whom they perceive as their inferiors. Indeed, the Ladinos refer to themselves as residents only of the municipio, not as "T'ojnameños." The local expression "*gente del pueblo*" (people of the community) is synonymous with *indígena* (indigenous person). By and large, the Mam natives regard the Ladinos as resident aliens.

The Sexual Division of Labor

T'oj Nam's variable economic mixture of interdependent subsistent and cash activities is reproduced in the lives of most Mam individuals regardless of their sex. Occupational status is flexible and does not lend itself to rigid classification since formal employment is intermittent or rare. To understand the position of women in this economic system, we need to know the nature of their participation in both the subsistence and exchange spheres, including the relation and importance of each sphere to the overall economic system.

The Subsistence Economy

Women's roles in the subsistence economy have a traditional character. One might combine the descriptions of women's contributions to each subsistence activity and extrapolate to reconstruct an image of the economic role of women in a pre-Conquest or pre-monetary T'oj Nam. While such an endeavor may have heuristic value, it is not my present objective. Further, it cannot be assumed that all subsistence production in T'oj Nam has pre-Columbian origins. "Tradition" is used here simply to refer to practices which are old and accepted among the Mam population, even if they have colonial or later origins (specified here whenever possible).

Traditional subsistence production is losing ground in contemporary T'oj Nam. Permanent Ladino settlers in the town and regular labor contracting for the plantations have brought many changes, as have improving transportation and communication. Nonetheless, T'oj Nam continues to rely on subsistence food and clothing production using preindustrial technology. Continuity between production for use and production for exchange is evident since even the most self-sufficient households habitually use the marketplace and cash as means of exchanging surpluses for a variety of other goods.

The traditional division of labor by sex in subsistence activities ranges from nearly absolute in some tasks to pragmatic flexibility or interchangeability in others. Within each household production unit there is a general division between field work and work in or near the house, which roughly corresponds to a division between male and female activities. Cultivation using hand tools or plows is basically a male responsibility, while food and clothing preparation are female responsibilities. In maize production, the sexual division is strict. Although women help with harvesting and gleaning, they do not take part in the planting and cultivation of maize in T'oj Nam. When asked if they ever help to hoe the maize even for a short while, the standard replies are, "That is what we have men for," or "No, the women here are weavers." In symmetrical fashion, men do not help at all with the daily handgrinding of corn or its preparation in the form of *tortillas*. Men identify themselves as agriculturalists.

A parallel to the sexual complementarity of work involving maize is found in the traditional division of labor for manufacturing cotton clothing. Much of the characteristic clothing of both Mam women and men is handwoven. It is highly distinctive and identifies the municipal origin of those who wear it. The tasks of spinning and weaving cotton are performed exclusively by women using pre-Columbian technology, the spindle and the backstrap loom. Skill at weaving is an important part of the Mam woman's identity. Women weave the cloth for men's shirts and pants as well as their own *huipiles* (loose-fitting blouses), heavily decorating the garments for both sexes with bright colors. When the weaving is finished, men hand sew the garments for themselves and the women. They typically stitch a decorative neckpiece on the women's huipiles. Men's sewing duties are probably also related to their slack-season handiwork of crocheting sisal or cotton *morrales* (carrying bags) for use by both sexes. Sewing appears to be a traditional responsibility of men, since all but the most acculturated Mam women claim that they do not know how to sew and that their husbands always sew for them. Similarly, the men do not know how to weave using the backstrap loom. Thus, the characteristic textiles as well as the characteristic food of the Mam require the direct labor input of both sexes to prepare them for use.

Despite the strict sexual division of labor regarding the most fundamental and time-consuming forms of subsistence production, it is important to point out that women are not completely barred from cultivation, nor are men completely barred from weaving. However, both cultivation by women and weaving by men take place in contexts that are post-Conquest in origin. For instance, it is common for women in T'oj Nam to perform substantial heavy labor in planting potatoes using a hoe or digging stick. None of the Mam women interviewed indicate that field work devoted to a potato crop is seen as inappropriate for women. However, potatoes are only a supplementary crop, often destined for sale, and are not esteemed the way that maize, the central food crop, is esteemed. The division between women's and men's work appears to weaken in both directions when people work outside T'oj Nam in the coastal areas as wage workers or subsistence farmers. On the coast, some women do work in the fields using the hoe to cultivate maize, and some men make their own tortillas if women are absent.

Men's weaving similarly occurs in a form that does not challenge the central subsistence traditions. Men weave home-spun wool for an overgarment called a *capixay*. Both the weaving and spinning techniques differ from those used by women for cotton weaving. The spinning wheel and large foot loom used for woolen textiles have colonial Spanish origins. Mam women do not use wool. As in the case of potato cultivation by women, weaving by men is at best a supplementary activity. Although it was once common among the men in this region (See Oakes 1951a: 243; Wagley 1941), it has declined greatly. Today, it is practiced in only a few T'oj Nam households by older men. Most men now buy woolen jackets or capixays that are produced in another town. Still, it appears that there is no prohibition on male weaving per se as long as it does not encroach on the traditional duties of Mam women.

1. *T'oj Nam: Town Center*

2. Market Day at T'oj Nam

3. Maya Cotton-Spinning Technique

Sheep raising is a common economic supplement in traditional rural households, but it is only partially a subsistence activity. Sheep raising also has obvious colonial origins and is not rigidly sex-typed. Adults of either sex may own and pasture sheep, although the shepherds are often teenage boys and girls. The value to the household lies in the semiannual sale of wool to Momostenango merchants (worth about Q. 60[7] per year for a herd of 50 sheep), the production of organic fertilizer in the fields, and the occasional sale or use of the sheep for meat and hides. In former times, more wool was probably used for local weaving (since many of the foot looms in the rural areas are now inoperative). Sheep raising is almost always seen as a supplement to rather than a substitute for agriculture. Other additions to the household economy include raising chickens, turkeys, and pigs. These tend to be the responsibility of the women, who feed them leftovers. More exceptionally, a household may possess mules, a horse, or an ox. These are used for plowing and transport, and are mainly the responsibility of men.

Another major, if infrequent, subsistence activity is house-building. This is a male responsibility and may involve collective volunteer labor, particularly in roof-raising when neighbors and kin join to get the task done quickly (applicable only to thatch roofs). This work is generally done when field work is slack. The collective labor of men in roof raising is matched and motivated by women's collective labor in cooking a feast for the crowd.

Washing clothes and hauling water are women's tasks. There is almost a cultural prophibition against male use of the water holes, particularly when women are present.[8] Only if all the women of a household are seriously incapacitated will a male carry water to the house. For example, a small boy might be sent if his mother has recently given birth, or an old man may go if his wife is sick. In general, however, males avoid approaching the water holes where women fetch water and wash clothes. Even if they wish to engage in conversation with one of the women, they stay at a distance and shout. As one man explained, they fear the women would gossip or taunt them with remarks such as, "What is the matter, are there no women in your house to fetch water?" or, "You had better get a wife!"

Similarly, the drudgery of providing the house with firewood is a male responsibility, yet occasionally women find themselves forced to do it if their men are away and have not cut enough in advance. Women often carry home heavy loads of sticks and small logs; such gathering is normal when a woman goes out for a walk to procure wild plants. Going up the mountainside specifically to procure heavier firewood with a machete is a task women are reluctant to perform unless unavoidable.

Other basic concerns in the subsistence economy are child care and health care. Small children remain in women's care because of their dependence on breast feeding, while older children are recruited to help care for younger siblings. From ages six to eight, children begin to contribute to the family work force. Fathers train sons and mothers train daughters. Pragmatism encourages a certain amount of cross-sex training, particularly if a family has children of only one sex. In such cases, daughters can be recruited sporadically to help in field work, irrigation, construction, and the use of pack animals. Similarly, young sons can be recruited to help with hauling water, tending babies, deseeding cotton, winding thread, building the fire, or turning tortillas. However, major dividing lines for the central subsistence tasks are rarely breached. I did not observe a single local exception where males worked at a backstrap loom or milled corn, or where women plowed or planted corn.

Local marketing is not usually considered a subsistence activity, yet it deserves mention here because it is an intimate part of the traditional subsistence economy. Marketing in the semi-weekly town market gives both Mam women and men the opportunity to exchange small surpluses of locally produced goods for other local goods and some articles imported from other regions. Even though cash is involved, local marketing does not generally increase the "income" of the members of a household as much as it increases their satisfaction. For most peasants, the market is a means of simple commodity exchange mediated by money. In the local market, there is no absolute differentiation between the types of products sold by women and men, but men are more likely to sell corn and potatoes, while women sell a variety of vegetable greens, beans, fruit, and eggs, as well as potatoes. The peasants in the market tend to sell their goods in small quantities that may yield around Q. 1.00 which, in turn, goes toward the immediate purchase of other goods. With the exception of a small number of urbanized Mam and itinerant peddlars from other villages, trade does not constitute a means of earning a living.

Figure 3-1 summarizes the sexual distribution of work in the subsistence economy of Mam households.

In general, women's tasks are intermittent, yet performed nearly every day. Women typically spend the morning grinding corn, preparing the meals, and washing clothes, while the afternoons are for weaving until it is time to prepare the evening meal. If the household is located far from the town center, hand-grinding of corn is necessary; it can take

FIGURE 3–1. The Assignment of Tasks in the Traditional Subsistence Economy According to Sex

Rigid Segregation

Women	Men
Grinding corn, making tortillas, & cooking foods	Planting, cultivating corn & other foods (beans, squash)
Spinning, weaving cotton cloth	Sewing manually, weaving wool
Washing clothes	Crocheting carrying bags
Feeding, caring for young children & infants	Feeding, caring for large animals (mules, horses, or oxen)
	Building house & furniture

*Partial Integration**

Mostly women	Mostly men
Hauling water	Getting firewood
Feeding, fencing small animals (chickens, pigs)	Using pack animals
Gathering herbs, wild plants	Making adobe bricks
Cleaning cotton	Irrigating fields

Both
Pasturing sheep
Planting potatoes
Harvesting crops
Marketing produce

* Tasks classified as "mostly" one sex are those which I observed the opposite sex performing without exciting comment.

up to five hours per day to prepare food for the average family. Washing may take five or more hours per week, depending on the household's distance from the washing place, family size and the number of infants, and the frequency of trips that are needed. Weaving generally consumes from three to five hours per day. It takes about one and one-half months working at the normal rate to make a man's shirt. Mam women have a work load that can keep them busy all day long, but the diversity of tasks also gives them flexibility in scheduling work and rest periods, and reduces monotony. In contrast, much of men's work in cultivating, building, or fetching firewood involves the concentration of a whole labor day or successive days on a single, repetitive activity. There are fewer changes of pace in their work, although they tend to enjoy a more complete relaxation at home and at mealtimes. Depending on the size and sexual composition of the household, women may similarly specialize in a single daily activity such as sheep herding, weaving, or field work during periods of peak demand.

In general, the sexes work under different kinds of constraints. For women, a major constraint is the daily need to prepare and schedule meals in a way that enables men to work for long periods of time without interruption by the need to prepare food. For men, the main constraints are the climatic and seasonal ones of planting, watering, weeding, and harvesting crops under intense pressure during critical periods in the crop cycle. During these critical periods, the man who fails to work long hours will jeopardize the household economy. Similarly, the woman who fails to prepare meals for her husband when he is working hard jeopardizes his ability to continue working. Apart from such obvious constraints, however, each sex has its respective periods of leisure.[9]

The social aspects of both female and male subsistence work are similar in that they are largely defined by the domestic mode of production. Basically, women and men tend to work alone or with their children in independent nuclear households, or with kin in extended households. Although men go outside the house to perform most of their work, the organization of this work cannot be accurately described as being more "public" than women's work. Except for the walk to and from the fields, pastures, or forests, much of men's workday is spent in a solitary setting with a few family co-workers. The degree of women's isolation in work similarly depends in part on the location of their house (e.g., in a hamlet or near a road) and the social composition of their household. Although they do their milling and cooking indoors and their weaving on the front patio of their houses, they are certainly not secluded or restricted to a "private" sector. Trips to do laundry, draw water, market, or carry lunch to their men in the fields give them a variety of opportunities to socialize. The work relations of both sexes in the subsistence economy are thus comparable in the way they are centered on the needs and labor force of the household.

In sum, there are clear principles regarding the responsibilities of each sex in the major areas of subsistence work. These principles establish a fairly equitable distribution of work as well as a complementarity or interdependence between the sexes. Exceptions to the formal division of labor by sex occur most frequently in subsidiary tasks, or when the Mam must work outside their community (in which case subsistence traditions are already broken). Generally, those who transgress try to maintain at least a token distinction between the way they perform a task and the way it is performed by the opposite sex. For example, men who make their own tortillas when alone on the coast contrast the large size and thickness (the crudeness) of their tortillas to those made by women. When men or boys carry water, they try to use containers that differ from those women use, and when women carry wood, they load it differently than men do. It is clear that a certain degree of cross-sex activity is acceptable as long as it can be viewed as a temporary deviation due to unusual circumstances rather than a deliberate rejection of traditional sex role complementarity.

The Exchange Economy

In T'oj Nam, economic activity[10] is largely intermittent and irregular. Intermittency is due to the alternating seasonal demands for wage labor on plantations and subsistence labor on local lands. Irregularity derives from fluctuations in market and domestic demand such that households may either decide to sell or consume their produce depending on the current mix of opportunities and constraints. For the Mam, there are essentially three ways to acquire cash: wage labor, cottage industry, and commerce. Each involves different kinds of assets and different degrees of involvement with the market economy. To understand the dynamics of women's economic position, it is necessary to consider the relation of both sexes to the exchange economy, noting that some economic activities take a distinctly new form while others are merely the traditional forms directed toward market exchange rather than home use. First, however, the approximate minimal cash requirements of peasant households should be considered.

Even the most traditional households must combine cash income with subsistence production, both because of the land shortage and because certain necessary goods must be purchased with cash. In this category are common household tools: machetes, hoes, grinding stones, pottery, weaving sticks, and spindles. Also included are certain clothing materials: factory-made threads, shawls, jackets, skirt material, straw hats, and shoes. Foods that are commonly purchased are salt, sugar (*panela*), lime, coffee, and chiles.

According to budgets of town-dwelling Mam who buy *all* their food, the cost of food for an adult is around Q. 130 per year (see Appendix Three). Farming families that do not have to buy maize, beans, or potatoes are able to reduce their expenses by around 50 percent, or even more if they exclude meat and eggs from their diet. But even with subsistence agriculture for staples, households need to spend about Q. 50 per year per adult for other essential food supplies.

Clothing materials are also a major expense. The cost for raw materials and factory-made clothing combined comes to roughly Q. 25 for one complete outfit of new clothing, which is typically an annual expense coinciding with the town fiesta. Many people make do with less. Combining the minimal cash expenditures for clothing and food, annual cash expenses for basic subsistence needs amount to *at least* Q. 65 per adult in the traditional peasant economy. Of course, many households have a greater dependence on cash. Additional cash expenditures, too complex to consider here, are necessary for long-term investments in tools, housing, land, and animals.

Given that the population requires a certain level of cash income, but not necessarily full-time employment, who is directly involved in this quest, and how do they go about it? Among men, it was found that in both rural and town areas, all had some means of acquiring cash income (including men who would be past retirement age in our society). Among Mam townswomen, 100 percent were found to earn some cash. Table 3-1, however, shows that rural women may lack opportunities, since 40 percent of those sampled earned no cash income. Table 3-2 shows the distribution of different types of economic pursuits among the Mam women and men who produce cash income. I shall examine the significance of this distribution as it relates to Mam women and their evolving role in the exchange economy.

Plantation wage labor. The most important means of compensating for an inadequate subsistence base in T'oj Nam is seasonal migration. It is so widespread, that villagers say the only time the whole population is present is in late October, for the harvest and fiesta, and at Easter time. During the remainder of the year, roughly half the rural population may be absent at any one time due to wage work on coastal plantations or to maize cultivation on rented lands in more fertile areas.[11] Plantation wage labor is an obvious step toward fuller integration into the market economy. It not only alters the peasants' economic

Table 3–1. Proportion of Economically Active Mam Women (earning cash income), 1974–75*

| Residence** | Earning Cash Income | | Sample Size |
	(%)	Number	
Rural	60.0	15	25
Town	100.0	35	35

* This table includes any kind of recurring economic activity producing cash income: wage labor, craft sales, or commerce. The duration and frequency of this activity varies considerably, as well as the amount of income produced.

** In this and subsequent tables, rural and town samples are not added together since they are stratified rather than random samples of the Mam population, and would over represent the smaller urbanized component which is about one-tenth of the municipal population. See Appendix Two for description of data collection.

Table 3-2. Paid Economic Activities among Mam of Each Sex Earning Cash Income

Type*	Women				Men			
	Rural		Town		Rural		Town	
	(Number)	(%)	(Number)	(%)	(Number)	(%)	(Number)	(%)
Weaving	3	20	22	63	—	—	—	—
Food preparation	—	—	7	20	—	—	—	—
Domestic wage labor (includes market kitchen help)	—	—	6	17	—	—	—	—
Health care, ritual, divination	2	13	3	9	—	—	3	14
Rental income	1	7	—	—	—	—	3	14
Commerce, stores, market stands	3	20	8	23	3	14	8	36
Agricultural wage labor (includes plantations)	7	47	8	23	11	50	5	23
Commercial farming	—	—	—	—	11	50	8	36
Sewing	—	—	—	—	1	5	2	9
Carpentry, masonry	—	—	—	—	1	5	1	5
Labor contracting	—	—	—	—	1	5	1	5
Forestry agent	—	—	—	—	—	—	1	5
Missionary interpreter/aid	—	—	—	—	—	—	2	9
Teaching	—	—	—	—	—	—	1	5
Scholarship student	—	—	—	—	—	—	2	9
Total subsample	15**		35		22		22	

* The number and percentages of economic activities exceeds the number of persons in each subsample, since many people combine several part-time or seasonal activities. This table draws on a sample of 50 women and 44 men.

** These 15 women represent only 60% of the rural women sampled. Out of 25, 10 were found to be without cash income.

perspective, but brings them into contact with another climate, an alien culture, and migrant workers from other parts of Guatemala.

The extent to which women participate in plantation labor is related to the types of plantations which are contracting workers (Schmid 1973:238). Sugarcane plantations contract few women workers (mainly as cooks), while coffee and cotton plantations are generally willing to hire women as an integral part of their seasonal labor force. The fact that most of T'oj Nam's migrants are recruited by coffee and cotton plantations means that there is demand for female as well as male wage labor. Virtually all of the agricultural wage labor performed by women occurs on commercial plantations as opposed to local peasant farms which hire occasional labor.

The incidence of plantation wage labor for each sex has been measured in two ways. First, participation in migrant wage labor during the year of 1974–75 was recorded, and, second, work histories were examined to discover the incidence of plantation labor experience among the female and male populations. Table 3-3 presents the rate of participation in plantation work by sex and residence for 1974–75. It shows that in both rural and town areas, roughly one quarter of the women performed plantation wage labor. Men in the rural area show a noticeably higher rate than women, with half of them migrating to the plantations, while town men participate at roughly the same rate as women. The data clearly indicate that Mam women form a signficant part of the migrant labor force. Interviews with three Mam labor contractors support these results. One contractor who recruits in an aldea of T'oj Nam estimated that half of his workers were female. Two others furnished absolute numbers so that I was able to calculate percentages. One showed that during the months of December through March, women were 25 percent, 25 percent, 16 percent, and 15 percent respectively of the total labor force contracted each month. The other showed that women were likewise 25 percent for December and 15 percent for January.[12]

Table 3-3. Plantation Wage Labor among Mam of Each Sex Earning Cash Income

Residence	Female			Male		
	(%)	(No.)	(Sample Size)	(%)	(No.)	(Sample Size)
Rural	28	7	(25)	50	11	(22)
Town	23	8	(35)	23	5	(22)

The work histories of 39 women and 35 men indicate that nearly nine tenths of the men and seven tenths of the women have experienced plantation wage labor at least once in their lives.[13] While the percentage of women affected is slightly less than that of men, it is evident plantation labor is almost a general feature of the work experience of both Mam men and women. We may then draw several conclusions: (1) Women of T'oj Nam are exposed to a relatively consistent seasonal demand for their labor on coastal plantations, and (2) the indigenous culture of T'oj Nam does not prohibit agricultural wage work by women.

Both coffee and cotton plantations typically pay on a piece-work basis, a practice which means that personal incentive is more important than sex in determining one's earning potential. A typical wage rate on cotton plantations is Q. 1.25 per hundred pounds, an average day's work. At this rate of pay, some women earn Q. 15 per month while others earn as much as Q. 50, more than many men are able to earn. For instance, one man who migrated with his thirteen-year-old daughter and a twelve-year-old son reported that he himself picked 120 pounds per day, his daughter picked 150 pounds, and his son picked 100 pounds. "She, the young female, picks more than we do," he said, noting her contribution to the Q. 111 they brought home from the cotton plantation after one month's work.[14] Two months of plantation work can, in many cases, suffice to cover most of an individual's cash needs, but depending on the labor, it can fall well short of a whole household's cash needs.

Within this context of relatively equal demand for the labor of both sexes, why does women's participation rate remain somewhat lower than men's? Conventional explanations might attribute this to cultural factors such as male authority and an unwillingness to permit wives to work for a wage, or to female preference for other types of work. However, such facile answers are considerably weakened by the overall high rate of female participation; nor were they cited by the people I interviewed. Another possibility could be the preference of *some* plantations for male labor, which could affect overall participation rates. While this factor seems to have a strong effect on other indigenous communities which supply labor to sugar plantations, its impact in T'oj Nam appears to have been slight. A more realistic explanation lies in the general working conditions on the plantations.

Working conditions on the plantations are infamous. They are roughly comparable to those described for the *cuadrilleros* (migrant workers) at El Cañaveral (see Chapter four). The conditions endured by migrant workers in Guatemala have been documented (Pansini 1980; Schmid

1973; Hoyt 1959; Dessaint 1962; Melville and Melville 1971; Richards 1981). They include: fatiguing low-paid work, poor housing and sanitary facilities, exposure to malaria and insecticides, transportation in overcrowded trucks exposed to the elements, child labor and lack of educational, health, or daycare facilities for children of migrants. Migrant women face additional problems. If they migrate with male relatives, they are usually expected to provide laundry and cooking services for their kin group in addition to their work in the fields. They may also be encumbered with small children who still need breast feeding.

One of the principle reasons that fewer women than men take part in the labor migration is undoubtedly its harmful effect on small children. Most people believe that the coast kills babies, and several of my informants reported that more than one of their small children had died while they were working on coastal plantations. This is the reason most frequently cited by the women themselves for remaining in the village while the rest of the family migrates. For families of T'oj Nam, the death of a child is not only an emotional loss, but also the loss of future labor power and security for the parents. They cannot afford to risk losing children just for the short-term gain of the mother's labor in the cash economy. Hence, whenever possible women keep young children in the village. This solution is economical not only in terms of the household's investment in children, but also because it leaves a household member at home to guard the supplies of corn and other household effects, and to tend the animals and crops. These activities have an economic value that is difficult to compute in cash terms.[15] Nonetheless, people make decisions which indicate their own evaluation of their situation. Here, it is highly significant that the labor system of the coffee and cotton plantations offers the same work and the same earning potential to both sexes. While the income from one or two months of plantation labor is generally very important to households short of cash, the opportunity cost for families with young children is high and acts as a deterrent to the participation of women during their reproductive years.[16]

Other wage work. Although plantations are clearly the major source of wage work for T'oj Nam as a whole, some local wage work opportunities arise. For men, these generally take the form of sporadic work as *jornaleros* (day laborers) in unskilled manual jobs, primarily field work. Often they are hired by other Mam households that are temporarily short of male labor. The standard pay rate is 50 cents per day plus lunch, or 75 cents per day. Combining local wage work with plantation work, virtually all Mam men have at one time worked for wages.

4. *Barrack Housing for Migrant Coffee Workers*

5. *Maya Girl Helping to Prepare Food for Migrant Work Crews*

6. *Barrack Interior*

For women, fewer but slightly more stable jobs may be found as domestic employees in Ladino homes, or as kitchen help in the market kitchens (*comedores*) run by Mam women. More rarely, they find work in Ladino homes in the capital or the coastal cities. This is a limited option that pertains almost exclusively to town women. Table 3-4 shows that only 6 percent of the rural women, but 40 percent of the town women sampled had wage work experience in the service sector. In the cities, the wages are from Q. 15 to 20 per month plus room and board, while local wages are considerably lower: Q. 3 to 5 per month plus meals and a place to sleep. Locally, the value of the meals would make the wage close to 50 cents per day, or two-thirds the standard local wage for male labor. Working conditions vary and can include skimping on meals by the employer, or excessive hours since employees are not paid by the task. For those with experience in Ladino homes, the opportunity to learn Spanish can be profitable.

Table 3-4 shows that the combined total of women with wage work experience in the plantation and/or service sectors includes nearly all women in the town sample. It also shows that during the year 1974–75, approximately one-third of the rural women and one-half of the town women were active in some kind of wage work. It is evident that women form an important part of the labor force of this community, and that wage labor is important as a source of income for women.[17] However, given the sporadic nature of employment, it is not possible to estimate accurately the proportion of working time that women or men dedicate to wage labor on an annual basis, nor the extent to which they experience unemployment as they shift between periods of peak demand for labor in the wage and the subsistence sectors.

Table 3–4. Distribution of Wage Work Experience (Past and Present) for Rural and Town Mam Women

Experience	Rural (16) (%)	Town (25) (%)
Service sector (household & kitchen help)	6	40
Total wage work (plantation & service sectors)	69	88
Total active wage workers 1974–75* (plantation & service sectors)	31	52

* This refers to wage work that lasted for at least one month, although in many cases, it did not last much longer than that.

Note: The sample for work experience, based on longer interviews, is smaller than that used in Tables 3–1 to 3–3 for *current* economic activites.

The wage work opportunities of both Mam women and men are almost exclusively low-skilled, manual jobs where minimal wages are paid. There are a few exceptions and significantly these all involve men. These positions include employment by international religious institutions for work as sacristans and social organizers, government employees such as the forestry agent or the town mayor, and private sector employees such as labor contractors. Referring back to Table 3-2, it is seen that out of 94 economically active people of both sexes, only six men hold nonmanual positions (missionary interpreter, forestry agent, labor contractor, teacher) that involve greater responsibility and higher status. These positions are noteworthy because they involve privileges and powers deriving from external institutions, which distinguish their work from that of plantation workers, jornaleros, or domestic employees.

Apart from the labor contractors, earnings in these positions are steady and higher than local wage rates. Wages for the interpreter are Q. 40 per month, while the forestry agent and alcalde earn Q. 60 and Q. 75 per month, respectively. Labor contractors usually earn well over Q. 100 per month in season, and their season's earnings can climb to Q. 1,000 when related benefits are included. While their income is variable, labor contractors are among the wealthiest Mam in the municipio.

Nonmanual employment opportunities are still very limited in T'oj Nam, but it is portentious that women are not beneficiaries. Their absence raises questions regarding the values that are transmitted through the private, governmental, and religious institutional structures that do business in T'oj Nam.

Commercial farming. In spite of the continued reliance on subsistence agriculture in T'oj Nam, commercial influence is clear given that land, labor, and crops all have established monetary values. Using the 1975 price of corn (Q. 8 per quintal) and Stadelman's estimated labor inputs of four to six days per cuerda (1940:168), an ordinary yield of one quintal per cuerda means that the cash value of one day of labor on one's own corn fields is between Q. 1.30 and 2.00. Given that the local price of field labor is from 50 to 75 cents, it appears that roughly half of the return to a landowner is a return to capital. Thus, the few who own sufficient land enjoy higher returns for their field work, or are able to use hired labor and still sell their crops for a significant return. For example, one T'oj Nam landowner has twenty-four cuerdas of high-altitude land which he plants with potatoes, using about a dozen hired laborers for planting, weeding, and harvesting. By transporting and selling the crop in Quetzaltenango, he is easily able to meet all the normal cash needs of the household, including roughly Q. 500 per year for food. Such complete dependence on commercial farming is rare (only one household among those sampled).

The degree to which commercial farming is practiced by households of T'oj Nam is difficult to determine, since there is no sharp division between commercial and subsistence farming techniques. Almost all cultivated land in T'oj Nam is planted with food crops (corn, beans, and potatoes) and the same appears to be true for most of the land that the Mam rent or sharecrop outside the municipio. The peasants of T'oj Nam are known as exporters of grain, yet the average landholdings are so small that even the combination of farming one's own land with income from one or two months of plantation labor is usually inadequate to meet either the cash or food requirements of most households. With extremely low-paying and limited job opportunities within the municipio, most households seek to expand their agricultural production by renting more land.

Land shortage most directly affects the male role in the household production unit. In my sample, roughly three-fourths of the rural men and two-fifths of the town men migrated in 1974–75 in order to rent or sharecrop additional land outside the municipio. Those who did not migrate were generally older men who had younger sons going, or town men who had petty bourgeois occupations.

The rate of return to agricultural labor on rented coastal land is perhaps slightly higher than on one's own land in the municipio. On the coast, land rents are high, but yields are usually five times as great as yields in T'oj Nam. Assuming that the average household has enough local land to produce one-third to one-sixth of its subsistence requirements,[18] rental of an additional fifteen cuerdas on the coast should guarantee subsistence needs, barring crop failure, and in good years could yield a cash surplus of around Q. 100 after all expenses are met. This can be calculated to give a return that is between Q. 2 and 4 per day.[19]

The rental of coast land is a means of enabling T'oj Nam men to continue their traditional corn farming. Yet this does not mean that the cash value of the crop or the surplus can be attributed to male labor alone. First, it is common for the land rental to be paid with money that was earned during the preceding months on the plantations. This money typically includes the wages of women and children. In addition, living conditions on rented land are rude. The migrants must provide their own food, shelter (makeshift shacks), water, and washing services. These services of labor maintenance can be an extra cost if they are not performed by female family members who accompany the men. Women not only make possible increased labor time and efficiency for the men, but also contribute their own labor at peak periods. On the whole, the sexual division of labor that characterizes the subsistence economy is reproduced when the household migrates to rent land on the coast. In contrast to plantation labor, which involves women directly in the cash economy through their labor contract, major farming surpluses are generally transacted by men as an extension of their traditional role.

In this partially monetized situation, the input of women is not easily quantified in relation to the cash value of the crop. Since field work is traditionally the man's primary responsibility, there is a tendency to attribute the income from surplus corn sales to men. This is a common conceptual shortcut in the transition to a cash economy. Rather than compute the numerous and diverse inputs of all family members and credit them with a fraction of the final cash value, the individual who is traditionally responsible for the final, saleable product assumes control of the cash income. Examining the commercialization of weaving will permit us to assess the effect of this transition on Mam economic sex roles.

Commercial weaving. A comparable area of control for women has developed with the commercialization of traditional textile production. However, the demand for maize is much more universal than the demand for the local style of hand-made clothing. Only with the growth of the tourist trade in recent years have the Mam women begun to discover a sizeable market for their woven products, albeit one which mainly affects women living near the town center. The participation rates of the rural and town women are indicated in Table 3-5.

Ethnographic reports from thirty years ago do not mention commercial weaving by Mam women in this region (Oakes 1951a, 1951b; Stadelman 1940). One informant claims she was the first to begin this practice some twenty years ago by filling orders for friends of a North

Table 3-5. Proportion of Rural and Town Mam Women Engaged in Commercial Weaving

Residence	Commercial Weavers		(Sample Size)
	(%)	(Number)	
Rural	14	3	(22)
Town	69	22	(33)

Note: Subsample for this table is smaller than Table 3-1 since data on commercial weaving is incomplete for five women.

American priest. During the last five years, the sale of indigenous clothing has become sufficiently lucrative to spur the organization of a weavers' cooperative whose female membership has fluctuated from around twenty-five to one hundred individuals.

The weaving cooperative, however, is only one of a number of different options for the sale of textiles, and as such its size is not an accurate reflection of the number of women involved in commercial weaving. At least ten of the town women with outside contacts are involved in filling orders for clients, including the major tourist shops in the national capital. More than a dozen others are involved in buying and reselling new and used textiles to tourists in the town center of T'oj Nam. These women tend to congregate around the bus stop in order to catch the tourists as they step off the bus. Another practice is the putting-out system, whereby a few women with a little capital and experience with tourists supply materials and contracts to other women to weave garments for resale. Sometimes commissioned textiles are not woven for tourists, but for local Mam women who are better-off or specialize in other activities and lack time for weaving. Finally, there are many sporadic sellers who exchange a garment out of some pressing need or simply because a husband did not appreciate the way the collar was decorated. All of these aspects of commercial weaving indicate that women are aware of the potential cash returns and are keen to obtain a cash income for their weaving.

Weavers work at different rates due to the differential pressure of other family duties, but an average return for weaving is around 4.5 cents per hour. Women typically have about four hours per day to devote to weaving. As long as the traditional male-female division of labor is in balance within a household, women do not have much free time for commercial weaving. However, if males are absent or if there is a surplus of females, such weaving becomes more feasible. Commercial weaving can also be increased by devoting less time to weaving for the family, in which case cheaper textiles are substituted.[20] Women who dedicate the most time to weaving (up to 45 hours per week) are able to earn up to Q. 2 per week if they have steady orders or good sales. The women who can (or must) do this are women who do not have to maintain a man by cooking, washing, or weaving for him. Yet earnings from full-time weaving alone are inadequate to support a women, much less a woman with dependent children, if she has to purchase all her food.

The commercialization of subsistence activities such as weaving and corn production has not brought high cash returns to labor. In general, current returns are scarcely sufficient to support an individual, and are inadequate to cover the costs of reproducing the labor force or maintaining the aged. However, those who control some capital, as in the ownership of land or the cash to rent land, are able to enjoy slightly higher returns. One cuerda of land is worth Q. 200 in T'oj Nam, while a weaver's total capital is worth only around Q. 10 to 20. Here is where the commercialization of production and the informal assignment of cash income to the individual who produces the final product works to the disadvantage of women as weavers. The value of hand-weaving is not augmented by returns to capital, while at the same time the price for local textiles is strongly affected by the availability of cheaper substitutes from the international textile industry. Weavers (like corn farmers) tend to discount the diverse inputs of family members to their final product and are in charge of the income from the sale of any textiles. However, the different cash values which accrue to these two products, corn and clothing, mean that commercialization greatly increases the value of traditional male activities relative to those of the women of T'oj Nam.

Commerce and petty capitalism. For the urbanized and bicultural Mam, several kinds of petty bourgeois entrepreneurial and service occupations are growing in importance. These include various specialities ranging from permanent stores and market stands which are operated by both sexes, to the comedores and periodic food vending that are conducted by women. In contrast to peasant farming which requires members of both sexes to maintain a production unit, commercial enterprises can be run by *individuals* of either sex. There is a high proportion of town women without partners engaged in operating commercial food services and small stores. Table 3–6 shows the percentage of each sex earning cash income through commercial occupations.

The small businesses of T'oj Nam are not subjected to rigorous cost accounting procedures. They typically bring an irregular income; some of the return may be a cash surplus, while a substantial part may take the form of food or goods which are withdrawn from the store's inventory for household consumption. Further, the work may be distributed among all members of the household who may or may not engage in other activities while tending the store. All these factors make it an extremely complex problem to determine the returns to the varying inputs of labor and capital, or the extent to which disguised unemployment or varying opportunity costs affect labor allocation.

The most successful commercial entrepreneurs who manage large capital investments tend to operate in family partnerships where both spouses and even children contribute to the enterprise. This often entails both diversification and economies of scale as when purchasing is

Table 3-6. Mam of Each Sex in Commercial Occupations in 1974–75*

Residence	Women			Men		
	(%)	(No.)	(Sample Size)	(%)	(No.)	(Sample Size)
Rural	17	3	(18)	20	2	(10)
Town	41	14	(34)	44	8	(18)
Total subsample		17	(52)		10	(28)

* Includes market stalls, stores, comedores, and a regular food vendor, but does not include women active in commercial sale of textiles only, nor men active in commercial sale of crops only.

Note: This table is based on a reduced sample of 52 women and 28 men due to incomplete data on supplementary commercial pursuits for 8 women and 16 men included in Table 3–2.

done on one trip for two separate business interests. Four examples of successful commercial households include the following combinations of business ventures where total capital investments in inventory range from Q. 200 to around 1,000:

1. Two separate stores, one operated by each spouse.
2. One store and one comedor operated by a husband and wife, respectively.
3. One store operated by a women and her daughters plus a large permanent market stand operated by her husband and herself with regular help from the two daughters.
4. Two vegetable stands operated by a husband-and-wife merchant team.

In these cases, there is a great deal of cooperation in buying, selling, and transferring goods and labor between the separate parts of the business as well as between the business sphere and the household sphere.

The smaller businesses tend to be those run by women without partners. One typical small store has a capital investment of around Q. 30 that turns over roughly twice a month. The old woman who operates it claims that she never has any real cash surplus, but that she simply reinvests Q. 30 every two weeks and is able to draw part of her food costs from the store. Although she is regularly in attendance at the store, she must complement this livelihood with plantation labor and weaving for sale to maintain even a low standard of living for herself and her grandson. Given the strain of plantation labor for the aged, it is clear that her store offers only a very marginal gain. Roughly the same is true for the women who rent small kitchens in the marketplace. Some can barley feed themselves and their children, while others may accumulate cash surpluses slowly at the rate of around Q. 5 per month, which can go toward clothing.

In general, a single individual suffers disadvantages in business, both from an inability to accumulate significant capital and an inability to profit from cooperation and economies of scale. The initial capital for many business ventures was derived from plantation labor by both spouses. Hard-working young couples with few or no children are the most effective at accumulating the first venture capital upon which a substantial business can be built. Other critical factors for success are access to property in the town center or on the main road, familiarity with the Spanish language, mathematical skills, literacy, and knowledge of urban markets.

Major commercial ventures by urban Mam are in their first generation in T'oj Nam. Women are active in almost all of the most successful ventures, although they have less success as individual agents.[21] A crucial issue will arise with the transfer of wealth to the next generation. Is the accumulated capital to be distributed equally among the offspring of both sexes, or is it to be treated like land and willed primarily to sons?

Ladinos

A brief look at the local Ladino population will clarify the economic significance of ethnicity. Table 3–7 shows that 77 percent of the women and 95 percent of the men earn some cash income—a high incidence of labor force participation by both sexes. As with the Mam, there is a tendency for Ladinos with irregular revenue to combine different forms of economic activity rather than pursue a single occupation.

The high incidence of labor force participation by Ladinas, most of whom are married, indicates the local Hispanic culture does not prevent women from earning a cash income. A glance at Table 3–7, however, reveals that most of them work at informal, self-employed, or home-based occupations. Only the teacher and one comedor operator work regularly away from home. *Atole* (a hot drink) vending is part-time work, often shared by a mother who prepares the atole at home and a teenage daughter who sells it in the outdoor market. In contrast, more of the men's occupations involve working outside the home, particularly the salaried positions. Carpenters work partly at home, and also travel to construction sites throughout the municipio. Overlap between Ladino women's and men's occupations occurs mainly in teaching, sewing, and storekeeping, with roughly equal participation by

Table 3-7. Paid Economic Activities by Sex among Ladinos in T'oj Nam (earning cash income)

WOMEN		MEN	
Type	(Number)*	Type	(Number)*
Self-Employed/Family Business		*Self-Employed/Family Business*	
Comedor-pension operator	4	Carpenter	9
Baker	4	Corn mill operator	3
Baker's apprentice	2	Butcher	2
Dressmaker	2	Tailor	2
Storekeeper	2	Storekeeper	2
Atole vendor	2	Plumber	1
Cantina operator	1	Leather worker	1
Domestic employee	1	Blacksmith	1
Healer	1		
Salaried Employees		*Salaried Employees*	
Teacher	1	Teacher	2
		Postal chief	1
		Telegraph messenger	1
		Municipal secretary	1
		Municipal scribe	1
		Tractor driver	1
		Pensioned employee of international firm	1
Total receiving cash income:	17 (77%)	Total receiving cash income:	21 (95%)
Total not receiving cash income:	5 (23%)**	Total not receiving cash income:	1 (5%)**
Total sample:	22	Total sample:	22

* Many activities are less than full time. Total number of activities exceeds number of individuals sampled since some individuals combine several occupations.
** Inactive women are 3 housewives, a retired baker, and an unemployed teacher; the inactive man is a retired weaver.

both sexes. There is an obvious difference, however, in the percentage of women and of men who hold full-time salaried positions. Apart from the teaching profession, all the remaining salaried positions in the civil service bureaucracy are held by men. Women assert that regardless of their educational attainments, they would not be considered for positions in the municipal office, post office, or telegraph service.

The relative level of income for Ladino women and men depends greatly on whether they are salaried employees or self-employed. Female teachers are on a government pay scale that does not discriminate by sex. They earn as much as the highest paid men (from Q. 85 to 125 per month). However, women bakers, dressmakers, and comedor operators earn considerably less. Demand for their products is relatively low, for none of these occupations provide full-time work for the women who engage in them. Futhermore, limited employment options as well as competition from Mam women have resulted in an oversupply of women trying to earn money in these areas. The rate of return for labor is about Q. 1 per day. However, an individual baker does not bake daily, and thus earns only Q. 2 to 4 per week; comedor operators average the same or less per week; and dressmakers find so little demand that they earn only about Q. 1 per week. In most households, female specialists earn from Q. 15 to 30 per month as mother-daughter teams, or Q. 10 to 20 per month for an individual. Although some women might prefer part-time work, it is more likely that none of them can capture enough of the market to work full time. Some of the women combine two of these options, so that they are, in effect, working full time. Others who have skills and work experience have dropped out because of the competition and low returns.

For men, the income from most types of craft work ranges from a low of Q. 1.50 per day for tailoring up to Q. 2 or 3 per day for carpentry, with occasional contracted work that pays Q. 25 to 30 per week. Male artisans are also affected by problems of irregular demand and competiton, so that many of them practice several skills. In particular, the blacksmith, leather worker, plumber, and tailor all practice supplementary occupations. Further, several of the carpenters reap a little extra income through barbering on market days. Rough calculations indicate that normal earnings for a male artisan are around Q. 50 to 60 per month. The apparent income differential between the sexes in the realm of crafts and trades becomes even more striking when salaried employees are considered, for most salaried men earn a secure income of at least Q. 65 per month. The Ladino male's advantage in obtaining employment obviously contributes to an overall discrepancy in the earning power of the sexes. Capital assets in a store, cantina, corn mill, or rental property, of course, make it possible to receive more income, but it is difficult to attribute this income to a single member of the household. Usually both sexes contribute to the accumulation and management of such capital.

The Ladinos of T'oj Nam are more completely dependent on cash income than the Mam, but most of them also enjoy a higher standard of living. The Ladino weekly food budgets are significantly higher, ranging from Q. 6 per week for two people up to Q. 16 per week for nine. Not only do they buy nearly all their food, but they buy ready-made clothing and fabric in the cities. Income that is not needed for food and clothing is often converted into investments in business, housing, education, and consumer goods. T'oj Nam is not noted for its entertainment facilities. Aside from drinking, which is usually moderate among the Ladinos, there are few ways for an individual to squander family funds.

The occupational characteristics of T'oj Nam Ladinos have been steadily changing over the last generation. The previous generation was more active in labor contracting, blacksmithing, wool weaving, leather working, candy manufacture, candle making, cigaret making, chocolate making, and even sewing. Now, labor contracting is dominated by Mam contractors. Many of the old Ladino crafts have almost completely died out as mass-produced commercial products have replaced the home industries. Increasingly, Ladinos seek salaried employment. There are indications that men receive preference, if not exclusive access, to a wide variety of salaried positions (with the exception of teaching and nursing), while women try to concoct new forms of local self-employment.

One particularly innovative old woman has a history of experimentation with many trades: making tamales, cigarets, and candles; baking; running a cantina and butcher shop; and sewing. She was the first to sell *arroz con leche* (a hot rice-milk drink), the first to sew skirts using a sewing machine, and the first to sell refreshments made with ice. Over the years she has given up most of these activities because of competition from local people and cheap, imported factory goods. Now she concentrates on a comedor and pension that caters to tourists (the first one to open).

The economic role of Ladinas, Ladino women, is not vastly different from that of Mam women. Economic activity and enterprise characterize women of both groups, particularly in the town center where they run stores, cantinas, and comedors. There are a few areas, however, where their activities do not overlap. Ladinas do not weave, and generally do not sell in the marketplace, nor work in the fields. Conversely, Mam women do not become bakers. These differences reflect, in part, the cultural pluralism in T'oj Nam, as well as the relative wealth of the two groups.

Within the realm of domestic responsibilities, we again find similarities. More than 70 percent of the 19 Ladino households sampled did not have domestic employees; in those that did, the Ladinas were themselves economically active. Thus most Ladinas, like Mam women, are expected to cook, wash, and provide child care. They are not a leisured class. One ethnic difference is that Mam women have more work weaving family clothing, whereas Ladinas either buy it ready-made or buy cloth to sew. A change in this direction is seen among

81

some urban Mam women who no longer weave for themselves, but commission the weaving by other women. Some differences in domestic work appear to be more related to an urban lifestyle than to ethnicity. In town, housework is lighter with running water, the market, and power corn mills at hand. While Ladinas benefit from these conveniences, they are burdened by the custom of ironing Western clothing. Another factor of importance is that Ladino families generally send children to school and encourage higher education. This deprives women of child labor in the home.

For the most part, the Ladinas have a higher standard of living than the Mam women, but work mainly at home. Mam women are more mobile in their marketing and plantation work. They also have security from the fact that their contribution is of crucial value in a poor household which relies on subsistence production. While in many Mam households women's labor contribution is considered comparable to the men's (in subsistence or cash values), the Ladina is much more directly confronted by a condition of lower earning power coupled with a lessening of her subsistence functions. The higher wages and salaries to which most Ladino men and a minority of Mam men have access suggest the evolution of an imbalance in economic power between the sexes in the most urbanized or modern households of T'oj Nam, be they Ladino or Mam.

Technology

Any technology corresponds to a cultural and economic context which includes the sexual division of labor. The technology of T'oj Nam combines pre-Hispanic, colonial, and modern elements. Some rather rigid distinctions in the types of tools used by women and men date back to pre-Hispanic society. The importance of hand looms, hearthstones, milling stones, and washing stones to women, and of the hoe and cutting tools to men are examples. But it is not clear that these manual implements give a productive advantage to the sex that customarily uses them.

Introduced elements of Spanish colonial technology favored an increase in male productivity. The exclusively male use of ox and plow in agriculture and the large foot loom for wool weaving originate in Spanish culture. However, the terrain in many areas of T'oj Nam is not well-suited for plows. The sheep-wool-weaving complex did develop the use of female family labor in herding, but wool weaving never became an important source of livelihood in this region. The use of mules as pack animals became an important innovation in transport, but this was not an exclusively male activity since women often joined the men in transporting family produce to the cities by mule. Thus, due to some specific conditions of the T'oj Nam economy, pre-Hispanic technology combined with the later colonial technology appears to have persisted with an overall complementarity between the sexes, without major advantages for either sex in production.

Given that modern technology can greatly increase the productivity of an individual, differential access to it by sex could foster significant inequalities. Modern technology in T'oj Nam has appeared in various forms, particularly in modern automotive transport and utilities that serve the town center. Improved transportation has facilitated the entry of many new industrial products: metal, rubber, and plastic goods; factory threads and cloth; metal roofing, glass windows; flashlights, watches, radios, clocks, and many similar goods. Significantly, the overwhelming effect of this technology is to alter and increase consumption patterns rather than production patterns. Notably, there are still no tractors used for agriculture (small plots and rugged terrain discourage their use). Weaving, washing, cooking, and carpentry for the most part continue to use pre-industrial technology. But some productive innovations include the corn mill and the water hose. The former permits women to devote more time to commercial weaving, while the latter permits a household to slightly increase productivity on some small plots. But for the most part both sexes are still tied to the domestic mode of production based on manual labor and the use of simple tools. The most important effect that modern technology has on T'oj Nam's production has probably been to make local production less profitable through increased competition with cheaper industrial products produced elsewhere.

While a few local and nonresident Ladino males have begun to own or operate modern technology (such as the buses, trucks, the power corn mills, and the electric plant), the Mam population of both sexes and the Ladinas are largely confined to the role of consumer. The one relatively cheap instrument of modern technology which they have claimed is the sewing machine.[22] Hence, it appears that modern productive technology has not yet had a major impact on the traditional sexual division of labor.

Origins of the Sexual Division of Labor

The sexual division of labor in T'oj Nam has its origins in pre-Hispanic peasant society but has been modified by colonial and modern influences. Physical isolation inhibited a thorough-going alteration of indigenous lifestyles, although there is ample evidence of eclecticism in technoeconomic behavior, religion, and even clothing styles. While colonial and national power structures have been superimposed, the agents of these powers were never sufficently numerous to completely transform rural family customs or the domestic mode of production of the Mam. The introduction of large-scale commercial agriculture in Guatemala added new burdens and new forms of production to the experience of the Mam peasants who were drafted for labor, but it did not eliminate subsistence peasant farming, which provided an inexpensive way to maintain the labor force. In some indigenous communities, only males were recruited for public labor, but in T'oj Nam both sexes have been drawn into the plantation labor pool. This dismal fact has been of major significance in preserving a rough equality between the sexes in the Mam population.

Large, national institutions have not yet had much direct influence in T'oj Nam. This has probably also been a positive factor in maintaining a degree of sexual economic equality, since these structures show few signs of equal recruitment and participation. Private, civil, and religious institutions have admitted relatively few local people into ther hierarchal structures. In the private sector, the plantation contractors are all male. In the religious institutions, only males have been hired as local aids, social promotors, or interpreters. In the civil sector, women participate only in branches dealing with primary education and health.

While sexual divisions are one aspect of these institutions, ethnic divisions are another aspect such that the interplay between the two types of discrimination is complex. In the private sector, the job of labor contractor or *caporal* (boss) has been converted into an indigenous specialty. In the government sector, Mam men have begun to assume a small percentage of the positions as elected mayors, teachers, and development agents, while Ladino men continue to hold most salaried posts. In the religious institutions, again, Mam men have been the prime recipients of positions and training in diverse capacities, such as social organizer, paramedic, and cook. We see, then, that a double discrimination against women and indigenes is in operation. Some openings have been found by people in each category, but the group that suffers a double discrimination—as women and as indígenes—is not finding any place in the institutional structures that have been and are establishing themselves in T'oj Nam. Significantly, one national institution that has not yet established itself in T'oj Nam is the military. The absence of a military draft of Mam men or of a stationed unit of the national police has meant a lower degree of institutionalized male dominance both economically and politically compared to other communities (Bossen 1975:599).

Economic Strategies

In the peasant economy of T'oj Nam, production depends upon sexual and generational cooperation within the household, the primary unit of production. There are a few economic alternatives to familial interdependency. Economic strategies for both sexes hinge upon their relationships to their parents, siblings, conjugal partners, and offspring. Each relationship represents a distinct economic outlook involving different claims and obligations, and different measures of control or subordination, leisure or labor, security or insecurity. These household relationships naturally change their character over the life cycle. They are also modified by changing economic opportunities. In this section, women's economic strategies and options will be examined in the context of the social and economic conditions of household membership and organization.

Two general conditions should be noted. First, Mam women are not a surplus labor force in T'oj Nam. The sex ratio is equal, and women's traditional work is still largely unmechanized and labor intensive. In terms of traditional subsistence activities, Mam men who lack sufficient land to work are more likely to be underemployed than women. The labor of Mam women is considered an indispensable and valuable contribution to the traditional household; it is not easy to replace without drastically departing from Mam culture and identity.

Second, children represent future labor power and security in old age, particularly in the rural area where ill health and the strain of continuous manual labor could mean a miserable existence for old people were it not for the support of their children. Both Mam women and men expect that they will one day depend on their formerly dependent children. These facts are important for women both as workers and as the major agents of reproduction, in that they imply that intersex dependency is balanced in most of the Mam community. Men and women are mutually dependent. Under these conditions, few women would profit from a strategy of submissiveness toward men in order to maintain their economic position. Faced with domineering husbands, supply and demand conditions should normally enable women to reestablish themselves as valued members of other households, whether through remarriage or by returning to their natal kin groups.

Women's strategies may coincide or conflict with those of other members of the household. Their choices depend on the household composition and assets of their own and their spouse's kin groups, as well as on their personal assets and liabilities as workers. In order to appreciate the complexities of their situation, I will first describe women's strategy in what might be called the canonical form of household in the traditional rural sector. This will be followed by illustrations and examination of economic strategies that women develop in other traditional contexts as well as in the more transitional, urbanizing sector of Mam society.

The Traditional Rural Household

In the prototypical rural household, children learn to work under their parent of the same sex. In mid-teens a young woman marries and typically joins the household of her husband. Both she and her husband are subordinates in this situation. The young wife must work under the authority of her mother-in-law who controls the household management and budget, while her young husband works under the authority of his father on whom he depends for access to productive capital, usually land. In this situation, a woman's strategy may coincide with her husband's. Lacking other economic assets or alternatives, they may both feel it is best to obey and cooperate with the aims of the senior generation, and to build up the family estate in the expectation that over the long run, they will be rewarded with control over a fair portion of that estate.

While a young wife and husband share a position of subordination as workers, they do not initially have the same relation to capital. A woman has the special problem of entering a strange household where she initially has no claim on the capital resources of the household, while her husband has a vested interest in that particular household because it represents his unique hope of inheriting land. In this sense, a young woman is economically more mobile than a young man since there is some choice regarding the nature of the household where she will invest her energies. If she finds a particular household a poor choice, she can often leave and seek a better situation. (This option is discussed further in the section on social organization.) When a woman has children, however, the situation changes. Her children's future inheritance is bound to her husband's estate. This gives her a vested interest in the capital assets of the household. It also reduces her mobility since taking her children to a new household entails the risk that they will not receive an inheritance from either their father or step-father.

Although children entitle a woman to greater autonomy and security within the household, she has little control over her daily budget until she and her husband reside in a separate house. This may or may not occur prior to the death of the senior generation, depending on the resources of the joint family. Similarly, a man may have to wait until his parents' death before he has full control over the disposition of productive capital (See Wagley 1941:67). Establishing a separate residence and receiving an inheritance thus have special economic significance for each sex with respect to their ability to direct their own labor and receive its rewards. Their shared long-term goal includes one more step that completes the life cycle: becoming the senior parental generation and controlling not only capital, but a labor force of young, strong adults. Men look forward to the assistance of hard-working sons in agriculture, while women look forward to the assistance of hard-working daughters and daughters-in-law in the household. Having described a general framework for women's economic strategies, we can now consider the dynamics of women's economic position in specific households that illustrate common situations in the traditional sector of T'oj Nam.

The Extended Family Economy: The Seniority System   1. Paula Ramos and Juan Tomas are heads of a joint family of twenty-six persons, representing four generations and sharing three houses. There are eight other adults: two married sons and their wives, an unmarried son and daughter, and one married grandson and his wife. The sixteen minors are two children, thirteen grandchildren, and one great-grandchild of Paula and Juan.

This family maintains a collective economy with all capital assets under the formal control of Juan Tomas. His sons turn over almost all of their income to him and he redistributes and reinvests it according to the diverse needs of the group. Thus, one son specializes in raising corn on the coast which he brings back for the entire family. Another is a shepherd who provides the others with meat. A third son was educated to become a teacher to earn a cash income, while some of the grandsons are muleteers who transport firewood for the family and for hire. Juan himself is primarily a farmer who raises corn and potatoes, and has worked on plantations in the past. Depending on labor needs, he and his sons transfer their labor from one area of work to another.

While the sons' labor remains under Juan's control (even with one son aged forty), the daughters-in-law enjoy a measure of autonomy from Paula's authority. Each resides in a separate house on distant landholdings. They are relatively free to manage the day-to-day disposition of the household supplies of food, cash, and child labor. Their autonomy is limited by the size of the budget allocated by the senior parents, and by the fact that as a joint family, any of the members of the other houses are entitled to meals and lodging if their work or errands bring them to the vicinity. On the other hand, Paula's married children and grandchildren are often in temporary residence for various reasons.

Paula joined this family as a daughter-in-law forty-five years ago and has passed through the stage of "junior" parenthood, acquisition of a house, productive capital, and dependent labor, until now she is a senior parent of a large, productive family economy. Paula has never had to perform plantation labor (her family was wealthy enough to give her land), and neither she nor her daughters have ever worked for wages. Her main economic tasks have included cooking, washing, weaving, childcare, raising and marketing small animals, but she has also helped with harvests and has planted and dug potatoes. She has two daughter's at home to assist her. Although Juan exercises more overt economic control over their property, Paula's opinions are not disregarded and she has considerable authority over her grown children. She is in a position to strategically distribute food and hospitality to a wide network of kin and guests. She also has freedom to maneuver with the household supplies, selling potatoes, eggs, poultry, textiles, and other goods to reinvest the money as she sees fit. However, she asserts that her husband supplies the household well and gives her all she needs.

Paula's case illustrates successful accomodation between women's individual economic strategies and the collective advantages of overall family cooperation and diversification in production. Competitive tensions are reduced by the specialization of sons in different tasks, and the specialization of daughters-in-law in different houses. The area for potential economic conflict in this type of household appears to be found less between the sexes than between the generations. The potential for an individual of either sex to divert income or assets to purely individuals ends is limited by the system of interdependent production for use and by storing wealth in relatively nonliquid traditional forms: food stores, houses, land, and animals. Although women's work in this household is highly differentiated from men's work, both sexes seem conscious of the advantages in interdependency and reciprocity between the sexes and of respect for senior authority.

The following example concerns a poorer rural family where women as well as men migrate to earn money.

2. The Rosario household includes two married sons, a married daughter, their spouses and children, all residing under one roof with their father, mother, and another child. The family sends its female and male members to work annually on the plantations. Augustina, the senior women at age sixty, migrated for many years with her husband and can list more than ten different plantations where she has worked. She and her husband no

longer migrate, but receive the money their children earn and control its distribution for household expenses "because we are still here." Augustina spends only Q. 2 to 3 for the household each market day on items such as salt, sugar, chiles, meat, and thread. Regarding the use of money, she says: "Men like to spend money for their cigarets. Women spend for their fruit or earrings. Men can spend more because they maintain the family. They provide maize, beans, potatoes. But men also depend on women. They need each other."

When Augustina worked on plantations, her earnings were collected by her husband who used them to buy land for their children. Since the children are her security as well as his, she agrees with this investment. When the family disperses for work outside T'oj Nam, she may remain at home alone to pasture sheep and guard the house. Even if the others are gone for a long time, she is secure: "Here there are corn, beans, potatoes, squash, salt, sugar, and firewood. I do not worry. I have all I need thanks to my husband and children." Augustina weaves, markets, and is also a traditional midwife-curer. In this capacity, she earns an independent income for a practice that requires a high degree of mobility, day or night. When she must go out on call, she can delegate household responsibilities to her daughter and daughters-in-law.

Women like Paula and Augustina have contributed to the accumulation of joint capital, have female help in the household and sons who have reached adulthood and married. They enjoy the security of senior status and authority, as well as a high degree of independence.

The position of a junior women in a joint household offers quite a contrast.

3. Maria Patricio joined her husband's household fifteen years ago. Before that, she used to pasture sheep and go to the coast to pick cotton with her father who collected her earnings. Now, with three children, she still goes one month each year and her husband collects her pay (around Q. 1.25 per day). Last year she worked as a cook, supplying tortillas for forty workers, while she was pregnant. She worked from 3 A.M. to 9 P.M., washing clothes in her spare time. Her husband gives her back Q. 1.50 to spend on personal items each market day, but he gives all the rest of the money to his widowed mother. Maria says of her mother-in-law: "She is in charge of everything. She is *dueña de la casa y jefe de gastos* (owner of the house, and chief of expenses)." Nonetheless, Maria feels her relations with her mother-in-law are good.

Here we observe the hard work and sacrifice expected of the younger women, while income is always passed along the hierarchy to the senior parent, in this case a woman. In these extended households, the annual migrations provide a periodic break from the daily contact with their mother-in-law which help the relationship endure.

Not all women must wait until old age to assume the role of senior woman in the household. Some young couples succeed in establishing an independent household shortly after marriage.

The Nuclear Household: Cooperation and Autonomy 4. Candelaria and Manuel are each twenty-five years old, have been together for seven years, and have two young children. At first they lived together with his parents, but by working together on plantations, they earned money to buy land and build a house near Candelaria's father (the two men have the same surname). This year, due to childbirth, Candelaria did not migrate. Her husband turned over his earnings to her to guard and use, keeping only a few dollars when he returned to the coast to work again. Candelaria spends only Q. 2 to 3 per week for potatoes, salt, coffee, panela, lime, chiles, and soap. Occasionaly she spends Q. 10 for thread, but Manuel also brings back raw cotton from the plantations which she spins by hand. They are poor, but they get along well. Candelaria is free to visit and go out as she chooses: "He is not jealous. I do not have to ask him permission to do something."

Young women in independent households often enjoy considerable autonomy. This seems due, in part, to the major contributions they make in plantation labor, sharing the travails of migration with their husbands. When they decide it is best for the woman to remain at home to care for children and local assets, the man and woman must learn to accept each other's independence. If the husband is responsible, a woman's best strategy is economic cooperation. The absence of domineering behavior by a husband may grow out of rational cooperation and mutual respect, but an additional factor may be an important guarantee of the status of young women in independent households. Frequently, a woman's father is still alive and will accept her back if a marriage becomes oppressive. If a man's wife has the option of leaving, he must treat her well. The contrapositive of this statement is illustrated in the next case.

Subordination 5. Flora is forty years old, married, and has seven children. She fears to take any independent decisions lest her husband beat her. Her husband farms and does not need to work on plantations. He makes it clear that he is jealous and does not like to be "apart" from his wife. Flora claims that he often does not give her *gastos* (household spending money). Instead, he gives their daughter the money to go to market. Elaborating, she says: "He beats me a lot. I would leave him if it were not for the children. There are many children, and they would die of hunger. I would have left at the beginning, but he did not want me to go. Now I have no father or mother. My father is dead, and my mother died a short while ago."

Flora's story shows that rural woman with dependent children who cannot count on parental support may see no alternative to an unsuccessful marriage. She cannot easily run off with another man because such action would jeopardize the future support of her children whether she took them or left them. Flora's endurance of her husband's dominance is not unique, but it is certainly not a part of prescribed feminine behavior. I encountered numerous cases of daughters who had returned to their natal families rather than submit to mistreatment or stinginess in their husband's households.

Special Situations In the traditional economy of T'oj Nam, women are generally expected to have a male economic partner, produce children, and contribute their labor to the household. We shall now consider variations from these roles expectations produced by widowhood, childlessness, and illness.

Widowhood. As long as senior parents of both sexes are present, the structure of the family economy appears to be patriarchal with economic control vested in the father. Senior men specialize in long-term management of major capital assets, while senior women supervise the day-to-day administration of the household. It appears that economic control of the household is a function of sex. However, cases of widowhood such as the following (and case three above) show that a principle of parental seniority can override sex.

6. Dominga is a fifty-year-old widow. Her household includes two sons and two daughters-in-law, and four grandchildren. Her work includes weaving for use and for sale, household management, and care of her grandchildren while her sons and daughters-in-law migrate. She also works in the fields planting and hoeing potatoes.

Dominga has migrated annually from age four, "walking behind my mother and father" through all the years of her marriage which began at age eighteen. She had six children, but only two survived. About 10 years ago, when her sons were still young, her husband died. Dominga continued to migrate for two months each year, picking cotton with her sons. She received the pay from the boss, both for herself and her sons. As her sons grew up, she helped them pay the bride price for their wives. She also purchased a small house in town (next to her own kin rather than her affines) where they now live together.

As a grandmother, Dominga no longer migrates, but she is still head of the household. "My sons give me their money and I guard it for them. They say, 'Here, you know what we need to buy,' and they deliver the money they get from selling corn or from working on the plantations. I buy for all of them." She even makes the purchases for her sons' personal clothing, and she hires workers to hoe the local corn fields when her sons are working on the coast.

Widowhood gives senior women overt economic control of the household if they have adult children. Grown sons defer to their widowed mothers in economic matters much as they deferred to their fathers. The widow of a junior male is in a weaker position if her children are young, or if her husband did not own land. The junior widow can remain in her in-laws' home depending on their good will, but her position is a weak one without a male partner and is seen as temporary. In many cases, she returns to the area of her (consanguinal) family ties, or seeks work as a domestic employee. If she leaves, she is often pressured to leave her children, for their inheritance claims are with their patrilineal kin. It is also easier for a woman to make a fresh start unencumbered by children; but by leaving them she not only suffers another emotional loss, she also loses her investment in them as security in old age.

Childlessness. In the preceding cases, we have seen that childbearing is an important part of women's strategy to increase their economic autonomy and security over time. Examination of the case of a rural woman who was barren helps to highlight the economic significance of motherhood.

7. María Lazaro is about sixty years old. She first married at age eighteen and lived twenty years with her husband, but never had children. They both did traditional subsistence work and did not have to go to the coast. When he died, she returned to her father's house. She soon married again and lived with her second husband for about fifteen years. She still had no children and they finally separated; her husband brought another woman home, they fought, and María returned to her father again.

After a few years, her current husband, Efrain, came to ask for her and she accepted. Efrain is poor, old, widowed, has many children, and must support his ancient mother. The household includes a married son, daughter-in-law, and their baby, a daughter who has separated from her husband and kept her baby, two teen-aged daughters and a younger son. Efrain's household is short of land and healthy male labor. His eldest son died several years ago, and his married son has malaria. The entire household migrates to the coast to pick cotton and raise corn, with the exception of Maria, who stays behind to look after the house and care for Efrain's mother.

Efrain has little to give María for personal expenses, although he provides staples such as corn, beans, sugar, and coffee. He gives her but ten or fifteen cents to spend on market days. María earns any other income herself, by weaving for clients. Sometimes she can earn Q. 6 per month from weaving since she does not have children of her own to care for. Although she is the wife of the senior male, she does not manage the household budget for the group. Efrain gives gastos separately to his daughter-in-law and children. Several years ago, María "adopted" a small orphaned girl whose mother had died working on the coast. The girl performs errands for her, and will not go to school "because she has no father," meaning that Efrain does not assume the role of foster father.

This case illustrates the plight of the childless woman in T'oj Nam. There is little doubt that the failure of her second marriage was partly due to childlessness, so that her husband, wanting children, had brought home another wife. Maria's third husband already had children. Remarriage brought her a new place to live and work, and a man who would provide her with maize and staples, but Maria did not gain the economic authority that a senior wife generally holds. Control of the household budget, then, appears to be reserved for mothers (or other women) who raise children to make major contributions to the family ecomony. Without children, Maria's economic insecurity resembles that of the orphan she adopted. Supporting the child is clearly part of a strategy to establish a reciprocal claim on the labor of a youthful girl who might help support Maria when she is too old to work.

Illness. The following case illustrates failure by both sexes to conform to expected roles that involve cooperative effort.

8. Martina Rojas is forty-six years old. She married without parental consent at age eighteen. As is the custom, she went to live in the young man's house together with his parents. At first, she liked him and was happy there. But the family was poor. "There were no gastos, nothing, neither clothing, nor food." Her husband himself had almost no money, but what he had was "only to drink and to spend on another woman. There was no money for my clothes or food." He also beat her when he got drunk. His family did nothing about this, they only looked on. Her husband gave the money he earned to his parents, not to Martina. Hence, when she lacked food and clothes, it was the fault of his parents as well. She had a daughter by this man. Martina's father wanted her to come home so she finally ran away for good, taking her daughter and her clothes back to her parents' house. After a year, her husband came to her house to take their daughter. Maria let her go because she did not have the money to maintain her, explaining: "Before, there was no money; there was no sale of shirts, huipiles, or collars; there were no cars, buses, nor motors to mill corn."

By letting her daughter go, Martina was free to work or remarry. She went to the coast to work as a maid for many years, and learned to speak Spanish. When her father died, she married again. After three years, she became seriously ill. Her stomach began to swell as if she were pregnant, but she was not. She went to the health center, to local curers, to doctors in the city, and was even operated upon, but no one could cure her. It became even more difficult for her to work, or even walk. When she got sick, her husband no longer wanted her. "At first he thought it was a child. Then he was angry because I could no longer work: neither mill, draw water, nor wash clothes. How he beat me with a stick!" He finally sent her away and she went to ask shelter with a distant relative who was always a friend. For the present, Martina depends on the charity of her friends and kin when she is too sick to work; she guards their house for them when they migrate. During this time she has also been active as a founding member of the weaver's cooperative, although her activities have decreased with the progression of her illness.

Martina's history indicates the importance for each partner of making the expected economic contributions. She would not endure her first husband's failure to provide for her, nor would her second husband endure her failure to work when she became permanently ill. In both cases, the men used physical violence, knowing that she was either outnumbered or too ill to defend herself except by leaving. With her father dead and no hope of remarriage due to her illness, Martina would have been totally dependent on charity were it not for the founding of the weavers' cooperative by women with similarly limited options.

The Transitional Urban Household

The break between the rural subsistence economy and urban commercial activity is not a sharp one, for many of the recently urbanized Mam modify only a part of their behavior to conform to modern economic constraints. The following cases illustrate some of the different effects that the increasingly important new sources of cash income can have on sex roles.

9. Fabula is age forty-three. She joined her husband at age fifteen, and for the first two years lived with his parents. Then she went with him for the first time to work in a coastal coffee plantation. She was miserable and cried a lot. They worked for six months the first year, and every year thereafter they went for two months. She would harvest coffee, clear the groves using a machete, and carry firewood. For about ten years, they migrated to the plantations.

About fifteen years ago, they had enough money saved to buy land for a house and store on the town's main street. Their first capital for the store came from the sale of potatoes they had grown. They started with only Q. 30 and now have between Q. 100 and 200 in inventory. They both tend the store (cantina) days and evenings, and they both make trips to the city, together or independently, to buy stock. Fabula also shares the work in potato cultivation. Comparing field work to storekeeping she says: "I like planting, irrigating, and harvesting potatoes—all of it! I like to work in the fields. I am no more than a prisoner here in the store."

Fabula has born eleven children. Notably the six that have survived were all born in the last fifteen years since their parents ceased their annual migrations to the coast. Fabula weaves and cooks for the family, but this is not too burdensome because she lives near the power corn mills and also has two teen-aged daughters to help. Her husband gets intermittent work in construction which supplements field work and storekeeping. When his son is busy, he recruits the two teen-age daughters to work as his assistants in making adobe bricks. Modern stereotypes of femininity do not deter these young women as they work on the main street of the town with their skirts hitched up, knee deep in the mud, which they shovel into brick molds. With the three of them working together, they can earn Q. 35 in one week of adobe making, but the work is irregular.

Fabula and her husband spend about Q. 12 per week for food and related expenses. Although her husband generally keeps the money and decides what to buy, she is content because he buys her skirt material and shawls, and because they can both make purchases. Her husband is not jealous or possessive. If she wants to go somewhere, she just decides she is going, and "off I go."

Fabula's case illustrates a successful transition to a commercial economy based on a sexual partnership in hard work. The overall impression given by this household is that sexual differentiation in terms of productive labor for a cash income (on plantations, in potato cultivation, storekeeping, and brick making) has been minimal. However, it seems possible that a hidden cost to the joint accumulation of capital in the early years of their marriage was the high infant mortality rate that coincided with their plantation work, a cost born more heavily by Fabula.

The next example shows how some commercial opportunities increase women's options for autonomy.

10. Antonia is age thirty. She was raised by her grandmother after her parents separated. At age sixteen, Antonia united with Carlos and they went to work on the plantations. She has a son by him, but they stayed together only one year until he joined with a Ladina. Carlos' mother kept their son, and Antonia went to work as a live-in maid for Ladinos. Without her son, she was able to work hard, but earned only Q. 4 per month for six months, followed by two years alternating plantation work and domestic work in local Ladino homes.

Then Antonia united with Mingo. She worked with him on the coast for two months. He collected both his and her pay, as is customary. She knew she had earned about Q. 45 the first month, but he said it was only Q. 10. "I kept silent and worked another month. When we returned I was pregnant. At this time Mingo began to be the *bailador* (dancer) around town. He was dressing well, going out drinking, and got another woman. I was thinking that he was doing this with the money I had earned. Then he started to treat me badly because he wanted me to leave so he could bring the other woman home." Antonia was mad about the money and the other woman. Fortunately, she had left Q. 25 of her own money in her mother's care, for when she left Mingo she had nothing despite her hard work on the coast. She took her daughter and went to work in a comedor, as a live-in employee, earning only Q. 1.50 per month. She had to supplement this with periodic plantation work. She found she could not do domestic work very well with a child. Also she could earn more on the coast.

On the coast, she met Pedro and united for a third time. At this time, she worked mainly on plantations. She picked coffee and cotton, weeded with a hoe and chopped with a machete. She also "maintained people," making tortillas for workers, earning five cents per worker. A fast worker, she would feed around forty people daily for Q. 2. Even picking cotton, she would pick around 150 pounds daily, which yielded about Q. 2. She often earned more than Pedro who averaged Q. 1 per day. When she joined Pedro, she did not know he already had a wife. Although polygyny occurs in T'oj Nam, she did not want to join Pedro's household, and opted to stay in the house she inherited from her grandmother. Pedro became a part-time consort. He brought her maize, treated her well, never tried to beat her, and was not jealous if he saw her out walking around the town. She continued to go to the coast with him every year, since his first wife, an older woman with more children, did not migrate. When Antonia was with Pedro on the coast, she collected her own pay, but since she earned more, she helped him buy soft drinks and small items. He would then take his cash home to his wife.

Antonia has had three sons by Pedro. The oldest died while she worked on the plantations. When they began to organize the weavers' cooperative, Pedro advised her to earn her living by weaving, for she is a good, fast weaver. "He did not want me to go to the coast anymore. He was afraid another son would die." Pedro has continued to bring maize and child support money when he visits, although he has since taken a second wife. He gives Q. 5 to 6 every month or so, or Q. 25 every six months. When he comes Antonia may send him off or feed him, and let him spend the night. She is pregnant again.

Antonia would like to return to the coast to work now because she is strong and can earn more there, but with small children she will not go back. Mingo wants to take back his ten-year-old daughter, Tomasa, but Antonia wants her to stay. Tomasa does a great deal of weaving, child care, and housework, in addition to attending school (Mingo pays her school expenses). When Antonia must go out, she can leave the younger children with Tomasa. Pedro wants to take her older son, but Antonia does not want to give him up either.

Since she has no land for crops, she spends around Q. 5 to 6 per week for food. At most she can earn Q. 6 per month from weaving. Even at this rate, there are nights when she must work until midnight, using a kerosene lamp. Pedro's contributions are irregular, and provide less than a quarter of her living expenses. The remainder of her income comes from her activity as an intermediary in selling textiles to tourists. She sells both as a member of the coop and as a free agent on the street. This is also an irregular income. Although she can count on good sales during the annual fiesta, during the off season she often has to borrow money.

Antonia's story illustrates how a woman has used wage labor and commercial opportunities to maintain herself independently through a series of unsuccessful conjugal relationships. She lacks the traditional support of her father, but at least had access to her grandmother's house. Beyond this, she shows ingenuity and determination in her efforts to support herself on her own terms in the cash economy. Domestic employment and plantation work were effective strategies for her as a single woman, but were imcompatible with raising children. The former paid too little, while the latter was dangerous to the children's health. Ultimately, by combining commercialism, weaving for sale, and economic claims upon the fathers of her children, she has been able to maintain herself and her role as a mother to her children. Her energy and efforts to improve the position of commercial weavers have earned her the respect of many Mam women who have chosen her for leadership roles in the cooperative.

The two preceding cases have shown how Mam women respond to new urban economic opportunities. Another aspect of the transition to a modern market economy is women's response to the appearance of major inequities in the earning power of the sexes in the money economy. The fact that some Mam men have found employment that gives them unusually high (by local standards) incomes as *individuals* is bound to affect the traditional pattern of mutual interdependence between husband and wife. Such cases are still few, but the ones that I encounter showed tensions between the sexes that seemed closely related to this transition.

11. Elena is age thirty-eight and has seven children. Her husband Enrique, is a wealthy labor contractor who spends at least four months each year on the coast. She used to work on plantations when they were poor, before he was a contractor, but she has not gone for many years.

Elena and her husband do not get along well. She knows that he has lovers on his trips: "He goes to the coast one year with one woman, the next year with another. Women want him now because he has money. He spends a lot of his money drinking and on other women. I have always had friends who would be on the same truck with him who would tell me what he does when he is on the *finca* (plantation). I assume he does the same. He used to tell me to go so that he could bring another woman home, but I would not go because I like this house. Another woman would not treat the children well. But for my children, I have wanted to go with other men. He (Enrique) says that one of the children wasn't by him, but by another *tata* (father) and he forgot that child."

Enrique and Elena have jointly bought land and built a new house with a store front; but Enrique does not give Elena any money for gastos. Any personal expenses for herself or the children are paid for by her. She earns a moderate income as a curer, for she knows how to give injections (She combines traditional techniques, divination, and modern medicines).

Hence, they share material or subsistence goods (Enrique still farms part-time), but have completely separate cash incomes and budgets.

In this instance and others, it appears that the transition to high *individual* cash income upsets the balance of mutual needs. The higher-earning husband begins to feel that his spouse is rather expendable and that he could easily replace her. He tries to provoke her to leave. Some women tenaciously remain, knowing that they could not independently accumulate enough capital for a comparable standard of living, but they try to find independent means of raising their own cash incomes. Eventually, the household standard of living seems to become two-tiered, with wives and children sharing a relatively high degree of comfort in terms of traditional subsistence standards—housing and food supplies, but a notably lower standard in terms of personal spending money.

Social Organization

Formal Community Organization

Some aspects of formal social organization in T'oj Nam date back to colonial and possibly precolonial times, while others clearly represent the recent intervention of national and international agencies. Formal organizations serve various purposes, but to a large extent they can be seen as responses to outside pressure. This section examines the extent to which women of T'oj Nam take part in formal organizations pertaining to politics, religion, education, and miscellaneous socioeconomic services.

Politics. The sphere of organized politics combines traditional and modern features adapted to the characteristics of different parts of the community. The most traditional form of political organization in T'oj Nam appears to be the cargo system, which has been well described for many indigenous communities of Middle America.[23] The cargo system is a hierarchical structure of political and religious offices that are filled by men of the indigenous community through a combination of election and appointment by the elders. It reflects an earlier social order in which community religious and political activities were not viewed as distinct or separate concerns. The religious officials, headed by the *alcalde rezador*, or chief prayer maker, are responsible for the maintenance of *costumbre* (Maya ritual and religious customs) in the municipio. Their duties include maintenance of the church, calendric rites performed at sacred spots in the hills of T'oj Nam for the health of the community and the crops, and guardianship of the *Caja Real* (Sacred or Royal Chest), which contains documents belonging to the Mam community. Accession to this position is a function of age and a man's previous record of service.

The highest political office is the elected position of *alcalde*, or mayor, who is charged with local civil and judicial administration. Since this position was made elective, it has been held by Mam men who receive a salary (as do the Ladinos who hold appointments as municipal secretary and treasurer). The bulk of the unpaid civil positions are treated as obligatory service to the community and are distributed in rotation among eligible Mam males. All Mam young men are expected to fill at least the lower positions in these community service hierarchies when called upon. With advancing age and service in the highest offices, a man can attain the status of *principal*, or elder, which confers great respect and political influence within the Mam community.

Women are almost completely peripheral to this system of formal community organization. They neither hold political and religious offices, nor do they participate in the selection of officeholders. They are, of course, affected by these formal organizations. If their husband holds an office, their household economy is strained since everyone in the household must compensate for this loss of domestic labor power and the expenses incurred by community service. At the same time, their household receives prestige and potential political advantages.

Community politics in T'oj Nam are linked with and modified by national politics. Because national policy determines that the position of alcalde be filled by popular election, progressive young men can be elected who have not worked their way up through the cargo system, and who may have little sympathy for the preservation of the old political order. National political influence is also present in the form of modern political parties organized to elect national and local slates of candidates. Each of the four major national parties has its formal representatives in T'oj Nam; they are Ladino and Mam men of modern urban occupations. Although there were no elections during the period of my research, informants reported that women are not active in party organizations, and even the men were activated only at election time.

My limited information on voting patterns also points to a minimal role for women. In twenty-nine Mam and Ladino households, I found only one case of a woman who had voted, whereas voting in at least one election was nearly universal among the men.[24] The exceptional woman who voted was an outspoken Mam widow who had recieved social assistance from the wife of the Guatemalan President whom she had spoken to during a visit by the latter to T'oj Nam. The widow quite clearly felt obliged to return the favor by joining and voting for the President's party. Beyond this case, the only women reported to have voted were the Ladina teachers, who are largely commuters to T'oj Nam and who vote "because of their jobs." A number of men also vote for that reason. In general, it is reported that people are interested in the mayoral elections and apathetic toward the national presidency. This difference in local versus national orientation definitely appears in the political awareness of the women. While most of those questioned could name the local alcalde, roughly one-third of the Ladina and Mam women could not name the current national president. Further indirect evidence of the low level of participation by women comes from the electoral register which enumerates *eligible* voters (those with citizenship cards). These figures show that somewhat less than 4,000 (literate and illiterate) people are eligible to vote and that of these just under 9 percent are women. Admittedly, this figure probably greatly exceeds the number of active voters of both sexes, but it serves to document the extent to which women are not yet integrated into the electoral system.

Another level of formal community organization is found in the aldeas. One particularly well-organized aldea has a committee that appears to be based on clan-like affiliations present in the community. This aldea, like other districts in T'oj Nam, is known by the patrilineal surname shared by its dominant families. Most residents of the aldea are patrilineal descendants of three brothers, grandfathers of the present senior men, although some outside men have married into the group. The membership in their committee numbers about seventy-five men, "heads of households." No women have ever participated in their meetings, which are held at the house of the president. It was implied by the president that an old widow or single woman with no man to represent her would probably be "sick or crazy," or else she would be living in a family group that included men.[25] The main purpose of the committee is to organize improvements in the aldea. The committee has formal leadership positions and membership lists, meeting records, and records of contributions. They have been able to tax themselves for money and labor to construct a system of piped water, and to purchase land to protect their water source and provide common pasture for sheep.

Despite the image of ancient Mam traditions suggested by the appearance of patriclan affiliation, there is much that is modern and recent in this committee organization. The particular aldea is known as a stronghold of active Catholics who have struggled against the *costum-bristas* (Mam religious traditionalists). Their committee is only five years old, and its water project was undertaken with the financial and organizational assistance of three outside organizations: *Desarrollo de la Communidad*, A.I.D., and CARE. Previous attempts by the president's father to get water for the aldea had failed. In this particular case, it appears that a relatively weak association of paternal kin was substantially revitalized by modern institutions and formal organization.

Another significant aspect of political organization in T'oj Nam is the absence of national police or military personnel in the municipio. Compared to other indigenous municipios in Guatemala where young men are drafted quarterly, the men of T'oj Nam are relatively unaffected by national military organizations. Although I lack data on the army's reasons for passing over T'oj Nam and other Mam villages, a local Ladino ex-soldier explained that indigenous men are drafted only from the more "advanced" communities where the men do not wear indigenous clothes and where many are educated. Although T'oj Nam Ladinos are eligible for the draft, few of them are ever drafted either. Some Mam men have enlisted for military service, and at least one became a member of the President's guard; but military service is quite rare.

Religion. In T'oj Nam, religion reflects the main streams of cultural influence. There are three major religious orientations: (1) a traditional Mam religion that has syncretized Maya and Christian elements; (2) Catholicism; and (3) Protestant Evangelism. The first is practised exclusively by the Mam, while the latter two include Ladinos as well. We shall briefly examine women's role in each of these religious systems.

Many aspects of the traditional Mam religion, locally called "*costumbre*" have been described by foreign observers. In some cases, ingenious methods were used to overcome cultural barriers and distrust to obtain information. Oakes (1951a), for example, worked indirectly through a Ladino male informant who studied with the Mam to become a shaman. Most of the data on Mam religious customs focuses on male activities: the hierarchical system of religious offices, the agricultural and calendric ceremonies. Relatively little information has been collected on women's activities, beliefs, or rituals in the traditional Mam religion. Indeed, since few Mam women speak fluent Spanish, and few investigators or their interpreters have been women, this data has been neglected. My investigation did not deeply probe Mam costumbre, but I shall attempt to integrate my own information with that available from other sources.

One of the major figures in Mam religion is the *chiman*, a religious intermediary. The term *chiman* is often translated as "shaman," but it also means "grandfather" in Mam. Chimanes are ritual specialists with knowledge of the Maya calendric system whose activities include conducting agricultural rituals, healing, divination, and magic. Unlike Western religions, the Mam do not strictly separate the specialists for spiritual and physical well-being.

Although most chimanes are male, there are exceptions. According to Oakes, there were women chimanes in the Mam region in the 1940s. In one area, they were said to have died out, while in another area Oakes had limited direct contact with a woman chiman who gave her calendric information (1951a:92, 114). My informants also reported that there were formerly a few women chimanes. An old midwife claimed that one still lived, although she was very old and lived up in the mountains. She was said to cast *mixes* (sacred beans) for divination. Unfortunately, I was unable to make direct contact due to the migration of my informant. Hence, the characteristics of female chimanes and the reasons for their disappearance remain largely unknown. Although knowledge of curing, calendrics, and divination are reported for women specialists, the role which some chimanes play in community ritual and in the community religious hierarchy has not been reported for any women.

Women perform important ritual functions in other contexts. As midwives, they supervise the birth event. There are suggestive parallels between the midwife's supervision of birth rituals and the chiman's supervision of agricultural rituals. Like the chiman who practices costumbre, the practising midwife must abstain from sexual intercourse. She must take a series of therapeutic steam baths with the mother and infant during the 20 days of confinement after childbirth. Furthermore, the "call" to become a midwife occurs in much the same way as the call to become a chiman.[26] In part, it seems to be a hereditary office. One woman, whose mother and grandmother were midwives, fell sick and was told that the only way to become well was to become a midwife. She had already successfully cured a few sick people, and decided she must obey the calling. Significantly, in Oakes' report, an old woman who was descended from a long line of shamans who inherited the office of *Chiman Nam* or Community Shaman, was herself a midwife who was extremely knowledgeable in ritual practices (1951a:19, 57, 184). Today in T'oj Nam, traditional midwives are extremely closed regarding their practice because Catholic missionaries have been campaigning against their methods and their right to practice.

Another aspect of women's ritual activity, and one which is neither diminishing nor clandestine, occurs during house-finishing ceremonies. When a house is completed, using collective male labor from among kin and neighbors, the corresponding women collectively prepare meals and a final ceremonial feast. This is a highly formalized occasion that involves the blessing of the house. On this occasion, the ten to twenty women who collectively prepare the feast form a procession, in order of seniority, to go to draw water. They do not go to the nearest waterhole, but to a special spring with sacred water where the chimanes conduct ceremonies on certain occasions. There, the leader prepares a sweetened herb drink with the fresh water. Each of the women, in order, takes four sips of the fresh drink. The leader fills each jug with water and after a rest, the procession returns to the house and a rocket is set off to celebrate their return. Then they offer the drink to each of the men who similarly take four sips each. No explanation could be elicited, except "*costumbre*," but the women's processions to the sacred spring are regarded as an indispensable beginning to the house-finishing ceremonial feast.

Midwifery and the water-drawing procession are examples of autonomous roles for women in ritual. The former involves a dyadic relationship between an individual and her midwife, while the latter extends to a larger collectivity based on kin and neighborly ties. Women also participate in costumbre with their husbands. Many of the rituals of planting and harvesting are conducted by men and women as couples. Women are expected to accompany their husbands to their fields to perform rites and to pray for a good crop. If a woman is wife of a chiman, she assists him actively in ceremonies, and partakes of the food and drink that is brought to the chiman by his client.[27]

For the most part, women's religious activities seem to be concentrated on the well-being of individuals and the household. This is also true for most men, but some men have an additional concern with the well-being of the clan and community which is expressed in collective ceremonies led by the chimanes. During my research, many of the community aspects of costumbre were moribund. The chimanes scarcely used some of the most central shrines; they no longer held community processions for rain, and there has been no Community Chiman for the last fifteen years since the last one died. Old costumbristas complain that the rains do not come like they used to since the people are no longer united behind their chimanes and since costumbre is expensive. Women also note that some of the customs for the birth of a baby have been foreshortened or replaced by a visit to the church to burn candles.

Roughly half of both the town and rural Mam described themselves as costumbristas or else "nothing" when questioned about their religious preferences. Confusingly, some people first say they are "Catholics," and explain that they mean "Catholic, as it used to be," indicating that they practice costumbre.[28] Chimanes have traditionally made use of the church, since T'oj Nam has rarely had a resident priest, and they have incorporated certain Catholic customs. Also, many of the people who describe themselves as "nothing" continue to practice costumbre. A few have lost faith in all religious claims, but maintain loyalty to their autochthonous customs. Religious preferences in T'oj Nam are shown in Table 3–8.

In recent years, both Catholic and Protestant missionaries have begun to agitate against traditional costumbre in T'oj Nam. They have won the formal allegiance of roughly half the Mam population sampled in both rural and town areas, with Protestants representing only about 6 percent of the total. Conversion to modern Catholicism appears to occur mainly through the men. Several of the women interviewed said they had converted mainly because of their husbands. One described how, as a Catholic, her husband had strongly fought her attempts to save her dying babies when she wanted to call the traditional midwife-curer to help them. Another woman who practiced Catholicism to please her husband returned to "nothing" when he died. In contrast to the men who profess to be Catholics, the women are very little involved in church activities. They attend mass and marry in the church, but their husbands are the ones who become active as catechists and occupy various posts at the church, as well as receiving special training courses outside the community. However, a recent attempt to retrain midwives has been undertaken by a group of foreign nuns, and has registered some 25 Mam women for the local course.[29]

Table 3-8. T'oj Nam Religious Preference by Sex and Ethnicity

Religion	Mam		Ladino	
	Women (%)	Men (%)	Women (%)	Men (%)
Costumbre	34	30	0	0
"Nothing"	17	15	0	0
Catholic	43	48	86	83
Evangelist	6	7	14	17
Total	100%	100%	100%	100%
(Sample Size)	(35)	(27)	(14)	(12)

Attendance at Mass in T'oj Nam is predominantly Mam, with men and women seated separately. Ladinos of both sexes are largely inactive Catholics, often dissatisfied with foreign priests who devote their attention to the Mam community. Public participation in religious pageants reflects the cultural pluralism of T'oj Nam. The organization of the Christmas pageant is predominantly Mam, whereas the Good Friday pageant is predominantly Ladino. In these events, both men and women act out the traditional parts assigned to them in Catholic tradition. It may be coincidential that in the Christmas tradition, a birth celebration, Mam women have more public roles to play than do Ladinas in the Easter tradition, commemorating a state execution. Apart from such religiosocial occasions, some of the significant implications of adherence to Catholicism for women include acceptance of the Church's promotion of formal Church marriages, prohibition of divorce and polygyny, opposition to the bride price,[30] and to traditional midwifery (including the twenty days of sweatbaths).

Evangelism affects only a small minority of the population of T'oj Nam, as it is the most recent religion to appear, encouraged by North American missionaries. The congregation numbers around one hundred. It is predominantly Mam, but includes some Ladinos and mestizos as well. Women are encouraged to take an active, speaking role in the meetings. Singing songs is an important part of their meetings and the songs are sung in both Mam and Spanish so that Mam women know the words. As in other parts of Guatemala, women seem to appreciate the prohibition on alcohol. One practical Mam woman reports that she converted for her husband because he used to be an extreme alcoholic and polygynist. Ladinas also report improvements in their family life when their husbands convert.

Women are affected by religious change in T'oj Nam, but in many ways the impact upon them is less direct than it is for men. Some women convert to Western religion for the sake of their husbands. They participate in and enjoy some of the public events, yet for the most part they have remained marginal to the conversion process. Mam women may voice loyalty to a Western religion and moments later begin to speak of the *"dueños de los cerros,"* the "lords of the mountains" who control events. For men, a more direct pressure for total conversion has come from its being coupled with employment opportunities, training programs, contacts with influential people outside the community, and political programs and alliances within the community. Men seem compelled by these pressures to accept and *propagate* a new system of beliefs. Women, who are more superficially exposed to the rationale (and economic benefits) of Western religion "go along" with their husbands, withholding public judgment and privately seeking reconciliation between the old and new systems.

Education. The comparison of levels of literacy between the sexes in T'oj Nam indicates that education has not been equally available. Municipal literacy statistics for 1964 do not report sex differences, but do show urban-rural inequities. For the population aged seven and over, there was 7 percent literacy in the rural areas and 33 percent literacy in the town area, with a combined 10 percent literacy rate for the whole municipio. In the 1973 national census, municipal literacy had risen to 11 percent of the population (Guatemala 1974). My data from 1975 show how literacy levels differ for each sex by ethnic group and place of residence.[31] In both ethnic groups and in both rural and town populations, women are significantly less likely to be literate than men of the same group. Rural Mam women (roughly 44 percent of the adult population of the municipio) fall well below the municipal average, and even below the 1964 rural average for literacy in T'oj Nam (see Table 3-9 below).

Formal education in T'oj Nam is entirely secular. The only schools are government primary schools. These are distributed throughout the municipio, with the largest school located in the town center. Out of ten schools, only three have classes beyond the fourth grade. As shown in Table 3-10, girls attending school in the town center are only 29 percent of the total. The low percentage of female attendance holds for the municipio as a whole, with only 32 percent female students out of a total of 709. This disparity appears to grow stronger in the higher grades. Out of 118 students in grades 4-6 in the municipio as a whole, only 23 percent are girls.[32]

The factors that discourage primary school education for girls are complex. Among the factors to be considered are: the sex of the teachers, the need for child labor in the home, the perceived value of edu-

Table 3-9. T'oj Nam Adult Literacy Rates by Sex and Ethnicity, 1975 (age 14 and over)

| Ethnic Group | Literate | | | |
	Women %	(Sample Size)	Men %	(Sample Size)
Mam				
rural	4	(26)	35	(23)
town	21	(28)	56	(16)
Ladino	72	(18)	100	(17)

Table 3-10. Attendance at the Central Primary School of T'oj Nam by Grade and Sex

Grade	Number			Percentage Girls (%)
	Boys	Girls	Total	
Beginners' Spanish	24	12	36	33
First	34	16	50	32
Second	37	15	52	29
Third	21	5	26	19
Fourth	31	9	40	23
Fifth	9	9	18	50
Sixth	11	2	13	15
Total	167	68	235	29%

Source: Figures from the school director, March 1975.

cation for each sex, the ethnic background of the children, and legal constraints.

The composition of the teaching staff does not give evidence of sex bias as much as ethnic bias. In 1975, the staff included twelve women and nine men, but none of the teachers were Mam. A more probable explanation for sex bias would seem to be the demand for child labor in the home. Observation suggests that Mam girls begin to perform useful work in the home at an earlier age than boys. At the age of seven, they draw water, babysit, tend the fire, assist in cooking and washing, clean cotton, and begin to learn tasks related to weaving. Boys of the same age rarely accompany their fathers to the fields, but are subject to occasional demands to run an errand or help get firewood. Serious work in the fields does not begin until around age ten. However, it is likely that field work would also pull boys out of school before they reach the higher grades. Indeed, the rate of attrition in attendance is high, with a total of 202 students in first grade and only sixteen in sixth grade.

Among the Mam population, education is not perceived to have very great value. With few exceptions, the Mam do not see education as an avenue into better occupations for their children, although they are aware that it is useful for keeping records of transactions and for reading signs in cities. Literacy itself cannot change the fact that they must farm and weave at home and work on plantations elsewhere for most of their lives. Although some of my female informants had attended school as children, none of them had any use for literacy in their daily lives.[33] A minority of Mam men have found use for literacy skills on becoming labor contractors, merchants, employees of the missionaries, or officeholders in formal organizations. But literacy alone is not enough to secure these positions. Conversely, some relatively wealthy and influential Mam men are illiterate.

Ethnicity may also have a bearing on the sex ratio of primary school children. Ladinos, as a group that speaks the national language and depends upon urban occupations requiring literacy, are thought to be more committed to educating their children than indigenes. National statistics show that literacy rates are higher among Ladinos in all major regions of Guatemala, and that female students are 44 percent of all students registered in primary schools. (Whetten 1961:262; Guatemala 1970:251). These two figures combined suggest that Ladinos in general are more likely to send their daughters to school.

However, attendance figures for three small T'oj Nam schools that serve a peripheral Ladino district (and hence lack introductory Spanish classes) show that of their 56 students in the first grade, only 18 percent are female. In contrast, the attendance in the first year of *Castellanización* classes (designed to teach Spanish to monolingual Mam children) show that of 139 students, 48 percent are female. At the same time, the director of the largest and most central school in T'oj Nam reports that 10 percent of the students are Ladinos, evenly divided by sex. Further, the urbanized Ladino households I observed seemed to have less need for female child labor and to routinely send all their children to all grades of primary school offered. With the information available, it is not possible to draw firm conclusions about different ethnic attitudes toward the education of daughters. One of the most important factors in school attendance for either sex is probably the economic position of the household; only better-off town households among the Mam and Ladino populations can afford to invest in their children's education.

Legal factors also affect school attendance. Fathers are sometimes arrested and fined if they do not send their *sons* to school. The truancy law is officially neutral, but in practice the sanctions affect males only. Although the truancy law is only sporadically enforced, it may influence the sex ratio of students.[34]

School activities themselves do not show much evidence of sexual discrimination, except in the area of organized sports (There are twenty-four boys' teams and only two girls' teams). In class, both boys and girls are taught to crochet, embroider, and grow garden vegetables, as well as the standard elementary school subjects. Students who have gone on to secondary school complain that basic literacy skills are not adequately taught.

Secondary school introduces a new dimension into the relationship of formal education to modern sex roles. First, it entails a much greater economic investment, since students must be supported in the city where the secondary schools are located. Second, it involves preparation for careers. The cost factor (roughly Q. 300 per year) is obviously prohibitive for almost all Mam households. Altogether only seven Mam students have attended secondary school outside T'oj Nam. Of these, only one is a girl. Most attend with substantial economic assistance from government scholarships and the church. All the Mam students are Catholic, and in at least six of the seven cases their fathers had worked closely with the Catholic priests. Thus far only one young man has graduated to become the first professional, a teacher, among the Mam population of T'oj Nam. Significantly, two Mam families with sons who have attended secondary school have also had daughters who graduated from primary school but were not sent outside for secondary education. Although some of the parents are dubious about the advantages of a costly education for their sons, their doubts are even stronger regarding the advantages for their daughters. It is possible that the traditional pattern of "marrying out" (joining the husband's household) for daughters makes parents less certain of the potential returns for their sacrifices.

Among Ladinos, it is estimated that around thirty to thirty-five have gone on to secondary school, including eight girls.[35] Most of them have become teachers. Only the wealthier Ladino families send children to school outside T'oj Nam, and usually they send *all* their children, often maintaining a second, urban residence near the schools. In contrast to Mam children who are expected to retain strong ties to their kin groups and establish patrilocal residence, Ladinos anticipate occupational and residential mobility (hence neolocality) from children of both sexes. Many of the adults have grown up in other municipios and their children in turn have dispersed to find employment in other areas.

In sum, it is difficult to determine the extent to which sexual bias is present in the system of formal education as it affects children of T'oj Nam. Bias clearly is present, given the consistent numerical superiority of boys in almost all phases of schooling. Yet the causes appear subtle and complex, combining considerations such as the earlier utility of girls' labor, the wealth of the parents, the cost and sources of financial support, and the expected returns for an educated woman and her parents.

Other organizations. T'oj Nam has a number of small organizations which serve a variety of purposes. These are groups that organize events and activities for the annual fiesta, and groups that have received outside aid in order to promote modern social and economic services. The fiesta groups are the most traditional inasmuch as the town has been celebrating its fiesta for many years without national or international assistance. These groups include "heads of households" who plan for the fiesta, and Mam groups that provide the traditional entertainment events of the fiesta: the *corrida*, or horseback riding event, and the *bailes*, ceremonial dances which are performed by masked, costumed dancers. All such fiesta preparation is organized exclusively by men.[36]

The organizations that have received outside aid have had more recent origins and more practical purposes, but have proven less durable. Two of these were a Savings and Credit Cooperative and a Mother's Association. The former was supported by a national development agency, was targeted toward a male membership, but has been essentially inoperative because very few people have anything to save. The latter was organized by Ladina schoolteachers, and is said to have included roughly 100 mothers (eight of whom were Ladinas, the remainder being Mam women) who provided snacks to school children. The directors of the mothers' group were all Ladinas, and the food supplies were acquired from CARE. This group folded four years ago when the leading Ladinas moved away.

One remaining organization that has been of particular importance to the Mam women of T'oj Nam is the Weavers' Cooperative. A brief review of its history will reveal some new dimensions of formal social organization among Mam women.

The Weavers' Cooperative was formed to assist Mam women in marketing their textiles, both through a cooperative village store and by making commercial contacts in the cities that would give them larger orders, steadier work, and make it worthwhile to purchase threads wholesale. The cooperative was founded in the early 70s in response to a widowed weaver's request for commercial assistance from the wife of the Guatemalan President. This woman along with two other women without male partners were the most active early organizers, presumably because their economic needs were the strongest. Since its inception, the cooperative has received outside organizational and economic assistance from two national and one international organization. It may be of some significance that the field personnel of these agencies in T'oj Nam were males until 1975, when the Peace Corps sent in a woman.[37]

During its early years, the cooperative had a female directorate, employing a male scribe, and a membership that varied between 70 and 100 Mam women. However, it began to break into two factions. The accusations that were made are revealing. The original leader was accused of favoritism toward her relatives (particularly her son who was selling co-op textiles in his store in a large city). She in turn accused the other faction of trying to take over the cooperative, arguing that it was intended for poor, single women, not for men and women from wealthy families. The faction that opposed her was indeed headed by several men who had been trained in cooperativism by outside agencies; two of the men were relatively wealthy labor contractors and brothers whose wives were weavers in the co-op. In both factions, it appeared that male kinsmen of the women weavers had private commercial interests in textiles and were attempting to manipulate the cooperative in their favor. Ultimately, some co-op funds were stolen, and the president's family was blamed. After a furor of accusations, the co-op split apart. The original president kept the official co-op statutes and about twenty-five members seceded from the co-op with her, remaining loyal to her as their *jefe* (chief). The other faction reorganized with about thirty members, and elected new officers. The new president and treasurer were two men who had been trained by and allied with the outside agencies.

Observation of the male-led co-op meetings after the split indicated a number of problems. The factionalism had seriously reduced membership and confidence. Meetings were attended by only about fifteen women accompanied by their children, and three to five men. The president dominated the meetings with lengthy speeches filled with modern Spanish expressions that the monolingual Mam women (the majority) could not possibly grasp. Few women paid attention until the subjects of weaving orders or money matters were raised. For example, after hearing a long speech from the president regarding a larger order for shirts, they were adamant that they would not fill orders that would give them only a 95 cent return for thirty hours of work. These meetings were generally conducted with minimal female participation, however, even though women's interests were, theoretically, its *raison d'être*. The fact that few of the women were fluently bilingual and none were literate were obstacles to a more democratic structure; they were unable to read correspondence and orders for textiles, nor to read and write co-op records regarding each woman's earnings. Many women were dissatisfied with male leadership but felt that without literacy skills or leadership training they would be unqualified to do the job. The few adult Mam weavers in town who could read and write had separate commercial outlets or belonged to factions that would not join this co-op.

The weavers' co-ops face problems of language barriers and illiteracy, kin-based factionalism, and the tendency for acculturated male kin to usurp too many marketing and decision-making functions from the weavers. Unlike the men's aldea committee, which was built upon preexisting kinship links, the initial weavers' cooperative was designed to cut across them in accord with Western ideas of democracy. It is not clear how successful this has been. During a period of low membership in early 1975, there were still twenty-eight contributing weavers, one quarter of whom were single mothers in the co-op receiving Peace Corps assistance. This suggests that commercial weaving through the co-op may still be an important means of support to women whose economic position is weak.

The Domestic Sphere

To a certain extent, the preceding discussion of formal community organization concerns the social links between T'oj Nam and the larger social world to which the municipio belongs. These "vertical" links with outside institutions and agencies are clearly influential in some spheres, yet in the daily life of the Mam, they seem very superficial. The majority of the Mam, and particularly the women, have never been to the nation's capital and have a very limited conception of what life is like outside their municipio and the coastal regions where they have worked. Guatemala as a nation has little meaning for them. To many of the Mam (and the older people openly assert this) T'oj Nam is the center of the world. The informal "horizontal" links and social relationships within this world of T'oj Nam are the focus of this next section. Specifically, the organization of the household and family relationships, which are of central importance to the people of T'oj Nam, will be examined.

Household structure. It is generally held that in peasant societies, the family structure tends to be complex, or extended, with families of more than two generations and/or more than one conjugal pair residing under the same roof. T'oj Nam is no exception. Complex family households were found to slightly outnumber nuclear family households in both rural and urban areas. In contrast, among the Ladino population, nuclear families outnumber complex families eleven to two.

Among the Mam large families are thought to offer greater security. They permit economic diversification and access to a large labor supply at peak periods. Individualism and the failure to marry is not considered a viable economic or social strategy for either sex in rural T'oj Nam. As in many peasant societies, the rural Mam find the idea of living alone profoundly disturbing. Marriage is almost obligatory. An unmarried adult of either sex is an anomaly and is persistently reminded of the advantages of marriage.[38]

The urban situation differs in that new commercial opportunities permit some enterprising individuals or "reduced" families (those that lack a conjugal pair) to maintain themselves adequately. Approximately one-third of the town Mam group sampled consisted of households formed by a single woman or man, mothers with children, or grandmothers with grandchildren. Significantly, all of the adults in these households were parents over age thirty; six out of seven were separated rather than widowed, and six out of seven were women. This may indicate that older women with children find it more difficult to remarry, or alternately that the need to remarry is weaker when an adult can count on assistance from children, particularly in the town area. The Ladino population shows a similar incidence of reduced families. Roughly a quarter of the Ladino sample (17 households) were reduced households headed by three old widows and a widower. It thus appears that the commercial opportunities and social milieu of the town weaken the traditional rural imperative to remarry or live with an adult of the opposite sex. A heterosexual pair is needed to maintain an efficient unit of domestic peasant production, but it is less essential for town dwellers who rely on other sources of income. Both the Mam and Ladino town residents who live outside nuclear or complex family structures are largely self-supporting economically through a mixture of commercial activities.

Mam patterns of inheritance and residence have an important relation to women's position in the household and in the community. Inheritance is predominantly patrilineal with most land and housing inherited by sons. In families with little land, daughters may receive only small plots or no land at all. They receive large land inheritances only if their parents are wealthy or if there are no sons. Logically related to patrilineal inheritance of real property is a preference for patrilocal residence. In 44 Mam marriages, 86 percent began in patrivirilocal residence. The remaining 14 percent had the opposite pattern of initial residence among the wife's parents or kin. This latter pattern occurs when the wife's family is significantly wealthier than the husband's family, when the husband has few kin, or when he does not get along well with his own father. While the vast majority of marital unions start out in patrilocal residence, other options may develop after a few years. Not infrequently, households that are initially patrilocal later reestablish themselves on land inherited from the husband's mother or the wife's father or mother, or on land they acquired independently.

This is particularly true for Mam families that have moved to town to exploit new commercial opportunities.

The combination of patrilineal inheritance and patrilocal residence contributes to the formation of informal clan-like groups within the Mam population. The alliances that grow out of patrilineal affiliations can have strong influence on an individual's position within the community. Through intermarriage, a woman contributes to the formation of alliances between (or within) the patriclans. She is in a strategic position to learn intimately the characteristics of two households and patriclans. This can make her an effective intermediary for promoting cooperation and extending favors between two kin groups. Her husband and her father and brothers may thus find occasion to cooperate in the fields, in house building, in lending draft animals, or in selling land to each other. It is her relationship with each of them that guarantees trustworthiness.

Although women generally "marry out" and do not receive title to land from their patrilineal kin, they remain members of their natal kin group. They are known all their lives by their patrilineal surname, for they do not change it upon marriage. In any crisis involving her relationship to her husband, a woman will turn first to her father and brothers unless her children are old enough to help her. In marital quarrels, separation, or widowhood, women can return to their parents' or brothers' house where they are entitled to defense, shelter, and maintenance. Women in many of the households sampled had returned for extended periods of time to live with their father or brothers. Sisters who have married out (or a mother who has remarried) usually cannot offer much support for they would generally have to draw on the resources of another patrilineal group. Even though their respective spouses can drive them apart, brothers and sisters tend to maintain supportive relationships throughout their lives.

Marriage and family. In T'oj Nam, Mam marriages are endogamous by municipio and ethnic group. Marital unions take a variety of forms. Formal marriages in the Western sense, known as *casamientos*, are found mainly among those who are actively involved in the Catholic catechist movement or in Evangelism. Frequently, the marriages are legalized after years of stable cohabitation and parenthood during which, for all traditional purposes, the pair had the status of a married couple. As in other parts of Guatemala, those who have not been married in a civil or religious ceremony describe themselves as *"junto"* (together) and are the majority of the adult population.

The distinction between couples who are *casados* (married) and juntos is not simply a distinction between formal marriage and de facto marriage or common-law marriage. Most Mam couples who are not casados follow a set of traditional marriage arrangements. Some of these customs are disdained by Ladino culture and condemned by Western missionaries. Marriage patterns are changing in T'oj Nam, particularly in sectors that are responsive to the modern religions and their rules regarding marriage. I shall deal with this diversity by first describing marriage practices among the more traditional Mam households and then discussing the changes that are occurring in other households.

In traditional Mam marriages, parental influence is strong. This is to be expected in a society where extensive domestic cooperation is essential. One of the most important issues is whether the marriage was arranged by the parents or undertaken solely on the initiative of the couple. In typical arranged marriages, the wife is said to be *pedida* (asked for), meaning that the man or his parents have spoken with the woman's parents and have made a settlement. Marriages formed without such a settlement are described as *voluntario* (voluntary) or elopement. These are not necessarily mutually exclusive options, where one is a "forced" marriage of parental convenience and the other a "love-match." In practice, there are many compromises among all the parties concerned. On the one hand, young people of either sex may wish to marry yet may not know any suitable partner; they then ask or trust their parents to take the initiative in selecting a worthy spouse. On the other hand, some young people initiate a relationship voluntarily, hoping that their parents will ultimately accept their choice and make a settlement. In still other cases, parents may try to force either a son or daughter to accept a partner that has been chosen for them.

Traditional Mam marriage negotiations between the two sets of parents typically involve a marriage payment (bride price)[39] from the husband's household to the wife's household. This payment is considered a compensation for the removal of the woman from her parents' house to the groom's house. The payment usuallly consists of money and goods such as livestock, corn, and liquor. When the amount to be paid is agreed upon and delivered, the marriage is considered formalized, settled as far as the parents and the Mam community are concerned. There is no other ceremony beyond the negotiation, payment, and the sharing of alcohol that accompanies (and possibly facilitates) the agreement. Data from 30 Mam marriages indicate that two-thirds of them involved a marriage payment to the wife's family. The going rate for cash payments of bride price is from Q. 100 to 150, plus varying quantities of goods, including alcohol. Over the last thirty-five years, inflation in the cash payment for bride price shows an overall correspondence to inflation in the price of corn (roughly a seven-fold increase), suggesting that the payment is not merely a social formality, but bears a real relationship to the cost of living.

Numerous case histories indicate that the negotiation and payment of bride price do not necessarily precede the commencement of regular sexual relations and cohabitation. Frequently, the relationship begins casually. A boy may start to regularly spend the night at his girlfriend's house or vice versa before the parents begin negotiations. If the couple are serious and happy together *and* if they impress the parents with their willingness to work, the parents of the boy visit the parents of the girl to ask for her.

The fact that she has been spending months or even a year living in his house is no guarantee that the boy or his parents will succeed in the petition (although it is assumed that if the girl is happy, her parents may let her go for less). Many complications can arise. The parents of the boy may prefer a different wife for their son or they may have already begun negotiations with another household, while the parents of a given girl may also have already accepted a petition from someone else. In such cases, there may be a great deal of anxious parental visiting, petitioning, money raising, and bargaining. The daughter may run off to her boyfriend and be brought home again, or the son may be unhappy with the alternate wife selected by his parents from a family that would accept their offer. In some instances, the son runs off to the coast to join the woman he prefers. It is difficult to estimate the extent to which the raising and lowering of bride prices reflect the social or economic interests of the parents, but when the woman's parents appear overly mercenary, they are strongly criticized.

Mam marriage arrangements reveal a number of interesting aspects of women's social position in T'oj Nam. These can best be understood after examining a few brief accounts of actual marriage arrangements.

12. Pedro Venancio's first wife joined him voluntarily. She stayed with him for almost two years. Her father caused problems because Pedro never paid for her. Finally, the father took his daughter back home. Pedro was very sad and alone for two years. Then his father went and asked for a girl. Pedro had never seen her before. His father paid Q. 30. The girl stayed with him for only three months, and then she left. She did not like it there and did not work well. Pedro did not like her very much either. "She would take things from other people's baskets." But when she left, he did not get his Q. 30 back. Pedro's next wife was also pedida, but he knew her beforehand. The payment was Q. 20. They have been together for 12 years and are happy together although none of the children born to them have yet survived infancy.

This case illustrates that if either the wife or her parents are dissatisfied with a marriage, it is not likely to succeed. Yet if the wife stays more than a few months, the marriage payment is not redeemable. The following case concerns a woman with similar difficulty in establishing a stable union.

13. Ana Maria is twenty years old. In her mid-teens she worked as a domestic employee in the city, but returned to T'oj Nam after several years of work. She had an affair with a young Mam student who was not prepared to marry. Then her mother arranged a marriage for her with a man, and received a bride price. Ana Maria says she went willingly, "*por gusto*," but she continued to secretly receive visits from her old lover. Her husband beat her because "he was very jealous" and she left him after six months, returning to her mother. The marriage payment was not returned. Within a year, she was married again. Her mother received another bride price, Q. 90. Ana Maria is happy with her current husband. He does not beat her, and she limits her relations with her former lover to verbal flirtation. She does not yet have any children.

Here we see that previous sexual experience or marital failure do not jeopardize chances of remarriage for either sex. On the other hand, Ana Maria's mother, a poor widow, put strong pressure upon her daughter to marry and was herself the bargaining agent in her daughter's marriage. Women generally seem to play an influential role in the marriage decisions affecting their children.

Marriage payments are made not only for young women of childbearing age, as the following case demonstrates.

14. Maria Lazaro, roughly 60 years old, is married to Efrain who is about the same age. Both have been married twice previously. Efrain's first wife ran away with another man after she had had two children with Efrain. His second wife bore more children and died, leaving him with young dependents. Maria Lazaro had also been widowed, first, and then separated from her second husband. She was in her mid-50s and living with her father when Efrain came to ask for her. She had never had any children and at any rate was beyond childbearing age when Efrain came to ask for her. He officially petitioned her father, although it is understood that the father cannot command a grown daughter, only a young one. Efrain, a poor man, made a marriage payment of Q. 35 and liquor, and Maria went to live with him willingly.

In Maria Lazaro's case, it is obvious that virginity, youth, or childbearing capacity could not have been considerations in the marriage payment. Most important is that Efrain had an urgent need for a help-

117

mate. Maria Lazaro still had a place in her father's house, but given his age she had good reason to consider remarriage.

There are a number of aspects of traditional Mam marriage that seem important for understanding the position of women. First, none of the women who went to live with their men without prior parental arrangement mentioned violence, rape, or intimidation as a factor in the initiation of the union. They say they went voluntarily, por gusto, or because they liked the man. This seems realistic since some of these women clearly describe subsequent violence from men as a cause of separation. Second, there appears to be little interest in virginity. Previous sexual experience is not a significant factor in selecting a marriage partner or in marriage negotiations. What is more important to the man and his parents is whether or not the woman's parents and the woman are sincere in the negotiations. The parents of the young man fear that they may pay the bride price, and yet after a short time the young woman may run away and they may lose their money. A third aspect of traditional Mam marriage is that it is not considered indissoluble. Both women and men are able to separate and remarry without much social disapproval, although they may have solid disagreements with their parents over the issue. If people of either sex repeatedly fail to establish a stable union, members of the other sex will regard them as a poor risk. However, scope for trial and error is built into the system.

The mechanisms for parental control of marriage, and particularly the marriage payment, are the subject of controversy both for outside observers and for the Mam themselves. This is an area in which their customs differ sharply from those of Western society. The bride price appears to Westerners and local Ladinos as a "purchase" of a wife since it involves a monetary transaction. It is interpreted as an index of low status for women since it is assumed that women are being equated with property and treated as chattels. Mam parents who have been converted to Western religions declare self-righteously that they will not "sell" their daughters for a bride price, that their daughters "are not animals." Part of this disapproval of bride price rests on the notion that parents will "sell" their daughters to the highest bidder so that daughters have no choice in the matter.[40]

This interpretation of traditional Mam marriage practices makes certain assumptions that are not justified. First, women are not "bought" in this system, since, unlike property or slaves, they can run away and cannot legally be forced to return to their husband. Indeed, the traditional Mam marriage system probably offers women a greater chance to make an informed choice in marriage since they are not required to remain forever with the original choice if it turns out to be unfortunate. Further, women view the bride price itself as an indication that they are valuable to both kin groups. They are ashamed of a low price; even women who are presently Catholic are careful to assert that 35 years ago a price of Q. 15 was equal to Q. 150 now. By bringing their parents a high bride price, women feel that they repay their parents for feeding and clothing them, and they maintain their good standing with their natal kin group. Finally, the implication that the bride price shows that women have lower status and less choice than men is also misleading and exaggerated by focussing on the exchange of valuables for the release of a daughter. This ignores the fact that young men may also lack a voice in their initial marriage arrangements. They may also be married without having first selected their partner, and they too run away when their parents make a choice that displeases them.[41]

Some Mam households practice an alternative to the patrilocal/bride price marriage system. This alternative is matrilocal marriage where no bride price is paid, but the groom comes to reside with his wife's people and agrees to work with his wife's father. As a permanent arrangement, this was probably a traditional option for men from poorer households. Also, before the availability of money through plantation labor, temporary bride service may have been a significant alternative to bride price as a means of acquiring a wife.[42] Given Western religious opposition to bride price, this traditional option appears to offer at least some households a means of complying with new religious expectations and fulfilling the traditional parental expectation of receiving some recompense for raising a child to productive maturity. The following case illustrates how this can work.

15. Anastasio is a wealthy traditional agriculturalist with land and sheep. He and his wife Olga are Catholics and pride themselves that their three daughters were married in church. There were no bride prices paid, but each of their sons-in-law became *hijos de casa* (sons of the house—an expression often used for foster children). Anastasio went and "spoke with" the families of the prospective sons-in-law before the marriages. The sons-in-law came to live in his house and worked cooperatively with Anastasio as if they were his own sons. After a number of years of such cooperation and joint economy, Anastasio gave them lands of their own and they built separate houses. Given the long period of joint residence in which the parents could observe the compatibility of the daughters and sons-in-law as well as the willingness of the latter to work hard, and given that Catholic marriages are considered indissoluble, Anastasio could decide to trust these sons-in-law to act as members of the family. Significantly, the transmission of lands to his daughters' households meant less land for his later son who went to colonize new land in the jungle.

This case shows a compromise between Mam and Catholic marriage patterns. Although bride prices were not paid, there was no loss of parental control.[43] This option depends on uniting daughters who have an inheritance with young men who come from weak families (orphans raised by distant kin) and lack an inheritance. In poor households that cannot attrack a resident son-in-law, it is a more difficult choice for parents to let a daughter go without any repayment just when she has come of age to make her maximum economic contribution to the household.

Plural marrriage. Polygyny is said to exist among the Mam and it is established that there are a small percentage of men who can be described as polygynists. Once again, one must be careful how one defines and uses this value-laden label before coming to conclusions about its implications for women. None of the Mam men in T'oj Nam are legally married to more than one woman. But in terms of traditional marriage, it is not uncommon for a man to be *junto* with, or even to have paid for, more than one wife. Usually, one wife has left already before a man makes arrangements to bring another wife home. But in some cases, this action itself is an inducement for the first wife to leave (a ploy by the husband to terminate a marriage since he cannot afford to abandon his wife by leaving her to stay in his house). Although a man rarely lives with both women simultaneously for more than a transitional period, this circumstance may be described as having "two wives" by the Mam, since they know it runs counter to Catholic teachings that a man and woman must marry only once. Most anthropologists would describe this as serial monogamy rather than polygyny.

The more germaine cases are those in which a man simultaneously lives with and supports more than one woman on a more permanent basis. Unlike the Ladino tradition, the Mam do not distinguish between the legitimate wife and the "concubine." In their view, the critical question appears to be whether a man and woman are exchanging husband-wife services which include not only sex, but the provision of shelter and food supplies by the man, and cooked food and children by the woman. The following is an example of the arrangement between one man and two women.

16. Hilario is a prominant and wealthy Mam businessman. He has a number of children by his first wife, Gloria, for whom he paid a bride price many years ago. Together they worked to build up capital for their businesses. Later, Hilario took as a second wife Victoria, who was jilted by her husband after many years of hard work and childless marriage. (Her husband brought home a second wife and she left, although he wanted both of them to remain in the same house.) Victoria lives in a separate house

provided by Hilario (and indirectly by Gloria), runs her own business, and now has a child. Hilario continues to maintain a joint economy with his first wife, and spends nights alternately with each wife. Although Gloria was angry and at first fought with Victoria, fear of retaliation from Hilario has now silenced her. Both women work for cash income and enjoy a relatively high standard of living.

The Mam community considers both women as wives of Hilario. Although this does not conform to the Ladino legal system, Hilario is relatively immune from prosecution since he is not formally married (he is not a Catholic), and since a man is not held guilty of adultery unless it occurs in the same house where he lives with his first wife. In Mam custom, the first wife, Gloria, does not have a recognized complaint as long as she is adequately supplied with food, clothing, and shelter for herself and her children.

Reports of such polygyny whereby a man supports two women and children living in separate houses are not uncommon. The men involved are generally wealthy through successful commercial activity. When a man joins with another woman, his wife's options are generally to steadfastly hold her position in the house or to leave to live with her kin or another man. Catholic and Protestant women are under extra pressure to stay since their religions do not permit them to remarry. Many traditional women simply leave a man because of "the other woman," but there are some cases in which they do not leave, even when the second woman comes to reside in the same household. The following case is an intriguing one:

17. Pedro is in his mid-40s and has been married for many years to Amparo. He goes to the coast every year to work on plantations and grow corn. Amparo used to go with him until there were small children to raise. Pedro continued to go alone, but he met Antonia on the coast and they were *junto*. On returning to T'oj Nam, Antonia declined to live with his first wife, as she had inherited her own house. Pedro supplied corn to both women, and Antonia continued to migrate to the coast with him until she too decided it would be healthier for her children if she worked in T'oj Nam. Then Pedro met Lucia working on the coast. Lucia returned home with him and joined his household. Pedro paid a bride price for her of Q. 100, for which he went into debt. The two women and Pedro live together for part of the year, and Lucia and Pedro go to the coast to work for the other part of the year while Amparo remains at home caring for the house and children. Pedro supplies what they need to each of them and continues to make contributions to his sons by Antonia.[44]

One of the most interesting aspects of this case is that there is no conflict over marital arrangements; the household is tranquil. The wives get along well and do not fight with each other nor with Pedro. Neighbors of both sexes appear to respect Pedro as a hard-working and responsible man. His practice of acquiring a helpmate while working on the coast is not remarkable; this is relatively common for both women and men if they have to migrate alone. It is related to the belief that neither a man nor woman is capable of living alone. Pedro is not regarded as promiscuous, but his neighbors acknowledge that in general having two wives is more difficult and more costly. One traditional old man commented:

> I have only one wife. Why have two? It doesn't work. You have to wear shirts made by both wives. And it is hard to earn enough money to support two wives, to make another pedido (pay the brideprice). Now money is expensive.

A traditional old woman with first-hand experience of polygyny with a rather promiscuous man also describes the situation pragmatically rather than moralistically:

> 18. I was married for many years to Satiro. He always sought a lot of women. He brought Sylvia home and the three of us lived together for four years. She was very friendly and we got along well. There were two beds, one for each woman. He slept with one of us one night and with the other the next night. But he also sought other women. Sylvia left and he brought home Teresa. She stayed only one year. She fought a lot. Satiro would also come home drunk and would beat us. He always fights when he is drunk, I put up with a lot from Satiro. Finally, I left him when my son was 14. Satiro's last wife was young and strong. When he beat her, she gave it back to him. She beat him up good and then left him. This never goes to court. This last woman lives alone now. And so does Satiro.

Open discussion of plural marriage in T'oj Nam invariably involves a man with more than one "woman" (*mujer* or *xu'j*) without specifying "wife" and without concern for formal legal definitions. The connotation of married status or being "junto" is derived from the services that are exchanged between the sexes. When a woman resides in a man's house, that is evidence that she is "junto" with him. If such residence is a criteria for plural marriage, then there were no reverse cases of plural marriage by women where they resided in different houses owned by different men. On the other hand, women also form sexual and exchange relationships with more than one man simultaneouosly, although this is generally done in secret or with greater discretion. A woman living with her mother-in-law does not have much freedom to form other relationships, but women in separate houses have greater independence, particularly when their husbands migrate. Sometimes when a woman's husband goes to the coast, he does not leave her enough food, money, or firewood for herself and the children. Under these circumstances, a lover may become important, or necessary. He may bring her maize or something else she needs, or may give her 25 to 50 cents (a day's wage). She may give him coffee and food, and sleep with him. But women also have affairs just because they like a man. Such "extramarital" relations are not uncommon, although men generally try to prevent their wives from having them.

Sexuality is not rigidly controlled, and it is generally agreed that prostitution does not exist in T'oj Nam. There are no women who support themselves principally by selling sexual favors indiscriminately. Young Mam men are said to have their first sexual relationships with ordinary young Mam women. The concept of prostitution seems confusing to some Mam women. They realize that a pejorative Spanish term is applied to women who have sexual relationships for money, yet are not certain if it applies to the quasi-marital relationships they are involved in. They seem unfamiliar with the treatment of sex primarily as a commodity.

Among the Ladino population, there are no reports of plural marriage. Sexual relationships are more carefully divided into legitimate and illegitimate ones, and it is considered unacceptable to have more than one spouse at a time. This is not to say that the incidence of separation, common-law marriage, remarriage, or marital infidelity is much different among the local Ladino population. However, legitimacy does have a bearing on the effectiveness of the claims that a woman can make on behalf of herself and her children upon the father of the children.

As with marriage, the Mam do not distinguish between legitimate and illegitimate childbirth in any formal way. For women, no stigma is attached to becoming a single mother. Nor is there a belief that mother-child bonds are sacred and unbreakable. In cases of conjugal separation, unweaned children usually stay with their mother, but when they are older their father may claim them if he has contributed to their support, or alternately, their mother may leave them with their father if she remarries or takes a job as a domestic employee. When a young father or mother remarries, often the maternal or paternal grandparents raise the grandchildren of the earlier marriage as if they were the parents. Men tend to keep their sons and women to keep their daughters, but there are exceptions to this principle.

Mam women and men welcome the birth of their first children, for this contributes to adult status and in joint households confers the right to greater autonomy in some household matters. Given the high rate of child mortality, most women desire at least three or four children representing both sexes to guarantee that some will reach adulthood and be able to assist their parent of the same sex in their work. After four children, however, many traditional women show a keen interest in birth control if they are still of childbearing age. Even monolingual Mam women have heard that foreign women know some methods, and a number of my informants anxiously sought information on *remedios* (cures) against pregnancy. Unfortunately, international and national religious and political groups have made the issues of forced sterilization, abortion, and birth control very controversial with the result that Mam women have very little choice; they are still largely denied access to information and methods of birth control which *they* can control. One informant recounted her unsuccessful attempts to abort through falls and self-inflicted abdominal beatings. According to information available through the health center, only a tiny percentage of women are receiving birth control pills or injections. Most cannot afford it, while it appears that some have become ill because the doses are too strong.[45]

Informal Social Behavior

Most of this discussion of social organization has centered on the major structural indices of women's position among the Mam: the forms of community and domestic organization. These indices facilitate regularized comparisons with women in other areas, but they omit other interesting aspects of women's role in society which are more spontaneous in appearance. The areas of informal social behavior that will be briefly considered here are communication networks, violence, and entertainment. This treatment of informal social behavior is intended not to be comprehensive, but merely to yield supplementary information and insights on women's position in T'oj Nam.

Communication networks. In their informal relations, women control a great deal of information, which includes the evaluation of people and events. In a community that lacks newspapers, the gossip networks are very powerful and can strongly influence an individual's standing in the community. Both men and women take it quite seriously when gossip touches them.[46] On a day-to-day basis, women of different families and clans gather at the water holes to do laundry and exchange news, complaints, and jokes. Women who live anywhere near a water hole tend to do a little laundry every day rather than miss any news of current events. They are also vigilant in defense of their neighborhoods and in search of economic opportunities. If strangers pass through their area, women watch them carefully and if they pass close by, they will usually receive friendly greetings and inquiries of where they are going and what they are doing. Foreigners are often amazed by the friendly interest of the Mam men and women alike, never realizing that they are being carefully interrogated. Since the men are often away on the coast or in the fields, women note carefully whether those that pass have come to buy, beg, or steal, or have a legitimate destination. In this sense, they are an informal police force and are not very bashful about the role.

The existence of informal communication networks is favored by the fact that women enjoy a great deal of freedom to socialize and move about in the community. Sometimes a wife will find herself amongst kin that attempt to restrict her mobility, but this is difficult to effect without interfering with the work processes. T'oj Nam has a strong work ethic and neither men nor women typically depart from it unless they have an "errand." Yet an errand can be an extremely flexible excuse to leave the house, and during the day women traverse the community to get medicine for a sick child, to visit a sick relative, to take lunch to their husband, to gather wild plants and kindling, to buy an egg, return a borrowed item, go to market or consult a diviner. As they go, they pick up and transmit the latest news.

Violence. The extent to which women are subject to violence or are themselves agents of violence is a reflection of their place in the social order. As indicated earlier, domestic violence toward women is limited by several factors: (1) women are able to return home if their husband is violent (since their labor is considered useful); and (2) it is not especially difficult to find another marriage partner, if there are not many children.[47] Thus, violent behavior by a husband is usually met with desertion by the wife. One Mam man reported that when he was an alcoholic, three different wives left him because he used to come home and fight with them. A woman reported that when she was young, her husband would try to beat her but she would run home to her father and then the two men would fight. A few older women stated that their husbands had hit them during the early years of marriage, but that they later stopped this.[48]

Cases where women have no recourse but to endure a husband's violence are a small minority. In case 5, above, a middle-aged woman with many children and essentially no kin support endured her husband's physical (and economic) tyranny because she had nowhere else to go *with* the children. A similar case involves a middle-aged woman whose husband beat her when he got angry over the children and her defense of them against his beatings. She did not want to leave because (1) they were economically well-off, (2) her parents were both poor and separated, and (3) she did not trust him to care for the children, for she claims he said, "Go ahead and leave. If the children die, don't worry, I'll be here to bury them." Moreover, they are Catholics and therefore she is not permitted to remarry. Since her husband has been a local political leader, she does not expect justice from municipal authorities. Her hope for a better life rests on an alliance with her sons whom she hopes can be financially independent of their father.

Mam women are not conditioned to passively submit to beatings or violence. They usually try to flee, fight back, or bring their case to court. The factors that force some of them to endure violent relationships are lack of other options (kin support) and lack of confidence in a judicial system which is always controlled by male coteries. In discussing physical violence between spouses, women feel that the odds are against them. It is not simply a question of physical strength, but one of social structure as well: Women are more vulnerable when they are alone among their husband's kin so that they then try to avoid physical conflict. This extends into the different reactions expected of each sex in cases of adultery. People say that a husband might kill if he discovers his wife with another man, while they believe that a lone woman would not be capable of violently killing a man. On the other hand, indirect methods of coercion remain an option, for both sexes believe in and are said to practice witchcraft.

Although reports of violence between the sexes do not credit women with autonomous physical assaults on men, there are cases in which they are reported to participate with men in such attacks. Further, women are found to physically assault each other over a variety of grievances. As among men, economic competition and property rights are an important source of conflict for women. In recent times, some strong verbal and physical attacks have occurred between women textile vendors over business practices. In one case, a street vendor attempted to sell weavings to tourists who were standing outside another weaver's store. The storekeeper was furious at this competition, and she rushed outside to beat the street vendor, injuring her. In another case, two women fought each other over the missing funds of the weavers' cooperative. Significantly, sexual competition per se does not appear as an overriding theme in conflicts between Mam women. Prostitution is not a serious threat; locally women do not face competition from a class of unemployed or displaced women who undercut their position as wives, while their husbands do not control enough disposable cash to attract prostitutes from outside the community. Hence, expressions of sexual jealousy among Mam women are not greatly amplified by economic fears; women do not customarily adopt desperate measures of submission toward their husband or violence toward the other woman to retain their husbands. In general, it appears that economic competition among traditional women is focused on the mother-in-law and daughter-in-law relationship where men are pressed to be mediators.

Women must also deal with violence or threats of violence in other contexts. Women do not like to go out alone after dark for fear that men may harm them. If they are home alone or with small children when their husbands are on the coast, a man may try to enter their house to molest them. Many houses are not entry-proof, but women know how to brandish firewood against an intruder and they usually have vicious dogs. Also, if a woman is temporarily alone, she can usually borrow a neighbor's or relative's child to spend the night with her as a deterrent to intruders. The one context in which women are most vulnerable to male abuse is the fiesta when both men and women drink too much. First- and second-hand accounts from the assailant's and victim's point of view concur that at large fiestas where there is massive drinking, groups of men plot to isolate a particular woman from her companions or male protectors, getting them and her extremely drunk until, semi-conscious, they can take her away for a gang rape. The reports of men and women do not concur in the extent to which this should be treated as a crime. As in our society, men tend to feel that a drunken woman collaborated in the assault and that a small monetary payment for sex is adequate compensation. Women feel that it is a much more serious crime, but know that their opinion does not influence a male-dominated judicial system. Informants report that one or two such cases occur at every major fiesta. They are treated legally as minor offenses against public decency with the men and the woman usually being jailed for a day or so.[49]

Entertainment. Compared to more modern communities and urban areas where commercial entertainments such as movies, dance halls, and sports events are more commonplace, the market days, house-finishing ceremonies, and especially the annual town fiesta of T'oj Nam loom large as forms of entertainment. During the fiesta, the *entire* Mam community celebrates with nearly a week of intense, continuous activity, which includes horse races, ceremonial dances, traveling amusements such as rides and games, plus 24-hour marimba music, dancing, and drinking.

Women do not participate in the costly displays of horse racing and ceremonial dancing where rented horses and costumes consume men's savings, but they are avid spectators. Women have conspicuous displays of their own in the form of the elaborate and costly new garments that they weave for themselves and their families especially for the fiesta. These bright garments are important status symbols that reflect upon the woman who weaves them. In almost all other fiesta activities, participation is open to both sexes. Mam women can mingle in the crowds, drink and dance in public, or spend their money on rides. Unlike Ladinas who do not feel free to drink or dance in public, Mam women celebrate openly and are scarcely more restrained than the men, although they participate in lesser numbers. Their participation is more limited than men's by the simple fact that they often have less money to spend (or less credit) and they are responsible for children. Women commonly get extra cash for the fiesta delights by selling last year's huipil or handwoven shirt to tourists. During the fiesta, it is common to see at least a few women dancing all night long—wherever a marimba still plays—sometimes with a sleeping baby on their back. Both old and young, women and men may stay out all night drinking together and wailing a plaintive Mam song until they pass out.

Ladinos are largely spectators during the fiesta, or busy earning money in their stores and cantinas (bars), or by providing tourist services. Compared to the Mam, Ladinos have more access to modern entertainment when they visit larger cities. Locally, the entertainment of Ladinas is largely confined to domestic gatherings.

Summary

The economic position of Mam women is complex and changing due to the partial and uneven integration of the local economy into the national and international economic spheres. In the more traditional subsistence sector, women make a vital contribution to the local economy according to a clear sexual division of labor. In the domestic mode of production that characterizes subsistence agriculture, women and men are mutually dependent for survival. Their balanced contributions and needs prevent either sex from becoming more valued than the other and, hence, promote sexual equality. Although their work routines follow different rhythms by day and by season, both sexes work hard; neither women nor men are viewed as surplus laborers or idle dependents. Economic success and decision-making power for both sexes are achieved within a seniority system. For women, a critical factor is their ability to produce children, while for men, a critical factor is their ability to acquire land. The combination of these two funda-mental assets—dependent labor and land—provide a basis for the eco-nomic security and authority of senior men and women. Although the traditional economic system appears to vest more emphasis on the male role as the controlling one, this control is limited by the generally high demand for female labor in all households and the freedom for women to transfer allegiances.

In the cash economy, it is essentially happenstance that the people of T'oj Nam are recruited by plantations that employ female as well as male labor. In contrast to other indigenous villages, this supplement to the subsistence economy does little to upset the balanced sex roles of the peasant economy. Paid by piece rates, women's labor is still perceived to be as valuable as men's even though a new cash standard is applied.

The cash standard, with respect to the products that women and men produce for the market economy, yields quite different results. The agricultural products of Mam men are in greater demand than the handmade textiles of the women. The scarcity of land for food crops raises the price of men's traditional activity whereas the abundance of cheap factory textiles lowers the value of women's weaving. Although neither agriculture nor domestic textile manufacture are absolutely uni-sexual activities, there is a tendency to attribute the product and its cash rewards to the sex that oversees production and brings the most special skills to the task. Hence, this is an area in which market forces upset traditional subsistence values.

However, as long as subsistence production remains important, tra-dition tends to counteract market-induced imbalances in the value of labor. Even in the incipient commercial sector, family businesses that do not individualize their cash income can maintain an aura of tradi-tional sexual balance despite their modern occupation. Overall, the Mam peasant economy maintains a high level of economic equality between the sexes. This seems strongly linked to the persistence of the subsistence economy as a substantial portion of total economic activ-ity, and the persistence of the domestic mode of production.

Marked differences in earning power by sex are developing in con-junction with formal, individualized, and salaried positions linked to the modern economy. Despite the scarcity of such positions, the fact that Mam women do not yet have any access to them suggests an evolv-ing gap between the sexes. This gap is more fully developed among the local Ladino population who represent the most immediate link be-tween the Mam and the nation. Although local Ladinas, like Mam women, show a high incidence of participation in the cash economy, they show significantly lower returns to their labor than men (except in teaching, where they are equal), and fewer career options.

The transition to a dependent, modern economy is underway in T'oj Nam. To a certain extent, women take part in this transition by participating in plantation labor and informal commercial activities. But as national integration increases, and opportunities for formal employment with large institutions increase, women are prevented from integrating at the same pace and in the same form as men. This is true for Ladinas and Mam. The two-fold change toward individual cash incomes and toward exclusion of women from major avenues of modern employment leaves women in a weakened economic position.

Women's role in the social organization of T'oj Nam is related to the political and economic position of the municipio within the nation as well as to the economic structure within the municipio. In formal organizations with national affiliation, women play a decidedly secondary role. In formal politics and the cargo system, for example, women are almost totally marginal. This may be interpreted partly as a survival of traditional Mam sociopolitical organization, or as an *adaptation* of traditional Mam society to centuries of political domination by an alien culture that refuses to accept women as political representatives. Regardless of the questionable input of Mam culture into a male-dominated political apparatus, it is clear that modern voting procedures and political parties have done little to increase the participation of Mam women. The distribution of opportunities and benefits from formal religious and educational institutions also show that these national organizations are more concerned with male involvement. In other formal organizations, a patriclan-like neighborhood alliance has been adapted to modern organizational purposes for men, while women must overcome male kin ties and lack of formal organizational experience to maintain their own new organization of weavers. The fact that within a few years women have been able to meet and organize publicly *as women* in order to promote their economic interests indicates a significant measure of social "openness" and potential for women in the public sphere.

In the domestic context, certain criteria suggest a definite male bias: preferred patrilineal inheritance of land, patri-virilocal marriage, bride price, and the existence of polygyny. On the other hand, female autonomy is suggested by the lack of interest in virginity, the lack of stigma for unwed motherhood, the right to divorce and remarry, the right to return to one's natal kin group for support, and the nonrefundability of bride price after a short trial period. These latter features mitigate the impact of male bias in household formation.

In this system both sexes are subject to some of the same general principles of social organization. The woman or man with a strong family is protected. The woman without kin can be more completely dominated by her husband or affines, while the man without kin (hence land) is likely to live in uxorilocal marriage, where he can be dominated by his wife's kin. In general, women appear more vulnerable because the dominant marriage pattern physically separates them from their kin, but the real possibility of desertion by wives plus the fact that bride prices are expensive act as deterrants to mistreatment of women by affines. Seniority, as a function of age and parenthood, brings high status to both sexes within the household. While women assume the major responsibility for the care of young children, children prove valuable as workers at an early age and are considered assets by both parents. Natural mothers are not held exclusively responsible for raising children. Typically there are other matrilineal and patrilineal kin willing to raise them if the mother finds they hinder her in arranging work or remarriage. Although polygyny occurs, it is not necessarily a disadvantage to the women involved. In the traditional subsistence sphere, it may be viewed as a way of expanding the household labor force without prejudicing anyone's position. However, in households where the husband controls a substantial and individualized cash income, a second wife resembles a form of conspicuous consumption for a wealthy husband and tends to reduce the income or standard of living for the first wife.

The transition to Western religious and cultural values presents a new package of social freedoms and constraints which are thus far only partially accepted by the most urbanized Mam. These include greater individual freedom in initial marriage choice, but much more rigid controls on household composition (no divorce, remarriage, or polygamy) and on female sexuality. Although the new restrictions on social relations do not theoretically impose unequal sex relations, they remove precisely those safety valves by which women could escape exploitative marriages. When this is coupled with an increasing imbalance in the economic value of the sexes in the market system, then the weight of these restrictions is likely to fall most heavily on women.

In informal social relations, Mam women enjoy considerable freedom. As marketers and workers, they have mobility. If they do not join the migrant labor force, they are often left in charge of the house and fields when the men migrate. In situations of conflict, women tend to use kin support and informal means of protection, since the legal system does not play a strong protective role. They are entitled to circulate in the public sphere in relation to work, market, fiesta, or kin functions.

In conclusion, women seem to enjoy considerable social freedom, autonomy, and respect at the grass roots level of Mam society, but they are deprived of representation in the more formal organizations which link T'oj Nam to the nation. As modern socioeconomic integration increases, the prospects for Mam women to improve or even maintain their standing relative to Mam men do not seem auspicious. Conservatism in both social and economic matters may be the rational reaction to the changes that confront them.

7. *Some members of a Mam household in hand-loomed clothes. Other members are away working on the plantations.*

CHAPTER FOUR

El Cañaveral: A Large Sugar Plantation

Introduction

El Cañaveral is a large, privately owned sugar finca of roughly 13,000 acres (more than 5,200 hectares) located in the plantation belt on Guatemala's southern coastal plain.[1] Like the archetypical plantation, El Cañaveral is very much a world-market-oriented enterprise employing large amounts of capital and specializing in a single crop. Although still largely family-owned, it is organized as a public corporation and functions as a modern business organization. It uses its land intensively and is committed to the use of modern technology whenever possible. The only major characteristic it does not share with the typical plantation is its practice of paying its workers in kind as well as in cash wages.

The physical layout of El Cañaveral includes several distinct areas devoted to various productive and residential purposes. Most of the agricultural land is dedicated to sugarcane, but about 5 percent is in coffee plantings. The sugar refinery, which has a large patio for vehicles loading and unloading cargoes of sugarcane, dominates the entrance. Nearby are the main administrative offices and above them, on a rise, an area which includes the *hacienda* (the owner's house), administrators' housing, the school, the health center, recreational facilities, and the stables. Along the edge of this central area is a residential section known as *barrio de los empleados* (the employees' district) where salaried employees have their houses. Although these houses are not as large as the houses by the hacienda, they are comfortable middle-class homes with several rooms, gardens, and modern conveniences.

The *rancheria*, a collective term for the various workers's barrios, or residential districts, extends behind and below the central patio.[2] Here one finds mainly standardized company housing with cement block construction, corrugated metal roofs, cement floors, electricity, access to running water, and outhouses. Within these barrios there are small stores and a variety of social service centers—a food co-op, a credit co-op, several churches, a company maintenance workshop, a social club where movies and dances are held, and a union hall. In one of the more distant barrios near the coffee groves is a coffee *beneficio* (a processing installation) where coffee is sorted and dried.

At the fringes of the workers' barrios and in areas set back from the roads or down in the ravine are the *galeras* (barracks), long rectangular buildings that provide mass housing for crews of temporary migrant workers. While the main structures have cement floors and electricity, they do not have private rooms or kitchens. Around the galeras are a number of rude shacks of cane, cardboard, and plastic sheets constructed by migrants and temporary workers who seek somewhat more privacy.

As a business, El Cañaveral is well-integrated into the national and international economies. It conducts commercial agriculture for export, and thus its owners and directors are very much involved with associations of exporters for similar commercial crops, with international prices and sugar futures, with the competition of other large plantations, with scientific experiments in agricultural techniques and sugar processing, and with investments in, and loans of, equipment to other plantations. It is one of the largest sugar plantations in the country, producing close to 50,000 tons per year. The owner and top managers belong to an international elite: They are well-traveled, frequently bilingual, and educated at foreign universities.

Those below management level, the resident wage workers and their families, are not directly involved with the international market economy and culture, yet both have an influence on their lifestyle. The wageworkers live in a community defined by common residence and employment rather than by distinctive cultural elements such as language, dress, social patterns, or economic specialties. Within the rancheria, the permanent residents speak Spanish and wear Westernized clothing. They belong to Western-style voluntary associations, the sugarworker's union, Protestant and Catholic religions, cooperatives and banks. They buy modern appliances on credit, and lack distinctive local crafts. They send their children to modern schools; to doctors for medical care; to movies or Boy Scouts for entertainment. They characteristically use buses, motor bikes, or bicycles to reach the nearest urban center, which is located only several miles away. Radios are commonplace, televisions are not rare although still a luxury, and most people who can read have ready access to newspapers.

The total population of the plantation is difficult to determine because it is seasonally variable, and because the administration does not keep precise records of the number of residents who are not directly in the employ of the company. At the time of my research there were 565 permanent workers, "heads of families." Of these, eighty were salaried employees and the remainder were wageworkers. Together with their families, the population of permanent residents can be estimated at nearly 3,000 assuming an average household size between five and six members.[3] In addition to the population of permanent residents, the number of seasonal workers varies from several hundred to a thousand workers. The majority of these workers require temporary housing within the plantation since they migrate from distant departments. Very few of them come with families, and the work crews, apart from the cooks, are exclusively male. Most of my research was conducted during the off-season when there were only about 400 migrant workers. (Fieldwork in El Cañaveral is described in Appendix Two.)

The plantation workers belong to different categories that determine the nature of their relationship to the plantation. At the top of the hierarchy are the owner and administrators who spend much of their time in the company offices in the capital city. Among the local residents, the highest employment category is *empleado*, or salaried employee. Most of the salaried employees work in administrative, professional, or white-collar jobs and enjoy the benefits of high pay and company-provided middle-class housing.[4] Below the salaried employees are the *rancheros*, the permanent, unionized work force. These workers are guaranteed year-round work and receive benefits such as small two-room houses, daily food rations, rights to use a small plot of land for personal cultivation and to pasture several cows on company land, rights to free education, free health care for their immediate families, and severance pay or a pension when their employment is terminated. At a lower level are the *voluntarios* (generally sons or relatives of ranchero families) who are guaranteed only six months of seasonal work during the harvest and receive benefits such as food rations, health care, and education for their children only during the period of their employment. These workers do not receive company housing, although some fifty of them have permission to construct their own *covachas*, or shacks, on company land. At the lowest level of the employment hierarchy are the *cuadilleros*, or work gangs of migrant laborers, who are contracted in groups for periods of two months. Cuadilleros are housed in large, crowded barracks and paid by piece rate or at the legal minimum wage. These workers come from many different departments of Guatemala, but the majority is indigenous, and typically they are unable to read or speak Spanish fluently. Although they have theoretical rights to health care and education for their children while working, the nature of their periodic recruitment means they are largely unaware of or unable to use them. Their contracts are intentionally limited to two months since, according to national law, longer periods of employment obligate the employer to pay severance pay when employment ends.

Economic Organization

Occupational Structure

El Cañaveral is both a business enterprise and a community. As a business enterprise, its occupational structure crosscuts residential boundaries; many of its employees reside outside the plantation. Conversely, as a community, many of its members are not employed by the company. Viewed from either perspective, El Cañaveral is characterized by hierarchical divisions in socioeconomic status. In the discussion which follows, women's position in the economic structure of El Cañaveral is briefly examined from each of these perspectives. Given marked differences in women's opportunities according to socioeconomic status, I chose to concentrate on one segment of the plantation population: the ranchero community. This community can be distinguished from other plantation residents such as the empleados by class status, and from other plantation workers such as the cuadrilleros by resident status. While all ranchería residents clearly share a direct or indirect affiliation with the company, their occupational status, particularly in the case of women, is not entirely determined by the company.

Of all the distinctive sectors of El Cañaveral, the ranchería community most completely represents a population whose social and economic identity derives from the plantation system. The managers, professionals, and clerical employees often maintain residence, business contacts, and social networks outside the plantation, while the migrant workers typically have a home community to go back to when their contracts terminate. In contrast, work, residence, and social ties for the ranchería population are all centered in El Cañaveral.

Economic Activity by Sex

Within the ranchería, there is a substantially higher rate of employment among males than females (Table 4–1). In this sample of thirty-one households, 88 percent of the men were economically active in the cash sector, as compared with 50 percent of the women. Among the women, the category of housework assumes its usual ambiguity, obscuring both the level of unpaid work and the level of unemployment among women who might seek paid work if it were open to them. Moreover, "economically active" does not imply *full* employment; it means only that an individual is directly engaged in earning a cash income.

One of the remarkable differences between the sexes in Table 4–1 is the percentage of workers employed by the company. Only 6 percent of the women as opposed to 76 percent of the men are on the company payrolls. Further, a large proportion of the households covered in this sample come from the central barrio where workers have more seniority. Since the company has not been hiring women in recent years, the central barrio with its three rancherías overrepresents the employment

Table 4–1. Economic Status of Each Sex at El Canaveral

Status	Women			Status	Men		
		(%)	(Number)			(%)	(Number)
Employed		50.0	24	Employed		87.8	43
rancheras	6.2		3	rancheros	46.9		23
other*	43.8		21	voluntarios	28.6		14
Retired		4.2	2	other*	12.2		6
Disabled		4.2	2	Retired		2.0	1
Housework		41.7	20	Disabled		2.0	1
				Unemployed		2.0	1
Total Subsample		100.1	48	Volunteer			
				fireman		2.0	1
				Unknown		2.0	1
				Student		2.0	1
				Total Subsample		99.8	49

* "Other" includes informal employment, self-employment, and employment outside the plantation.

137

of women in the ranchería as a whole, which is less than 1 percent of all company employment of rancheros.

Underemployment

Among those listed as employed in the preceding table, there are some who can best be described as "underemployed" since steady work is not available to them. (Underemployment can be distinguished from part-time employment where a worker is not available for full-time work.) Among the men, underemployment is fairly easy to observe. Fourteen of the men in the sample are voluntarios, who are guaranteed only six months of work each year during the harvest season. Of these, five appeared to be largely unemployed during the nonharvest season, also known as *tiempo muerto* (the dead season). The others found supplemental employment as laborers on other plantations or in various artisan trades. The company's demand for male labor is so great during the harvest season that there is virtually no male unemployment among residents at that time. Over the course of a year, then, the pattern of male underemployment is one of an extended period of unemployment alternating semiannually with an extended period of full employment.

For women, the extent of underemployment is much more difficult to calculate since there are so many more variables involved.[5] With only a tiny percentage of the women employed by the company regardless of the season, most women are found in informal occupations where their work lacks regular hours, tasks, income, or clientele. Generally, female underemployment does not take the form of the males' alternating periods of full employment and unemployment. Rather, it involves varying degrees of chronic underemployment. For example, a woman who could cook for fifteen to twenty workers at lunch time can count on only one or two regular clients. One who could make one or two dresses per day finds she has only one or two clients per week. A woman who could spend five hours per day doing take-in laundry finds she has only one hour of work per day.

Women's employment, much of which is self-employment, also fluctuates with the harvest cycle and the incomes of their clients. In tiempo muerto, when clients have to cut back cash expenditures to a bare minimum, the women's services are in much less demand. Seamstresses, storekeepers, and those who sell specialty foods especially experience marked fluctuations in demand depending on the season.

Another factor which affects the level of economic activity among women in particular, and which relates to the issue of underemployment, is that women do not always act as individual economic agents. A mother may share her work as a tortilla maker or laundress with her daughter, thereby dividing what could be one fully employed worker into two part-time workers, leaving neither totally unemployed. This occurs several times in the sample, as is shown in Table 4–2, presenting the income of economically active women of the rancheria. Finally, it should be added that at least nine of the twenty-four women listed as economically active are not fully employed.

The ambiguities of women's position in the labor market and the uncertain level of underemployment that is masked by family housework both make quantitative measurement of market employment extremely risky. Nevertheless, it is evident that women in the ranchería face a significantly lower level of demand for their services in the labor market and that they experience higher levels of underemployment than the men. And, unlike the seasonally employed voluntarios, who are typically sons of rancheros and can expect to become rancheros themselves as older men retire, the women have no such expectations.

The Range of Incomes

There is no simple way to calculate the average monthly incomes of women who work in El Cañaveral. Not only is there the usual distinction between full- and part-time workers, but again the informality of most women's work means that they are subject to a degree of fluctuation that does not characterize formal plantation jobs.[6] Thus many women's incomes are found to vary with the season, the duration of the annual harvest, and their clients' personal fortunes, such as their health, courtships, bouts of drunkenness, unemployment, and so forth.

Table 4–2 presents the average monthly income of ranchería workers, divided by sex. Although best viewed as estimates, the figures nonetheless provide an idea of the magnitude of the earnings from the different kinds of work performed by each sex. A major consideration is that the rancheros receive a set of benefits which, if translated into monetary values, would greatly increase the level of their monthly wages. Some of the benefits are:

houses (generally two rooms with cement floors, block walls, electricity, running water, and maintenance);
daily food rations: 2 lbs. corn, ½ lb. beans, 2 oz. salt, 2 oz. lime;
free primary education for the children of rancheros;

Table 4–2. Average Monthly Cash Income of Employed of Each Sex by Occupation*

Women		Men**	
Occupation	Income (Q.)	Occupation	Income (Q.)
Company nurse/midwife (R)	100	Tractor operator (R)	132
Storekeeper: beer & prepared		Factory operator (R)	125
food; baker, poultry & pig		Factory foreman (R)	106
raiser; butcher; corn miller;		Timekeeper (R)	105
soap maker	75	Electrician (R)	103
Factory laundress		Mechanic (R)	98
(R)/meat vendor	50	Welder (R)	93
⌈Cafeteria operator	50	Assistant welder (R)	86
⌊Cafeteria operator	50	Metal worker (R)	84
Factory laundress (R)	46	Refinery operator (R)	79
Corn miller	37	Crane operator (R)	77
Storekeeper	30	Sugar dispatcher (R)	76
Seamstress	22	Field worker	75
Tortilla maker/laundress	20	Assistant mechanic (R)	70
Semi-retired midwife	15	Warehouse dispatcher (R)	62
Domestic employee	15	Sugar warehouse worker (R)	60
Laundress	12	Assistant mechanic (R)	57
Laundress/food sales	12	Refinery worker (R)	57
⌈Tortilla maker/laundress	8	Refinery worker/tailor	50
⌊Laundress	8	Guardian (R)	46
Seamstress	8	Field worker (R)	45
⌈Laundress	7	Field/factory worker (R)	41
⌊Laundress/tortilla maker	7	Field/factory worker (R)	41
⌈Baker/cook	7	Fieldworker (R)	38
⌊Baker/cook	7	Voluntario	38
Domestic employee/laundress	6	Voluntario/apprentice mechanic	34
Storekeeper	6	Voluntario/shop worker	33
Seamstress	5	Voluntario/field worker	33
	——	Voluntario/field worker	33
Total income for		Guardian	30
24 women: Q.	603	Voluntario/shoe repairer	25
Average monthly income		Voluntario	18
of women = Q. 25		Voluntario	18
		Voluntario	18
		Voluntario	18
		Voluntario	18

Total income for 36 men: Q. 2122
(income unknown = 7)
Average monthly income
of 36 men = Q. 59

NOTE: (R) indicates ranchero status. 22 male and 3 female employees listed above thus receive housing, food rations, education, health care, and other bonuses as part of their remuneration. Brackets indicate a mother-daughter work team.

* Earnings estimates were based on: (a) direct statements by informants and (b) calculations based on job status reported by the informant using official wage rates listed in the agreement between the union and the company. Average monthly income refers to an estimated average over the whole year where the harvest is assumed to last 6 months and those who work in shifts receive 11/8 times the base pay rate.

** For men, 7 whose income is unknown have been excluded from this tabulation.

free health care for the rancheros and their immediate families;
retirement pensions of 45 cents per day, or rights to severance pay;
use of 0.13 hectares (around ⅓ acre) of land, and pasturage.

These benefits should probably be calculated as having an additional value of at least Q. 20 per month.[7] The rancheros, as unionized workers, have a much stronger economic position than nonunionized workers, regardless of sex. The vast majority of the women do not work for the company, however, and are not eligible for such benefits.[8]

While the equal levels of pay and privilege accorded to the three women rancheras in the sample indicate that the company does not sexually discriminate against those women within the ranks of unionized workers, it seems fairly obvious that there is discrimination in hiring women for such positions. The fact that male cash income averages more than twice female income (and with noncash benefits exceeding female income by a factor of 2.5) is largely related to the males' near-monopoly on ranchero positions.

The Sexual Division of Labor

The market economy. The sexual division of labor in El Cañaveral is fairly rigid. As we have seen, the pattern of employment set by the company itself accounts for the strong associations between males and formal employment on the one hand, and females and informal employment on the other. Beyond this, none of the women are employed in field or factory work: The few women rancheras employed by the company work in laundry and health care. At the same time, none of the men are engaged in occupations that involve laundering, health care, or food preparation. The main areas of overlap occur in the informal sphere in such individual specialities as sewing. (See Table 4–3.)

Only one of the occupations of rancheria women involves a high capital investment, specifically the corn millers who have machines that are worth between Q. 500 and Q. 1,000. Fourteen women have a medium level of capital investment ranging from about Q. 25 to Q. 200 invested in sewing machines, store stock, bakery ovens, and/or refrigerators. Three women have special skills without capital (health specialists) and 20 women lack any special capital or skills. In the occupations of the men, only the truck owner-driver has substantial capital invested in his work. However, at least twenty-four of the occupations involve some special skill.

The conclusions that can be drawn from Table 4–3 are that: (1) there is more occupational specialization among men than women; (2) men's

Table 4-3. Occupations by Economically Active of Each Sex*

Occupations	Women Number	Occupations	Men Number
Food Seller	19	Field worker	12
Laundress	14	Refinery worker	6
Storekeeper	8	Mechanic	4
Seamstress	5	Welder	3
Baker	3	Dispatcher	2
Midwife/curer	3	Guardian	2
Corn miller	2	Carpenter	2
Domestic employee	2	Crane operator	1
		Blacksmith	1
Total subsample	39	Warehouse worker	1
		Tailor	1
		Shoe repairer	1
		Tractor operator	1
		Assistant mayor	1
		Truck owner-driver	1
		Electrician	1
		Timekeeper	1
		Factory foreman	1
		Total subsample	39
		(unspecified)	(4)

* Table 4-3 is based on an expanded sample of occupations of 90 women in 63 households which includes the smaller sample of Table 4-1. The sample was expanded to correct for overrepresentation of economically active women from the central barrio. The sample for men is the same for both Table 4-3 and 4-1. The number of occupations listed exceeds the number of economically active persons since some pursue more than one type of occupation.

specialties are very much related to the needs of the company while women's are related to the needs of the community; and (3) men's occupations more commonly entail the use of modern machine technology.

The domestic economy. As I have maintained in other chapters of this study, the division of labor encompasses specialization not only within the market economy, but within the domestic or subsistence economy as well. Here the pattern of ranchero households conforms to the traditional model of Latin and other European cultures. In general, men take almost no responsibility for child care, laundering, cooking, or housekeeping. They expect their wives or female kin to keep them provided with clothes that are clean and ironed; they expect meals to be served when they come home; and they expect that they will be able to go out during their nonworking hours without the encumbrance of children, or reproaches from their wives.

The contribution of men to their households is largely monetary, usually combined with other primary economic resources such as housing, or crops which may be planted on plots allocated by the company. Most men turn over a regular portion of their earnings to women for household expenses. The budgets vary widely, but women generally receive an allowance ranging from a low of Q. 12 to 15 monthly to about Q. 50 monthly. Exceptions are several extended households in which the pooled income of the various members can amount to around Q. 100 for a senior woman to spend on behalf of the group. Rough calculations indicate that the women's budgets range from 30 to 70 percent of a man's wages. In two cases, the separated wives of rancheros are guaranteed Q. 30 per month for child support by court order. In general, such allowances cannot be construed as payment for a woman's domestic services until the costs of feeding and maintaining other members of the household (husband included) are subtracted. In some cases, a woman has nothing at all left over or can barely manage food expenses on the amount she is allocated. Another variable factor is the extent to which men use the remainder of their wages for personal or for household consumption. In El Cañaveral, men usually pay the monthly installments on household appliances such as televisions or refrigerators, and they might also pay for clothing and for children's higher education. In general, it appears that the wives of rancheros have a *potential* to live better, by receiving an allowance from a responsible husband, than by entering the labor force as unskilled women.

The duties of women as wives and mothers are more or less outlined by all of the above tasks that men will not do for the household, which must then be done by the women. Further, the opportunities for women to earn money are largely extensions of, or derivative of, the very same skills which women acquire as houseworkers; only a few (8 out of 39) women in the sample have work that takes them outside of their homes regularly, and the work itself does not fall outside stereotyped areas of female responsibility: food, health, domestic work, and laundry.

Women of other categories

The employment opportunities of the women of the ranchería contrast with those of other women within the plantation community. Empleados are higher in socioeconomic status than rancheros, while cuadrilleros are lower in status. Although in some respects neither of these two categories is as completely integrated into local plantation life as the rancheros, they both represent to the rancheros alternative living standards to strive for or avoid.

Women of employee households. The company has about eighty salaried employees on its payroll. These people cannot belong to the union and do not receive the guaranteed benefits that rancheros enjoy. However, they do have individually negotiated benefits which might include housing, a maid, meals, free gasoline or use of a car. Empleado is a company payroll category that includes a wide range of income levels, from secretary and guard up to the highest administrators, with benefits distributed according to status. Unlike rancheros, the salaried employees usually have a closer or more intimate relationship with top management, a proximity which entails higher pay and status, and certain privileges that serve to maintain company loyalty in crucial positions.

While some of the eighty empleados reside outside the finca in the nearest town or even in the capital city, there is a barrio of empleados which houses many of them. Out of a sample of twenty such households, only five women are economically active. The jobs they fill are those of a teacher and school director at the company school, a seamstress who sews the school uniforms, a storekeeper who runs a popular and well-stocked store in the ranchería, and a part-time shopkeeper in the neighboring town. The women in the remaining fifteen households are housewives. Older daughters who still live at home are studying for higher degrees or help with housework rather than work outside the home. The types of work found among the few economically active women require either professional skills or access to capital to become established, and they are limited to conventional feminine fields. At the same time, there is a strong demonstration of domesticity in the fifteen households (75 percent of the sample) where women do not enter the labor market.

This general absence from the labor market cannot simply be explained by the burdens of housekeeping; three-fourths of the twenty households in the sample have at least one domestic employee to do cleaning, washing, and tortilla making. Yet these women are not without household functions. They tend to be active in another "class" of family-centered work—supervising the higher education of their children, and acquiring and maintaining the symbols of a higher status and standard of living. Some of these symbols are interior decorating suited for social entertaining, refrigerators, televisions, telephones, stereos, stylish clothing, and gourmet cooking. Another symbol seems to be that of a leisured lifestyle for wives.

What image does this class present to the women of the rancheria who make them tortillas, do their laundry, and send teen-age daughters to them to work as domestics? Rancheria women see that in empleado households, women who enjoy good food, clothing, health, and education for their children are mainly economically dependent women who stay home to supervise the household rather than work outside it. Thus, this type of domestic lifestyle may be perceived as a condition of obtaining higher social status and a higher standard of living.

Migrant women. The majority of the migrant workers at El Cañaveral come not in family groups, but as single males or fragments of families, leaving other members behind to care for their homes, children, crops, or whatever interests they may retain in their home communities. The particular recruitment policies employed at El Cañaveral mean that the migrant labor force is overwhelmingly male. Cane work is very rigidly assigned only to male workers on the logic that women are unable to do heavy work with a machete.[9] But even in its coffee operations, the company almost never employs female labor, despite the fact that coffee is commonly picked by women throughout Guatemala.

The number of cuadrilleros at El Cañaveral varies according to season with as many as 1,000 during the sugar harvest and at least several hundred during the off-season. The only women recruited are the *mantenedoras* (maintainers), also called *molenderas* (millers), who are essentially camp cooks, and are hired in a ratio of about one woman to twenty men. There are also small numbers of women who accompany their men to cook and wash for them but are not paid by the company. These women and their children may pick up odd jobs in the ranchería, particularly if they have returned to this plantation many times.

A molendera works with a male partner, usually her husband, who is referred to as *almorzero* (lunch man) or as a *plonqui* (a corruption of the English "flunky"). Her partner does the pick-up and delivery of the prepared food, tortillas and beans, to the men in the fields. Depending on her energy, a woman usually contracts to prepare food for around twenty workers. Some that I interviewed make tortillas for only sixteen men, while other strong workers maintain up to thirty-five and forty men. These women earn 5 cents per day per man. They live in galeras where men, women, and children of different households share a single room of bunk beds at one end, while the groups of molenderas do their cooking at the other.

Working conditions of these women are unenviable. They rise at 3 A.M. to begin making tortillas, and their work finishes at 7 P.M. If they have free moments during the day, there are clothes to wash—by hand.

145

The labor of making tortillas while standing over hot wood fires is extremely intensive. Poor ventilation of the smoke from numerous fires produces burning, tearing eyes and probably respiratory problems among the women. The standard pay for a molendera is roughly the same as that for a man doing field work, around Q. 1 per day. But a woman with experience both as a molendera and as a field worker asserts that field work is better because there is no smoke and there are fewer hours of work (from 6 A.M. to 4 P.M.).

What is the image that the women of the cuadrillas present to the women of the ranchería? It is an image of poor women who must work all day standing in smoke, living without privacy, possessions, or home, without security in their work, or educational opportunities for their children, and without the possibility of accumulating material goods. It is clearly not an image conducive to the idea that a woman's economic independence improves her standard of living or health.

Origins of the sexual division of labor

The observed division of labor in El Cañaveral could easily be regarded as a manifestation of the so-called Latin tradition of male supremacy (machismo) and female domesticity. However, it is important to consider just why such a value system should be viable in a particular context. Surely El Cañaveral as a company and as a community operates within a cultural milieu where male supremacist values are frequently voiced. But the acceptance and utility of such values must bear some relation to local institutions. In the present case, it is hard to ignore the impact that the company, El Cañaveral, has upon the occupational structure of available roles for each sex. Does El Cañaveral simply conform to local cultural stereotypes in determining hiring, recruitment, and training of workers, or are its policies determined at least as much by the economic priorities of the company and/or the cultural stereotypes of management as opposed to those of workers?

The company and the place of women. The highest level of the staff at El Cañaveral, the administrators and managers, together with engineers and agronomists, is exclusively male. Except for a female secretary-receptionist, all the white-collar office workers are male. In the health center, the highest professionals, the doctor and the pharmacist, are both men while the nurses are all women. In the school, there are ten female teachers, including a female director.

At the lower levels, all types of factory and field work are performed exclusively by men. The same is true for other miscellaneous jobs such as cattle and stable caretakers, gardeners, guardians, and various maintenance crews. For nonprofessional women, the only possibilities for company employment are those of washerwoman, midwife, and molendera. In addition, a few women employed as domestics by the management receive their pay directly from the company payroll.

The range of incomes within the company. The range of incomes for women on the company payrolls is fairly narrow—from around Q. 20 to 30 per month for cooks, or molenderas, to around Q. 80 per month for teachers and nurses. The two highest salaries are Q. 130 monthly for the secretary (a nonresident) and Q. 160 per month for the school director.

The range of male incomes is much broader. Some unskilled men earn as little as the women at the bottom of the payscale, around Q. 20 to 30 per month for cuadrilleros, gardeners, and watchmen. Most factory workers and skilled workers earn around Q. 50 to 100 per month, while foremen's wages are over Q. 100 per month. Finally, among the higher level administrators, salaries may be as high as Q. 800 per month or more in cash, plus a variety of other benefits of considerable economic value.

While company employment entails a minimum wage (established by national law) for both sexes, the lack of equivalent numbers of job openings for both sexes belies this apparent equality at the lower end of the pay scale. At the higher levels, division of work opportunities by sex involves substantial differences in earning potential, as women remain excluded from equal access to jobs generally, and to high positions of any sort.

Historical changes in company policy. The older women of the ranchería claim that formerly the finca offered more employment opportunities to women. Women used to be employed for a variety of tasks that included such outdoor work as cutting and binding cane leaves (for roofing), picking beans, and cutting *rosa de jamaica* (a plant used for beverages, which also has medicinal properties). Other paid work that women performed for the finca included making and repairing sugar sacks, and washing filters, denim cloth and sugar sacks in the river. In coffee production, women were also employed to manually clean and sort coffee beans. All of this work seems to have been done at piece rates. Women with a history of working with the sugar sacks report that they used to work in a regular group of eight to ten women and that they were directed by a *caporala*, or forewoman. There was continuity in this work force. Some women report working twenty to forty years washing sugar sacks. Others report starting out at the side of their mothers and taking over the job when their mothers grew too old.

Gradually, however, most of this work has been phased out. From the early 1940s, long-term sugar-sack workers who quit or died were not replaced. Today, the company laundering and sack repairing occupies only three middle-aged women, two of whom inherited the job from their mothers; all of them have worked at the job for many years. It appears that humanitarian considerations entered into the company's decision to retain these few women, since each is a major source of support for her family (two being divorced or separated mothers, and the third married to a worker who lacks ranchero status). Other opportunities for the local women to work directly for the company have disappeared. The roofs of cane leaves have been replaced by metal roofs in company housing, the coffee sorting is done by machines, and the sugar sacks are factory-made outside the finca. The company has not supplied new opportunities for women to work in the field, the factory, or the office. During a time period in which the number of rancheros has doubled to reach a figure of 500, both the relative and absolute numbers of women employed by the company have sharply declined. Today, women in the rancheria simply do not have employment opportunities with the company.

The coffee-picking policy at El Cañaveral illustrates that employment practices affecting women are not simply a response to values emanating from the worker's community. Coffee picking is done by both sexes in many parts of Guatemala. A number of ranchería women have done it in the past, and some still pick their own coffee grown on household plots in El Cañaveral or in private holdings outside the plantation. In view of the general scarcity of work opportunities for women and the plantation's need for such labor, I found it strange that the women did not pick coffee for wages at El Cañaveral. The women said they did not pick coffee because the company does not hire women, but hires male cuadrilleros instead.

It seemed possible that in the central part of the ranchería alternate sources of income combined with cultural prejudice and distance from the coffee groves might discourage women from seeking manual labor in coffee. However, this did not seem likely in the peripheral area of the plantation located near the coffee groves where alternate sources of income are scarce. In fact, in that area I discovered that some young women cross over to other plantations to pick coffee on a day-work basis since such work is not available in El Cañaveral. Occasionally, they report that a girl might pick coffee as an *ayudante* (assistant) of an older brother working for the company, but girls or women are not hired in their own right. Despite these reports, the personnel director

8. *El Cañaveral: Sugar Refinery and Large Cane Fields*

9. *Rancheria women with temporary work transplanting coffee trees.*

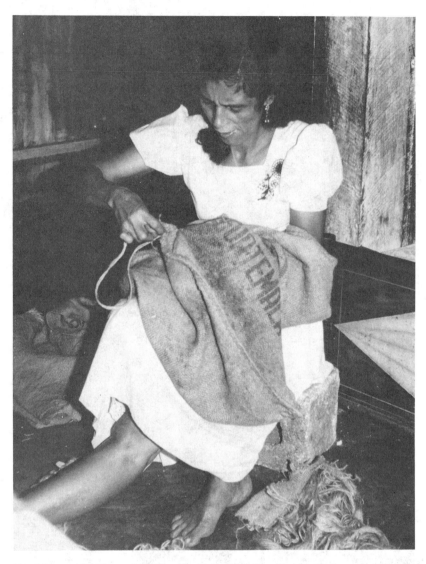

10. *Woman Worker with Obsolete Job: Mending Sugar Sacks*

at El Cañaveral insisted that local women could get work cards if they wished, but that none of them wanted to work.

Given the two contradictory explanations, I was inclined to believe the women since some of them did in fact go outside to pick coffee on other plantations. Their version was later given greater credence when, on a return visit, I learned that a new, young administrator of the coffee sector had hired a number of resident women to work picking coffee, and later in the off-season he had a team of resident women working in the fields transplanting coffee seedlings. When I interviewed this administrator, he confirmed that he had instituted this new policy because in his prior experience on other plantations women had participated in coffee production. Once such work was clearly offered to them, women did step forward to take it. The women stated that they were quite pleased to have these jobs, for there was no other work available that paid as well (roughly Q. 1 per day, by piece rate). One woman who had searched a long time for a good job as a domestic employee was tempted to quit her job for the higher-paying field work, but aware that it was only seasonal she opted to continue the domestic job, which gave her greater security of work the year round. Pleased at the change in company policy, the women who wanted to work were to be disappointed again when this new administrator died in an accident and the company abandoned his policy of offering field work to women.

Access to modern technology and training. El Cañaveral has been described as a modern sugar plantation *cum* refinery tuned in to an international economic system. Unambiguous evidence of its commitment to modern technological developments can be seen in the company office, which has a computer, an air-conditioner, and a radio hookup with the modern offices in the capital city. While the use of modern technology in company operations could be described at length, here I am more concerned with modern technology as an aspect of the lives of the people of the ranchería: in their formal work activities and their informal household activities.

The management of El Cañaveral is extremely interested in applying the latest developments in science, agricultural technology, and engineering to keep its operations up-to-date and competitive. One result of this had been the growth of the *ingenio* (refinery or sugar mill), also called the *fábrica* (factory) by the workers. From a dominating position at the entrance to the plantation, the factory buildings and patio have been expanding into the ranchería, requiring the demolition of some workers' housing.[10] The growth of the refining operations has been accompanied by a growing need for skilled workers to operate the machinery to its maximum 24-hour capacity during the harvest, and to repair it during the off-season. The male ranchero population was called upon to meet this need and the company has been providing the necessary training for many workers. This is apparent from the job specialization that can be found among the rancheros: welders, mechanics, crane operators, electricians, and so forth. Many of the jobs require literacy and some mathematical training. Although not all the rancheros are employed in skilled labor, the majority work within the factory at least during the harvest period. Some 30 percent of the rancheros return to less-skilled field work during the off-season, but in general the unskilled field work is performed by voluntarios and cuadrilleros, the temporary workers.

The significance of the acquisition of skills by rancheros at El Cañaveral is not only in the pay raises they receive. The training and experience with modern machine technology increase the workers' employment options outside the plantation and add to their general confidence that they can function in an industrializing world. When the workers are unionized, their skills increase their leverage in the event of a strike since it is more difficult for management to find adequate replacements. For the few women rancheras, there has been no attempt to provide special training for the washerwomen, although the nurses did receive specialized training. However, since nonresident nurses are also hired, the actual investment in training resident women for specialized occupations in the plantation is practically nil.

Although women are denied opportunities to join a modern industrializing work force, their work within the home has not escaped the impact of modern technological change, and in some respects is quite modern compared to the majority of Guatemalan rural and urban populations. For instance, most ranchero households have the benefits of electricity and running water. They also have gas or kerosene stoves, or have their firewood delivered by truck. This means that women are not burdened with the daily labor of hauling water or searching for firewood. They have relatively cheap bus transportation to the nearest city where they are able to make most purchases for the household without the great physical exertion of carrying things to their homes. There are several power corn mills on the plantation so women no longer have to spend hours daily in milling corn by hand; they pay for milling. With ready-to-wear clothing and factory-made cloth available, relatively few women make their own clothes and none of those that do start by weaving their own cloth. Most women hire one of a few seamstresses with sewing machines. There are only seven bakers on the entire plantation, but with commercial bread available in the stores, these women make and sell mainly specialty breads and cakes. Clearly, the domestic work of women has been lessened in many ways. It is physically lighter, but does not involve many new skills or creativity, especially compared to the craft production of textiles and clothing by women in many indigenous communities. And it does not create much confidence that they can control or work with sophisticated technology.

Unquestionably, a few women have been able to capitalize on some aspects of modern technology in order to turn their free time to economic use or creative activities. Good examples of this are the seamstresses, the corn millers, the women with refrigerators who sell cold drinks and beer, and the women who have developed special cooking skills. But the majority of women have not been able to use modern technology to increase their economic value or bargaining power, for there are few new economic roles open to them. While women's increased leisure may improve the quality of health care and education they can provide for their children, the company also provides for the education and health care of workers' families so that even in these traditional spheres the average woman finds her contribution has been diminished.

Economic Strategies

A selection of brief vignettes from the lives of individual women illustrates important aspects of the economic situation of women that do not readily emerge in the analysis of economic structure. In particular, the economic structure leads women to develop certain strategies in marriage and work. Here I examine the economic context of submission, competition, violence, and prostitution as they pertain to women's strategies in El Cañaveral. Again, none of the cases that follow should be construed as "typical." Each illustrates some patterns that are common within the rancheria while each has idiosyncrasies. These exceptions are instructive when they reveal the kinds of constraints that operate to make some kinds of behavior more common than others.

For women, the most striking feature of the economic structure is that opportunities are severely limited both in number and in kind, with almost no access to formal-sector jobs on the plantation. Given this scarcity of employment options, women can be expected to place a high value on relationships with men that can give them economic support and security. The best strategy for most women would be to emphasize relationships with men like the rancheros who have the means to support a family.

151

The economics of scarcity are relevant here. Despite a demographic surplus of males in the plantation area, the percentage of men who are rancheros, unionized semi-skilled workers with secure jobs, is low. Thus, women have good reason to be competitive over such men. Once they have established a marital union, many women will go to great lengths to maintain some kind of "hold" on the man who can support them. The implications of this situation for women of the ranchería are: (a) a tendency to tolerate and endure perceived inequities and injustices in their marriages for lack of better alternatives, and (b) a tendency for wives to react violently against other women who are competing for support from the same man.

Submission Toward Men

Without implying that submission toward men is unique to El Cañaveral, it appears that it takes extreme forms among some of the women of the ranchería precisely because of the striking inequities in economic resources available to each sex. The case of Benedicta illustrates this.

1. Benedicta is age thirty-nine and was married at the age of fifteen. Her husband is ten years older than she, and a ranchero. She has suffered with him because he drank a lot and went with other women and did not give her money. He also used to beat her, but she never left him. Although they have both been Evangelists for many years, he would frequently "fall" back into his worldly ways and go out drinking, dancing, and wasting money while she stayed "in the house waiting for him with his dinner, with his clothes cleaned, and with his children." She was miserable and suffered for many years. She has had ten pregnancies resulting in six children. Two children died, and two were aborted.

Since she has been married, Benedicta has not worked outside the house. She is an affable person and would like to work, but her husband will not let her. She would like to have her own business, but he said it would not be profitable. She earns some cash at home by selling cooked foods to the neighbors, and washing. Benedicta says it would be nice to be able to go for a walk alone, to be single, or to be so fortunate to have a husband who lets her go out. Her husband is jealous. He does not want her to go anywhere alone, only with the children, the youngest of whom is nine. While married men are free to go out alone, she says that married women generally are not.

Relations with her husband, now nearly fifty, have been better in the last few years. He does not drink anymore or run around as before, and he is kinder. Nonetheless, Benedicta is still afraid to go for a walk without the children, or to go visiting without her husband's express permission. The fear of provoking a violent reaction is still very great. Clear evidence that her husband has become more economically responsible toward his family can be seen in the home. It is modest but well-furnished. Signs of economic well-being include a refrigerator, an electric iron, a collection of about twenty books, pictures on the wall, and well-dressed children.

Benedicta's case is thus one in which submission to economic hardship and extreme authoritarianism yielded fairly high economic returns in middle age. A similar case is that of Lydia:

2. Lydia is thirty-six years old. She has lived for fifteen years with a ranchero and has four children. She has never had a job, having been raised on a nearby finca until she united with her husband. Her husband used to be a heavy drinker and spendthrift who abused her. He used to beat her and even sold her sewing machine for drink. She endured it rather than leave. Several years ago he converted to Evangelism and stopped drinking. Although he still beats her occasionally, they are now able to acquire household conveniences and they spend evenings attending temple services together.

Lydia's husband earns around Q. 100 per month and gives her slightly less than half his pay to cover daily household expenses while he pays for durable goods such as clothes, shoes, and installments on the television or refrigerator. Lydia earns a few cents a day by selling popsicles to the neighborhood children. Her daily routine is one of housework and washing in the morning, preparing lunch for her husband and children, followed by a few hours of relaxation in the early afternoon when a neighbor visits and they watch TV together. Around 4 P.M. chores begin again with the preparation of dinner.

Lydia's placid lifestyle at present involves relatively little conflict over the economic structure of sex roles. In exchange for housing, food, and clothing provided by her husband, she provides cooking, washing, child raising and sexual partnership. If her life appears unexciting, one notes that it conforms to the old European adage regarding ideal female behavior: "A good wife is one that nobody talks about." In the case of both Benedicta and Lydia, we find women constrained to a narrow range of behavior by their husband's economic control, physical intimidation, and the burdens of children. As economic dependents, these women lack the "collateral" for defiance and they have no means with which to compel the "good behavior" of their husbands. They opt for a tactic of patience and endurance, hoping that with time their husbands will come to place a greater value on family life.

The following case is similar to the preceding one in fundamentals, but here a younger woman is not yet resigned to submission as a tactic and is looking for an alternative:

3. Berta is twenty-four years old. She has been married for five years and has one child. Her husband is a ranchero who earns well and gives her Q. 25 every two weeks for living expenses. Berta was raised in El Cañaveral and has never worked. She resents being married. Her husband never helps her with anything in the house. He has other women and goes out often with male friends. He is extremely jealous about her and does not let her go out, nor does he invite her out with him. When he argues with her, they both end up hitting each other and come out in a draw. All the same, he is the one who gives orders. Berta is looking for an opportunity to leave. Her relatives are not in a position to help her, but she hopes that two friends in the capital may be able to find work for her as a domestic employee.

Compared to the preceding cases, Berta has less reason to endure a situation where she is miserable in her dependency. With only one child it is still possible to become a domestic employee if she leaves her home in the rancheria. Like Lydia, who also grew up on a plantation, she has had no work experience and does not expect to find work in the plantation region, but looks to the city as an alternative.

Competition Among Women

In the three cases presented above, it is clear that the wife of a ranchero faces considerable outside competition for a share of her husband's wages. While alcoholism and male peer groups may be contributing factors, wives generally perceive their real competition to be other women: prostitutes in town who are interested in a worker's paycheck, and local women who may just be after his cash or who may also hope to establish a more permanent support relationship. An insecure wife is reluctant to jeopardize her position by directly attacking her husband when he wrongs her by distributing his earnings among other women; this would challenge his authority or drive him even more surely to the comforts of a new partner. Instead, women who feel severely threatened are prone to attack the competition. While such attacks may begin with verbal abuse, they may well culminate in physical violence.

Yolanda, age sixty-five, reports her reaction to competition some thirty years earlier when she was living with a ranchero and had several young children:

4. My husband was mad at me because he had another woman. Once when I was washing clothes by the stream, I saw the other woman and I grabbed her and started to beat her. I left her all bloody. That night he came home very drunk when I was asleep and grabbed me by the hair and started to beat me. I fought back. He had me down on the floor, but I got

a knife and stabbed him in the thigh. We were both put in jail for three months. I had two children in jail with me, and made my tortillas there. . . . We each had to pay a large fine. The other woman was not put in jail, but my husband had beaten her also. After this, we separated.

Yolanda attempted to control the competition since she could not control her husband, but in terms of keeping the latter the effort did not succeed. One of the issues was clearly an economic claim.

Yolanda always had to work to support herself and her children because her husband drank and did not give her money. After they separated, she was advised to go to the judge in town. The judge said her husband would have to pay her half of what he earned and he agreed. For several years, Yolanda received Q. 15 per month from him. The plantation administrator also let her remain in the ranchero house where she sold foodstuffs. Her husband had to erect a shack in the ravine.

A similar case is that of Reina:

5. Reina is twenty-six years old, born in another region. After a childhood of broken homes, work in coffee plantations, and domestic service, she began to live with a young ranchero at El Cañaveral at age eighteen. Within five years, she had five births, but two children died. Her husband beat her when she was pregnant with one of the children. She was sick after its birth and the child died in infancy.

Reina never lived well with her common-law husband because "he likes women too much. He is always going and spending money with other women, lovers and *rocoleras* ("juke-box girls" or prostitutes). Some of the women are from El Cañaveral." Once, she fought with one of her rivals. After seeing the woman go off with her husband, she waited for her to pass by alone and then beat her. Next, Reina was beaten by her husband. She has been separated from him for three years. Reina went to the local alcalde in order to collect support money from her husband: She gets Q. 30 per month. Her widowed father-in-law has permitted her to continue living in the same house while his son lodges with friends.

Such physical violence toward other women is undertaken as a last resort where a woman feels very desperate. In both of these cases, the wife had an acknowledged position as "the" wife and was able to make successful legal claims to ensure some support after the break-up. Obviously, the rancheria sample favors the women who are successful at such claims, for the unsuccessful women must move on to other areas where they can find a livelihood.

Attacking the "other woman" places the blame for the failure of marital unions on exogenous factors. While a woman may very well feel that her rival is to blame, if the relative economic resources of the spouses were more equal, such desperate attacks would be exceptional even if marital reshuffling remained common.

We now consider the case of a woman who neither became submissive to maintain a relationship, nor did she fight her competition.

6. Matilda is forty-seven years old, born in a small village. After a childhood of broken homes and abuse, she came to work at El Cañaveral as a domestic employee. At age seventeen she went to live with a young cane worker who was a *voluntario*. Expecting some easing of economic hardship, she found instead that:

"After this my life was the same. My life has always been centered on material needs. Soon I was a mother. We were all right because as a mother I had the hardship, and he would bring me wood, maize, and little things for the house. But no. He started to drink and go to town. He was chasing women. He no longer looked at the house. I was left. Always washing for other people to be able to sustain myself. I had no help, not even pennies with him."

Matilda returned to work and their relationship dissolved because he was already involved with another woman. After about five years, Matilda was tired of being alone and did not want to work so much. She became involved with the father of her last two children. The situation repeated itself. He stayed with her until the first child was born and from then on he would come and go but mostly they were separated until her last child arrived. Then they stayed together until he died in an accident. This man also drank and chased women.

"He had a *monton* (a heap). Every little while, another woman. They didn't love him. They were just women of the street. It was for money. Here, that is what they look for first. They see that a man has money and they leave the worker with nothing. And when he does not have money, they no longer want him. If a man doesn't have money, women don't look for him."

Neither of Matilda's men ever beat her. She says that if they had, she would have gone to court. She did not submit. "Other women only endure. Me? No! For this I am known as *delicada, brava* (angry)."

Matilda's oldest son, age twenty-four, has never helped her economically. He withdrew because he now has his own family with three children to maintain. Meanwhile, Matilda continues the work she has done all her life, making tortillas and doing laundry. She has never had a house from the finca, but only permission to build a shack.

In Matilda's case, the competition with other women was a factor in the break-up of her relationships with men, but it appears that these relationships were never sufficiently rewarding for her to come to blows in defense of her position. One important consideration is that as seasonal workers, neither of the men was able to give her the advantages of being a ranchero's wife. They themselves only lived in covachas. Matilda found that the added income brought by such a man did not really offset the extra work it involved and the added costs of maintaining him.

Matilda's comments on the competition for a man with money in his pocket are echoed by innumerable women within the ranchería. Particularly on payday, there is strong competition from the town prostitutes. Berta, discussed above, describes the situation as follows:

> The men spend a lot of money on the women in town. Twenty years ago they say it was different; there were not so many restaurants in town like now. The restaurants are like bars where the prostitutes are. . . . Women who are left without money for food go to fetch their husbands in the restaurants where they are spending. The men are drunk and the wives go to hit the prostitutes. The prostitutes fight back with them.

Like many women, Berta knows the price range for services in the various establishments. Herminia, age seventy, expresses a similar view:

> In general, the men only go making trouble for poor women and abandon them. They go to town and drink in the restaurants where there are prostitutes and waste their money. They do not give their wives expense money. There are husbands who on receiving their pay go straight to town and forget they have women and children. Then they come the next day or in the middle of the night. The woman remains with no choice but to make claims. And there are women who fight with the men because they do not give them a home.

It should be understood that there is no rigid line separating the wives from the "other" women. One ranchero household with five daughters reports that four of them married and the fifth is a prostitute in town. Neither the mother nor any of her daughters are literate, nor have they had any work experience—which may help to explain why prostitution was an alternative to the daughter who did not marry. It is not uncommon to find families in the ranchería whose daughters are single mothers living at home because they have not yet been able to establish stable relationships with responsible men. To draw an analogy: Just as rancheros have sons who are only seasonal workers but hope to join the ranks of permanent workers when a vacancy appears, there are daughters who are irregular wives hoping to join the ranks of permanent wives. The number of desirable positions for both sexes is limited and those that do not make it generally leave El Cañaveral. An important difference, however, is that wives are not unionized and cannot control their competition or their working conditions. The best they can do is exert social pressure within the ranchería where, with some help from the local alcalde and the administration, they are able to prevent the operation of the kind of forthright prostitution prevalent in the town.

Exceptional Women

This discussion would not be complete without giving some consideration to the exceptional women who manage to live without resorting to tactics of submission and are not threatened by competition from other women. Apart from the three rancheras, very few women in El Cañaveral manage to escape from a position of economic dependency which leads to submissive behavior toward men and competitive behavior toward women. Even when they are able to contribute small amounts of cash to the weekly budget, it is usually not enough to alter the economic imbalance between husband and wife.

However, there are some exceptional cases:

7. Belinda grew up near the capital in a stable home where her father, a skilled worker, saw that his daughter acquired both educational skills and a variety of work skills, albeit informal ones that were taught at home. Belinda married young to a boy even younger than herself. Although she soon had a child, she worked both before and after its birth to enable her husband to finish secondary school. As a factory worker, management encouraged him to continue studying at nights in Guatemala City, and over the years Belinda engaged in a variety of entrepreneurial activities to make his further education and advancement possible. Her work included working in a store, running a lunch-kitchen, laundering, dress making, raising chickens, and slaughtering pigs. Now, in middle age, Belinda's husband has become an empleado and also has a repair shop outside El Cañaveral. Belinda no longer runs any businesses, since profits have gone down for chickens, food services, and dressmaking as the supply of such services has increased. She does informally help her husband in his repair shop and does not mind getting dirty to remove a motor.

Although she is not currently economically independent, Belinda feels economically secure. Her husband is faithful, responsible, and drinks very little. She has never had problems with him, saying, "He is good because I helped him." When she is ill, he is willing to cook and make tortillas, wash clothes and dishes, and he used to help her with the housework and chicken business. Their house and goods show careful investment, and their children are well-educated.

8. Yolanda (of case 4 above) has become a successful entrepreneur after the failure of her first union. When she formed a household with a second ranchero, she continued to pursue a variety of entrepreneurial activities. She claims she decided it was better to continue working than to resort to the manipulative tactics of other women. Since she had three children by her previous marriage to support, her husband did not object to her con-

tinued economic activity. As her sons grew up, some migrated to the United States and were able to send her money, which she invested. Today, her varied economic concerns include corn milling, the sale of cold beer and soft drinks, pig and poultry raising, sale of prepared foods, bread baking, and soap making. Although she is illiterate, she is shrewd when it comes to barter, trading goods with other housewives without the use of money as a medium of exchange, and skilled in the investment of her capital.

9. Matilda (of case 6 above) has been mainly self-supporting for all the time that she has lived in El Cañaveral , despite two tenuous unions with men who were not rancheros. After years of steady, hard work as a tortilla maker and washerwoman, she had been slowly investing her small savings in a piece of land outside the finca where she hoped she and her children could live with some security. Having fallen ill for a period, she was unable to make the payments and was forced to sell her land at a loss. Currently, she is still beset with problems over housing, as her permission to keep her covacha in El Cañaveral is rescindable. She recently lost her right to stay on one lot when the house changed hands because a ranchero retired. At that point, she had to move down into the barranca and set up her shack in an undesirable location, full of refuse, too far for her customers to reach her, and where the nearest neighbors are two men whom she fears will attempt to seduce her teen-age daughter. Despite the fact that she has worked diligently all her life, all she has is a small, flimsy shack with cardboard walls, a dirt floor, and no electricity.

In the preceding cases, women who are exceptional for the level of their economic activity are seen to be unable to single-handedly accumulate significant capital. The two women who are economically well-off have had the benefits of a company income, home, education and health care for their children acquired through their husbands. Greater independence came with old age and the accumulated benefits of the husband's work, or the assistance of grown children. In contrast, the third case of a single mother without formal company benefits shows the extreme difficulty for a working woman with children to do more than just get by from day to day on her own.

Social Organization

The participation of women in the social organization and activities of El Cañaveral, will be discussed under three broad headings: domestic or household organization, and formal and informal community organization. The household shall be considered first, followed by the formal organizations and activities as they are customarily subdivided into such elements as politics, religion, and education. Finally, the more informal areas of kinship and friendship ties in the community will be discussed.

Domestic Organization

This section begins with an examination of women's position in domestic organization because it is the sphere at El Cañaveral in which women assume central roles both formally and informally. The nature of women's participation or lack of participation in community organizations is strongly conditioned by their domestic roles. Domestic social organization is examined beginning with the structure and composition of the household, proceeding to an examination of women's position in marriage and the family, and finishing with some observations regarding the factors reponsible for shaping such groupings.

Household structure. The nuclear family is usually defined as a conjugal pair with children. In a sample of thirty-two ranchería households, only half fit the definition. In the sixteen nonnuclear households, twelve have members of three or more generations and one has two generations of married couples, qualifying them as "complex" in organization. The remaining three households could be considered "reduced" in form in that they do not contain a conjugal pair, but consist of: a mother and children, a grandmother and grandchildren, a divorced man with no children.

Although the right to a company house in the ranchería is generally determined by the husband/father's status as a worker, there are many couples who do not have rights to their own houses. Out of fourteen cases where married couples live with one or both parents, eight are uxorilocal and six are virilocal. Couples are not restricted by unilineal descent principles in seeking housing: Pragmatism prevails where good housing is at a premium.

Many of the conjugal unions initiated in El Cañaveral are terminated (whether by abandonment, separation, divorce, or death) before the children are grown. As a result, it is common for children to be brought up by only one of their natural parents. Fourteen of the households in the sample, or 44 percent, contain stepchildren. There are five households in which the natural fathers have retained responsibility for the children, and nine in which the mothers have kept the children. Significantly, none of the fathers has taken the responsibility for the children without the assistance of another woman: four had remarried and one man relies on his married sister who lives in the same household. Of the women taking such responsibility, six live alone or with female kin, two have remarried, and one lives with her father-in-law. This suggests that, as with housing, pragmatism may prevail over the natural parenthood of either sex in determining the placement of children. (Only three of the fourteen cases involved the death of a parent: one of the father and two of the mother.) It also suggests that women, but not men, may be induced to assume the responsibility for child care without the help of the opposite sex.

Marriage and the family. In El Cañaveral, there are various ways to interpret marital status, so that the boundary between marital and other relationships needs some clarification. De jure marriages, civil and religious, are not the predominant form of marriage in the rancheria. In fact, 59 percent of all established marital relationships are simple unions or de facto marriages.[11] The preference for common-law marriage seems related in part to the cost of a formal ceremony (one woman estimated it would have cost her more than Q. 100), as well as to the feeling that one should not marry unless one is certain it will last—especially when religious traditions prohibit divorce. Common-law marriages occur both with and without the consent of the parents.

The legal advantages and disadvantages of de jure as opposed to de facto marriage are not clear cut. It is said that if a woman is legally married, then she can go to court to get support for her children if the husband fails to support her. A woman with children of an informal union who was only "united" (*unidos*, a common usage for common-law marriage) contrasts her situation where she receives no child support from the children's father with that of her sister, also separated, who was legally married and is receiving child support money. However, based on other separation cases, it is clear that de facto marriages can also be legally recognized by the court and that some women are aware of the procedures. For example, Reina, cited earlier, never legally married her husband in spite of his wish to marry, because his father said he was "no good." When the relationship deteriorated and her husband went to live with other friends, Reina was nonetheless able to go to court to receive a legal settlement of Q. 30 per month for her children.

An important variable in determining the woman's status is whether or not she has "united' or established residence with the man. Without such joint residence, sexual relationships are referred to as being "*en la calle*" (in the street). There are numerous young, single mothers in El Cañaveral who, never having established joint residence, are unable to claim economic support for their children. Another important factor that affects child support is whether or not the father agrees to legally "recognize" his children. In one case, a woman who had legally married and divorced her ranchero husband reconciled with him several times after the divorce. The man did not recognize the resulting children until years later; meanwhile they did not enjoy the rights of ranchero's children to free health care or attendance at the company school.

A marital relationship, whether de jure or de facto, is considered the only proper context in which a woman may consent to sexual relations and/or bear children. Prostitution is the recognized institution for the regulation of nonmarital and hence improper sex relations. The two institutions, marriage and prostitution, are conceptually polarized such that a woman who consents to sexuality outside of marriage risks acquiring the reputation of a prostitute. For men, there appears to be no such restriction of sexuality or conceptual polarization between men who have sex with wives and those who go to prostitutes. It is recognized that they are the same men. Actual prostitution by women of the ranchería is rare and results in legal sanctions, because neither management nor residents condone it within the plantation. However, it is clear that significant numbers of women do not conform to the marital ideal. Single mothers are not uncommon. My sample shows that about 20 percent of the mothers of the ranchería are single, separated, or divorced. Some of these women are older, economically independent women, but most are young women supported by their parents or just their mothers. Although single motherhood is not an approved status, there are enough women in this situation to dilute community reaction. Such cases are not confined to the rancheria but include daughters of empleados as well.

While single mothers are one indication of the occurence of extramarital sex, sexual affairs are said to occur frequently both among the young single women and among married women. Despite an emphasis on virginity for women in order to avoid jealously or recriminations from their husband when they marry, young women assert that sexual affairs are common for girls beginning around age 14 to 16, and that few enter marriage today with no sexual experience.

In most cases, women who do not conform to the marital ideal are under considerable social pressure to change their behavior, particularly if they persist in unregulated sexual relations and bear children. Nonconformity results in criticism of varying sorts, depending on the type of relations the woman maintains. For example, several young women with children continue to have sporadic relations with their lovers without being able to induce them to accept the economic responsibilities of fatherhood. This might be related to the man's lack of a steady job or to the fact that he is making commitments to other women. In the former case, the young mother may hope that with time he will get a steady job and accept his responsibilities, while in the latter, she may hope he will come to prefer her over her rivals. In such cases, the young woman is generally considered foolish, but among women there is some sympathy for her plight. However, if the relationship persists a long time and the woman continues to bear children without getting any economic security, then sympathy wears thin.[12]

As a contrast to this situation where sympathy is possible, women are extremely critical of the wife who takes lovers. In part, their criticism is based on the assumption that a woman will never consent to sexual relations without receiving money. Thus, the woman who is married and seeks other men is considered "*maniosa*" (manipulative), and is condemned for depriving other wives of their due.

Given that women both as wives and prostitutes provide sexual gratification in exchange for economic benefits (not to deny that there may be different degrees of affection involved) wives are at some pains to show that in exchange for their greater economic benefits and security they are providing other services to their man. While bearing his children is one such service, there is a point at which this is no longer possible or advantageous for women, as when a man already feels he has enough children to support. For this reason, a wife's claim to superior status becomes dependent in part upon her provision of personal services such as cooking and laundering. Women who receive economic support from a man without cooking for him are considered akin to prostitutes. Criticism and gossip directed by women against other women often assert that the woman does not even cook for her man.

An interesting example is an elderly divorced woman who earned her living through food sales and supported her daughters and grandchildren through her efforts. She was the steady sexual partner of an elderly worker who gave her Q. 25 per month. This woman was criticized and under pressure to provide other services to the man for his money. Specifically, she was expected to go to live with him and cook for him. The woman resisted for a long time, mainly because she did not want to sacrifice her independence and ability to support her daughters.

Cooking is symbolic of wifely status to a man. In an account of a husband's jealous behavior, a woman recalls that once her husband came home when a woman friend was visiting. Her friend poured him a cup of coffee but he was angry and insisted his wife pour it for him, at which point he flung the cup at her and began his accusations that she was a faithless wife.

In the ranchería, motherhood is taken for granted as a normal part of adult womanhood and the responsibility for child care falls almost exclusively on women. Until they are old enough for school, children spend nearly all of their time under the care of their mothers or other women. Fathers enjoy their children, but do not like to be encumbered by them; one rarely sees a man outside his house accompanied by young children. In contrast, married women who leave the house generally must take children with them both for the sake of the children and for their own reputation as responsible mothers and faithful wives. Women have few opportunities to escape from the daily burden of childcare unless their mother or sister lives nearby and comes to help. Even so, there is no regular sharing of child care responsibilities. Only in exceptional cases does a mother pay someone else to look after her children while she works, and the only cases of this that I encountered were of short duration. Furthermore, El Cañaveral lacks any day nurseries. Because men are permitted to work at relatively high-paying jobs on the plantation that are highly incompatible with the presence of young children, women take full responsibility for child care and tend to be unemployed or confined to only those types of paid work which, being both safe and intermittent, permit sufficient attention to the young.

The ranchería mother's prime concerns are to provide for the health and well-being of her children by making sure they are well-fed and clothed. Formal education is provided by the schools, and mothers informally instruct their children in daily chores, generally allowing them much free time for unstructured play with neighborhood children. Children are charged with many errands by their mothers and often act as messengers or reporters regarding community affairs, since they generally have greater freedom to come and go than their mothers. Women whose jealous husbands restrict their mobility exhibit great interest in their children's reports of activities outside the house.

While child raising is a normal part of marriage for almost all women, many feel a need for and attempt to practice some form of birth control or family planning. Out of a small sample of twenty-two ranchería women of childbearing age, eight do not practice any form of birth control, while thirteen do use some method, and one is infertile. The breakdown of methods is as follows:

Abstention	5
Sterilization	4
Pills	2
Injections	1
Rhythm	1

Abstention is practiced by three women who sleep in separate beds from their husbands (with varying degrees of success) and by two who are separated and consciously avoid any involvements which could possibly leave them with responsibility for more children. Abortion could also be listed as a form of family planning for it occurs even though it is illegal.[13]

At El Cañaveral the idea that a woman's place is in the home does not just refer to the idea that women should not be in the work force, or that they should retain major responsibility for children. Particularly with young wives, there is often a strong desire on the part of the husband to limit his wife's contacts outside the house, and hence her opportunities for sexual infidelity and/or greater independence. More than a third of the married women with whom I discussed this issue assert that they cannot go out without their husband's permission or they risk a beating. Another quarter of them indicate that on account of their children they hardly ever go out. These and other women who stay mainly in their homes could be interpreted as women who know and accept "the rules," not attempting to engage in independent activities outside the home that might be considered unsuitable for a wife and mother. Of course, there are some married women who are free to come and go. As one would expect from the above, most cases of independent behavior by wives were those in which the women were older and economically active.

Company policy. At this point it is useful to review and interpret some of the ways in which the company influences the structure of the family in the ranchería. (1) As seen in the section on economic organization, the company encourages a position of economic dependency for women by restricting most forms of wage work to male rancheros and male migrants. (2) The company provides housing, food rations, health services, and education to rancheros and their families. These are benefits "in kind" which favor the economically dependent family members in that, unlike cash, they cannot be easily converted to individualistic consumption. (This contrasts with the plantation's effect on migrant workers where men are physically separated from their families and are not provided with adequate housing or other meaningful benefits for dependents.) (3) The company health center encourages the use of birth control.[14]

The second and third policies can be understood in a relatively straightforward way. The company has an interest in promoting family stability among skilled workers, not only to ensure a stable supply of workers at present, but also to ensure the reproduction of the next generation of workers with the necessary skills and good health. The company also has an interest in encouraging birth control so that the population of workers' children does not greatly exceed its needs for future labor. Overreproduction of the population is costly both in terms of the provision of services, and in terms of the potential disturbances that could arise with a large pool of unemployed young workers.

It is more difficult to account for the company's policy of avoiding the employment of women even in areas where it would seem there is little cultural prohibition: seasonal coffee picking, office work, and some kinds of factory work. Several interpretations are possible, assuming the company has adopted this policy after rational consideration. A conventional approach is that by paying one wage, the company in fact gets the work of two people: the husband as worker and the wife who works to restore her husband for another day's work and to reproduce the next generation of workers. This argument is weakened by the fact that the rancheros do receive higher wages and more benefits than migrants, which may be interpreted as a wage that covers the cost of the women's labor as wives.

An alternate explanation is that the dependent family and the differentiated status of women act as a restraining force on the worker's power to rebel against the company. The dependency of the wife and family keeps a man tied to his job since there is rarely an alternative income to fall back on. Further, the wife as a nonworker does not always understand or feel solidarity with the worker's point of view, thus creating a division between men and women within the working class. Also, it may be some consolation to a dissatisfied worker that at least he is not a woman, since he can command personal service within his home.

Another possible concern of management is that if women were given a share of the work that is now performed by migrants, it would be more difficult to maintain the conceptual separation between seasonal and permanent workers which enables the company to hire the migrants for less. Unlike migrants, women could use their influence with ranchero husbands and hence the union to press for greater benefits and solidarity.

These explanations all make some sense, yet do not seem sufficiently powerful to explain the acceptance of strongly dichotomized sex roles with males as wage earners and females as economic dependents and family workers. One can never be certain of the extent to which management has rationally calculated the various pros and cons of employing women and decided to pursue policies that are in the company's best interest. To an extent, company policy may be determined not by a calculation of interests, but by reflex or unconscious reproduction of the macroculture (or by both reason and reflex, if they are consistent). One key consideration is the widespread Western assumption that women are needed as housewives in order to reproduce the labor force.[15]

Although the factors influencing women's position in the family system of El Cañaveral cannot be conclusively determined here, a consideration of the parameters involved shows that current economic decisions both in the rancheria and in the head office are very important. This does not deny the importance of traditional cultural values nor the values of modern international culture, but relates the family and its values to a specific economic context.

Summary. Marriage and the family are social institutions that include both sexes in their membership. This does not mean that both sexes are equally involved in and dependent upon these institutions in either social or economic terms. In the section on economic relations, we saw that because of their restricted options in the labor market, women find marriage an attractive alternative as an economic base. Marriage may be seen economically as an exchange of material values (provided by the husband) for service values (provided by the wife). In El Cañaveral, husbands may be said to enjoy a "sellers' market." That is, the material values which they can provide are sufficiently scarce that husbands can make additional demands on wives. One of their options is to demand a high degree of control over their wives' activities, typically seen in a curtailment of sexual freedoms and social relationships outside the family. Husbands legitimately command fidelity from their wives. I found no evidence that women can command loyalty or sexual fidelity, or restrict the mobility of husbands; if some men are faithful, it appears to be of their own volition. (In my experience, it has never even been hinted that women can successfully command fidelity or that faithful men are fearful of their wives.)

Apart from the social effects of economic inequality in marriage, there are also social effects attendant upon the nature of the work performed by each sex. Men's work takes them away from familial relationships and requires their participation in larger social relations with peers and with the plantation hierarchy. These relationships cannot be challenged, for they are part of the material basis for the household. In contrast, women's work as wives involves contact only with children and other members of the immediate family; other contacts are gratuitous. Housework is largely an individualized responsibility of the wife. Even in an extended household, each woman may have her own hearth; each woman will cook and wash for her own man and children.

Additional features of women's situation in El Cañaveral imply limited social contacts for the wife compared to women in other areas. For example, the public water fountain and washstand is a central locus reserved for all-female social contacts in many other parts of Guatemala. This is absent in El Cañaveral because most homes have a private source of running water. Similarly, in many peasant areas the role of market vendor is a legitimate extension of a wife's role which provides a context for wider social relations. There is no marketplace in El Cañaveral. Rancheria women have little to sell; they produce few garden or craft products beyond those that are for household use. Their role in the markets in town is largely limited to that of consumer.

Formal Community Organization

Beyond the household is the community, the sphere of public activity. Such activity occurs in both formal and informal contexts. Formal activities involve defined organizations having publicly recognized status, identifiable membership, a specified sphere of interest and some specialized leadership roles. Informal activities occur without benefit of defined organization, or at best involve organizations of flexible membership having no established leadership roles. While this formal/informal schema does not allow completely unambiguous classification of all types of social organization, it is generally possible to distinguish organizations or activities according to the extent to which formality or informality prevails.

Politics. Politics in El Cañaveral encompasses several levels of interest, which include the local union, formal political authority, and elections. In terms of effective participation by the ranchero community, the union stands out as the most important formal organization. The power of the union as an organized force was demonstrated with a major strike that occurred during the period of research. The relevance of the actions and issues of the strike to the women of El Cañaveral will be examined.

The union. Membership in the union encompasses essentially the entire permanent work force of rancheros, some 470 persons. Predictably, female membership in the union is negligible since so few women are rancheras. The union leader said there were only six women members: the two washerwomen and the four nurses. However, the women themselves are not certain of their position. One woman knows the union took down her name, but still thought she might not really be a member. Further, when asked if they ever speak in the union meetings, the women rancheras said they did not. One woman explained that women do not know how to speak publicly, and that she did not know the proper words. Another said that, "Women do not talk in union meetings, they only go to hear. Men talk. If women have something to say, they talk it over with the men before the meeting and then the men say it for them in the meeting."

Since the union hall is a structure with open walls located in a central part of the ranchería, union meetings are hardly "closed door" affairs; anyone in the community can follow their proceedings simply by standing in the yard or street outside the building. Attendance was high shortly before and during the strike. During one meeting, the hall was filled to capacity with about 500 men and 25 women inside.

The women came in pairs or small groups. Only one or two appeared to be accompanied by men. Quite a few women brought children and did not stay for long stretches. Obviously, not just the women rancheras, but the wives of some of the male workers were sufficiently concerned about the possibility of a strike to attend. In most meetings, women and girls tending younger children clustered around outside the building, standing and chatting amongst themselves, occasionally turning an ear to the proceedings within. As predicted, no women spoke publicly at any of the meetings I attended.[16] On the eve of the strike, some women still did not know the meaning of the term *huelga*, or strike. Within the hall, when the votes for a strike were taken, the women in attendance did not join the men in shouts of "strike" or affirmation, although they stood up with the men when the final vote for a strike was taken and was unanimous.

The major issues behind the strike include housing rights of rancheros (who were demanding certain compensation and guarantees in the face of company demolition of worker housing to enlarge the area for refining operations) and job rights for the "sons" of rancheros. The latter point could have been of particular interest to women, and they way it was handled revealed the complete lack of influence that women have in matters relating to company work. The question of job preference is explicitly treated in the union-management pact:

> Article 3b: Hijos de rancheros. It (the pact) is also applicable to the *hijos de rancheros* (children/sons of rancheros[17]), men or women, in that which refers to the preference to work for the Company and salaries for minors of age.

The grievance, as expressed by a worker who spoke, was that the grown sons of rancheros were not getting preference as in the agreement. Instead, the temporary workers, the cuadrilleros, were working for 80 cents per day, less than the minimum wage. It was argued that the Company should get rid of 100 or 200 cuadrilleros, hire the unemployed sons of rancheros, and pay all workers the same legal minimum of Q. 1.12 per day. It should be noted that although the worker-management agreement appears to explicitly include daughters of rancheros (in the same way that they are included in the health and education benefits), there was no intention by any of the workers or negotiators for the union to press this issue as far as daughters were concerned. Jobs for their "*hijos*" became a major rallying point among the workers, and a point they eventually won from management.

Some incidents during this period further reveal lack of concern for women as members of the community to be affected by the strike and its outcomes. After a succession of local union members had voiced their grievances, small and large, a union organizer from the union central office gave the most stirring speech, which he closed with very strong lines:

> ¡Hombres tienen que luchar como hombres!
> ¡O Mañana tienen que llorar como mujeres!
> (Men must struggle like men, or tomorrow
> they must cry like women!)

At least two other leaders closed in a similar style with references to "hitching up their pants" because tomorrow it will be too late. It is certain that statements such as these associating action with maleness do little to make women feel that they have a potential interest in the struggle.

Only at one point, on the eve of the strike, did the men remember that women might be able to contribute. They called on the women to come the next day and shout that they want jobs for their hijos. Tellingly, the women remained largely at home the next day and throughout the strike, doing their usual household tasks. Apart from listening in at union meetings, they never openly participated or supported the strike proceedings.

Formal political authority Since the plantation is a private enterprise, many of the political functions that one expects to find in a civil community are attenuated and/or performed by company management. For the most part, political decisions affecting the ranchería originate in the administrative offices and are carried out by employees of the company. The company assumes responsibility for maintaining order by hiring a number of night watchmen and guards. The two local *alcaldes auxiliares* (assistant mayors) are selected by the town alcalde from among four candidates proposed by management. The lack of democratic procedures here largely excludes ranchero men as well as women from the political process. However, ranchero men have slightly more influence, both through union representation and because the employees assigned to keep order on the plantation are always male.

Voting While the significance of voting in national elections as an expression of popular will cannot be taken for granted, one may nonetheless view the act of voting as an indication of some degree of participation in political rituals. In this respect, we find that despite the granting of the vote to all citizens in 1958, very few women of the ranchería vote. Twenty-four out of twenty-five women questioned in the ranchería have never voted, compared to only two out of twenty-four men. While voting is mandatory for men, and few would want to admit noncompliance with the law, this does not diminish the fact that it is socially and legally acceptable and expected that women do not vote. Women's reasons for not participating include statements such as:

"It never crossed my mind."
"I know I have the right, but I have no inclination."
"I do not have a *cedula* (identification paper)."
"My name was not on the list."
"Here they do not ask women to vote. By constitution it is an obligation, but they do not enforce it."
"I do not like to stand in line because there are almost all men. You feel it is ugly when there are just a few women and many men."
"I have not voted. Women do not vote much, almost not at all . . . . Mainly the women who work as teachers or who work for the government vote."

Other politics Apart from the formal political structures, political activity in the past has included guerrilla movements and at present includes threats and assassination attempts against management. This issue was too sensitive to investigate at the time of my research due to the tension surrounding the strike, so that I do not have information on the extent of women's participation or complicity.

Religion. The two major forms of religious expression and organization within El Cañaveral are Catholicism and Evangelism.[18] Within the ranchería, a small survey shows that the two religious systems are roughly equal in terms of numbers of adherents, with only a few people claiming no affiliation whatsoever. However, levels of active participation are notably different. While most Catholics rarely attend reli-

171

gious services, at least half of the Evangelists sampled (Table 4–4) attend services regularly, often several times a week. Discussions of religion with informants give the impression that for Catholics religion is largely a passive affiliation or part of their identity rather than a part of their activity; for Evangelists activity is essential.

Religion provides one of the few formal organizational milieux in which women of the ranchería are welcomed and where they can participate directly. However, Roman Catholicism and Evangelism differ in their modus operandi and it is worthwhile to examine the relative attractions that they hold for women.

Many people of the ranchería claim firm allegiance to Roman Catholicism, yet strongest and most regular attendance at Mass is provided by the indígenes who populate the migrant labor gangs. Among the permanent ranchero population, only about ten women and four or five men come regularly to Sunday Mass. During the week, masses are attended almost exclusively by indígenes. The priest explained the high attendance among the indigenes as follows:

> The church is a diversion for them. They have no movies, bars, or casinos in the galeras. So they go to drink beer in the stores or some go to Mass, some go to Protestant sessions. They go to Mass not so much for religion as for diversion, since they do not have to pay for church.

One might speculate that the general lack of attendance by permanent residents at routine celebrations of the mass is, in part, related to a desire to maintain social distance from the poorer church-going indígenes who clearly occupy the lowest position in the local status hierarchy.

For the people of the ranchería, Catholicism is centered less on the mass than on the celebration of special occasions, rituals and holidays such as funerals, marriages, girls' fifteenth birthday celebrations, Christmas *posadas*, fiestas, the patron saint's day, and other special

Table 4-4. Religious Affiliations of Each Sex at El Cañaveral

	Evangelists		Catholic		Neither	Total Sample
	Total	Active	Total	Active		
Female	16	8	15	1	1	32
Male	11	7	14	1	1	26
Total	27	15	29	2	2	58

holy days. The priest asserts that among rancheros there is an emphasis on images, candles, and superstition within the home, but very little knowledge of the "real" religion.

While most Catholics in the ranchería are largely inactive in the institutionalized form of religious expression, there is a *hermandad*, or religious committee, composed of both sexes, which organizes processions and the care of the patron saint. The committee has a membership of seven women and nine men, some of whom belong to the empleado category. This committee is dominated by a woman of the ranchería. Thus, despite a generally low level of activity, it seems that women of the *ranchería* are as likely as men to participate in Catholic religious organization.

The system of *compadrazgo* (godparenthood) is also evident in El Cañaveral as a means of establishing ritual kinship in the context of Catholic sacraments such as baptism. While most Catholics have compadres, it appears that the relationship is not a very binding tie.

Evangelism generally involves a stronger commitment than Catholicism among people on the ranchería. Many of its followers are converts, as opposed to Catholics, who have stayed with the religion of their parents. Conversion implies that individuals have made a personal commitment to behave in accordance with their newly adopted religious beliefs. Attendance at religious functions is one manifestation of this commitment.

There are two Evangelical temples within the central areas of workers' housing, located roughly two blocks apart, and memberships are distinct. I have detailed information on one of them, which claims a membership of about 115 people, although not all of these attend regularly. This church has meetings both during the day and at night. During the day, women dominate the meetings since the men are at work, while in the evenings the meetings are mixed.

This church has organized two special subgroups. One is a "Feminine Society" of about thirty members and the other is a mixed youth group of about thirty-five members. The women's group meets one day each week. They have an executive committee of seven elected officers. Their activities include organizing fiestas, visiting and "activating" nonbelievers, studying the Bible, and organizing trips to visit churches in other areas. They also visit the sick and collect money and food which they give to people who are experiencing special hardships such as death or illness in the family. Educational activities have ranged from teaching the "message" to teaching women how to sew, cook, and make flowers. Although men do not have an equivalent "Masculine

Society," there have been classes to teach the men to play music: accordion, harmonica, and guitar.

Like the Catholic church, which is always headed by a male priest, the Evangelical congregations are also headed by male pastors, but since the latter can be married to women active in the church, it does not appear that leadership is as remote from women as it is in the Catholic hierarchy. Although the Catholic church has a larger following among those of lowest status, the indígenes, the Evangelical internal organization is more democratic. In the latter system, both women and men preach. Due to their differing work schedules, women generally preach during the day and men preach at night. A different person preaches each day of the week. On an average night, one of the temples has twenty-five to thirty women and men in attendance while the other generally draws well over fifty. As in the Catholic church, women and men sit on opposite sides of the room. The Evangelists generally have less than 10 percent indígenes in attendance; in this they are clearly more community-based than "catholic" in their membership. Children also attend services, some of them sleeping through very loud and lively meetings.

Although one of the Evangelical congregations is fairly subdued, the other is noted for its rousing singing and clapping. On some nights they not only have a lead singer with a microphone, but a complete back-up of guitar, bass, and drum. The whole congregation sings, while non-members gather outside (which is not really necessary since the music can be heard clearly throughout the neighborhood) to listen and enjoy the music. If the local priest believes the Mass is a form of entertainment to many of its participants, there is no doubt the Evangelists offer stiff competition in that regard. On the other hand, Evangelists prohibit certain kinds of entertainment that are acceptable among Catholics, such as drinking and dancing. Although both religions prohibit divorce and adultery, the more organized membership of the Evangelists exerts more social pressure against those who "fall into vice."

In a community where women do not normally participate in organized public activities, it is significant that they play an active role in religious organizations. It appears that their participation is possible because the religions present in the ranchería are in no way threatening to the status quo of male control over the family. The religions support the family organization and encourge women to endure a bad marriage. For this reason, attendance at religious functions is often tolerated by husbands who otherwise oppose their wives' desires to work or engage in social activities outside the home. One woman described her husband's reaction as follows:

Since he knew me—that I was not a woman who went chatting with other men for pleasure—he was not so suspicious. He would say, "I know when you are talking with some man, you are talking of Evangelism, and not talking of other things."

It is interesting that many of the most economically dependent women in my sample are Evangelical converts. In cases where their husbands are also converts, women associate real material benefits with the change.

Organized religions, particularly Evangelism, in El Cañaveral can be seen as institutions which mitigate the social and economic inequities that affect women when they become economically dependent on men and when the family is just one among many competitors for a man's wages. Without threatening the economic base of marriage, Evangelism provides women with an arena of legitimized social activity outside the home, and even the opportunity to travel to other towns for religious meetings. Indeed, it strengthens the social and economic base of the family by prohibiting competing activities such as drinking, dancing, and (directly and indirectly) other women. Perhaps more important, Evangelism provides a social alternative to male "street culture." In the ranchería, many men seek recognition by demonstrating that they can buy more drinks or more women than the next man. These are "street" activities which severely hurt the economically dependent women and children. Evangelists combat this, providing an arena where men who lead virtuous lives can gain recognition and respect from the congregation when they participate in preaching and leading the hymns at the nightly meetings.

Catholicism and Evangelism can be seen to have different kinds of appeal within the ranchería, despite the fact that both are religions that provide socially acceptable forms of extra-domestic activity for women. It appears that the local Evangelists offer more creative assistance in solving severe social problems that arise in this workers' community due to the uneven distribution of economic power between the sexes. Women's gradual loss of subsistence functions and general lack of access to jobs has coincided with a gradual increase in the modern skills and cash income of the men as rancheros. As opposed to benefits in kind such as food rations and houses, cash wages are easily converted to individualistic purposes by those with paid jobs. If the family is to survive with only one wage earner, some social controls have to develop to pressure that earner to consistently share wages with dependents. Religious organizations such as the Evangelists in El Cañaveral attempt this type of social control. Yet as much as Evangelism permits women formally to meet to help each other, preach, and sing, it joins Catholicism in its opposition to divorce and the promotion of monogamy with domestic, dependent roles for women.

Education. The primary school at El Cañaveral is free for the children of those who are employed by the company. Children of salaried employees, rancheros, and voluntarios make up the school population, although the latter are disadvantaged in that their education suffers discontinuities corresponding to the seasonal nature of their fathers' work. Children of migrant workers are rarely brought to El Cañaveral, and when they are brought they do not enroll in school since their stay is so short. As can be seen in Table 4–5, the sex ratio in the school is nearly even, and there appears to be no discrimination against girls regarding their right to an education at the primary level at El Cañaveral.

Equal enrollment does not always mean that the educational content is the same for each sex. Certainly, literacy and basic mathematical skills are of great importance in the modern world, and the school at El Cañaveral appears to teach these skills with equal emphasis for both sexes. But the school also provides orientation and preparation for adult jobs and careers, and it is precisely in this area that classes are divided by sex. For example, girls receive classes in "education for the home" in all grades. They learn to make tablecloths, place mats, and bags, as well as to crochet and embroider, and to sew on a sewing machine. Boys, on the other hand, learn carpentry. They paint and make furniture for the school. They learn to measure, to use hammers, saws, and files. Sports activities are also divided by sex. Thus, while both sexes are provided with some educational tools needed to survive in a modern world, they are also prepared to accept sexual segregation. The fact

Table 4–5. Primary School Attendance by Boys and Girls at El Cañaveral

| Grade | Number | | Total | Percentage Girls |
	Boys	Girls		
First	64	53	117	45
Second	60	43	103	42
Third	43	50	93	54
Fourth	37	53	90	59
Fifth	45	33	78	42
Sixth	45	33	78	42
Total	294	265	559	47%

that the teaching staff is entirely female further reinforces segregated role concepts.

To continue their education beyond primary level, children must commute to schools in town, where they have to pay school fees which may range from Q. 3 to 15 per month. Although children of salaried employees usually continue in school, not many children of the ranchería are able to continue unless their fathers earn fairly high wages. Significantly, a few of the older teen-age boys are able to get seasonal work with the company and thus can contribute to the costs of higher education. Since there is greater career specialization in secondary school, it would be interesting to know if greater differentiation between the sexes occurs at this level. The experience in most industrializing countries suggests that sexual discrimination and segregation are maintained at the highest levels of any educational system even though they are dropping at lower levels of the system as education becomes available to the majority of the population (Deckard 1975; Sullerot 1971; Boserup 1970). However, the small number of children in secondary school in my sample, combined with their dispersion to a number of different secondary schools in the town meant that I was unable to verify this hypothesis for the ranchería population.

It has often been suggested that there is a correlation between the lack of education and the lack of job opportunities among certain population sectors. In El Cañaveral, the available data on the adult ranchería population indicate that education is not a major factor in the unequal distribution of job opportunities by sex. A sample of forty-nine adult women and thirty-one adult men of the ranchería, showed that 67 percent of the women as compared to 74 percent of the men are literate.[19] Secondary education among the adult ranchería population is exceptional for either sex, while the number of years of primary school completed is not notably higher for men. Thus, illiteracy or lack of education cannot be taken as important reasons for the exclusion of ranchería women from formal plantation jobs.

Acquisition of job skills Although formal educational levels are not highly differentiated between the women and men of the ranchería, semiformal education and the acquisition of jobs skills are differentiated by sex. Semiformal education includes on-the-job training where young, unskilled workers become apprentices and gradually acquire skills that are needed for a better economic position. In El Cañaveral, on-the-job training is common among the men who work in the refinery. As the refining operations have grown, the need for skilled workers has been largely met by training rancheros and their sons for the new jobs. In many respects, the skills which the male workers possess are the result of acquiring jobs from the company, rather than the result of prior training. This allows for a certain mobility within the ranchero status and even on occasion from ranchero to empleado status.

Women of the ranchería do not have access to such on-the-job training with the company. For one thing, the few positions that the company holds out for women are either unskilled (laundering) or professional (teaching, nursing, and secretarial), with no intermediary range of skilled jobs. Nearly all of the professional women employed at El Cañaveral grew up and received their training independently outside the plantation community, and continue to reside outside as well.[20] Compared to men, it is much more difficult for women of the ranchería to improve their personal socioeconomic status within the plantation. Some young women receive on-the-job training as domestic workers, or, if they have the means, they invest in sewing courses in town. Beyond this, women of the ranchería who seek training or education for better jobs must direct their efforts toward an external milieu and a job market with which they have had little contact.

Social Services and Recreation. There are three cooperatives in El Cañaveral that are organized to provide services to the community: a credit cooperative, a food cooperative, and a bus cooperative. The bus cooperative is definitely a boon to the entire community because it provides cheap and frequent transportation from the various workers' barrios to the town where people can utilize a full range of urban services such as markets, stores, banks, and restaurants. This is particularly important for women, who more often than men lack other forms of transportation.

The food cooperative is a similar service designed to be of community benefit by providing cheaper food. It has only some fifty members. Women whose husbands paid the membership fee report that they prefer to shop in town markets because it is cheaper.[21]

The credit cooperative is essentially a credit union enabling its members to accumulate savings and to receive loans. Its membership is drawn from the rancheros, empleados, administrators, and other members of the plantation community, plus a small percentage of outside town residents with indirect ties to El Cañaveral. Data on membership shows that out of 509 members, only 65, or 12 percent, are female. Some of these are the economically dependent wives or young daughters of empleados and rancheros; others are company employees such as the secretary, nurses, and teachers; and others are economically active women of the ranchería and the town. Although I was unable to establish the exact number of women of the ranchería who benefit from this service, it is clear that only a small fraction of them are able to put aside some personal income as savings.

In addition to the cooperatives, there is a small library in the workers' barrio that was established by a voluntary organization called the Progressive Youth Club. This library has scheduled two hours of service in the afternoons for women, and two hours in the evening for men, but was not opened as scheduled during my research. Very few women were aware of the library, and none that I interviewed had used it.

An important aspect of these four organizations is that in each case, the executive committee (*junta directiva*) is made up of men only. The Progressive Youth Club is an all-male group composed of ranchería youths who are active in the union, while the leadership of the cooperatives includes men who are empleados as well as rancheros. Two relevant considerations are that (a) in general, male members of the El Cañaveral community have more capital to invest in organizations, such as the credit and food cooperatives, that require an initial deposit as a condition of membership, and (b) in their job-related activities in the office, factory, field, and union, men have more expeience in organized groups and have regular contact with each other in ways that permit them to develop the habit and skills of working together for common ends. Women lack both of these preconditions—surplus cash and organizational experience—and are thus largely unprepared to take part in such community service organizations. Significantly, these organizations have created a small number of paid jobs which replicate the plantation job structure such that women are only employed as clerks in the cooperative food store, while men are exclusively employed as bus drivers, assistants, and office personnel for the credit cooperative. It is interesting that women are included as consumers of these services, but they have no role in the decisions governing their operation.

Different degrees of formal organization can be seen in the recreational patterns of the sexes. Sports are an illustration. Soccer is the dominant sport in El Cañaveral and, as in most of Guatemala, it is played only by males. Boys learn to play in the street, in school, and in Boy Scouts; older boys and men continue to play in organized teams and sports clubs. El Cañaveral has its own soccer teams and hosts regular Sunday matches with teams from other companies and other cities. Crowds that are predominantly male, ranging in ages from small boys to old men, gather to watch. Soccer players enjoy a certain prestige in the community[22] and participation allows young men to compete for social status and recognition.

179

Women and girls lack comparable sports clubs or athletic activities where they are able to receive the admiration of the plantation community. Basketball and volleyball are sports that are considered acceptable for young women, although they are also played by males and occasionally are played in integrated groups. Girls learn to play basketball and volleyball in school. There were reports that an informal group of girls and young women from both the ranchería and empleado barrios played weekly basketball games amongst themselves, but they did not play at all during the period of my research. In sharp contrast to the organized soccer games of boys and men, and the weekly volleyball games held by the men of the administrative staff, I did not personally observe any athletic activities for women or girls, whether on the basketball court, soccer field, or volleyball and tennis courts. Athletic activities are not as prestigious for girls or women as they are for boys and men. Some of the young women who like to play basketball indicate that it is not considered entirely proper beyond a certain age, or when a woman is married. They add that only a few women continue to participate in sports after leaving school, and the one or two married women who do are considered exceptional.

The annual fiesta at the end of the sugar harvest emphasizes the differences in the ways the sexes can gain prestige in recreational contexts. Although I was not present for these events, numerous informants described the triumphs of young men in sports and athletic competitions, while young women were remembered only for their role as competitors or winner of the election for "Queen of the Fiesta."[23]

Scouting activities show a similar sexual asymmetry. There are Boy Scouts in El Cañaveral, but there are no Girl Scouts or comparable organizations for girls. Boy Scouts are given active support by the top management and are linked to an international organization. Within El Cañaveral, the scouts organize regular outings such as overnight camping or climbing a volcano. The boys who participate come from both the ranchero and empleado divisions of the community. While a few mothers and teen-age girls participate in chaperoning activities, the focus of the organization is undisputably that of offering recreation and organized cultural experiences to all-male groups.

Informal Community Organization

Kinship. Many households in the ranchería are related to each other by kinship and marriage. Ranchería endogamy is fairly common, while the migration of one member of a village to El Cañaveral has often been followed by other relatives in search of work. It is jokingly said that with so many relatives and intermarriages, there are really only five families in the ranchería. Indeed, certain surnames are extremely common. Kinship is bilateral and the maintenance of kinship ties beyond those of parent, child, and sibling is largely voluntary. Kinship is important for favors and contacts, but there is no evidence of corporate groups based on kinship. This is consistent with the fact that the workers, as tenants, have little control over property and their economic position is based on individual wage work.

For women, kin are important for exchanging such favors as small loans, occasional help with child care, or help with illness. Closest relations are between mothers and daughters and between siblings. When asked about their friendships, women with relatives on the finca frequently claimed that their relatives, especially sisters were their best friends. Sisters tend to be cited in the context of "true" friends, or *amigas de confianza* (trustworthy friends). The tendency to place greater confidence in relatives is reflected in some of the following statements:

Yolanda, age thirty:
>I visit my sisters almost daily. I go to talk. I have friends in some of the barrios, but we do not visit each other. We talk when we pass by. I do not get involved. I don't want to have *revoltijos* (mix-ups).

Davida, age thirty:
>I have eight brothers and sisters here. They are my only friends. One married sister who lives up the street visits each day. I get along well with my neighbors.

Several women with young children maintain that when they wish to leave the house, they can leave their children in the care of their mother or a sister, but that it is not customary to ask the neighbors. An important consideration in relation to the emphasis on kin for friendship and trust is that some women go straight from their parents' guardianship to their husband's house. Lacking any nonfamilial work experience, these women also lack experience in forming outside friendships.

Neighbors and friends. As compared to close kin, women seem reluctant to extend their confidence to neighbors. Many conversations with informants reveal a basic distrust or coolness toward neighbors. One word which recurs frequently in the context of neighbors is to be "*evitada*," which means to avoid trouble, not to meddle or get involved. The sentiments expressed by Matilda were echoed by other women:

My neighbors have always treated me very well. I will do favors but I stay out of quarrels. I am *evitada*. If someone needs me, I will do a favor. I will help if there are sick people: I help in the house if they do not have help; I wash their clothes. But I never go from house to house criticizing the life of other people. From that come quarrels.

The force of gossip repeatedly enters into women's concerns about their relations with neighbors. According to Natalia, age thirty-five:

Neighbors do not do favors like watching each other's children. There is a lot of gossip. If one asks a favor, people gossip. If a woman dresses well, they gossip. If a woman dresses poorly, they gossip. There is jealously and envy. A woman cannot walk alone with a man or everyone says they are lovers or something.

One way of mitigating the possibility that gossip might disrupt a marriage is to limit one's excursions outside the house to the most "legitimate" contexts, such as visiting kin or going to church, where it is difficult to make accusations of infidelity. Jacinta, age forty-seven, describes some other aspects involving friendship and gossip:

I have a sister here. We visit occasionally. Married women do not have friends. I have only one friend. She is an *amiga de confianza* and comes to visit. She helps if I am sick. If a true friend helps you, they do not advertise it to everyone . . . . A true friend does a favor and keeps it to herself. You can trust her with your things. You cannot hire someone to help you when you are sick because they have to *guardar la boca* and *guardar las cosas* (keep their mouths closed and keep your things safe). Most people are not like that. The reason there is so much gossip is that there is not enough work in the house.

This statement reveals the delicacy with which a real friendship must be handled. Jacinta also suggests that underemployment for women is an important factor contributing to the weight of gossip and social pressure within the community.

Yolanda, mentioned above, gives an account of one *revoltijo* or quarrel she was involved in with her neighbors. The married woman who used to live next door was her friend. When her fifty-year-old husband decided he preferred a twenty-year-old wife, her friend left and came to stay temporarily at Yolanda's house. The second wife was angry at Yolanda and began to gossip about her. According to Yolanda, the young woman was an extremely quarrelsome neighbor.

Women who grew up together on the plantation, attended school together, or migrated from the same village are more likely to include some nonkin in their circle of friends. Flora, age thirty-one describes her friendships as follows:

> One is a sister-in-law, some are sisters and nieces, and others are women whom I used to play with when we were single . . . . We go to movies together once each week, and sometimes we go to fiestas.

Perhaps because Flora is separated from her husband, she seems freer than others to maintain a wide circle of friends, some of whom are also single or separated.

Virginia and Matilda are an example of two women who migrated from the same village and who have maintained a close friendship for many years. Matilda is remotely related to Virginia's husband. Some of the favors they have exchanged include the lodging of Matilda and her husband with Virginia's family one year; Matilda's physical defense of Virginia one night when Virginia's husband came home drunk and attacked her with a machete, followed by Matilda's taking Virginia to her house for refuge until Virginia could safely return. Day-to-day favors include casual exchanges of food, or perhaps a cutting of a decorative plant, doing laundry when one of them is sick, sharing an iron, and so forth. Such close friendships appear to be rare.

"Wine, men, and song." Amusements in El Cañaveral include drinking, dancing, and movies. Not many married women participate in these activities. A few of the women I interviewed occasionally go to movies with their husbands, but they do not go with other friends of either sex. More commonly, women said their husbands go out to movies without them. One young wife reports that her husband goes to the movies each week in town, but he does not let her go. She says:

> The single life is happier. When you are married, you cannot go out. I used to love to go to dances and when I was single he [her husband] invited me to dances in town. Now he no longer does that. He does not like to dance.

On the same theme, another woman explained the situation in a roundabout way:

> I do not like to go to movies. My husband does. I do not like to go because there is no money. My husband goes every week or two. If I go, then there is no money to buy food. Single women go to the movies, but husbands do not let their wives go . . . . If I were to go to the movies without my husband's permission, he would hit me. I do not ask permission because he would not give it. And he does not want me to go out with him . . . .

183

Men do not ask permission of their wives. They say, "You are not my mother."

Movies, dancing, and drinking seem to be acceptable social activities for men, and to some extent for single women or unattached women, while women who are currently married rarely participate freely. Three-fourths of the married women said that they did not go out to movies or other types of entertainment.[24] The explanation given by half of them referred to their husband's restrictions, while the remainder cited their Evangelical beliefs or the problems of child care. Indeed, very few women and girls attend the Saturday night movies shown in the social club. The crowd resembles that at the Sunday morning soccer field.

The sale of hard liquor is forbidden on the plantation. Those who drink or go to bars for entertainment do so in town. This is an aspect of plantation life that I did not observe firsthand. My female informants did not go to town for this purpose, but they described it as a habitual male activity on payday. Drinking beer on the plantation is done openly by men, but the only women I observed doing so were several who are economically self-supporting. These exceptional three or four women would sit outside on the front patio of the house where beer was sold and buy each other a few rounds on payday.

Apart from the social forms of recreation and leisure activities so far considered, a number of households in the ranchería have been able to purchase modern conveniences and luxuries which also enhance leisure. Televisions are not uncommon in the ranchería. They provide a particularly important form of entertainment for women, for they are a part of a *domestic* setting. Women with televisions in their houses typically have one or two regular female visitors, such as a sister or close neighbor, who stop in during the afternoons or evenings to watch favorite programs, usually *telenovelas* (soap operas). Women bring their children with them and hence do not deviate from the role expectations that a wife and mother belongs indoors with her children.

Bicycles and motorcycles are other modern luxuries that are common in the ranchería. These vehicles, designed for outdoor use and individual mobility, are almost never used by females. A few of the young women and girls know how to ride them, but as with other outdoor activities, after a certain age they stop because they are ashamed. In all of the households I visited, there was only one case in which a female owned a wheeled vehicle. This was a sixteen-year-old girl who won a big motorcycle in a raffle. Although it was undeniably hers, she never used it. Her older brother took it over "to break it in" with some half-hearted promises to teach her how to ride it. She wanted to ride it, but made excuses that it was too big for her to handle and that people would gossip about her if she rode it. Throughout the ranchería, I found households where men and boys owned bicycles or motorcycles, but the women were uniformly unable to use them. One married woman explained:

> In the afternoons, a few of the girls here ride bikes. I used to ride as a child with one of my girlfriends. People here talk if a woman rides a bike or motorcycle. They think they are for men only. Now I only ride behind my husband on the back of his motorcycle.

An indication of the wide use of bicycles and motorcycles by men in the ranchería is the fact that on an average workday during the non-harvest season, I counted forty-two bicycles and twenty motorcycles parked by the factory. Since there is a regular bus service, it appears that bicycles are important for leisure, independence, and status as well as transportation. The social pressure against their use by women may arise because a woman on a bicycle is not "home with her children"; she is not restricted to a fixed route. Bicycles seem to imply more independence than the community is willing to tolerate from women.

Summary

In considering the economic situation of women at El Cañaveral, it has been shown that women generally lack direct access to plantation work and the benefits it confers. Informal work is available to a limited extent, but there is plenty of competition both within El Cañaveral and, of course, from the neighboring town. Women who have few economic options hope to share the income and benefits accorded to the privileged category of unionized (male) workers. In so doing, many of them adopt tactics of submission toward the former and competition among themselves to hold their position.

While the arbitrary or individualistic exercise of economic power by the men of El Cañaveral may seem to be just another manifestation of Latin American machismo, it should be clear that such exercise of power is effective for two primary reasons: (1) the denial of secure, well-paying jobs to women that are equivalent to those held by unionized male workers, and (2) the presence of a large pool of women in the neighboring town who are willing to provide services in exchange for minimal economic security and benefits. Essentially then, the male rancheros (not the migrant workers) find that with respect to female services and companionship, it is a buyer's market. One might note, finally, that while the management in El Cañaveral is directly responsible for the exclusion of women from their labor force, it is the cumulative effect of many such managements that ensures that women will be competing for very low rewards as they offer services to males in the plantation communities and towns.

Women's social relations outside the home have few formal bases for their foundation and legitimization. Because they are economically dependent on their husbands, women's most legitimate sphere of activity is in their husband's house, caring for children. In this situation, kinship is the most effective basis for friendship because its legitimacy is of the same order as that of marriage itself. Until girls began attending school in greater numbers, few of them were permitted to circulate among groups that were not kin-based. Frequently, marriage seems to entail a loss of freedom to associate, even with female friends who in theory should not be considered a threat to the husband's control of his family. Nonkin friendships for women appear from the community point of view to be ties that are competitive with the marriage. We have seen that in particular instances they provide an important refuge to a woman when her marriage is in crisis and in that sense can undermine a husband's presumptions of power over his wife.

Women's social relations are largely confined to people in the ranchería. Kin ties extend farther but are largely limited to annual visits. Very few women speak of friendships across employment categories. When they do, there is usually a kinship or ritual kinship (compadre/comadre) relationship involved if their friends are empleados. Ranchera women maintain that they have almost no contact with the women who come as migrant workers. These women generally remain in or near the galeras, which are located at a distance from the permanent housing, and given that their stay is of short duration, one could not expect many friendships to develop.

This discussion of formal and informal social organization in the ranchería shows that women's low level of participation in public life parallels their low level of participation in the wage labor force. Women are not absolutely excluded from either formal economic or social positions outside the home, but they are only found in very limited spheres which, by modern convention, are thought suitable for women. Similarly, in both the economic and social spheres, women who are active are most likely to operate in informal channels in order to circumvent (or survive) the restrictions imposed by other social and economic structures.

186

The dynamics that operate to keep women from attaining a greater role in the formal organizations of the community may be seen as a combination of two major forces. First, there is the exclusion of ranchera women from most forms of formal employment outside the home. This deprives them of the financial base and shared contacts which facilitate effective participation in public organizations. Second, the lack of economic options for women induces them to accept economic dependence in marriage. The stronger economic position of husbands enables them to personally restrict their wives' participation in public life. In this context, women's remaining options are to seek interstitial roles in the economy and to manipulate informal social ties in order to further their own interests as individuals.

11. Evangelist Rancheros: Bible Reading and Material Gains

CHAPTER FIVE

San Lorenzo: An Urban Squatter Settlement

San Lorenzo is a lower class *colonia*[1] (district) filling a ravine within one of the central zones of Guatemala City. It is one section of a larger squatter settlement, or shantytown, of a type common in Guatemala City and many other large cities in underdeveloped countries. The percentage of Guatemala City's population living in shantytowns during the 1960s was estimated to be around 15 percent (Roberts 1973:35). With continued rapid growth of the city, it is likely that this percentage is even higher at the present. (Fieldwork in San Lorenzo is described in Appendix Two.)

The population of San Lorenzo was roughly 2,000 according to a census estimate for the early 1960s (Roberts 1973:44) but a more recent census of squatter settlements places the population closer to 3,000 (Rojas and Marroquin 1970). A tabulation from the 1964 census shows that the level of literacy in San Lorenzo is relatively high, at 70 percent of the population aged seven and over. The sex ratio is essentially equal. There are 5.5 persons per household. Ethnically, the population is overwhelmingly Ladino, with only 2.8 percent of the population "indigenous" (Ministerio de Trabajo 1969). Roberts, however, points out that the city is a locus of easy assimilation, while the census definition of "indigenous" "pertains only to whether the respondent habitually speaks an Indian tongue or wears Indian dress." He gives a slightly higher estimate of the indigenous population, at around 5 percent (1973:21, 60).

San Lorenzo consists entirely of squatter housing. The invasions of the ravine where the shantytown is located took place in the late 1950s. There were early attempts by the government to remove the population and, when removal proved impossible, later attempts to establish greater legal control and regularity within these areas. Residents of San Lorenzo have struggled both to obtain legal titles to their house sites and to improve the quality of their housing. Nonetheless, household conveniences and urban services remain minimal. Conditions are comparable to those reported in a survey of one of Guatemala's vast squatter settlements where four-fifths of the houses have but one room, more than half have no sanitary facilities, slightly under half still use wood for fuel and lack electricity, and more than 90 percent lack running water (INVI 1968). The overall density of settlement in San Lorenzo is 780 per hectare, or more than 1,900 persons per acre (Cuevas 1965).

San Lorenzo is primarily residential. It includes small churches and social centers, but there is no school. Play space for children is located only at one extremity of the settlement. Children generally crowd the dirt paths, where they play games and where the laundry is hung out to dry. Commercial activity in the form of household stores and workshops is common, but there is no market center within the colonia. For most work, marketing, education, and recreational activities residents must frequent the adjacent areas up on the streets outside the colonia. Transportation within San Lorenzo is by foot. It takes about fifteen minutes' walking to reach the central commercial zones of the city. Bus service is available on the city streets.

The appearance of San Lorenzo contrasts markedly with middle-class or even working-class colonias up at street level. Despite its proximity to the urban center, the steep descent of the slopes of the barranca makes it an undesirable location for housing, one that had been rejected by builders who could afford to be choosy. The overall impression is one of crowding and poverty. Lacking streets for automobile traffic, there are dirt pathways which flood with mud in the rainy season. Some paths are quite narrow, strewn with garbage and excreta. Yet considering the density of residence and the lack of urban services, the colonia is remarkably clean.[2]

Houses are constructed of any materials that are cheap and available. The typical house has a roof of corrugated metal, rough wooden planks for walls, and a dirt floor. Many inhabitants have been steadily improving their houses since the invasion. The kinds of improvements that one notices are block or adobe walls, cement floors, stretches of cement sidewalk outside the house, an additional room or an occasional addition of a second story. Most houses have some sort of small patio for washing and cooking which may be adorned with plants if space permits. The general lack of running water means that households need to have water manually hauled from one of several public faucets located within the colonia.

Economic Organization

As an urban settlement, San Lorenzo has a population that is heavily dependent on the market economy and economic activities that produce a cash income. Service and trade occupations, along with crafts and skilled labor, are common, while professional, managerial, white-collar, and agricultural occupations are exceptional. Economically, the colonia is home to a population that can be described as working class, combined with people who are not stably integrated into the working class, the so-called lumpen proletariat.

Economic Activity by Each Sex

The population economically active by sex is shown in Table 5-1 for two samples from San Lorenzo and environs.[3] The percentages of males economically active are similar in the two, but the percentages of females show a large difference. This is probably due to different methods of data collection. The low level of female economic activity in the 1969 sample appears to result from underreporting consistent with prevailing cultural views of women's role in the economy.[4] However, Cuevas (1965) in a study of three similar squatter settlements in Guatemala City reports that women form 42 percent of the total labor force, a figure which is comparable to the 45 percent which I found for San Lorenzo in 1974–75.

Table 5-1. Proportion of Economically Active of Each Sex (Age 16 and Over Earning Cash Income) in San Lorenzo, 1969 and 1974–75

Sample	Females		Males		Total*	
	%	(Sample Size)	%	(Sample Size)	%	(Sample Size)
1974–75	70.1	(117)	85.8	(120)	42.0	(491)
1969	34.3	(67)	82.9	(70)	33.9	(254)

* Includes employed minors along with adults as percentage of total population including children.
Sources: 1969: Orellana and de León 1972; 1974–75: author's sample.

190

12. *Guatemala City: Squatter Housing*

13. *San Lorenzo Women Getting Water from Public Faucet*

Elaborating on the characteristics of the workforce in San Lorenzo, the economic status of the adults in the 1974–75 sample is shown in Table 5-2 below.

Table 5-2. Economic Status of Female and Male Adults in San Lorenzo, 1974–75

Women			Men		
Status	%	(Number)	Status	%	(Number)
Employed	70.1	82	Employed	85.8	103
Unemployed	6.0	7	Unemployed	10.8	13
Disabled*	7.7	9	Disabled*	1.7	2
Student	0.9	1	Student	0.8	1
Volunteer	0.9	1	Unknown	0.8	1
Housekeeper	14.5	17			
Total subsample	100.1	117		99.9	120

* Includes temporary and permanent disabilities such as recent childbirth and old age.

Within the category of "employed," ten of the women are part-time workers. Typically, they wash or do domestic work on a day-work basis, several days a week. Similarly, within the category of employed males, there are 14 who were working at the time of the interview but who recently had experienced unemployment and/or considered their present work to be unstable. In this respect, it is significant that when I asked women about their employment status, women who worked irregularly or something less than full-time often responded that they only did housekeeping, *oficios domesticos*, implying that they did not "work." In contrast, men typically responded in terms of an occupation even though further discussion might reveal that their work over a period of months had been quite irregular and less than what one could call "full-time."

Another interesting aspect of occupational status is that men exhibit a higher rate of unemployment. Here again, cultural categories affect economic perceptions. Housekeeping absorbs women who are not in the labor force, while there is no comparable classification or activity legitimately open to men. Men who are not in the labor force normally describe themselves as unemployed or disabled. Yet women who describe themselves as housekeepers often say that they would go back to work if a good job were available. Despite such distinctions between

191

women and men, the pattern of economic activity in San Lorenzo as shown by the 1974–75 sample exhibits a remarkable degree of similarity between the sexes. In pursuit of the areas of differentiation, we will now examine the occupational distribution for each sex.

Occupational Distribution by Sex

Table 5-3 presents the percentage of each sex employed in broad occupational categories for samples from 1974–75 and 1969 along with a sample modified from Robert's study during 1966–1968 (1973:38). It is extremely rare for residents of the shantytown to occupy positions in the white-collar, managerial, or professional categories, but when this does occur, men are more likely than women to step out of traditional working-class job categories. There is a fairly consistent level of 83 to 88 percent of the women employed in the "sales and services" sector, and only 12 to 14 percent employed as "artisans, skilled workers, and operatives." In contrast, between 33 and 39 percent of the men are employed in the "sales and services" category but they are much more heavily represented in that of "artisans, skilled workers, and operatives," where their participation ranges from 57 to 63 percent.

Tables 5-4 and 5-5 provide a breakdown of occupations that were classified into these two major categories for the samples of 1974–75 and 1969. In the sales and services sector, most women are employed in occupations that involve domestic maintenance, preparing and selling food, or washing and ironing clothes. Only a small percentage are engaged in selling other types of products such as shoes, or are employed by a large establishment such as a hospital. There are no women employed as guards or cab drivers. In contrast, men in sales and services more often work in formal jobs for large establishments as sales agents, civil servants, and military personnel, and in occupations such as those related to the care or use of automobiles, bicycles, or corn mills.

Although Table 5-4 shows a numerically strong position for women in the sales and services sector, there is significantly more diversity in the types of work that men perform and it is more likely to take place in a nondomestic environment. In the 1974–75 sample, more than 80 percent of the women are working in a domestic environment, although nearly half of these women are not working in their *own* homes. In the 1969 sample, roughly 70 percent of the women work in a domestic context, but it is not possible to state what percentage actually work in their own homes. Men typically work in a nondomestic en-

192

Table 5-3. Occupational Categories of Economically Active Women and Men, 1969 and 1974-75

Category	Females (%)	Males (%)
Sample 1974-75		
Professional & bureaucratic	1	3
Managerial & executive	0	2
Office work	0	2
Agriculture	0	1
Sales & services	85	33
Artisan, skilled work, & operative	14	60
Total	100%	101%
(Subsample size) (includes minors)	(91)	(117)
Sample 1969		
Professional & bureaucratic	0	0
Managerial & executive	0	2
Office work	0	0
Agriculture	0	0
Sales & services	88	35
Artisan, skilled work, & operative	12	63
Total	100%	100%
(Subsample size) (includes minors)	(24)	(60)
Sample 1966-68		
White collar	0	4
Agriculture	0	0
Sales & services	83	39
Artisan, skilled work, & operative	14	57
Unspecified	3	0
Total	100%	100%
(Subsample size) (heads of household)	(37)	(90)

NOTE: In this table the category of sales occupations is combined with service occupations. I also combine artisans, skilled workers, and operatives into one category. This is due to ambiguities in classification of certain occupations. For instance, a person who makes and sells tortillas provides a service and is involved in sales. Similarly, shoemakers and seamstresses may work at home, in small shops, or in factories.

In using Robert's 1966-68 data, I combine his categories for "workers in established enterprises (factories, bus companies)" with "construction workers" and "craftsmen (shoemakers, tailors, dressmakers)." I also combine his categories for "traders" and "service workers (police, domestic service, waiters, barbers)" into "sales and services."

Subsample totals refer to economically active individuals, not the entire samples of Table 5-1.

Sources: 1966-68: Roberts 1973; 1969: Orellana and de León 1972; 1974-75: author's sample.

193

Table 5-4. Sales and Service Workers of Each Sex, 1969 and 1974-75 (Including Minors)

Females		Males	
Occupation	(Number)	Occupation	(Number)
Sample 1974-75			
Domestic employee	17	Sales agent clerk	8
Tortilla maker	16	Miscellaneous sales:	
Washing	13	food, shoes, snacks	7
Household storekeeper	12	Guardian	4
Market cook & vendor	5	Auto repairer	4
Ambulant clothes merchant	3	Janitor	3
Food preparation & sales	3	Newspaper vendor	2
Domestic cook	2	Bill collector	1
Ambulant shoeseller	1	Bicycle renter	1
Snack & cigaret stand operator	1	Market standkeeper: firewood	1
Home candy sales	1	Household sales: firewood	1
Hospital employee	1	Messenger	1
Washroom attendant	1	Corn mill operator	1
Magazine sales	1	Cab driver	1
		Hotel kitchen employee	1
Total subsample	77	Milk deliverer	1
		Dectective	1
		City employee	1
		Total subsample	39
Sample 1969			
Tortilla maker	6	City employee: maintenance	4
Household storekeeper	3	Sales agent	2
Marketer (market & street)	3	Newspaper vendor	2
Food preparation & sales	2	Military serviceman	2
Domestic cook	2	Barber	2
Sales clerk	1	Bill collector/sales	1
Washing & ironing	1	Household sales: firewood	1
Waitress	1	Ice cream maker & vendor	1
Nurses' aid	1	Milk deliverer	1
		Letter carrier	1
Total subsample	21	Car washer	1
		Janitor	1
		Cab driver	1
		Marimbist	1
		Total subsample	21

Sources: See Table 5-3.

vironment. Only one of the men in the 1974–75 sample works out of a domestic setting. Men are generally working in established enterprises, in shops, or in the streets.

In the category of artisans, skilled workers, and operatives (Table 5-5), we find that women are typically involved in the fabrication of

Table 5-5. Artisans, Skilled Workers, and Operatives of Each Sex, 1969 and 1974–75 (Including Minors)

Females		Males	
Occupation	(Number)	Occupation	(Number)
Sample 1974–75			
Clothing factory operative	6	Construction worker/mason	20
Dressmaker	3	Mechanic or assistant	8
Embroiderer	2	Auto painter or bodywork	7
Cigar maker	1	Tailor	6
Factory operative: electrical	1	Shoemaker: nonfactory	5
		Bus or truck driver	5
Total subsample	13	Carpenter	4
		Factory employee	3
		Shoe factory operative	2
		Housepainter	2
		Baker	2
		Electrician's aid	2
		Blacksmith: balconies	1
		Road worker	1
		Typographer	1
		Varnisher	1
		Total subsample	70
Sample 1969			
Nonfactory seamstress	2	Construction worker/mason	8
Factory seamstress	1	Shoemaker	7
		Varnisher	4
Total subsample	3	Mechanic	3
		Factory worker	3
		Baker	2
		Truck loader	2
		Shoe factory operative	1
		Electrician	1
		Pump operator	1
		Blacksmith	1
		Weaver	1
		Watchmaker	1
		Candle maker	1
		Auto painter	1
		Tailor	1
		Total subsample	38

Sources: See Table 5-3.

clothing, whether at home or in a factory, and that they are few in number. In contrast, many more men are employed in this category and again they exhibit a much wider range of occupations. Men work in traditional areas such as baking, shoemaking, construction and candlemaking, but they are also found in more modern types of work as factory operative, mechanic, electrician, truck driver, and typographer. Within this work category it remains exceptional for a man to work in a domestic environment, while it is still common for women to do so.

The occupational categories used in this discussion do not include those economic activities considered socially and legally illegitimate, such as prostitution, pimping, thievery, illegal alcohol sales, and dope peddling. There is no doubt that such activities provide some income to a small percentatge of the shantytown residents, but they could not be included or measured because of their furtive, irregular nature. Of these different activities, prostitution is of particular significance to women. While professional prostitution appears to be relatively rare within the colonia, intermittent, casual, or part-time commercial sexual relationships may form an important economic supplement to the poorest women in times of hardship (see case 9 to follow).[5]

Although women have entered the cash economy to a large extent, very few have entered modern urban occupations. Apart from the relatively small number of women who work in factories (around 8% of all women employed), women are mainly involved in expanding a limited variety of informal selling and service functions to serve a larger urban market. Compared to the women, the men of San Lorenzo can be found in a much wider range of occupations. We shall now consider whether the differences in occupational distribution by sex are related to differences in earning capacity.

Average Monthly Income

It is conventional to calculate the average monthly income either for the head of household or received by the entire household. For example, Roberts gives Q. 55 per month as the average income for male and female heads of household in San Lorenzo (1970:488). A census referring to one of the larger squatter settlements in Guatemala City shows Q. 70 as the average monthly income per household, while the average income of household heads was Q. 43 per month (INVI 1968:73, 77). Another conventional economic index is the percentage of household heads or of workers whose earnings fall within a given range. For instance, calculations from Roberts (1973:39) indicate that the late 1960s, 80 percent of the household heads earned Q. 60 or under per month, while the census showed that 87 percent of *all* workers earned Q. 60 or under (INVI 1968:75). Unfortunately, the position of women workers in such calculations cannot be distinguished.

196

In Table 5-6, the monthly income of each sex is listed by occupation for both 1969 and 1974–75 samples. The average monthly incomes for adult women are Q. 20 and Q. 21 respectively, and for adult men they are Q. 53 and Q. 60 respectively. Hence, adult working women of San Lorenzo earn only about 35 percent of what men are able to earn. Taking the sexes together and including employed minors, we find that in both samples, 80 percent or more of those who work earn Q. 60 or under. Considering the sexes separately, however, reveals that two-thirds to three-fourths of the females earn Q. 20 or less per month. In contrast, less than one-fourth to one-tenth of the males earn under Q. 20 per month. Clearly, women are more concentrated at the low end of the pay scale.

Earning a living is somewhat more unpredictable than a glance at Table 5-6 would indicate. "Monthly income" does not bear any fixed relation to the amount of work performed, the regularity of work, or the provision of fringe benefits such as meals. These variables affect the interpretation of the marked differences in average earnings between the sexes in San Lorenzo.

One interpretation of the disparity in female and male income is that men work longer hours. However, examination of the rate of pay for a full day of work by low-skilled female and male workers reveals that the pay difference persists when the amount of time devoted to work is equal. For example, domestic employment and making tortillas are the most common occupations for women in San Lorenzo. The average tortillera earns about 50 cents per day for a workday that may run as long as 12 hours. Domestic employees average between 60 and 70 cents per day for a full day of work and are likely to have to commute to other zones, thus adding a transportation cost. For men, the most common occupation is that of mason or construction worker. Among masons and their assistants, the average daily wage is around Q. 2.25 for a 10-to-12-hour day. Thus, differences in the amount of time devoted to work cannot account for differentials in daily rates of pay.

One important consideration is that women are more likely than men to work in occupations where they receive meals in addition to cash payments. Both tortilleras and domestic employees commonly receive meals which are probably worth around 50 cents per day. Considered as a monetary benefit, this would still leave the average woman's pay well below that of the average man (probably 40% below at least). Similarly, those who are independent traders commonly take a part of their earnings in the form of food products from their own stock, while they calculate their earnings as that which remains to use for other purposes. Generally, these small storekeepers or traders do not

197

Table 5-6. Average Monthly Cash Income by Sex and Occupation (Including Minors)

Women		Men	
Occupation	Income (Q.)	Occupation	Income (Q.)
	Sample 1974–75		
Factory seamstress (U)	80	Factory owner	200
Hospital employee	75	Commission agent	130
Market vendor: dairy goods	60	Government detective	125
Tortilleria & storekeeper	50	Police tailor	125
Social promotor	50	Chauffeur (U)	120
Factory seamstress (U)	40	Mechanic	108
Factory seamstress	40	Assistant mechanic	100
Shop seamstress	40	Watchman (U)	100
Dressmaker (U)	40	Construction dispatcher	100
Cook (M)	40	Agricultural mechanic/sales	100
Storekeeper/sewer/craftswoman	40	Chauffeur	98
Market vendor: snacks	38	Military police	90
Washing & ironing	37	Hospital janitor	90
Assembler: electricial apparatus	36	Tourist hotel: maintenance worker	90
Domestic employee (2 jobs)	35	Sales agent	85
Cigar maker	32	Sales agent	85
Tortillera/seamstress (F)	31	Carpenter	85
Washing & ironing (M)	30	Mechanic	84
Market vendor: snacks	30	Chauffeur	80
Storekeeper	28	Shoe factory operative	80
Storekeeper	28	Bookstore employee	80
Seamstress	27	Bindery employee	80
Washing	25	Civil aeronautics, unspecified	80
Washing (M)	25	Factory tailor	80
Market vendor: vegetables	21	Factory tailor	80
Factory worker: shirts	20	Shoemaker	78
Storekeeper	20	Carpenter	72
Domestic employee/mistress	20	Auto bodyworker	70
Cook	18	Factory tailor	70
Vendor: snacks, cigarets	18	Construction worker	64
Vendor: tamales	18	Construction worker (U)	64
Domestic employee (½ time)	18	Construction worker (U)	60
Storekeeper	17	Construction worker	60
Domestic employee	17	Carpenter	60
Domestic employee (M) (J)	16	Carpenter (U)	60
Domestic employee	15	Factory tailor	60
Domestic employee (J)	15	Mechanic	60
Ambulant shoe vendor	15	Auto bodyworker	60
Washing & ironing (½ time)	15	Typographer	60
Domestic employee (M)	15	Shoe factory operative	60
Domestic employee (M)	15	Housepainter (U)	60
Washing	15	Baker	60
Domestic employee (½ time)	14	Tailor	54
Tortillera	14	Tailor	50

Table 5-6. Average Monthly Cash Income by Sex and Occupation (Including Minors)—
Continued

Women		Men	
Occupation	Income (Q.)	Occupation	Income (Q.)
Tortillera	14	Shoemaker	50
Tortillera	14	Factory employee: coffee	48
Tortillera	14	Truck driver	48
Tortillera	14	Chauffeur	48
Tortillera	14	Construction worker	48
Tortillera (J)	14	Construction assistant	48
Tortillera (F)	14	Construction worker	48
Ambulant clothing vendor	13	Ironworker: construction	48
Tortillera	13	Auto bodyworker	48
Tortillera	13	Mechanic (U)	48
Tortillera	13	Mechanic/electrician (U)	48
Cook/tortillera	13	City laborer	48
Fruit and candy sales	12	Construction worker (U)	45
Domestic employee	12	Construction assistant (U)	43
Washing & ironing/storekeeper	12	Construction worker	42
Domestic employee	12	Hat factory operative	41
Vendor: vegetables, snacks	12	Metal worker: balconies	40
Washing & ironing	12	Watchman	40
Washing (½ time)	12	Construction worker (U)	40
Embroidery/washing	12	Construction worker	40
Washing	11	Construction assistant	40
Candy sales	10	Construction assistant	40
Fruit, candy, crafts sales	10	Milk distributor (U)	38
Storekeeper/food sales	10	Housepainter	37
Domestic (J)	10	Ice cream maker/vendor	36
Rags, clothes sales	9	Mechanic (J)	36
Storekeeper	9	Shoemaker	36
Magazine sales/domestic	9	Bicycle rental	36
Washing (½ time)	8	Cab driver	36
Dressmaker (U)	8	Corn mill operator	32
Washing	8	Cinema candy vendor	32
Washing & ironing (disabled)	8	Construction assistant	32
Tortillera (½ time)	7	Food vendor	30
Tortillera (½ time)	7	Auto bodyworker	30
Apron vendor (U)	6	Auto bodyworker	30
Domestic employee (aged) (M)	5	Car washer/guard	30
Embroiderer	5	Corn mill operator	28
Domestic employee (J)	3	Varnishing assistant (J)	25
		Tire repairer (J)	24
Total income for		Apprentice mechanic	20
82 women:	Q. 1,695	Apprentice mechanic	20
(income unknown = 9)		Agricultural field worker	19
		Firewood vendor	18
		Vendor: snacks, cigarets	18
		Electrician's helper (J)	16
		Ambulant shoe vendor (F)	15

Table 5–6. Average Monthly Cash Income by Sex and Occupation (Including Minors)—
Continued

Women		Men	
Occupation	Income (Q.)	Occupation	Income (Q.)
		Bill collector	15
		Newspaper vendor (J)	13
		Electrician's helper (J)	10
		Construction worker (U)	10
		Magazine vendor (J)	9
		Janitor (J)	8
		Shoe gluer (J)	6
		Shoemaker's assistant (J)	5
		Kitchen helper (J)	3
		Kitchen helper (J)	2
		Total income for 100 men: (income unknown = 17)	Q. 5,401
Average monthly income of 82 women =	Q. 20.67	Average monthly income of 100 men =	Q. 54.01
Average monthly income of 5 minor females =	Q. 11.60	Average monthly income of 12 minor males =	Q. 13.08
Average monthly income of 77 adult females =	Q. 21.26	Average monthly income of 88 adult males =	Q. 59.59

Sample 1969

Women		Men	
Waitress	70	Shoemaker (shopowner)	150
Cook	50	Factory toothbrush maker	148
Seamstress	45	Janitor	100
Nurses' aid	40	Mechanic	95
Food & sales preparation	27	Watchmaker	90
Seamstress	26	Sales/bill collector	80
Cook	24	Letter carrier	80
Tortillera (F)	23	Barber	80
Shoe vendor	20	Barber	80
Tortillera	17	Shoemaker	76
Vegetable merchant	16	Baker	75
Tortillera	15	Mason	74
Vegetable merchant	14	Baker	72
Pensioner	13	Pump operator	71
Seamstress	13	Candlemaker/marimbist	66
Market vendor	12	Electrician	60
Vendor	12	Shoemaker	60
Washing & ironing	12	Milk deliverer	57
Vendor	11	Shoemaker	56
Tortillera	8	Mason	56
Tortillera	7	Sales agent	55
Storekeeper	6	Custom's office: truck loader	54
Providing room and board	6	Ironworker	52

Table 5-6. Average Monthly Cash Income by Sex and Occupation (Including Minors)—
Concluded

Women		Men	
Occupation	Income (Q.)	Occupation	Income (Q.)
Food preparation and sales	4	Sales agent	50
		Mechanic (U)	50
Total income for		City maintenance worker	50
24 Women:	Q. 491	Auto painter/furniture maker	46
		Tool assistant	45
		Tailor	44
		Shoemaker	42
		Unskilled city laborer	42
		Ice cream maker & vendor	41
		Truck assistant	40
		Shoemaker	40
		Mason	40
		Shoemaker	40
		Tailor	40
		Military guard	40
		Mason	40
		Weaver	40
		Military guard	40
		Street patcher	37
		Municipal laborer	37
		Varnisher (U)	37
		Mason	32
		Mason (U)	30
		Assistant mason	28
		Furniture decorator	28
		Cab driver	25
		Shoemaker	24
		Assistant mason	20
		Varnisher	15
		Newspaper seller	15
		Sales: firewood	11
		Odd jobs	8
		Total income for 55 men: (income unknown = 5)	Q. 2,904
Average monthly income of 24 women =	Q. 20.46	Average monthly income of 55 men =	Q. 52.80

NOTE: The letters in parentheses indicate the following:
F = Other family members also contribute labor.
J = The person is an employed minor.
M = Meals are an additional part of the remuneration (not necessarily three meals
per day).
U = Work is unstable, subject to layoffs.
Sources: See Table 5-3.

keep records of how much food they extract for their own family consumption, although this is obviously recognized as one of the benefits of running such a business. In contrast, male employees usually receive all of their pay in cash.

The regularity of work is another variable which can affect the interpretation of monthly incomes. For instance, the women who work in occupations such as washing, preparing food, or general domestic employment do not speak of fluctuations in the demand for their labor. They may change jobs frequently, but do not complain of difficulty in finding another job at the same low level of pay, provided they possess certain identification and health certificates. In contrast, many of the occupations in which men are employed are characterized by strong fluctuations in activity. Construction workers, in particular, seem to suffer from frequent layoffs and periodic unemployment. Sixty percent of those who were actively employed as masons or who had last worked as masons reported that their work lacked security, and that there are times when they are unable to find any work, or at most a few days each week.

Considering the fact that women tend to receive certain material benefits in addition to a cash payment, and the probability that women are less subject to sharp fluctuations in the demand for their labor, the gap between the income of women and men is not as great as it appears from the survey data presented in Table 5-6. Although I lack sufficient data to measure the importance of differences in long-term levels of employment and income, the fact that male unemployment was higher than female in the 1974–75 sample is consistent with the hypothesis that there is greater fluctuation in demand for male labor. Various informants reported that it is easier for women to find work than men, although women earn very little. Such statements refer to the relatively extensive demand for female workers as domestic employees. But it should not be overlooked that women have to work longer hours than men to receive the same amount of cash. Men do not attempt to compete for the low-paying jobs in domestic service, and even some women who want to work refuse to accept jobs as domestic servants at the going rate.

Overlap Between Women's and Men's Work

Although women as well as men actively participate as workers in the cash economy of Guatemala City, the types of work they perform are largely distinct. Women are most heavily represented in the sales and services sector where they perform tasks that are often simply extensions of standard domestic activities. Men do not wash clothes or make tortillas for an income. Blurring of the line that divides the realms of women's and men's work occurs principally in the area of self-employed trading, and in some kinds of craft and factory work. Beyond that, there is a wide range of occupations that seem to be options only for males. These are typically jobs in transport, construction, and various types of work in established enterprises that have no relation to domestic modes of production.

Housework

Within the home, there is a sexual division of labor. Women are expected to assume responsibility for preparing meals, washing clothes, ironing, and minding children. Men are responsible for maintaining or improving the quality of the dwelling. Although employed women may receive assistance from their husbands in some tasks, men will normally not offer much aid and women do not expect it.

The household in San Lorenzo lacks many of the production and consumption functions that characterize the household in other regions. Forms of household production, which are common in rural subsistence economies, must here compete with a wide range of industrial products. In the city, production tends to take place outside the home in specialized workshops and factories. Although some artisans in San Lorenzo work at home, they produce for a market, not for home use. Unlike urban middle-class homes, the home in San Lorenzo is not designed for high levels of consumption and maintenance. Middle-class standards of housekeeping, which involve more possessions and more work, are beyond the reach of most residents of San Lorenzo. By the process of elimination, then, the dominant activity within the home is simply the provision of services for those who work outside it. This activity is generally performed by women for other members of the family. When the workers fail to earn enough to support the family, these women seek outside sources of income. This may be a permanent arrangement, or one that occurs at times of special hardship. In compensating for unemployment or underemployment of other family members, women workers tend to remain in the same service sector, washing clothes or preparing foods for paying clients.

As mentioned earlier, housework is an ambiguous category between employment and unemployment. In any family, those least likely to find well-paying jobs outside the home typically assume the housework responsibilities. A woman who loses her job often returns temporarily to housework in her own home, if there are other wage-earners present. Clearly, there is a significant amount of work to be done, but the low incomes of the working people mean that relatively few families can afford to have a family member devote full time to housekeeping without earning any income.

Using the breakdown of economic status presented earlier, and assuming that unemployed and disabled women contribute to family housework, we find that at most 6.7 percent of the total population, or one out of every fifteen, is engaged in housework. Considering that it is extremely rare to find paid domestic employees working *within* San Lorenzo, this ratio appears remarkably low when compared to the ratio of one out of every four or five persons (family members and domestic employees) employed in housekeeping in the middle-class colonia of Villa Rosa (see next chapter). The low ratio of women available for full-time housekeeping within San Lorenzo is both an indication that households must manage with fewer services, and that women who work must often assume a double load that includes maintaining household services for other family members.

Origin of the Occupational Structure

The origin of the occupational structure in San Lorenzo may be examined from several perspectives. One perspective considers the broad patterns of demand for labor that characterize Guatemala's development into a modern economy. These patterns of demand are such that they are generally held to be responsible for major demographic imbalances in Guatemala in terms of the sex ratio. More specifically, the marked surplus of men in plantation regions indicates a high level of demand for male labor in commercial agriculture. The surplus of women in Guatemala City indicates that there is demand for female labor, particularly as domestic servants for the middle and upper classes that are concentrated in the capital.[6] These overall differences in sex distribution suggest that migrants are aware of the types of jobs available, or that they ultimately have to adjust their residence to the conditions of the labor market. In either case, if migration is a response to economic pressures, then it is clear that these pressures apply to men and women in distinctive ways to produce the national demographic imbalance (cf. Roberts 1973:67–68).

Viewed within the context of the nation and the city, areas such as San Lorenzo play an important structural role. San Lorenzo is a labor reserve for the modern economy. It accepts those who are redundant in the countryside and in the city, and helps them to preserve themselves until the economy needs them again. The shanty-towns are referred to by social organizers and politicized residents as *barrios marginales* (marginal neighborhoods), in recognition of their precarious position in the social and economic order. In an urban economy affected by fluctuations in national and international prices and markets, a flexible labor market must evolve that expands and contracts in harmony with the economy. This involves a complex adjustment on the part of the urban working class, which must be alive and well enough to provide a variety of labor skills when demand is high, but which must know how to adjust and maintain itself when demand for its labor skills is low. The observed sexual division of labor supports the necessary degree of structural flexibility on the part of the urban working class. Men provide the labor force in the sectors that are both more dynamic and more cyclical and hence subject to periodic setbacks, while women are generally employed in the service sector, which experiences relative stability.

A specific question concerning the demand for labor as it affects the residents of San Lorenzo is whether or not there are institutional biases in favor of hiring men in skilled jobs and established enterprises. As we noted in Tables 5-5 and 5-6 on occupational distribution, only a small percentage of women work in factories or large establishments. Most work in private households or are self-employed. Although many men are also self-employed or employed in small workshops, male representation in established enterprises is significantly higher. Based on the samples of 1969 and 1974–75, the percentage of women employed by enterprises or institutions with more than 10 employees is close to 13 percent, while for men it is twice as high, at about 26 percent.[7] This suggests that institutional discrimination may indeed be a factor in the establishment of new forms of sexual discrimination in a changing economy. However, the dispersion and low incidence of formal employment opportunities among the people of San Lorenzo make it difficult to establish a firm connection at present between institutional employment and sexual bias.

Technology

As residents of the metropolis, the people of San Lorenzo are surrounded by modern technology. As low-income residents of a shantytown, they have access to only a small share of it. Certainly their lives are affected by many modern technological innovations, such as motorized public transportation, electricity, and mass communications. But relatively few people can afford to purchase major consumer or producer technology. Small items such as radios, watches, and kerosene burners are common, but larger items such as televisions, sewing machines, refrigerators, or motorbikes are not. No one in San Lorenzo owns a car or washing machine. Nor did I find a single household with an investment of more than Q. 1,000 in any item of modern technology.

Most people of the colonia are still engaged in preindustrial types of employment. Construction workers still build houses using manual labor; laundresses still haul water and wash clothes by hand. Training in the use of large-scale or capital-intensive technology is very limited. To the extent that people work with modern technology, their skills remain focussed on small-scale and intermediate technology such as is found in small bakeries, auto repair shops, and tailor shops. A few people work in larger factories, but their jobs seldom require high levels of technical competance.

A review of the types of jobs that men perform suggests that they have some advantage in acquiring valuable technical skills, in part because they are more likely to be employed in large establishments. Several men, for example, have received driving lessons from their employers and have since received better-paying jobs as truck drivers. I did not encounter any women in San Lorenzo who know how to drive. The level of differentiation between the sexes is not great however; its impact is sporadic rather than systematic. The introduction of industrial products and innovations in the city has not created demand for or training of skilled labor in areas such as San Lorenzo. This is largely because Guatemala's position in the world economy is essentially one of recipient of the products of advanced technology.

Economic Strategies

While an analysis of demography and macroeconomic factors helps to explain the sexual division of labor, at another level the occupational structure is shaped by the historical experiences of individuals who by trial and error arrive at a set of arrangements whereby they can support themselves. In Roberts' study (1973), many of the problems of male heads of household are discussed in terms of their urban careers. Here, I shall consider the female experience in this regard in order to illustrate the distinctive qualities of the adaptive strategies employed by women, with the hope of providing a better understanding of how both sexes interact in San Lorenzo.

The cases presented illustrate various economic conditions women encounter. None of these cases can easily be taken as archetypical, since diversity is a dominant characteristic of the population. San Lorenzo houses Ladinos and indigenes, Catholics and Protestants, urban-born and rural migrants, extended families and fragments of families. While the diversity makes nearly every individual's case seem distinctive, I have selected several cases to illustrate the different contexts which seem particularly important in determining the economic position of women over the long run. These contexts are: the presence of stable male wage earners; the presence of irregularly employed males; the absence of male wage earners. The classification of women in terms of their relationship to men is not to imply that women do not make individual decisions regarding their best economic strategies. Rather, it highlights an important variable in the context of their decisions.

Stable male wage earners present. For women with children and very limited access to high-paying jobs, living with men who can provide a stable income has clear advantages. It enables them to reject low-paying jobs in some cases, and provide better care for the house and family. In other cases, however, women find their options more restricted because the relationships of the family may limit the ways they can dispose of their labor.

1. Marta, age twenty-five, was born in the capital. She has a husband and two children and lives in a partitioned house shared with her parents and unmarried sister. Their house is one of the better ones in appearance, made of finished wood, with cement floors, sturdy chairs, electricity, a latrine, and a new stove with an oven.

Marta's parents were among the original invaders. In a joint effort, her mother claimed the land while her father got the wood to build the shack. For twenty-one years her father worked in a flour depository until recently he was replaced by a younger man and given a small quittance pay. Marta's mother had worked as a cook before marriage, but afterwards only did occasional washing and ironing as an economic supplement. With her husband's unemployment, Marta's mother says she would now look for work if she did not have serious health disabilities.

Marta is relatively highly educated, having completed the third year of secondary school. She started to work at age seventeen in a shirt factory and worked there seven years earning Q. 60 to 70 per month in piece work. Although she had a child at around age 20, she continued to work several more years until she got married and had a second child. Her husband is also from San Lorenzo and works as a bus driver earning Q. 98 per month and contributing almost all of it to the household. Other support comes from Marta's sister who, with a sixth-grade education, now works in a factory that produces electrical apparatus; she earns Q. 36 per month.

Despite the present unemployment of Marta's father, this household has enjoyed a long period of steady male economic support. Important incomes have also come from the unmarried daughters in factory jobs. Currently, the role of principle earner belongs to Marta's husband, who, notably, earns more than either of the daughters was able to earn in factories. The conditions that favored Marta's withdrawal from the labor force include: the presence of a stable provider who contributes more to the household than she used to earn; the needs of her dependent children and disabled mother; and accommodations in the household of her parents. Given that the parents had invested in household improvements, the contributions of the unmarried daughter alone would probably be nearly enough for sustenance. However, with the addition of Marta's husband to the household they are able to afford additional improvements such as the new stove.

2. Herminia is about sixty years old, married, and lives with her husband and three grown children, all of whom are employed. She was one of the original invaders of San Lorenzo. Her house shows significant investments: a cement floor, block walls, a latrine, a stereo, a short-wave radio, a sewing machine, and a small gas burner for cooking. The dwelling's appearance would place it within the middle third of the economic spectrum in San Lorenzo.

Herminia grew up in an eastern province and until her mid-twenties when her father died, she never had a job. On her father's death, she came to the city to work and to help out her mother who had another child at home. Herminia knew people in the city who came from her province. She lodged with them at first, and worked as a cashier in a bakery. She met her husband at this job. Although she married, she continued to work for another four years. During this time that they worked, they began to have children, and they were happy. They were renting an apartment for Q. 15 per month. Herminia stopped working to care for the children. Later, her husband lost his job and they could not pay the rent. A neighbor woman in a similar situation told Herminia about the invasion. Then they came to San Lorenzo: "We grabbed our lot and built our little shack—in the same place where we are now."

Economically, this was a hard time for Herminia. Although her husband found work again, he started to drink and go out with other women. He had another woman and four children "*en la calle*" (in the street). Herminia told him to leave, but he did not go. He continued to live with both until the other woman died several years ago. He split his salary between them. Herminia had to supplement this as best she could by making and selling food from her house.

Herminia's current economic situation is much improved now that her rival is dead and her grown children are also contributing to the household.

Besides her own food sales, she receives income from three sources. Her husband gives her Q. 8 of the Q. 15 he earns weekly, while a son and daughter contribute Q. 10 and Q. 12, respectively, each month. Significantly, the son earns twice as much as his sister and pays for his studies to become an accountant. Another son, separated from his wife and children, currently lives at home and uses his wages to support his children.

Herminia's case shows that despite a durable marriage, a husband's economic contribution can be variable either through job loss, or independent decisions regarding the distribution of his earnings. Although Herminia has passed through trying times, her long-term position is that of a woman who has had fairly stable male assistance, even if it was not maximal.

In the past, the factors which influenced her economic decisions were: (1) the presence of four dependent children; (2) the inadequacy of her husband's contribution; and (3) the instability of her housing in San Lorenzo. While the need for cash alone might have driven Herminia into some other occupation than the low-income sale of foodstuffs around her house, the housing factor was an important part of her overall economic outlook, for she could not afford to both buy food *and* pay rent.

In San Lorenzo, defending one's house takes two forms: physically occupying the house, and politically organizing to defend the shantytown as a whole.[8] Herminia did both. By working out of her home, she kept watch over her house; and for many years she has been highly active in organizing the political defense of the shantytown against any threats of eviction.

At the present time, Herminia's economic position is fairly secure due to consistent contributions from several earners. With no dependent children, she is not pressed to increase her income through expanding her food sales, but continues to provide services for the working members of her family and for her grandchildren.

3. Alma is in her fifties. She lives with her husband and her last unmarried child of eleven, and has a friend and her child boarding with her. Her house has electricity, a latrine, and even a crude second floor, but is relatively simple within and could be described as an average-quality house within San Lorenzo.

Alma worked as a domestic while a teen-ager, but stopped work when she married at age eighteen and began to bear children. Out of fifteen births, four children survived; the three oldest are now married. For the first eighteen years of her marriage, she did not work. Her husband worked as a finca (farm) administrator, followed by several jobs as a guardian on fincas near the capital, and then a job for a sawmill where he worked for twenty-five years. The sawmill paid Q. 1 per day, but provided good housing and other benefits.

When Alma returned to work about twenty years ago, she worked at a coffee *beneficio* (processing plant) of a state-owned finca. Along with 348 other women, she worked selecting coffee beans, earning Q. 1.50 per day, paid by the pound. Men also worked there loading and unloading railroad cars, weighing coffee, and closing the sacks. Men earned Q. 2 per day.

When the state-owned beneficio was sold, she went to work in another coffee beneficio, again earning Q. 1.50 per day, although she was paid at a slightly lower piece rate. While she worked, her older daughter tended the youngest child. Alma stayed at that job until 1971 when it was eliminated by machinery. All the women lost their jobs. Some of the men lost their jobs as well, but many of them are still working there. In recounting this, she interjects: "That's why there are so many women in the bad life [prostitution]; they have to do something to earn."

For the last three years, she has not found work in factories. She says, "They don't want to give work to older people, so now I work at home." She earns about Q. 32 per month by combining sales from her household store with sewing various articles that are sold in the markets.

Although Alma and her husband had free housing at the sawmill where he worked, she worried about where she could live if he died, since he is considerably older. This led her to join the invasion. Since then, they have lived in San Lorenzo on and off, having someone live free in their house to guard it while they returned to the sawmill. They have been back in San Lorenzo for two years now. They are currently saving to improve their house further, now that her husband is working as a guard and earning Q. 100 per month.

Alma reentered the labor force at a time when the age of her children made it easier to work and when she was able to earn relatively high wages. Her contribution has been significant since that time, often exceeding her husband's in terms of cash. However, her income has gone down since modern technology eliminated her job at the coffee beneficio and she has become self-employed. It should be mentioned that Alma only learned to read as an adult in night school, and is still unable to write.

In the preceding cases, we have considered the economic characteristics of some of the original invaders and their children. However, San Lorenzo experiences a significant rate of turnover. The characteristics of the incoming population which *buys* into the neighborhood appear to be somewhat distinctive from those who originally settled it, although over the long run these differences may fade. Comparing invaders with those who came later, Roberts noted that, "The proportion of single females who come with their children to set up house in the shantytown has diminished from the earlier 34 percent to 18 percent

(1973:115). Two cases of this type, although less complex, are briefly described as follows:

4. Ernesta is a Kekchi Indian in her early twenties, recently *juntada* (joined, or married without ceremony) with a young Quiche man. They live in a poor, small house with a dirt floor, barely furnished, which they bought for just over Q. 300 several months earlier.

After only one year of school, Ernesta worked from age 10 in coffee harvesting and in private houses, until she moved into this house with her husband. At her last job she was receiving Q. 35 per month from the foreign family that employed her.[9] She says she left that job because her husband told her to. She is pregnant now, and feels that she cannot go out to work in houses or the market because someone may rob or occupy the house if it is left unattended. Her husband works in a coffee factory earning Q. 2 per day. He gives Q. 10 per week to Ernesta, and Q. 2 per week to his sister. Ernesta also earns about Q. 5 per month by working long hours embroidering huipiles and other articles for sale.

In this case a woman decided to give up a fairly high-paying job as a domestic employee in order to protect a joint investment in a house because she will soon have a dependent child.

5. Josefina is in her early twenties and her husband is five years older. They were both born in eastern provinces where they attended school for two and four years, respectively. They started living together four years ago and have a two-year-old child. Josefina has never worked. Her husband has a good job for an international company as a mechanic. He earns Q. 108 per month and belongs to a union. They bought their house a year earlier, paying Q. 1,100. Until then, they rented a house and sublet parts of it. They say they came to San Lorenzo because they could not afford to buy anywhere else.

Although their house is not conspicuous from the outside, inside it is one of the most decorative and well-kept in the colonia. It is made of cement blocks, with cement floors. The walls are painted brightly and colorfully. They have a refrigerator, a formica table with matching chairs, a stereo, and a TV, all bought within the last few years on sale or on installments. They are still paying for the refrigerator. Josefina says she might consider working if she does not have another child, but she would like to have one more.

Unlike the early invaders, this couple obviously did not come to San Lorenzo out of desperate need. Rather, they found that they could acquire an adequate house more cheaply in the shantytown than elsewhere. Their higher standard of living and aspirations for upward mobility make them appear remote to many of their neighbors who are older and not as well-off. However, others in the colonia have also done well and improved their homes. It should also be remembered that this couple has not yet had to invest much in children or their education.

The last two cases illustrate that: (1) those who can afford to pay significant sums of money for a house in San Lorenzo tend to be dependent on a stable male earner; (2) women who have or are expecting children tend to have a small or dependent economic role if their husbands are stable providers. We shall now examine some cases in which the men are not stable providers.

Discontinuous male contributions.

6. Luz is in her mid-forties and lives with her husband and nine children, ranging from twenty-three to three years old. Luz was born in another Central American country where she received a sixth grade education and considerable traveling and marketing experience with her family. She married a Guatemalan when she was around twenty and came to Guatemala to live with him and his relatives in an eastern province. At that time she was no longer working, but had children and was dependent on his family. Her husband himself was unreliable as a source of support both because he spent time in jail and because he tended to side with his relatives when there were money problems. The relatives did not like her and there were violent fights over money which she would lose since she had no relatives nor allies there. For a while, she left the three children with his family while she went to work as a merchant in a port town. When she was prospering again, her husband persuaded her to return with him but the situation repeated itself. She blames the death of one of her babies on the treatment of his family.

With the political upheaval in 1954, her husband was in danger and migrated to the city. She later followed, but received no help from him and found herself without resources. A woman migrant from the province who knew of Luz's desperate situation came to her aid. She lent Luz 50 cents as capital, showed her the market, and let Luz and the children, who now numbered five, stay with her in her shack. Luz bought vegetables the first day and sold them for double. Slowly she built up her business, taking her five children to market with her. At the time of the invasion of San Lorenzo, Luz went with her children and erected her shack. It was torn down by police, but once again she put up her cardboard house. By this time her relationship with her first husband had totally disintegrated.

In the shantytown she met her current husband. He helped her to get her citizenship papers, and she began to have children with him. Despite the arrival of five more children, Luz has always continued her marketing. Her second husband has had a discontinuous career as a self-employed shoemaker, an employee in the customs office, and a shoemaker for the police. He has been unemployed for the last two years and has had a drinking problem. Meanwhile, Luz is the mainstay of the household economy. She earns roughly Q. 15 weekly from her marketing. Her two oldest unmarried sons are also working and contribute together Q. 18 monthly for household expenses. They also contribute material and labor for improvements in the house.

Luz's house is quite crowded and disorganized, but shows some major purchases. For instance, there is a refrigerator used for Luz's marketing which cost Q. 700. Her husband helped her pay for it since he was working at the time. They also have a TV purchased on installments by Luz. Regarding her husband's reliability as a provider, Luz is fairly sympathetic. She complains not that he is unemployed, but that when he has been employed he has given money to his sons by another woman and has not given to his daughters by Luz, saying, "They have their mother." Luz claims that when she married him, she was unaware of this prior commitment to another family.

Luz's case is exceptional in that her sixth-grade education and travel experience as a child are unusual for women. However, her unsuccessful marriage which left her destitute with five children is not unusual at all among women in San Lorenzo, nor is the solution of choosing to rely on marketing to sustain her family. Her relationship with her second husband is also fairly typical with respect to the discontinuties in his employment and his obligations to his children with different women.

Some of Luz's views of work are enlightening. She knows she earns more in the market than she could earn as a domestic, but it is not only the money that is important to her. She loves marketing and being her own boss. She would not like to be mistreated by the employers in a house. She says that many employers beat their servants, order them around, and then do not pay them, when the women have children at home waiting for food. She cites at least six different occasions she has gone with some poor girl who did not get paid, and taken her to the judge to get the judge to make the employers pay. She believes she must help them because she herself was once in such dire need.

She would like one of her daughters to follow her in marketing and help her. Her oldest daughter, however, is not interested. The girl would rather find work in a factory. This would be fine with Luz if her daughter did, in fact, find such work. From conversations with Luz and other women, it seems clear that of the three types of work that they perceive as open to women of their class, factory work is the best, followed by marketing, followed by domestic work.

7. Sonia is close to forty years old, married to a man of the same age, and has had eight children, seven of whom are currently living at home. Sonia and her husband migrated from a coastal town. Although they do not fluently speak Cakchiquel nor wear traditional clothing, the children

consider themselves as indigenes because their grandmother maintains her ethnic identity. Sonia cannot read, but her husband is literate.

Sonia has worked all her life. She has gone out to do wash and iron; she has been a mess cook; she has sold clothing from house to house; and has sold *chuchitos* (corn dumplings with meat) and other things to eat. She currently works as a domestic earning 50 cents per day. She has always earned just about the same. Her husband has worked in construction and as a chauffeur. He does not have secure work. To work as a driver, he needs to pay Q. 10 to renew his driver's license. He has been out of work for three months, but when he has work he earns from Q. 3 to Q. 4 daily.

Sonia's children have all contributed to the household, with the exception of one handicapped child who attends a special school. The eldest daughter has worked in cafeterias, a pizzeria, and a chicken store. Her earnings have usually been around Q. 16 per month, although she earned Q. 45 monthly in the job at the pizzeria. This daughter recently married and no longer contributes to the household. Other earners in the family include a 22-year-old son who earns Q. 2 per day making metal bracings at home for house construction. A sixteen-year-old daughter is currently unemployed, although she had also worked in a cafeteria. Two younger girls work as domestics, one earning Q. 15 monthly, the young twelve-year-old earning only Q. 3 per month. Even the two sons under ten contribute by earning money selling a type of bread for a man in the neighborhood.

The family has lived in San Lorenzo for twelve years. They bought their lot, but the father built the house. It is made of wood with a cement floor, two rooms, an electric light, and a latrine. They do not have a radio or other costly appliances, but they appear to be within the middle third of San Lorenzo's economic spectrum.

In this household, it appears that the work of every member is important in maintaining a relatively constant standard of living in the face of fluctuations in the fortunes of individuals. The temporary unemployment of one of Sonia's daughters is probably partly welcomed since it means that she can take over many of the domestic chores. Notably, after about age fifteen, age and experience do not seem to increase the earning capacity of the domestic worker.

Male earners absent. In households where the women lack relationships with males which involve a regular contribution, or redistribution of their income for collective needs, the women are forced to rely solely on their own low earnings, and typically live at the edge of scarcity.

8. Faustina is in her fifties. Her household consists of two people, herself and a twelve-year-old granddaughter. Faustina is a tortillera and has been making tortillas for a living for roughly forty years. Faustina is indigenous, although the traditional clothes are too expensive for her to wear now. (She would wear them if she could afford them.)

Faustina had two children who are now grown and married, each with five children. Her husband abandoned her some fifteen years ago when she was sick and had to go to a hospital. When she came back she found he had gone with another woman. She supported herself and the children by working in market kitchens and renting rooms, or lodging with her daughter. Two years ago she bought the shack she lives in now for Q. 90, paid on installments. She paid for it herself with her tortilla money. She currently receives no economic help from her children and considers them ingrates. She has raised the granddaughter since infancy and finds her like a daughter. She currently employs another woman, and the two of them make tortillas for about 50 cents per day plus the tortillas that they are able to eat. She frequently has to buy on credit.

Faustina clearly belongs to one of the poorer households in San Lorenzo. Her crude shack has a dirt floor, wood walls, no latrine, one light bulb. It is small with nothing of obvious value in the room other than one bed and her cooking utensils. Faustina is illiterate, but has paid for her granddaughter to study so she will not have to work so hard in her life, and so that she can work away from *fuego y humo* (fire and smoke), the two salient features in a tortillera's life.

As in the other cases where male earners are absent, have left, or died, Faustina just barely manages to provide for her subsistence and little more. Improvements in the house are out of the question without at least occasional assistance from someone capable of earning more.

9. Juana is close to fifty years old and single. Her household consists of herself, two grown daughters, and two grandchildren. All three adults work. Juana was one of the original invaders of San Lorenzo.

Juana was born in a western province and is a ladinized Quichean. Her work history spans almost her entire life. She was abandoned by her mother at the age of three and left with a family as an *hija de casa* (literally a house child, that is, a foster child). She remembers that they scarcely fed her and that she was beaten. At age nine, she went to work in a household butcher shop. She was supposed to earn 40 cents per month, but actually received only food and clothing. At age twelve, she came to the capital with an older cousin who worked as a cook in a private house. Juana learned how to do housework, saying that here "there was another custom for sweeping and I did not know that kind of work." She worked there four months and learned "something." She was supposed to receive Q. 4 per month, but they did not ever pay *her*, only her cousin. She says: "I was very stupid; I did not know. Finally, I got to know other girls here who counselled me. I went to another house."

In her next job, Juana was to receive Q. 5 per month for child care. This too was a failure. She was sent to the market with Q. 5 for a 25 cent purchase and put the change in her dress, but it was gone when she returned. Being new to the city, she had not known how people steal things here. Her employer called her a thief, and she stayed eight months to pay the money that was robbed. Finally, a man in a store heard her story and paid off her debt so that she could come and work for him. She worked there for three years, learning more household skills such as cooking. She was well-liked and earned Q. 8 per month. It was good work because she was given enough to eat, she was paid on time, and was given responsiblity and time off. There were two reasons for leaving. First, she was offered more pay elsewhere. Second, the sons of the household were already men and they wanted to abuse her and take advantage of the situation.

Her next job of any duration lasted from age fifteen to eighteen. Her employer taught her to be a Catholic, to wear shoes and give up the indigenous style of clothing. When she left that job, she went to live with the man who fathered her first two children. He was older, a Ladino, and employed as a policeman. "At first I did not 'work', but I did business." That is, she began to sell *atole*, a hot drink, and *chuchitos*, steamed corn dumplings, as her mother had. She would sell at various construction sites and at times earned good money. Also, her *marido* (common-law husband) was giving her Q. 35 monthly, and she had no boss. But since she had her own money, he kept lowering the amount he gave her: "Q. 35, 30, 25, 20, 15, 10, . . . and I left!" At this point she returned to work as a domestic. She maintained relations with this man, but there were lots of fights because they were both very jealous. She left her daughter with her ex-consort and his other woman for several years. Then she returned to marketing and placed her children in a state-run daycare center. Since then, she has been marketing food and vegetables. Her youngest daughter claims to have an indentation on her head from the baskets she has carried since she was seven years old.

Juana took part in the invasion of San Lorenzo, coming alone with her children and erecting her own shack. Her relationships with men have been informal and have rarely involved living together for any length of time. Her youngest daughter describes how her father is gone most of the time and rarely comes to see them. He was gone for two years, came recently for a short time and then left again. He does not contribute to the household financially, probably because his earnings are too small. In describing her friend of the last thirteen years, Juana says that she lived with him for a short while but left because he was very jealous. Also, they ran a kitchen in the market and she had to work too hard. She prefers selling vegetables. At the moment, she had not seen him for three weeks, since he had lost his job as a guard where he had been earning Q. 2 per day. In Juana's view, it was expected that if he was not working he would not come to see her.

Juana's two daughters who live with her conduct their lives in a similar fashion. The oldest, Julia, is in her late twenties, and has five children and no husband. The father of the children does not help her at all with money. However, his mother takes care of three of the children while Julia works. One other child is in the state-run daycare center while Julia takes the infant with her to work. She usually works as a domestic, or washing clothes. The younger daughter, Yolanda, is scarcely twenty and has one child of two years whom she takes with her to the market where she sells prepared foods. She also reports that there is no help from the child's father. He left her when she was two months' pregnant and went with another woman. She had lived with him for several years in a coastal city, but has always worked since he did not earn enough. At times she sold clothes or vegetables. With a sense of humor, she gave the following description of her stay in the provinces:

"One could die of hunger there. Life here in the city is much better because you can at least earn your food, and sell something in order to live. Here you can sell your basket of vegetables, but there, you die of hunger. Two years I suffered there. I worked at a coffee plantation, earning 30 cents a day for harvesting coffee. They didn't weigh it, but paid by the basket, for a basket holds around fifty pounds. There were only bars there. You'd have to look a long time before you came to a pharmacy. One pharmacy, many bars!"

Regarding sexual affairs, Juana expresses the situation pragmatically. "The majority of women do it because—where does the money come from? But they must hide it, because if their man finds out, he hits her, practically kills her. But women have to give their bodies in order to support their kids—because the men drink too much."

Juana's hut is one of the poorer ones in San Lorenzo. It has plank walls, an uneven dirt floor, crude partitions within a small space. There is a light bulb, but they have not had electricity for a long time, since they cannot pay a Q. 15 bill. Between the three of them, they earn about Q. 65 per month.

To some extent, this family may be considered deviant in San Lorenzo. The women are looked down on for their irregular relationships with men, but they are not considered prostitutes since they are primarily self-supporting through other kinds of work. The fact that they do not have access to regular income from men means that they have not been able to invest in many improvements in their house or to provide personal services for their children. Comparing the time spent at home with that spent in the market, Juana says of the market, "I get bored being here, but I am happier here than in the house. In the house, there is nothing to do; a lot of hunger, but nothing to eat." The absence of anything other than the most episodic male economic contributions to this household leaves its members in a most precarious position, precarious even relative to that of the other residents of a lower-class squatter settlement.

Social Organization

Although San Lorenzo is a geographically distinct entity, it exists as an integral part of the city which surrounds it. The lives of its people are embedded in the life of the city, touching to varying degrees the lives of people of all social classes. For the people of San Lorenzo their contacts within the barrio form only part of the network of dispersed ties which link them to the rest of the city. These ties extend vertically and horizontally across the entire metropolis.

Symetrically of course, the larger city is linked to San Lorenzo. It is not a tie that the rest of the city always finds comfortable. To many politically powerful Guatemalans San Lorenzo is an unstable, volatile, chaotic place where the order and organization of the rest of the city hardly exist. Thus government and other organizations have often appeared within San Lorenzo as organizing forces, concerned to establish order and control over the community but generally unwilling to change the economic and broader social conditions which make San Lorenzo the place it is.

Formal Community Organization

Politics. The political concerns of the people of San Lorenzo are complex. Wedged into the metropolitan center, the colonia is directly exposed to and affected by a wide range of political and economic institutions that represent foreign, national, and urban interests. With a heterogeneous population, political activity in San Lorenzo is characterized by a high degree of factionalism, fragmentation, and competition for community and personal support from external sources. A detailed description and analysis of the variety and density of political linkages maintained by colonia residents is clearly beyond the scope of this study.[10] In this discussion, I focus on the nature of women's involvement in several political groups and types of political activity which represent the major forms of political behavior in San Lorenzo.

The electoral process. As a densely populated neighborhood within the national capital, the colonia of San Lorenzo is subject to intense political activity during national and municipal elections. Although the elections themselves are not necessarily valid measures of popular will, participation is important to the people of San Lorenzo. The degree of participation by women may be taken as a reflection of their level of consciousness of political events and of their integration into the formal political processes of the city.

Unlike other sectors of Guatemala, the colonia of San Lorenzo exhibits a relatively high level of electoral participation by women. In a sample of sixty-three adult women, exactly one-third of the women have voted at least once in national or municipal elections and some have been voting regularly since the vote was granted to women.[11] In general, the women of the colonia possess a high degree of political awareness. In contrast to women of rural peasant and plantation communities, the women of San Lorenzo know the names of current national and municipal leaders and can correlate the terms of various presidents with changes in the economic and political climate, particularly as it affects the colonia. This is not surprising, for the uncertain legal status of San Lorenzo encourges a high degree of sensitivity to any political parties or candidates that either reject or support the continued existence of the settlement. In a culture that stresses the importance of "*la mujer en su hogar*" (the woman in her home), women can be activated in defense of their housing.

With regard to party politics, there is relatively little information on the extent of women's participation or formal membership. Some women have stated that the party workers who canvass the neighborhood at election time are almost exclusively male. Others report instances when their votes have been actively solicited by pairs of women working for one of the national political parties. Few of the women (or men) wish to advertise their political commitments in an environment where the term "politics" is often associated with fraud, broken promises, shifting political patronage, and danger. Women sometimes disavow any political preference, stating that they voted for a particular candidate only because they wanted it stamped on their papers that they had voted.

Roberts has described the importance of patronage for particular men in San Lorenzo who are able to obtain employment opportunities and paid political posts as a reward for their political support. I found evidence that the patronage system applies to women as well as men, although it appears to be less extensive and to operate at a lower level. One of my informants claimed that she had to affiliate with a particular party as a precondition for submitting a job application, while several other women obtained places in municipal markets as a result of political contacts. With respect to more formal political positions in organizations with influence that extends beyond the squatter settlements, it seems that the socioeconomic background of both men and women effectively sets limits on their opportunities. However, the formal political structure of both the national and municipal governments is overwhelmingly controlled by men.

Local political organizations and groups. Shantytowns in Guatemala usually possess voluntary betterment organizations which attempt to organize community improvements. In San Lorenzo, a predecessor of this type of organization appears to have developed at the time of the invasion. The invasion of San Lorenzo was a planned event regulated by an ad hoc invasion committee. Roberts, whose work focusses on male activities and life histories, states:

219

> From the accounts of those who took a leading part in the invasion, it is apparent that the possibility of invading had been a topic of discussion *among men* in the contiguous legal neighborhood and informal meetings had been held to consider the possibility (1973:113). [Italics added.]

It is possible that Roberts did not intend to exclude women in this statement, for he has noted that single mothers formed a high percentage of the original invaders, and that women often took the initiative in securing housing in San Lorenzo. From the accounts of female participants in the invasion which I recorded, it is clear that the possibility of invasion had also been widely discussed in *female* networks in nearby neighborhoods. The original participants give conflicting reports regarding the leadership of the invasion, some naming a male and others naming a female leader, but this may be consistent with Robert's observation that in the early years "organization was informal and not instituted in committees with set procedures" (1973:312). At any rate, it is evident that women played an active role in the original organization of the invasion.

Following the early invasion period when defense of the settlement had been an essential basis for cohesion even without formal organization, an increasingly stable environment has permitted the growth of both formal organization and neighborhood factionalism, resulting in a plethora of formally organized groups and committees. These organizations have been unable to provide an ongoing comprehensive political structure, for they compete for the allegiance of different sectors of a heterogeneous population.

One formally organized group which evolved out of the earlier squatters' committee is the local Betterment Committee which claims to work on behalf of the community as a whole and to coordinate the activities of various other colonia groups. This committee is affiliated with MONAP (National Movement of Settlers) which in turn coordinates the activities of similar betterment committees throughout the metropolitan area.[12] Some of the direct concerns of the Betterment Committee include the provision of drainage and a sewer system, improvement of the streets, and the renumbering of the houses in the colonia. It also performs various social welfare services, and has been associated with some ambitious community projects which failed, such as an attempt to organize a school and a consumer's cooperative within the colonia, and the construction of a social hall, which collapsed.

The Betterment Committee is described by some residents as a group in which men dominate, while women participate. Indeed, at the time of my research, the elected officers of the committee consisted of seven men and two women. The four executive posts were all occupied by men, and two of the five assistants' posts were held by women. It is reported that in past years the executive posts have also been held by men. At the time of my research, the committee appeared weak due to factionalism and apathy.

At a routine meeting of this committee which I attended, only four men and four women attended, plus a woman social worker who belongs to another *"categoría"* (social status) and does not live within the colonia. During the meeting, the four women remained peripheral, both literally and figuratively, to the discussion. The men and the social worker sat at a central table and discussed the work of the committee. The social worker initiated almost all discussion. Two male officers responded to and elaborated on her proposals, and the women in the room eventually dozed, or simply listened while working at handicrafts. Indeed, one of the women was present only because meetings were always held at her house, while another came to accompany her husband. When I questioned the women about their lack of active participation, they explained that much of the committee work dealing with drainage, water, street improvement, and house enumeration are male concerns because men have more experience in construction.

Women who do not regularly attend the small weekly meetings of this committee, some of whom consider themselves alienated or opposed to the group, report that they have attended past public meetings of either the Betterment Committee or a comparable rival group called the Community Council where the women do speak out just as the men do. Some of the more active and vocal women report that women tend to be more reluctant than men to take the microphone at mass meetings, but when they have done so they have always been listened to and applauded by the men.

The squatter settlements have survived largely because of their unity in defense of their housing and because a threat to one is perceived as a threat to all. To a certain extent, the political potential of the women and men of San Lorenzo remains latent until a catalyst provokes renewed organization. An example of such a catalyst was the emergence of a dispute regarding the dispossession of several dozen established residents from their housing in a neighboring shantytown, and the alleged acquisition of false titles by outsiders. City newspapers carried the story of the residents who were threatened with eviction. Concern spread rapidly through the colonias via personal contacts and leaflets as well as the public media. With the support of the university students' association and its legal advisor a meeting was called to establish an Emergency Committee to deal with the problem.

This meeting, which I attended, was held at the university on a week-day morning on very short notice; yet it attracted roughly eighty women (accompanied by nineteen children) and thirty-nine men representing the several colonias concerned. The disproportionate attendance by women was explained by the fact that more men have jobs that do not permit them to attend. The meeting was chaired by the representative of the students' association. The nature of the emergency, the history of legal claims, and the plan of action were discussed.

To rally support, residents from the community, including those threatened with eviction, came to the stage and took the microphone to explain their situation. Those who spoke were about two-thirds women, and a significant number could be identified as "indigenous" by their clothing. Among these residents there was no noticable difference between the skills or reception of male and female speakers. A few were obviously experienced, articulate leaders. One such woman advised the others, "Do not worry, but come forth and explain what is happening. We are humble, but we should speak—all those who have been threatened."

As a result of this meeting, representatives from each of the allied squatters' settlement were selected to form a coordinating committee charged with helping the legal adviser present their case. The representatives of San Lorenzo included two men and one woman (all three being officers of the Betterment Committee), while the committee as a whole included seven women and five men from the various squatters' settlements. The woman representative from San Lorenzo described her activities as follows:

> My duty has been to be at the side of the legal adviser when we have an audience with some functionary of the government, in order to support him, to call on the people when they have to come, and to regulate them in front of the National Palace in the central park, always in an attitude of peace.
>
> . . . We went to the Secretary General of the President to see what had resulted from the petition we had presented to the President of the Republic and we invited many persons, around 500. Another man and myself organized the people who gathered, then we also made announcements by radio. In all, the major part who came were women. Men are less active in these associations because of their work. The man must earn the bread of the house, he has to be working, and these things are usually done only in the morning when the men are working. We [women] have to go out *patas arriba* (topsy-turvy) without having our sweeping done, the beds made, and with the fires that rats can pass over—because there is no fire. Many times we have had problems with our husbands because their clothes

are not ready, because the food is not ready at home, or else we have to make the food one day for the next.

I go from 8 A.M. to 1 P.M. because I have to stay in the office all day to send telegrams, to put announcements on the radio, to go to a hearing. In the afternoons, I have to advise people by going from house to house because some people do not listen to the radio.

The problem of eviction which arose during the time of my fieldwork was just a small skirmish in a long series of struggles to defend the squatter settlements since their foundation. The assemblies of settlers of the allied squatters' settlements may not have produced a massive turnout in terms of the total squatter population, but a turnout sufficient to show serious concern and the ability to rally much larger groups should the problem intensify. The strong showing of women and their active participation indicate that (1) housing is an issue of immediate importance to women, (2) colonia women are experienced in this type of struggle, and (3) women of the shantytowns are not stymied by cultural stereotypes that discourage public roles for women.

The important role of women in the Emergency Committee of the squatter settlements offers a dramatic contrast to the union meetings at El Cañaveral where women do not dare speak. Although it is rare for women of San Lorenzo to work in unionized jobs where they might become involved in strikes and political activity outside the colonia, some of them are experienced in a variety of informal political struggles that are not confined to neighborhood interests. Some have participated in demonstrations against high prices, and in support of a priest who is active in urban politics; others have participated in strikes organized by market associations. Some of the most politically active women are those who took part in the founders' invasion of the area; they have an informal network of loyal neighborhood supporters who can be activated for certain causes by little more than a shout from the doorway of their leader.

The politically active women of San Lorenzo are familiar with many types of formal and informal political expression, including the use of leaflets, newspapers, radio, television, and public demonstrations. They are also familiar with threats, tear gas, and other forms of violence as part of the political process of Guatemala. Although there appear to be effective limits on the entry of women into important leadership positions in the formal structures of political parties and government, the role of the women of San Lorenzo in the more informal political movements and organizations displays vitality and approaches sexual equality.

Religion. Religion is an important basis for social organization among the people of San Lorenzo. As seen in rural areas, religious expression in the urban shantytown is also characterized by divisions between Catholics and Protestants. In San Lorenzo, there is further fragmentation as a result of the diverse cultural and regional backgrounds of residents, and the availability of multiple modes of religious expression in the metropolis.

In 1966, Roberts found that the population of San Lorenzo was roughly 75 percent Catholic and 25 percent Protestant (1968b:755). My own findings from 1974–75, based on a sample of 48 families, show little change in this distribution.

There are three small Evangelical chapels and one small recently completed Catholic church located within San Lorenzo, but people from the colonia attend both Protestant and Catholic churches in other neighborhoods as well as those in their own community.

Protestantism. Roberts' study (1968b) does not distinguish among Protestant sects, but informs us that 60 percent of the Protestant families were Evangelists.[13] In my survey Evangelists also form about two-thirds of the Protestant families. Hence, this discussion pertains largely to the characteristics of Evangelical groups, as representative of the major Protestant denomination in San Lorenzo.

Evangelism offers many of the same attractions for women that were noted in El Canaveral. These include: frequent meetings in both evenings and afternoons where women are active participants; the organization of mutual aid groups among women which provide social and small financial aid to families in crisis; the prohibition of alcohol; and the organization of trips to visit other Evangelical groups around the capital.

Table 5-7. Family Religious Affiliations in San Lorenzo

Church	(%)	(Number)
Catholic	73	35
Evangelical	15	7
Mixed (Catholic and Evangelical)	4	2
Jehovah's Witness	6	3
Mormon	2	1
Total sample families	100%	48

In his analysis of the secular behavior of religious groups in Guatemala City, Roberts suggests that urban growth, migration and job instability in low income groups have created a situation in which:

> There are neither the geographical, economic, nor social bases for enduring secondary associations among low-income families. Under such urban conditions, a religious sect is one of the few forms of urban voluntary association available to low-income families. (1968b:754)

Emphasizing the role of Protestant groups in providing members with a definite social position and practical means to alleviate economic insecurity through sober habits, Roberts maintains that:

> One of the greatest dangers in Guatemala City is the temptation to alcoholism and petty crime. In this situation, the small Protestant groups provide a community of supportive relationships which can help individual members avoid drinking, smoking, and petty crime. (1968b:761)

The "moral community" established by Protestant groups such as the Evangelists is particularly important to women in San Lorenzo. As in El Canaveral, a religious organization that strives to curb the tendency for male economic providers to divert the family funds toward personal alcoholic consumption is attractive to women whose economic position is weak. A supportive social network is also particularly important to women when family relations founder and women are left with dependent children. Roberts found that "four of the five female heads of family who are Protestants converted to Protestantism when their husband's desertion disrupted their existing family and kinship links" (1968b:768). Significantly, half of the Evangelical families in my own sample are headed by women, and most of the women, whether married or single, have faced either widowhood, separation, or marital instability due to the husband's alcoholism.

Roberts has commented on the particularly active role of women in the Protestant religious groups of San Lorenzo:

> Families with no other relatives in the city, women whose marriages are broken, and people whose occupations expose them to exceptional uncertainty such as the small self-employed craftsmen or traders, are disproportionately found in these churches. One other striking feature of these churches is that their active members are females. Given marital instability and the greater difficulty that women experience in making and maintaining social relationships, the Protestant churches do offer a milieu where females can easily form relationships and where family cohesion is

emphasized and strengthened through constant interaction in the various church activities. (Roberts 1968b:768)

These observations regarding the attraction and advantages that Protestant groups hold for women and others who are economically vulnerable are largely consistent with my own interpretations of religious organization in San Lorenzo. I would only add that religious groups are still the most socially accepted or "legitimate" modes of extradomestic organization for women in a society that lacks other traditional organizations which invite social participation by women.

Catholicism. As observed in other parts of Guatemala, Catholicism in San Lorenzo does not necessarily refer to an active religious affiliation. Most Guatemalans consider themselves Catholic from birth, but many remain only nominally Catholic. Furthermore, Roberts notes that Catholic affiliations in the city are diffuse.

Guatemalans in the city do not regard their religion as centered around any one church and its community of believers. . . . The sacraments of the church, such as confession and communion, are infrequently taken. . . . A Catholic congregation in a city church does not form a stable set of social relationships, but a constantly changing set of individuals (1968b:760).

Roberts also points out that there is a scarcity of priests in the city, with only about one priest to about 30,000 people in low-income areas. Although Catholic congregations appear to be amorphous groups, too large and unstable to be an "interacting community," San Lorenzo does possess a core of organized Catholic activists, the Catholic Hermandad,[14] which bears some resemblance to the Protestant groups.

The Hermandad is an association of active Catholics dating back to the foundation of the colonia. It is noteworthy that the original invaders decided to name their colonia after a saint, and acquired a saint's image to serve as the focus for their combined residential, political, and religious identity. Although time has revealed considerable division between Catholics and Protestants, progressives and conservatives, old and new residents, the Hermandad persists as a subgroup identified with a particular constellation of interests in San Lorenzo.

Formally, the Hermandad is concerned with the care of the saint and with Catholic religious observations within the colonia. Its members organize a neighborhood festival and procession for the saint's day and elect a queen. They organize pilgrimage excursions to Escuipulas which may take as many as 200 people by bus to visit the famous shrine. They also conduct neighborhood-wide fund raising—through parties, dances, bicycle races, and sponsorship of wrestling matches—to support church functions and to construct a small church within the colonia.[15]

Like the Protestant groups, the Hermandad is a closely knit community group in which local women play a leading role. It is headed by a religious committee composed of twenty-two people, of whom two-thirds are women. The president of this committee is a woman who commands a significant loyal following. She is able to mobilize this following to support or boycott various other organizations within the colonia, as well as to mobilize them to participate in religious or political issues that have broader significance. This woman draws on the strength of common bonds among the invaders and a long history of mutual support among members of the Hermandad, also acting as chief intermediary between the colonia and an urban priest who is widely known and popular among the city's squatter settlements for his political positions and advocacy of radical change. The women of the Hermandad militantly support this particular priest on a variety of issues ranging from national, urban, and church politics to neighborhood organization.[16]

Roberts' assessment of the importance of women in the Hermandad is again one with which I largely agree:

> Despite radically different doctrines and practices, the Hermandad has some striking similarities to the Protestant sects. It, too, was dominated by women and by women who were either separated from their husbands or who could expect little support from them. These women interacted frequently, both in the organization of religious activities and in political activities and recreation. They helped each other out in small and large emergencies. . . . They are the only group of Catholics that worship as a locally based community (1973:188).

Religious groups are an effective form of social organization in San Lorenzo and permit an unusually high level of participation and leadership by women at the community level. Because religious institutions are formally associated with, and hence protected by, conservative ideologies, they possess a relatively high potential to innovate and invite the creative participation of people who might otherwise be considered unstable and/or dangerous members of society if organized. The religious organizations of San Lorenzo serve both to help stabilize the social and economic situation of people who have an insecure position in urban society, and to advance their interests, individually or collectively, in ways that are less likely to be considered "political" and hence dangerous.

Education. Various studies of Guatemalan squatter settlements such as San Lorenzo have reported literacy levels at around 80 percent of the population (Cuevas 1965:56; INVI 1968:19). Roberts (1973:38) reports that 77 percent of the adult males in San Lorenzo have attended school, but does not supply any data on female literacy. In my own survey of San Lorenzo (sample of 1974–75) and in the urban survey of 1967 (Orellana and de Léon 1972), sexual differences were evident in the literacy levels and the average number of years of schooling achieved by those over age 15. (See Table 5–8.)

The data in Table 5–8 clearly indicate that females are relatively disadvantaged with respect to education. In part, the differences in female and male educational attainments may be attributable to the conditions in rural areas from which many of the adults of San Lorenzo migrated.

Data on the contemporary education of San Lorenzo children by sex are not available. Since there is no school within the colonia, San Lorenzo children disperse to attend various city schools where they are mixed with children from other, often higher-status, neighborhoods. Roberts reports that 38 percent of the school-age children of San Lorenzo do not attend school (1973:335). It is likely that compulsory formal education for both sexes and the availability of public primary schools in the city are gradually reducing the differences between the sexes with respect to literacy and primary school education. Statistics for urban areas of Guatemala as a whole show that girls make up 46 percent of the primary school population enrolled in the first grade of

Table 5–8. Literacy and Average Education Among Females and Males (Age 15 and Over)

	Average Years of Schooling	(Sample Size)	Literacy* %	(Sample Size)
Sample 1974–75				
Females	2.2	(31)	67	(66)
Males	3.6	(25)	90	(62)
Sample 1969				
Females	2.5	(67)	66	(67)
Males	3.9	(69)	96	(69)

* Literacy for sample of 1974–75 was recorded according to respondents' own evaluation of their abilities. In the sample of 1969 (Orellana and de León 1972), the percentage who had received at least one year of formal schooling was used as a measure of literacy. Although both measuring techniques have weaknesses, the agreement between the results indicates they are resonably accurate.

Sources: See table 5–3.

public schools, with their proportion dropping steadily to 43 percent of those enrolled in the sixth grade (Guatemala 1970:251). On the other hand, there are indications that in the small percentage of cases where youth from low-income families can pursue secondary education, they are predominantly males. In my interview sample of fifty families, there were six families with a total of seven children enrolled in secondary institutions. All but one of these students were males. Apart from secondary institutions, several young women had enrolled for short vocational courses in sewing, typing, or nursing aid offered by various commercial institutes in the city. The INVI census of squatter housing (1968:10) supports this observation. Of 166 individuals who were recorded to have completed some secondary education (including those in progress), only 34 percent were females.

The social significance of sex differences in education is a complex issue, but there is little doubt that in modern society formal education plays an increasingly important role in job access. Roberts has shown that since the mid-1950s there has been a decrease in the importance of personal contacts and, inversely, an increase in the importance of literacy as a criteria for obtaining employment, particularly the better jobs in "established enterprises" (1973:125–130). If the possession of educational credentials is increasingly a condition for access to good jobs, then the observed lag in the educational qualifications of women is currently a limiting factor.

Other social organizations. The people of San Lorenzo participate in various social service, work, and recreational associations. As with other areas of social organization in San Lorenzo, these are characterized by fragmentation within the colonia and by dispersed vertical and horizontal links to people and organizations in the rest of the city.

At the local level, and of the most direct appeal to women, are the women's clubs. According to informants, the first women's club was formed in 1966 when a social worker from the Social Welfare service began to come to teach various skills to the women of the colonia. The group that formed eventually solicited municipal support for the construction of a club house. The women acquired an unoccupied lot and they themselves collaborated in construction by working with shovels and picks to level the land and by carrying the cement blocks to the work site while men hired by the municipality erected the building. At the time of my research, the San Lorenzo women's club had recently split into two rival groups which I shall distinguish as the Women's Club and the Mothers' Club. Each group claims that they hold a large active following in the colonia while the other is nearly defunct.

The Mothers' Club retains the keys to the club house, which also contains sewing machines donated by the municipality, while the Women's Club meets in a resident's home but has retained the services of the social worker from MONAP. The Mothers' Club President maintains that the other faction is an arm of the Betterment Committee and MONAP, which she feels are trying to control all other community organizations. She argues that as elected president she has delegated authority from the municipality to control the use of the club for Mothers' Club meetings.[17] The leader of the Women's Club claims that the clubhouse should be made available for community purposes, which include meetings of MONAP groups. The vituperative dispute between these two groups is a reflection of other splits in the community, such as those between factions that support or oppose the Betterment Committee and those between Catholic and Protestant groups.

In terms of their appeal to women, the Women's Club and the Mothers' Club are almost indistinguishable. They both offer regular meetings and organize lectures, courses, and activities for women. Some of the past programs have included evening literacy courses, sewing and cooking classes, and promotion of various handicrafts such as knitting and making candle holders and paper flowers. Before the split, the group had around two dozen active members. At the time of my research, both groups drew about a dozen women and teen-age girls to their meetings.

When I attended meetings of these clubs, they appeared disorganized or highly unstructured.[18] At the Mothers' Club which was currently lacking a social worker, the president simply led a very informal cooking lesson for the teen-age girls while some older members chatted and knitted. The president explained that she was trying to get other social workers from the municipality or Red Cross to come to teach useful crafts, and possibly literacy. She asserts that the women want to be productive, but that the social workers from MONAP were teaching them useless crafts that were unsaleable.

At meetings of the rival group, the social worker taught the women how to make mosaic pictures using seeds, how to make flowers out of corn husks, and helped some with their knitting stitches. The women claim that they are able to sell some of these items, but when they do not sell they are simply used at home. The desire to learn saleable handicrafts and to acquire new economic skills appears as a specific and strong motive among women in both clubs.

The women's clubs have been dependent upon external patrons, the municipality and MONAP, to provide financial resources, programs, and personnel. The intermediaries are generally middle-class social workers. Apart from factional problems, some women express disenchantment with the clubs because they do not teach skills which can help the women get better jobs or increase their cash income. The arts and crafts taught by the social workers require little skill and capital and have a limited market; they are of dubious economic value.[19] Their main achievement is that low-income women have an alternative source of low-income work which, like laundering and marketing, is compatible with their domestic responsibilities. To a certain extent, these novel domestic skills may also represent a more genteel form of work to women of San Lorenzo even if they are not very profitable. Middle-class women engage in similar crafts as hobbies and to a certain extent serve as a model to the women of San Lorenzo who would also like to decorate their crudely furnished homes with small items of aesthetic value.

A sexually integrated social group which meets in the colonia is a pro-family welfare organization sponsored by MONAP. This group organizes local programs to explain social problems such as health, venereal disease, and birth control. Some of their programs have been widely attended by as many as 50 people, and information on birth control appears to be widely disseminated among the women and men of the colonia.

Another significant example of social organization in San Lorenzo proved to be a failure, but I mention it here because it is extensively reported by Roberts (1973:240–282) prior to its failure, and my informants discussed it as well. This was the consumer cooperative organized in the late 1960s, again with the assistance of external oganizers. As in other colonia organizations, the women played an active role in the cooperative. The founding membership of twenty-one included nine (or 43 percent) women. Of the four executive officers, only the president was a man and some of the women emerged as important leaders of the group. According to a former participant and officer, the women were again hard-working volunteers, planting the posts for the construction of the building and later provisioning the store. She blames the eventual failure of the co-op on the president who was allegedly letting his family help themselves to the store's supplies so that the store was losing money. People withdrew from the co-op and the president moved out of the colonia. Although the co-op failed, it was another indication of the high level of participation and integration of women in community organizations. An even greater degree of female participation (84%) was observed in a consumer cooperative with 60 members in a neighboring squatter settlement (Roberts 1973:247), where the cooperative continues to function.

There are other small organizations in San Lorenzo that have less appeal to women. For instance, there are various informal sports clubs composed of young men who form soccer and basketball teams. Although some of the teen-age girls have played basketball informally since leaving school, sports are not an enduring basis of social organization for them. As in North America, young men in low-income areas of Guatemala look to professional sports as a road out of the slum. For young women, professional sports careers are virtually nonexistent.

Apart from community-centered organizations, a small percentage of the residents belong to work organizations outside the colonia. These include unions and market associations. Less than 5 percent of all employees in Guatemala are unionized (Piedra-Santa 1971:171; Roberts 1970:485). Since unionization occurs most easily in the larger establishments with formal jobs in which women are underrepresented, the percentage of unionized women is even lower. In fifty households in San Lorenzo, I found that only three men and one woman currently belong to unions. Women who worked in textile factories reported them to be nonunionized, in large part due to repression. One woman repeated a common observation, "At the factory, if you join a union, they take away your work. In order to have work, you have to avoid union activities and be in agreement with the bosses."[20]

San Lorenzo women appear to be somewhat more active in market associations where the economic situation is less formalized. Three San Lorenzo market women in my sample have participated in such associations. Two have been active in past strikes against increased market taxes, and a third has actively participated in the organization of an association for the defense of marketers.[21]

Domestic Organization

Household structure. During the fifteen years since its settlement in the invasion, San Lorenzo has been changing as social acceptance and investment in housing in the colonia have increased over time. Household size has increased. Census data from 1964 report the average household size at 5.5 persons (Ministerio de Trabajo 1969). Later studies from 1965 and 1968 show an increase to approximately six persons per household (Cuevas 1965; INVI 1968; Rojas and Marroquin 1970), while my own survey of 76 households in 1974–75 shows an average of 6.5 persons per household. Robert's study confirms the apparent trend toward larger household size. He found that the colonia has a constant turnover of population, approximately 7 percent a year, and that the average number of children of entering families increased from 2.7 families that entered San Lorenzo prior to 1961 to 3.4 in families that came later (1973:115).

Another change in the characteristics of households since the founding of San Lorenzo is a decrease in the percentage of female-headed households.[22] Roberts observed that since 1961 "the proportion of single females who come with their children to set up house in the shantytown has diminished from the earlier 34 percent to 18 percent" (1973:115). My data from 1974–75 show that approximately 16 percent of the households are headed by women. According to Roberts, the decline in the high proportion of female-headed households since the founding of San Lorenzo contrasts with a legally established low-income neighborhood of approximately the same age which was settled primarily through purchase. This neighborhood, called Planificada, was initially settled with only 9 percent of the households headed by women, a proportion which declined only slightly to 8 percent after the initial period of settlement (1973:110, 115).

The changing household structure appears to be related to the changing economic value of housing in the colonia of San Lorenzo. The original invaders who came to San Lorenzo were distinguished by the fact that they could not afford to pay rent or buy housing. They seized upon a risky and radical solution to their problems. Single mothers were disproportionately represented in this very desperate urban group.[23] As San Lorenzo has become a more established colonia where newcomers pay rent or purchase houses from previous residents, it is no longer an area of extremely low-cost housing; it is no longer within the reach of most female heads of household. Instead, newcomers to the colonia are more likely to be families that can count on male economic support (see cases four and five of this chapter), and in this they bear a closer resemblance to the households of Planificada.[24]

Family structure in San Lorenzo is predominantly nuclear, with 68 percent of the families in the 1974–75 sample taking this form.[25] Complex families which expand upon the conjugal pair with children to include three or more generations or collateral relatives comprise 20 percent of the sample, while reduced families which lack a conjugal pair are only 12 percent of the population. Each of the reduced families encountered was based on kinship links between women and children (or grandchildren) rather than between men and children. In the complex families, there are eight households with eleven married couples living in households belonging to their kin. Of these eleven couples, five are virilocal and six are uxorilocal, indicating the importance of bilateral kin ties for acquiring housing in an urban environment where cheap accomodations are scarce.

Marriage and the family. The incidence of common-law marriage in San Lorenzo is similar to that found in El Cañaveral. Only 42 percent of the couples living together are legally married (the same percentage found in El Cañaveral; see Chapter Four, Note 10), while the remainder are united consensually (Roberts 1973:40). While legal marriage undoubtedly reflects status concerns, it is difficult to assess its importance for women. There is little evidence that legal marriage is an effective guarantee of economic support for a San Lorenzo woman if a couple separates. Other factors such as male unemployment, job mobility, and alcoholism can make male economic support erratic regardless of legal obligations. At the same time, some men who have separated from common-law wives continue to make contributions for child support whenever they are able to earn a good income. Also as in El Cañaveral, many of the conjugal unions in the squatter settlement are short-lived due to abandonment, separation, divorce, or death. In a study of several squatter settlements in Guatemala that are similar to San Lorenzo, it is found that 73 percent of the household heads are married or united in free union, 12 percent are single, and 15 percent are divorced, separated, or widowed (INVI, 1968:20, 28).

Children in San Lorenzo are frequently raised without the benefit of continuous support from both natural parents. Both male and female parental relations may be interrupted not only by changing emotional commitments, but also by the instability of employment and the mobility needed to obtain work. In informal interviewing, it appeared that at least sixty-three children in twenty-four households (32 percent of the households in the 1974–75 sample) were living with only one or with neither of their natural parents.[26] The arrangements include children living with single mothers, with grandparents, stepparents, and foster parents. There are cases of children living with adult females, or adults of both sexes, but none in which children are solely under the care of adult males.

The flexibility with which some children are moved between various households and child care arrangements reflects economic necessity. Children are typically transferred to available kin whose opportunity cost in performing child-care is lowest, that is, those who have least to lose by caring for children. For example, in two cases in San Lorenzo, single mothers have gone to work in the United States, leaving their children in the care of the children's grandmothers and sending money for their support.

Some working mothers take their children to the Children's House run by the Society for the Protection of Children. For Q. 1 per month per child the children may be left from 8 A.M. to 5 P.M. and are given lunch and two snacks. Although it is located outside San Lorenzo, one working mother describes it as "very easy for the mother, and very practical." A laundress says that she simply locks her young children in the house when she must go out to work, while another leaves her children informally under the supervision of a friendly neighbor. Still others take their children to work with them if they are self-employed in trade or in the markets. Although market women find it easier than others to take their children with them to work, they are aware that the marketplace is not the most desirable place to raise young children. One woman wishes she could get her fellow market vendors to organize a market association which, among other things, would demand a day-care center:

> We desparately need a place for the children of all the poor market women who only hang around or interrupt their mother's business when they could be learning something. Most of the children cannot go to a regular school because their mothers do not have the resources. If such a *guardería* existed now, I would have my children in it.

The difficulty and cost of raising children in an urban cash economy discourage reproduction. Many, if not most, San Lorenzo women of childbearing age practice birth control.[27]

The treatment of children appears highly variable in San Lorenzo, depending to a large extent on the economic resources at hand. In the poorer households, the cash outlay for clothing, food, and elementary education for children is a severe burden, and children are expected to contribute economically by running errands and doing odd jobs from an early age.[28] The child that cannot or will not make a contribution is often resented. In households that are better-off (and in some that can barely afford the extra expense), parents may make great sacrifices to provide their children with secondary education in the hope that they will obtain good jobs. This means doing without the immediate economic assistance of their maturing children, hoping that they will repay their parents later on. Indeed, the risk seems justified, since the older residents of San Lorenzo tend to depend significantly upon the cash contributions of their grown male and female children, and some would face extreme hardship without such help.

When not working, the social life of teen-age girls is more restrained by parents than that of boys. Girls are discouraged from loitering in the streets the way groups of boys do. Yet their frequent errands give them opportunities to chat with friends *en route*. Female virginity and parental consent are seen as ideal conditions for a daughter's marriage. Such views conform to the widely disseminated "public morality" advocated by the higher strata in Guatemala. Informants' statements suggest that such ideal conditions are probably uncommon in San Lorenzo. Several conjugal unions that were established during my research indicate that it is a regular procedure for a girl to simply unite with a boy by moving into his (parents') household, particularly when pregnancy is suspected. Parental disapproval is voiced if the girl is young, if the boy failed to speak to the girl's parents, or if it was necessary for the girl's brothers to put pressure on the boyfriend. In two such cases where girls left to live with their boyfriends in the colonia, the mothers were extremely angered by the unions because they felt that the boys liked to drink too much and would not be responsible fathers. Remembering their previously expressed ambitions for their daughters to continue their studies in the United States to learn skills for high-paying jobs, their disappointment is understandable.

As in El Cañaveral, married women and common-law wives experience a good deal of competition from the women "in the street" and from alcoholism, both of which drain family resources. The young woman who has children but lacks a husband is often suspected of trying to lure someone else's man. Yet the illegal origins of San Lorenzo and the obvious need to create a niche where formally none existed seem to contribute to a somewhat tolerant attitude toward the woman who lives on formal or informal prostitution. One informant discussed the subject as follows:

> There are declared prostitutes and those who are "contraband," without permission. If you have to work, you take out your permission—they are like diplomas. One girl we know here turned to the bad life. She lives with a thief. . . . There are prostitutes here who are liked and respected by their neighbors. The majority have children. It is rare the one that does not have children. I know a woman who works in the park in Zone 1. She says that she earns about Q. 5 per day.[29]

Within San Lorenzo, informants claim that prostitution is not very common. This contrasts with the public image of the shantytown as the home of prostitutes and thieves (Roberts 1973:199, 205, 340). With respect to prostitution, a possible reconciliation between these two views is that San Lorenzo itself is not wealthy enough to support much prostitution; those from San Lorenzo who work as prostitutes tend to direct their activity toward more lucrative zones of the city.

In San Lorenzo there is relatively little evidence that men are able to control the social life of women or restrict them to a private domestic sphere of activity. The density of settlement means that there is very little private life. Many of the daily activities in the colonia—drawing water, washing clothes, stepping outside one's door—are very public acts simply because the small, flimsy houses on tiny lots, the shared walls, paths, and water facilities all impede privacy. This lack of privacy, the rudimentary character of many homes, and the unstable economic contributions of husbands make it difficult for men to impose social restrictions upon women. When this situation is compounded by the need for the woman's economic contribution, any attempt to confine a wife to the house becomes impractical.

The ideal that a woman's place is in the home finds little expression in San Lorenzo, but the cult of male domination and the right to command a wife is not entirely absent. I found it most explicitly expressed by Alida, whose husband earned a relatively high income and who had recently become a Jehovah's Witness:

> The husband commands everything at home. If I want to go out somewhere, I have to ask my husband's permission. If he says no, I do not go. The jealous man does not let his wife go out. If the husband knows that the wife is honorable, he lets her go out. But an honorable wife always goes out with the children, she does not go out alone. I always go out with the children unless I am going out to work. [She sells shoes.] Then I leave the children alone in the house. But if I am just going out for a walk, I take the children along.

Even here, accommodations are made for the working woman. Anabella describes the moderate attitude taken by her husband: "I can talk to men in the street, but he does not like men in the house." Despite such statements, I found that home visits from males as well as females are not uncommon in San Lorenzo. For instance, a woman engaged in religious and political activities freely invites men or women from these groups into her house for a cup of coffee when they drop by to discuss problems.

This does not mean that sexual jealousy and suspicion are less common in San Lorenzo than elsewhere, but that strong restrictions on female social activity are relatively inconsistent with women's vital role in establishing the colonia and earning a cash income. In general, the women of San Lorenzo achieve a relatively high level of social autonomy.

In an environment where women's experiences have taught them self-reliance and where they have successfully opposed violent efforts to dislodge them and their families, facing government opposition and public insult, they are not easily intimidated by their husband's attempts to control the domestic unit. An interesting case of a marital power struggle is that of a quarreling couple that I interviewed. Jorge and Isabella were part of the invasion. After many years of residence in San Lorenzo, Jorge decided to sell the house and use the money to move into a better neighborhood because their older children were ashamed of their home. Isabella opposed his decision, but he went ahead and sold it without her consent. She went to the authorities "to defend myself and the children," and contested his right to sell. The judge said that Jorge did not have title to the land, and that the whole family had a right to the house. Jorge was ordered to return the money to Isabella, who bought the house back and got it listed in her name. Jorge claims he wanted to buy a legal lot and build a new house.

An excerpt from their argument reveals not only their personal grievances, but something of the distinct perspectives of men and women in the colonia:

Isabella:[30]
> A lot costs Q. 1,500 to buy. He did not have enough income to buy a whole lot, much less to pay to build a house.

Jorge:
> When there is a contradiction between husband and wife, nothing works, nothing constructive results. The fault is hers because she did not agree with me.

Isabella:
> I need two incomes to maintain the family. He spent Q. 25 of the money he received.

Jorge:
> This is the responsibility of the man. There are times when the woman must help the man.

Isabella:
> But in another form.

Jorge:
> Imagine the woman who could help the man not only to work, but also to think!

Isabella:
> Imagine! We would be without a place to live and to eat.

Jorge:
> Or we would be better. The woman must give all her encouragement to the man.

Isabella:
> For four months he worked, but he did not give me any money. He buys the food, but gives me no money. I do not see any shoes, or clothes. I go out to work to buy clothes and shoes. . . .

Jorge:
> I used to give her all the money and make her happy.

Isabella:
> But you changed.

Jorge:
> There is a reason.

Isabella:
> There is not a reason. You and your dignity. You and your money. A wife does not deny her man at night. A typewriter and refrigerator had to be sold when he had no work. A woman needs more than bread and water. The man could destroy everything. The house is mine. He had the money in his pocket, minus Q. 20. I bought the house back with the same money.

Jorge is concerned with "progress," while Isabella is concerned with "survival." Isabella wants the security that, even if faced with the loss of male income, she will have a house for herself and her children. Jorge wants his relatively high but irregular earnings to go toward a more respectable dwelling. Enlisting an ideology of male dominance, he has withheld his earnings from his wife to save for a house, but this has been a source of irritation to Isabella. She expects, but does not count on, Jorge's contribution. Her long-term strategy takes into account the difficulties a woman can expect if death, desertion, or male unemployment leave her as the sole support of the family, dependent on her meagre earnings as a domestic employee. Her experience as an invader familiar with judicial disputes over housing probably contributed to her decision to defend her position in court.

This couple's dispute illustrates a common tendency for men to employ their greater economic leverage and an ideology of male supremacy to control the domestic unit and its collective resources. The woman's response is typical in that she does not directly challenge the principle of male leadership as much as ignore it while making independent decisions. Like many other women in the colonia, her contribution to housing and family income give her counter leverage so that compliance with her husband's decisions is not her only acceptable option.

In summary, the conditions of domestic life in San Lorenzo suggest that a high degree of flexibility is necessary in the face of an unstable job market where labor is cheap. Legitimization in marriage and in reproduction are relatively unimportant for long-term security when there is little property or status for children to inherit from their fathers or for wives to claim when their husbands have low incomes or are cyclically unemployed. Rather, child care and conjugal relationships are subject to severe economic pressures and a large measure of expediency.

With a high percentage of working women, marital relations often appear not so much an alternative as a complement to economic activity by women. The cash contributions of women remain much lower than those of men, by and large, but they provide an important margin of security and a basis for women's self-assertion in the domestic unit. In general, women do not adopt an attitude of extreme submission or deference in the presence of men, and they do not describe strong restrictions on their social contacts outside the home.

A further basis for female autonomy in the family is their direct claim to their housing. Women who participated in the invasion have created their own inheritance, their own capital, in the form of houses. That this has a bearing on domestic decisions was seen in the discussion of Jorge and Isabella. Mangin's observation regarding domestic relations in a Peruvian squatter settlement seems to have validity for San Lorenzo (1970:26):

> The fact that the couple has an investment in the ownership of a lot and a house probably holds some husbands who might otherwise desert. . . . If the husband does desert, particularly if he is a common-law husband, the wife is a good remarriage possibility since she is the "owner" of a house and a lot.

As a consequence of their economic role and position, women of San Lorenzo are not socially isolated or confined to the house with children. Even those who do not earn an income have many opportunities to socialize in the course of their domestic chores. They get their water at a public spigot, hang the laundry in the public pathways, and are generally part of an informal communications network. Their knowledge of each other's social situations and tactics contributes to their skills in solving domestic problems and provides moral support. Although public ideology and modern media stereotypes promoting male dominance and female submission in the family are not without effect in this colonia, to a large extent they are discordant with the realities of survival in a squatter settlement.

Informal Community Organization

Kinship. As San Lorenzo ages, kin ties among the residents are multiplying. Endogamous marriages are common among the youth, who sometimes live with their parents or acquire houses of their own in the colonia. Further, established migrants tend to help their relatives from the rural areas to settle in the colonia. Despite this gradually developing network of kinship relations among colonia residents, most people's kin ties remain widely dispersed as a result of the generally high mobility within the city and/or migration from the countryside. Colonia residents often have numerous kin and compadres[31] in their provincial home towns as well as in other zones of the capital. Sometimes their rural relatives serve as a destination for weekend visits or occasional vacations, providing a welcome chance to enjoy a rural environment. Although kin networks are somewhat weakened by dispersion (distant migration, family separation, and stepfamily relations), they remain an important potential resource for low-income urban residents who have unstable work and housing.

In general, the dispersed kinship system that characterizes San Lorenzo is bilateral and flexible. Kin are particularly sought for help during illness, but also for temporary lodging, loans, job contacts, and child care assistance. There is a tendency to view kin with greater trust than friends, but these relations must still be carefully managed and not overburdened with requests for aid. Women and men seem to differ somewhat in the types of assistance they can provide to their kin. Women are more likely to help during illness and to provide services and shelter to their kin, while men tend to give or lend money and material goods. However, neither sex appears to have a particular advantage in maintaining contact and receiving help from their relations.[32]

Friends and neighbors. The combination of high population density and poor housing means that much informal social life overflows into the streets. Intimate knowledge of one's neighbors is almost unavoidable. In this context, neighbors can be both an important source of social support and a source of friction.

On the positive side, people with relatively dispersed kin ties often turn to neighbors for friendship and assistance. The women of San Lorenzo enjoy a relatively high degree of autonomy in forming and maintaining friendships, irrespective of their marital status. Some of the women have become fast friends through the invasion experience, followed by shared religious and community activities. For others, neighborhood friendships may be more superficial, but they are important in certain contexts. Women report a variety of services and favors exchanged among their neighborhood friends: minding a neighbor's children or house when she goes out, providing loans of small household items or petty cash, reciprocal exchanges of special foods, help during illness or family breakup, and sharing the latest news and job information. I encountered only a few women who claimed to lack friends in the colonia. These were mainly recent residents with preten-

241

sions to high status, or women who spend most of their time working outside the colonia. The latter form their most important friendships with people whom they have met through shared factory work or domestic service, or through selling in the same marketplace.

The negative effect of living in an area of dense population and little privacy is that neighbors can be a source of intense irritation. For example, conditions in the shantytown are such that day and night one can hear one's neighbors speaking in the adjacent houses. Throughout the night there are bursts of noise as people come home late, or get up in the night to eat breakfast and leave for work in bakeries or other odd-hour jobs. Some people play their radios in the middle of the night, or walk through the streets talking loudly with drinking companions. One working woman was so upset by her husband's habit of coming home late, drunk, and playing music at 3 A.M. that she did herself and her neighbors a favor by calling the police and having him put in jail for a week.

Women are more constantly exposed to troublesome neighbors because they tend to spend more time in the colonia than men. The unsanitary habits of neighbors can be a source of extreme irritation. For instance, Telma complained that, despite warnings, her neighbor always emptied her chamber pots by throwing them at her house. The conflict intensified until one day the neighbor dirtied Telma's water supply. When Telma saw this, she responded by grabbing her neighbor by the hair and beating her. Both women were sent to jail. After that, Telma moved with her family to a different house in the colonia. Other women have also reported conflicts with neighbors which have caused them to switch houses. Competition between small neighborhood stores run by women is another source of bitterness. One woman complains that her small fruit store was doing well until her neighbors "selfishly" decided to open stores as well. Then the returns were so low that they all had to close.

As the home of a poor population facing severe job competition, San Lorenzo is characterized by social problems that typify the low-income areas of modern cities. Some of the residents resort to various illegal or quasi-legal activities such as petty theft and selling contraband drugs, alcohol, tobacco, or sex. These risky activities help some residents to survive unemployment and underemployment, but sometimes they do so at the expense of fellow residents. Various women of the colonia claim that they or their homes have been robbed of such items as jewelry, citizenship documents, clothes, household appliances, and bicycles. At the same time, women seem to account for a fair number of those who have had run-ins with the law. One of my informants casually revealed that she had been in jail for selling contraband tobacco, while four others cited brief jail terms for fighting. Since this information was not solicited, it is likely that my interview sample of fifty households contained other women with prison experience.

For the most part, San Lorenzo is a neighborhood of hard-working respectable people who are struggling to make ends meet with very low incomes. Inevitably, a poor population includes some who make their living through illegal activities and who would even take advantage of their poor neighbors. Knowing the poverty and the need which surrounds them, people tend to view their neighborhood with distrust. The informal environment of the colonia requires that women as well as men learn to "defend themselves" informally, and at times extralegally, against a wide range of social and economic problems. This response appears to be an important aspect of survival in a crowded city that can provide neither adequate employment nor adequate housing for the lower class.

Summary

An impressively large fraction of the women of San Lorenzo are economically active, albeit often engaged in irregular and poorly rewarded activities. Occupational segregation, particularly in access to formal employment in large estabishments, is evident. Women workers are largely confined to domestic services or self-employed trades where earnings are extremely low. In fact, it is argued that women in such circumstances create their own demand by offering services that are almost superfluous but cheap enough to stimulate consumption (Arizpe 1977). As little as these women earn, it is essential to their continued existence. This is immediately clear in the case of households lacking fully present male members, the more so when the general lack of financial resources of the people of San Lorenzo is considered. Even in households where an adult male is present, the instability of many male sources of income, and of many such households for that matter, means that most women must from time to time find sources of cash on their own.

The ability of the middle and upper classes of Guatemala City to absorb cheap female labor in service occupations gives women some independent cash income as a necessary alternative to total dependence on men with marginal employment. Over the long run, a woman's success at moving beyond day-to-day survival is largely dependent on her access to regular economic support from males (conjugal partners or sons) who receive higher incomes. Thus, by virtue of membership in a social category (lower-class female) that has very low cash income potential, women are induced to perform informal services for family members as a basis for claims upon their cash incomes. Often this unpaid labor comes as an addition to the work women perform for cash incomes. In a larger context, female labor both for a meagre cash income and for the maintenance of other family members provides a kind of "sub-subsistence," akin to the garden plot, and is in this sense essential as well to the continued existence of San Lorenzo as a *barrio marginal*, a source of labor for the more dynamic, rewarding, and volatile sectors of the national economy.

Women's social relations are conditioned by their direct participation in the market economy and direct involvement in the acquisition of housing through squatter invasion. As workers, women are necessarily involved in nondomestic social relations. In the performance of paid domestic services, they have personal contact with wealthier, usually middle-class, employers. In petty trades and marketing, they become involved with a diverse clientele from different parts of the city. The economic activities of these low-income women facilitate the formation of significant informal networks in the colonia and the city at large.

As members of a shantytown, the population of San Lorenzo has experienced some success through organization of their invasion to claim a place to live. Women were heavily represented among those who saw no other alternative than activism. They have had to collaborate with a heterogeneous population in an ongoing struggle to maintain their joint claim to inhabit a ravine. The activism of the women has persisted at the grass roots level of organization in political, religious, social service, and work organizations. Their participation is a clear indication that these women do not perceive their interests as being confined to the home and familial relationships.

Women not only participate in an active social life outside the home, but some of them have become integrated into the leadership of significant local organizations—witness the Emergency Committee, the Hermandad, the Consumer Cooperative, and, to a small extent, the Betterment Committee. Sex segregation persists in some organizations in San Lorenzo, but it is not highly unbalanced; both sexes do belong to small clubs that promote such activities as sports or knitting, designed to appeal to only one sex. While it cannot be said that women have achieved full social or political equality in San Lorenzo, they have assumed a relatively dynamic and important role in the community.

The important economic and social contributions of women to the survival of the family in San Lorenzo have their counterpart in weakened domestic and sexual control by men over their wives. The women of San Lorenzo belong to a class that has been referred to publicly as "*los desheredados*," the disinherited ones. The term aptly describes their position since they did not inherit the land or housing in the city where they now reside. With no inheritance, the concern for legitimacy in conjugal relations or parenthood fades. No doubt San Lorenzo men aspire to dominate women and conform to public models for masculine behavior, but for women there is little incentive to submit to strict social or sexual controls by the men of their class. Such submission does not convey substantial increases in their standard of living or security, while it could seriously inhibit a woman's capacity to feed herself, her children, and sometimes her husband. The fact that in many households neither man nor woman has secure employment or secure assets means that both may experience intermittent dependence upon the other. In this situation, it is difficult for men to maintain their claims to dominance.

14. San Lorenzo Vegetable Seller Keeping Child at Work

15. *Squatter Activists Gathering at University Before Formal Meeting*

16. *Villa Rosa: Private Gardens and Paved Streets*

17. *Villa Rosa Homes with Protective Walls*

CHAPTER SIX

Villa Rosa: An Urban Middle-Class Colonia

An Enclave of Suburbia

Villa Rosa is an orderly subdivision of new suburban-style housing constructed on a flat, elevated stretch of land not far from the commercial hub of Guatemala City. As a relatively affluent area, Villa Rosa is set apart from the neighboring colonias by its material standard of living and its physical boundaries. It is surrounded on three sides by ravines that divide it from poorer neighborhoods, including squatter settlements, located within the same administrative zone of the city. Despite its central location, Villa Rosa enjoys a certain insularity within the city. (See Appendix Two for a description of fieldwork.)

With a population of slightly over 4,000 people, the colonia has a marked preponderance of females, who comprise 58.7 percent of the population (142 females per 100 males). Resident female domestic employees account for nearly two-thirds of the imbalance. Ethnically, only 2.9 percent of the population are classified as indigenes, and observation indicates that these are probably all resident domestic servants. Villa Rosa also has a high overall literacy rate of 80 percent.[1]

Almost all the homes in the colonia are new single-family units built in the early 1960s, and paid for on a fifteen-year mortgage plan. The real estate values ranged from Q. 12,000 to 18,000 at the time of my research. The houses have numerous modern conveniences—six to eight rooms, electricity, modern plumbing, yards and gardens, carports, and front gates with buzzers to deter intruders. Modern appliances are very common. A 16 percent sample of census data (sample of 1973) for the colonia showed that 94 percent of the households have both radios and televisions, and 91 percent have refrigerators. Only 10 percent had telephones in 1973 but installations were increasing rapidly during the time of fieldwork.

The physical layout of Villa Rosa follows typical suburban forms. The streets are paved, lighted, and curvilinear to restrict traffic flow. There are parks within and near the colonia, but many urban services are located outside the area, making this a quiet neighborhood. Commercial activity is largely restricted to small neighborhood stores and home beauty salons, and is relatively inconspicuous. In a few homes, lawyers or accountants have private offices. The only two noteworthy exceptions to the general absence of commercial activity are a moderate-sized drugstore–medical center and a gas station. Significantly, both are located at the extremities of the colonia on the main road leading through it. Even the nearest marketplace is located in a neighboring colonia. Nor are any government or religious buildings located in the community. Nonetheless, Villa Rosa has ready access to urban benefits. An efficient highway and regular bus service connect it to the central commercial and administrative zone of Guatemala City. Although the direct car trip can take as little as five or ten minutes to reach the center, the roundabout bus route traverses the poorer neighborhoods and can take more than half an hour.

Economic Organization

Unlike the other communities examined, Villa Rosa is closely affiliated with the capitalist classes of Guatemala. The population includes some plantation and factory owners and a large proportion who are employed in professional, managerial, and white-collar occupations, which together form the basis for its affluence. There are also some petty bourgeois elements who operate small businesses serving the neighborhood or other parts of the city; these are a minority.

Due to the fact that this is all new housing, the origins of the residents are heterogeneous. Only 43 percent were born in Guatemala City, while roughly 52 percent come from a variety of provincial capitals and towns scattered around the nation. The remaining 5 percent were foreign-born, mainly in Central America, but a few in the United States and Europe, as well. Their class origins are also diverse. Based on parental occupations, class backgrounds ranged from the rural aristocracy (plantation owners), to provincial professionals, bureaucrats, business in-

247

terests, and petty bourgeois, and a few in low-skilled manual occupations. Among the City-born, most had parents with professional backgrounds.

Given this mixture, it is evident that some households are more accustomed to affluent urban life than others who can barely afford the lifestyle, or who are nouveaux riches and are not sure of the appropriate conduct. One unifying feature is that heavy physical or unskilled labor is virtually absent, apart from resident domestic servants. In this discussion, I treat the servants as a separate group, excluding them from the initial analysis of women's economic options. Although they form a significant percentage of the resident female population, their distinctive socioeconomic characteristics would, if included, distort the picture for middle-class women.

Economic Activity by Sex

The rate of activity in the cash economy for each sex is shown in Table 6-1 below.

The difference in the rates of females and males in the 1975 sample requires comment. This sample, my own, shows a 50 percent greater proportion of women economically active in the cash economy and about 15 percent less men. There are two possible explanations: differences in data collection and differences in the nature of the sample itself. Each explanation appears partly valid. The lower level of male employment in the 1975 sample is due to the fact that the sample includes more male university students. (It is unlikely that this represents a chronological trend of decreasing male employment.) By contrast, the higher rate of female economic activity seems at least partly due to underreporting in the other samples. I suspect that underreporting of female employment, due to cultural depreciation of the em-

Table 6-1. Proportion Economically Active of Each Sex in Villa Rosa 1969, 1973, and 1975 (Age 16 and Over Earning Cash Income)

Sample	Females			Males		
	(%)	(Number)	(Sample Size)	(%)	(Number)	(Sample Size)
1969	38.1	8	(21)	78.9	15	(19)
1973	36.7	72	(196)	78.1	132	(169)
1975	56.7	34	(60)	64.6	42	(65)

Sources: 1969: Orellana and de Leon 1972; 1973: author's extract from Guatemalan census, unpublished; 1975: author's sample.

ployment of women, might easily result from the census method of data collection. This seems especially likely in the case of female service workers or women who run small businesses from their homes.

The Sexual Division of Labor: The Market Economy

As a population that is highly integrated into the cash economy, the residents of Villa Rosa exhibit a wide variety of occupational specialties which are characteristic of the modern urban labor force. Table 6–2 groups occupations into general occupational categories and shows that professionals and bureaucrats form the most important category for both sexes, while agriculture is entirely missing. Sex segregation is extreme in such categories as service work, where no males participate, and transport, industry, and construction, where women are completely absent. In managerial and executive positions, men have a considerable edge, but the gap is not very great in the professions. Sales and office work are important for both sexes, but the higher employment rate for women noted in the 1975 sample is found chiefly in service occupations and commerce—occupations that often lack a specialized place of work and fixed hours and are thereby liable to be overlooked or not taken seriously as forms of economic activity.

Sexual differences in the professions stand out more clearly in Table 6–3, showing the constituent professional occupations. Education, particularly primary school teaching, is by far the most common profession for women.[2] In contrast, male professionals are spread over a much wider range of occupations. Although teaching is important for Villa Rosa men, they are more likely than women to hold higher-level posts in education. In business-related professions, a very few women work as accountant, analyst, or IBM operator, while men are heavily represented as accountants and auditors. Further, women are completely absent in a number of professions: the military, law, engineering, and music. In medicine, the typical modern Western division prevails whereby men are doctors, while women are nurses, nurse's aids, and lab technicians.[3] The distribution of professional occupations, definitely linked to higher education, supports the view that a modern Western occupational structure is affected by the diffusion of Western gender stereotypes, transmitted in part through educational institutions.

The hierarchical implications of the sexual division of labor are affirmed by examining the sexual division of earnings in the cash sector. In Table 6–4, the sample of 1975 shows that the average monthly in-

Table 6-2. Occupational Categories of Each Sex, 1973 and 1975

Category	Female		Male	
	(%)	(Number)	(%)	(Number)
Sample 1973*				
Professional & bureaucratic	43.7	31	48.0	61
Managerial & executive	5.6	4	9.4	12
Office work	35.2	25	7.9	10
Sales & commerce	11.3	8	18.9	24
Agriculture	–	0	–	0
Transport, industrial, & construction	–	0	15.7	20
Services	4.2	3	–	0
Total subsample	100.0%	71	99.9%	127
Sample 1975**				
Professionals & bureaucrats	32.4	11	44.4	20
Managerial & executive	2.9	1	13.3	6
Office work	23.5	8	20.0	9
Sales & commerce	17.6	6	17.8	8
Agriculture	–	0	–	0
Transport, industrial, & construction	–	0	4.4	2
Services	23.5	8	–	0
Total subsample	99.9%	34	99.9%	45

* Subsamples totals are slightly less than in Table 6–1 due to insufficient information on the nature of some occupations.
** Total number of occupations for males exceeds number of males (42) since three men combine two kinds of work.
Sources: See Table 6–1.

come for males is Q. 328, while for females it is Q. 136, or 42 percent of male earnings.[4] The sample of 1969 independently confirms the direction of inequality, with men earning an average monthly income of Q. 262 and women averaging only Q. 82 per month, or 31 percent of male earnings. Higher pay for both sexes in 1975 is probably due to inflation between 1969 and 1975.

Comparing incomes within fields, among office workers women earn an average of Q. 159 per month while men get Q. 207 monthly. In education, where men tend to occupy the higher-level positions, men

Table 6-3. Professional Occupations of Each Sex, 1973 and 1975

Profession	Women		Men	
	(%)	(Number)	(%)	(Number)
Sample 1973				
Education	67.7	21	24.6	15
School director		1		1
Professor		1		6
Primary school teacher		18		8
Sewing teacher		1		–
Music	0.0		3.3	2
Medicine & science	16.1	5	4.9	3
Doctor		–		2
Dental mechanic		–		1
Nurse		2		–
Nurse's aid		1		–
Laboratory worker		1		–
Lab assistant		1		–
Law	0.0	0	6.6	4
Lawyer		–		2
Legislator		–		1
Judicial transactor		–		1
Military	0.0	0	6.6	4
Chief of motor brigade		–		1
Army official		–		1
Colonel		–		1
Air Force pilot		–		1
Other	16.1	5	54.1	33
Engineer		–		1
Designer		–		1
Reporter		–		1
Publicity: advertising		–		1
Planner: telephones		–		1
Auditor		–		4
Accountant		1		17
Inspector		1		1
Analyst		1		2
IBM machine operator		1		1
Social worker		1		–
Assessor		–		2
Mapmaker		–		1
Total subsample	99.9%	31	100.1%	61
Sample 1975				
Education	82.0	9	20.0	4
Professor		1		1
Primary school teacher		7		–

Table 6-3. Professional Occupations of Each Sex, 1973 and 1975—Concluded

Profession	Women		Men	
	(%)	(Number)	(%)	(Number)
Typing teacher		1		–
Public health				
instructor		–		1
Curriculum specialist		–		1
Music teacher		–		1
Music	0.0	0	5.0	1
Medicine	0.0	0	5.0	
Odontologist		–		1
Law	0.0	0	15.0	
Lawyer		–		3
Military	0.0	0	15.0	3
Police chief		–		1
Air Force pilot		–		1
Army lawyer		–		1
Other	18.0	2	40.0	8
City official		–		1
Civil engineer		–		1
Auditor		–		3
Diplomatic service		–		1
Programmer		–		1
Accountant		1		1
Statistician		1		–
Total	100.0%	11	100.0%	20

Sources: See Table 6-1.

average Q. 302 per month, compared to only Q. 169 for women. In accounting, there is only one woman employed, half-time, who earns Q. 75 monthly. A male full-time accountant in the 1975 sample earns Q. 400 monthly, while one in the sample of 1969 was earning Q. 375 monthly. Not only do women earn significantly less than men within most fields, but there were no cases in which wives earned more than husbands. Although informants claim this can occur, it is clearly quite exceptional and probably temporary.

An examination of formal employment categories tells us little, in fact, about how this diverse group of women actually operates in the cash economy and why they are such a disadvantaged group relative to their men. These questions will be addressed later when we examine

Table 6-4. Average Monthy Cash Income by Sex and Occupation, 1975*

Women		Men	
Occupation	Income (Q.)	Occupation	Income (Q.)
Typing teacher (U.S. institution)	400	Advertising manager	800
Seamstress	250	Salesman	700
Teacher	215	Sales representative	600
Bilingual secretary	200	Expert in curricula	600
Sales supervisor	200	Factory manager	500
Teacher	180	Car salesman	500
Executive secretary	175	Finca administrator	500
Secretary	175	Air Force pilot	500
Teacher	170	Diplomatic service (pension)	
Teacher	170	/private business	495
		Head of accounting	450
Secretary	160	Government department	
Secretary	160	director	450
Commercial secretary	150	Accountant	400
Office worker	140	Office clerk	350
Secretary	115	Officer clerk	350
Professor	100	Store owner	350
Home beauty salon		Lawyer	300
operator	100	Pianist & teacher	300
Dressmaker	100	Office clerk	300
Kindergarten teacher	80	Programmer	290
Accountant (½ time)	75	Lawyer: Army (½ time)	250
		& private practice	(plus)
Storekeeper	70	Salesman	250
Beautician	60	Clerk	250
Teacher (½ time)	60	Public health instructor	210
Dressmaker	50	Office clerk	200
Handicrafts: knitting	45	Music teacher	200
Storekeeper	40	Professor (½ time)	200
Storekeeper	40	Court official	125
		Machine & radio	
		technician	120
Total income for		Machine operator	120
27 women:	Q. 3,680	Odontologist (½ time)	112
(income unknown = 7)			
		Municipal employee	100
		Controller of accounts	100
		Office clerk	100
		Bank clerk	90
		Total income for	
		34 men:	Q. 11,162
		(income unknown = 8)	
Average monthly earnings		Average monthly earnings	
of 27 women =	Q. 136	of 34 men =	Q. 328

* Not all individuals were willing to provide precise information on their income, so that some were excluded from this table. One such case is a man who combines employment as an auditor with administration of his own plantation for an income between Q. 1,000 and 8,000 per month. Some people have additional income from capital which was not included here.

individual examples. First, it is necessary to outline the nature of work in the domestic economy and its relation to women's options.

The Domestic Economy

Since the households of this colonia are entirely dependent on cash income, a conventional analysis would not consider as economic activity any additional forms of work which do not produce monetary income. Unlike those who work in the cash sector, wives who work to maintain the middle-class household are not awarded a direct, personal cash income. Since they purchase many goods and services, the market economy views them as consumers rather than producers or "active" members of the work force. However one labels their work, an analysis of women's economic position in Villa Rosa is certainly not complete until the nonmarket forms of domestic labor, which are mainly performed by women, have been considered.

It has already been shown that women's and men's occupations overlap in some sectors of the market economy, but that men have access to a greater variety of higher-order positions and receive higher incomes. When it comes to housework, there is very little overlap between men and women. Out of 125 households in the 1973 census sample, none of the men were housekeepers. Men who were not employed were categorized as students, retired, unemployed, or "other." Similarly, in the 1975 sample, no males were described as housekeepers. But getting behind the label (which is obviously gender-stereotyped), observations and discussions of the distribution of household responsibilities confirm that very few men assume more than a minute responsibility for domestic work and child care. Even when both spouses work outside the home, husbands do not attempt to assume equal responsibility for domestic work. The women generally attribute this to "Latin" culture, and repeatedly describe men generically as very well-served, self-indulgent, or egotistical (*muy servidos, comedon,* or *egoista*) concerning housework. The single case of reasonably shared housework was that of a progressive-minded divorced woman who, tellingly, was not legally married to the man she was living with.

Family housework. While housework is basically considered women's work, it is performed in two ways: by unpaid family members and by servants. In the 1973 census sample, 48 percent of the women over age fifteen are categorized as unpaid family housekeepers. All other women are employed, unemployed, students, or retired. In the 1975 sample, 28 percent of the women are occupied only with housekeeping, although many of those who have jobs are also responsible for much of the housework in their households. The two samples produce nearly identical percentages of resident female domestic employees, at just under 11 percent of the total population. Combining the numbers of live-in domestic employees with full-time family housekeepers, the census sample yields almost 25 percent of the total population employed in housekeeping, while the sample from 1975 shows 19 percent of the population so employed. Approximately one of every four or five persons is dedicated to the home maintenance of the rest of the population. This gives a rough idea of the importance of housework in the economy of Villa Rosa.

The availability of domestic employees is obviously a factor of some importance to the middle-class woman in that it lowers her work load and alters her responsibilities. Beyond middle-class standing itself, there does not appear to be any single factor which strongly predicts the presence or absence of domestic employees. Most households have them whether or not the adult women have outside employment. In the census sample of 1973, more than half of the households have live-in servants, whereas, in the samples from 1975 and 1969, over 60 percent have them. Households which *lack* domestic servants are generally characterized by one or more of the following features: lack of young children, lack of outside female employment, and the presence of an adult female relative with at least some time available for housework. In 1975, there was little correspondence between the outside employment of women and the hiring of domestic servants; some working women have not hired help, and some women staying at home do hire domestic workers. Evidently, households which manage without domestic employees either have less work per woman, or a tight household budget. Households that have servants may or may not have a greater amount of work per woman, suggesting that ability to pay is a key factor, whether or not the services are central to the well-being of the household.[5]

Housework includes a variety of tasks: washing and ironing clothes, buying food and household articles, cooking, washing dishes, general housecleaning, and child care. As part of their middle-class standard of living, Villa Rosa residents consume more elaborate meals, fashionable clothing, and home furnishings, and do more entertaining than most Guatemalans. Their consumption patterns entail extra time and effort for the housekeeper. This housekeeping is obviously facilitated by some forms of modern labor-saving technology such as ready-to-wear clothes, and the availability of stores, supermarkets, and processed foods and stoves and running water for cooking and cleaning.

At the same time, the fast-food industry has not yet transformed family dining patterns. In many households I visited, the husband and children return each day during the two-hour lunch break for a home-cooked meal together. Laundry also remains a labor-intensive task. Laundromats are scarce, and the few who own washing machines complain that they have broken down and cannot be serviced.[6]

Villa Rosa households are places of labor-intensive service work, but the link between this work and the productive processes of the modern economy is indirect. Production is removed from the home, and even from the colonia. Maintenance and reproduction of the economically active population is an essential form of work, but it is confused with a range of services and consumption patterns that go far beyond any biological requirements and extend into the realm of conspicuous consumption of luxuries and social reproduction of class position.

Calculating the "pay" or the economic return to the middle-class housekeeper is problematic and is not usually attempted. Yet such an exercise can help to explain why women choose to remain outside the labor force in the service of their families. One important consideration is that the middle-class woman resembles a "shareholder" in the household "corporation," and to some extent her fortunes rise and fall with the fortunes of the family as a whole.

With respect to her immediate economic position, the middle-class woman generally receives some kind of allowance from her husband with which to manage the household budget, including her personal expenses. Her husband typically pays the mortgage and utility bills, while she is responsible for food, small household items, clothes, and domestic servants. Women may receive from less than one quarter to nearly all of their husband's pay. The lowest amounts received by women interviewed are between Q. 60 and 80 monthly where the husbands earn Q. 300 to 400 per month. Several women whose husbands earn around Q. 500 per month have monthly budgets of Q. 200. Where the husband is a particularly higher earner, or the wife makes a substantial contribution to family income, she may manage sums of up to Q. 500 per month. The few divorced or separated women in the colonia receive from Q. 100 to 250 from their ex-husbands to maintain their households and children (while working to supplement this). Some households have no fixed budget for the housewife, or it may be quite small. In extreme cases, the husband doles out money item by item, thus controlling his wife in the manner that many middle-class women control their servants when they send them out to make small purchases for the household. While these allocations of income present a general idea of the way money is distributed to women for housekeeping, there are almost as many different arrangements as there are households. Further, the extent to which the wife's budget can be used for personal as opposed to general household expenses is a matter of informal arrangement and is extremely varied.

Despite the lack of precise economic returns for female family housekéepers in Villa Rosa, their overall range of income compares favorably with that which women achieve through labor force participation. In some cases, housekeeping offers the opportunity to manage significantly more cash than middle-class women can generally earn outside the home. But women who choose a housekeeper role at the expense of outside economic activity take a double chance: first, that their husbands will earn an adequate income, and second, that men will share a major part of that income with their wives. Of course, independent economic assets through inheritance can mitigate any such threat, but a substantial number of Villa Rosa households are nouveaux riches and lack solid support from the maternal side. The women who are in the labor force may not have the opportunity to earn as high an income as middle-class men, but what they do have, they control.

Domestic employees. Since domestic employees form a significant part of the resident population of Villa Rosa, I shall consider their affect on the gender division of labor in the home. First, domestic employees are exclusively female; they account for roughly five percentage points of the female majority of 58 percent in the colonia's population. Second, despite coresidence, they are clearly distinguished from the urban middle class. Their lower status is indicated by their subordinate economic position as employees, lacking vested interest in the real wealth or capital assets of their employer's household. Their relationship to the middle-class families with which they reside is an economic one which can easily be revoked. Domestic employees do not come from or return to homes in Villa Rosa when they are not working; their families are located in poorer rural communities or urban colonias, including shantytowns such as San Lorenzo.

Slightly more than a quarter of the domestic employees have an indigenous ethnic background, while their educational levels are quite low, averaging only 1.9 years for the seventy-two resident employees of households in 1973. The average age of employees is very young, twenty-one years old, indicating that there is high turnover. During fieldwork, a number of households were looking for replacements for *muchachas* (girls) who had left.

High turnover is clearly a function of pay levels, working conditions, and the nature of demand for such labor. In the 1975 sample, the average pay for live-in domestics is Q. 20 per month. The highest-paid woman receives Q. 30 per month, and the lowest Q. 15 monthly, excluding one young teen-ager who earns only Q. 1.25 monthly. These young women generally receive a place to sleep plus their meals, which may be considered as part of their wage. However, those who live out do not earn higher *cash* wages. This suggests that live-in employees receive higher total compensation because they are available to work longer hours.[7]

The task of the domestic employee is to perform or assist in the housework for which middle-class women are held responsible. With no males sought for nor seeking this work, these female assistants reinforce the notion that housework is the exclusive concern of women. In most cases, the middle-class woman supervises or herself performs some housework despite the presence of domestic employees, unless she is very pressed for time. A division of labor usually develops between the middle-class woman and her employee(s) whereby the middle-class woman maintains control over child rearing, money spending, and food preparation. Employees are assigned the more monotonous and less responsible tasks of washing clothes, ironing, sweeping, mopping, doing errands, and washing dishes. If the employee is trusted, she is permitted more responsibility for cooking and child care.

The nature of demand for domestic employees in middle-class households is complex. A rather larger proportion of the middle-class women are available (not being in the labor force) to perform necessary housework without pay for their families. The existence of this alternative is evident in the low demand (hence low pay) and high turnover for domestic servants. Yet a vast pool of cheap female labor drawn from the urban poor and from migrants is available. The low price of this female labor stimulates demand for increased domestic services in middle-class homes. The demand for domestic servants is thus extremely price-elastic. Although the difficulty of obtaining "good" domestic servants is frequently discussed by Villa Rosa's women, the demand for such servants is not expressed in higher wage offers.

Despite considerable overlap in the domestic tasks performed by unpaid middle-class housekeepers and domestic employees, their different relations to the work process and its rewards reflects their different class affiliations. The domestic employee receives her wage, which is very low, and little more. She does not have job security, nor the hope that if family fortunes rise, hers will rise proportionately. More likely a rise in the family fortune would mean that another domestic employee would be hired at the same low pay. Nor does the servant have an investment in her employer's children even if she is charged with their care. Children have duties to their mothers when they grow up, but not to their babysitters. Both the employee and the employer are well aware of this difference, which explains why most middle-class women do not wish to transfer responsibility to their employees.

The economic benefits of being a middle-class housekeeper are poorly defined and variable. Rigorous comparison with the wage of the domestic employee is impossible, for the budget of the middle-class woman is clearly not the same as a wage. Much of the money is spent on collective needs for food, clothing, household articles, and the children's education. How much remains as the personal reward for her work is unclear, but having the means to feed, clothe, and educate one's children is *part* of a higher standard of living. Although the majority of domestic employees are single and childless, their low wage does not permit them to maintain children or invest in their future. When they are older and begin to have children, they are forced to seek other economic arrangements. With these considerations, one can crudely compare the monthly budgets of middle-class women with the wages of their employees—suggesting that their returns are at least several times those of the servants.

How is the middle-class woman affected by the presence of a large labor force of lower-class women ready and willing to perform the same housework for much lower returns? In a world where occupations define value, how do middle-class women justify higher economic rewards? The questions are related. The presence of a depressed labor female labor force in domestic service undoubtedly affects the economic outlook and strategies of middle-class housewives. Cheap domestic labor, especially for the nouveaux riches, can undermine women's traditional economic functions, especially as households purchase more and produce less of what they consume. The middle-class woman knows that most of the daily housework is unskilled, and that there are scores of lower-class women willing to perform it for less pay. Both the changes in household technology and the domestic servants devalue housekeeping tasks. The market value of housework is so low that for the same budget money a husband could hire three to four live-in employees to replace the economic services of a middle-class housewife. Alternately, the middle-class woman short of personal cash knows that by dismissing the maid and doing the work herself, she only gains about Q. 20 per month.

This brings us to the second question: What are the special qualifications or skills of the middle-class housewife that fortify her claims to greater economic rewards and privileges despite the low market value of her work? Clearly, little training is involved in washing clothes, ironing, and mopping floors. She does not claim superiority in these areas.

259

Instead, she attempts to excel in new kinds of housekeeping skills that emphasize and reinforce superior class status for the household. She dabbles in gourmet cooking, fancy needlework and crafts to beautify the house, interior decorating, home tutoring of the children, and so forth. These diverse skills, stimulated by magazines and the media, are sought by middle-class women to demonstrate that they are valuable to their households in ways that cannot be matched by lower-class domestics. Such skills are actually more social than economic in nature. Even the prestige of "managing" domestic servants is eroded by the technological simplification of household tasks. Thus, the devaluation of domestic work poses a problem for many of these middle-class women which can be resolved by (1) either joining the labor force and seeking status on its terms, or (2) elaborating symbols and activities designed to enhance status ascription. If they take the second option, they ally themselves with a system that defends the prerogatives of legitimate wives, and the privileges of the well-born against occupational mobility.

Combining these views of middle-class women in the labor force and in the domestic sphere, it appears that women's *economic* position in the middle class is much more precarious and indirect than men's. In the market economy, women are more circumscribed than men with respect to salaries and occupational offerings. For housekeepers, there is no competition from men but a large pool of lower-class women ready to take over their economic functions. As individuals, the women of Villa Rosa have an ambiguous economic class standing, for neither women's pay scales nor their housekeeping skills suggest they could independently maintain themselves in the middle class. Moreover, if discrimination in the labor market is insurmountable, it may be in their interest as privileged women to emphasize their achievements in ascribing status (as mothers), rather than to achieve status by accepting ascription (to the female job ghetto).

Origin of the Occupational Structure

Large institutions. Many of the most economically rewarding occupations in Villa Rosa do not originate in either the traditional Maya or Ladino cultures, nor do they originate with community economic structure. For the most part, the occupations are urban and modern, presuming not just literacy, but higher education, mathematics, data-processing techniques, highly specialized knowledge, and technical skills. They are linked to a worldwide system of information processing and commodity exchange. Examination of the growing importance of large corporations and large institutional employers can shed some light on the observed occupational and salary structures.

Large institutions are a particularly important source of employment for Villa Rosa residents. Major business establishments plus the government, military, and educational bureaucracies employ 72 percent of the economically active population of the sample of 1975. The remainder are self-employed in individual or small family enterprises as storekeepers, free-lance professionals, and artisans whose homes are often their place of work. Table 6-5 shows a marked inequality in the sexual distribution of occupations according to the scale of the enterprise. Institutionalization of the workplace, implying greater scale and specialization, is associated with significantly lower participation rates by women.

Government employment accounts for a large proportion of the jobs in the sample from 1975 and, according to Roberts (1973:30) within the city as a whole. For Villa Rosa residents, the government provides jobs in a wide range of ministries: Justice, Labor, Public Health, Agriculture, and Finance. It also includes municipal posts, the armed forces and national police, and much of the educational system. In the private sector, banks and large corporations, some of them multinationals, account for most of the jobs. Large corporate employers for those residents sampled in 1975 include a variety of commercial interests: pharmaceutical, cosmetics, and food processing industries, foreign car imports, banana exports, textile manufacturing, international airlines and hotel chains, and the oil industry.

Table 6-5. Employment of Each Sex in Large and Small Establishments, 1975

Type	Women		Men		Total	
	(%)	(Number)	(%)	(Number)	(%)	(Number)
Large Establishments						
Government	18	6	24	10	21	16
Education	26	9	10	4	17	13
Military	0	0	7	3	4	3
Business	12	4	45	19	30	23
Subtotal	56	19	86	36	72	55
Self-Employed/ Family Business	44	15	14	6	28	21
Total Sample	100%	34	100%	42	100%	76

Large institutions have the capacity to establish recruitment policies that have major significance for the economic position of women. When hiring decisions become impersonal and standardized, institutional discrimination can severely restrict women's access to middle or high levels of income and can reinforce stereotypes that influence the educational preparation and orientation of both sexes. There is evidence that such institutionalized discrimination is developing, if not already highly prevalent in Guatemala's modern middle classes. (Gender-segregated help-wanted columns in the national newspapers attest to this.) While Villa Rosa women find some employment in large modern institutions, not only do they find fewer such opportunities as a percentage of women working, but they are also overwhelmingly confined to a limited set of jobs that receive low pay and little responsibility within the institutional structure. Teaching and secretarial work in both public and private sectors account for most of women's employment in large institutions (16 out of 19 cases in the 1975 sample).

The feminization of teaching and clerical work is part of a modern pattern of sexual segregation in employment. Its recent emergence is evident in a wider context of Guatemala's changing distribution of nonagricultural occupations. The national census data shows the proportion of women among clerical workers rose from 20 to 34% between 1950 and 1973, with women "concentrated in secretarial rather than in skilled or unskilled office work categories" (Chinchilla 1977:53). During the same period, the percentage of women in managerial occupations has been reduced to nearly half of its 1950 level, dropping from 36.2 to 18.8 percent of the total. The administrator-owner-manager category of employment has declined sharply for both men and women, with women disproportionately losing ground, a change Chinchilla links to the "recent period of foreign penetration" of capitalist enterprises (1977:53). Women have also lost ground in professional and technical employment as the female percentage in these occupations has dropped from 42.8 to 32.6 percent between 1950 and 1973. Moreover, the modern armed forces and police,[8] which provide important training and career opportunities to members of the middle class, remain an exclusively male preserve even though they have expanded into a wide variety of civic action programs since the 1960s (Chavarría 1975; Adams 1970; Dombrowski et al. 1970; Sharckman 1974).

Foreign influence. The emerging pattern of sex segregation in the modern institutional sector of middle-class employment can be interpreted both as an *endogenous* Guatemalan characteristic deriving from local cultural and historical development, and as an *exogenous* pattern fostered by the nature of Guatemala's relationship to the industrially developed nations of the West, particularly the United States. Clearly, a dialectical process is to be expected, but since culture-historical explanations are often uncritically applied to sexual divisions, I will turn first to the often neglected possibility that sex segregation in the modern sector of Guatemala is influenced by the international division of labor and the nature of dependent development. More specifically, this view would predict that capitalist expansion would replicate its socioeconomic institutions and their cultural embellishments in the capitalist centers of peripheral areas, and that the elites of underdeveloped nations—a relatively small proportion of the population—would be particularly sensitive to the models and management styles of advanced capitalist countries.

International management. Research detailing the influence of foreign institutions as well as individual entrepreneurs, advisors, and technical experts as a *direct* source of sexual discrimination in Guatemalan institutions has not yet been undertaken. However, indirect evidence supports the view that recent foreign penetration favors a particular division of labor by sex within the middle classes. The similarity between the emerging concentration of women in clerical work and elementary school teaching within Guatemala's modern sector and the concentration of women in the same types of employment in the developed nations of North America and Western Europe is unmistakable (Ginsberg 1977; Sullerot 1971). In the United States, women are 75% of all clerical workers and 86% of all elementary school teachers (Deckard 1975:87, 114). Needless to say, the observed occupational sex-typing in Villa Rosa does not appear to be particularly Guatemalan, nor a throwback to a Spanish colonial heritage.

With numerous avenues for North American influence in the modern sector of Guatemala, it would be naive to view development of the new occupational structure simply as a culturally neutral or parallel process. The dominant role of U.S. investment and recent corporate expansion in Guatemala is well documented (Adams 1970, Jonas and Tobis 1974; Quintana 1973; Butler 1981; Torres Rivas 1981). Between 1964 and 1974, the number of U.S. firms and affiliates in Guatemala increased from 58 to 126, representing 62.4 percent of all firms in Guatemala (Adams 1970; Cavalla 1981). Seventy-seven of these firms were listed in the *Fortune* one thousand with thirty-one among the top one hunded for 1974 (Cavalla 1981:119). By 1981, there were 193 U.S. firms and affiliates operating in Guatemala (Butler 1981). Among the seventy-seven largest U.S. corporations in Guatemala are various companies that provide work to people of Villa Rosa.[9] Indeed, the coincidence between the expanding influence of foreign corporations in the formal sector of the economy and the increasing concentration of women in clerical (secretarial) occupations suggests that international institutions do structurally replicate themselves when they expand into the peripheries. Assumptions about the gender of management and of secretaries (along with assumptions about age, attractiveness, and marital status) are in all likelihood transposed without question in the top-down formation of large institutions and bureaucracies. I suggest that this is not merely "picking up" attractive elements from a foreign culture, but a generalized response to the power that the foreign culture represents.

The military channel. American influence is significant in government as well as in business, through numerous military, financial, and diplomatic links. One might single out the modernization of the Guatemalan armed forces and national police as an area of strong U.S. participation and influence, with the United States providing military equipment and training (Adams 1970:262; Sharkman 1974; Dombrowski et al. 1970). For example, between 1950 and 1970 over 2,000 military and 30,000 police personnel are reported to have received training in United States-sponsored programs in Guatemala, in the United States, and at United States bases in third countries (Sharckman 1974:197–199). Moreover, of $242.6 million in United States assistance to Guatemala between 1970 and 1979, over $22.1 million, or 9.1 percent was directly for the military (despite a 1977 cut-off by the Carter administration for human rights violations). CONDECA, the Central American Defense Council, which represented a Central American military alliance under strong U.S. influence, was formed in 1964 and functioned until the fall of Somoza in 1979. This has been described as an example of the United States "superimposing a military structure on an undeveloped region" (GNIB 1982). Through CONDECA, the United States allocated substantial military aid, training, and advisers to each country in Central America, emphasizing counterinsurgency techniques and "civic action" programs. Military officers receiving U.S. military training also absorbed "U.S. ideas about development" (GNIB 1982). This influence is definitely felt in affluent areas like Villa Rosa where resident officers in both the military and national police have received technical training in the United States, and where a number of families have military connections. For instance, one Villa Rosa man with a highly successful career in the national police had received a six-months' "scholarship" to study police methods in Washington, D.C., while another highly paid military pilot also had a military scholarship to study in the United States, living

there long enough to become fluent in English. The fact that a significant portion of American influence and assistance is transmitted by a
preeminently male United States military establishment to an exclusively male Guatemalan military establishment means that this can be
another important route for the institutionalization of modern sex stereotypes in Guatemala. The central role which the armed forces play in
political and civil institutions must not be ignored; it is integral to the
growth of dependent capitalism. As Adams foresaw in 1970,

> The military, as part of its increasing corporateness and continuing poli-
> ticization, has been moving toward a regulating position in governmental
> affairs. It is, in a sense, taking over the ruling of the country. (1970:262)

Indeed, all but one of Guatemala's presidents since the C.I.A.-engi-
neered counterrevolution of 1954 have been military men, and in 1982,
after another presidential election was contested by military candidates
who claimed fraud, the military faction of Rios Montt staged a coup
that negated any pretense of electoral democracy. This is strong evidence that the elite military academy and military career shape the men
who exercise power in the Guatemalan government. The point to emphasize here is that the Guatemalan military and hence the government
itself, even when it postures as independent, is very much a creature
of dependent capitalism.

A more complete examination of the range and depth of influence
of United States and other Western capitalist institutions on the Guatemalan middle class is beyond the scope of this study. The purpose
here is not to track down the multiple paths of Western cultural and
economic influence in the new sexual division of labor in Guatemala.
But even this brief consideration of the nature of the relationship is
sufficient to suggest that powerful international corporations, financial
interests, and military institutions are active overseers of institutional
development in Guatemala, and that the middle and upper sectors of
Guatemalan society are most receptive to that influence. The working
relationship between institutional elites reproduces male–female dual
labor markets within large-scale institutions. This is compounded by a
high level of cultural influence through the mass media that disseminate Western values: movies, television, music, literature, and the whole
gamut of images created by modern advertising. Urban Guatemala,
and particularly its middle and upper sectors, is strongly exposed to
sexually stratified institutions and cultural-sexual stereotypes originat-
ing in Western capitalist nations.

What is proposed is not a simple "conspiracy theory" regarding United States corporate and military decisions to exclude women from access to higher-order positions. It would be difficult to argue that a consciously organized, concerted effort by foreign nationals deprives Villa Rosa women of an equal role in the emerging modern sector of Guatemala. Rather, it is suggested that the nature of economic domination is such that male-dominated occupational elites of Western capitalist society (in business, government, and military sectors) are influential both as cultural models and in their managerial capacities in the formation of comparable institutional elites in Guatemala. Guatemala's condition of political-economic dependence can be seen as an impersonal mechanism whereby the emerging pattern of sex segregation and inequality is imported from the developed capitalist economies. At the upper-middle-class level, such sexual stratification per se might not have an essential function in the maintenance of the capitalist hierarchy, any more than, say, speaking English. And, as individual cases to be examined will show, middle-class women are beginning to seek a larger role.

The Latin factor. Certainly not all of the sexual division of labor in Guatemala's large institutions and modern bureaucracies can be attributed to the current wave of foreign influence. The Spanish arrived nearly five centuries ago and the Latin heritage should not be discounted entirely. But it is again important to stress that the Spanish heritage is not simply a cavalier attitude of men toward women. It, too, involved the importation of a political-economic structure. An exclusively male military force and administrative bureaucracy was superimposed on a subjugated population. This Spanish-male bureaucracy ran the Audiencia of Guatemala for three centuries, and certainly left its mark on public life, laws, and institutions. (See Appendix One.)

However, Independence in the nineteenth century, the reorganization of power, the liberal reforms and the penetration of German capital to be followed by the penetration of U.S. capital in the early twentieth century mean that more than one and a half centuries of socioeconomic change must be considered. Foreign influence is greater in Guatemala today than it has ever been in the past.

It is not merely Latin culture, but also Western political-economic institutions corresponding to the worldwide expansion of capitalist economies that foster sexual stratification in the business and government sectors. The Latin patriarchal ideal at the personal domestic level was always linked to the maintenance of a predominantly male administrative bureaucracy which distributed political and economic

266

privilege. Contemporary Villa Rosa and its new suburban lifestyle are similarly tied to modern institutions that distribute privilege.

The significance of modern technology. The people of Villa Rosa live and work in areas where modern technology is virtually ubiquitous. Most men and women do not have much experience with heavy physical labor. Their occupations are concentrated in white-collar and service sectors where the work entails few of the old sex-segregating myths of strength requirements or grease-and-grime which elsewhere have been used to justify the exclusion of women. Given the diversity and pervasiveness of modern technology in the commercial and business districts of Guatemala city, it is impossible to single out a particular aspect of modern technological change which can account for the sexual divisions of Villa Rosa. The steady introduction of modern office equipment is a technological change transforming most white collar and professional occupations, but its relations to gender stereotypes is not definitive. The rapid growth in clerical occupations (Chinchilla 1977:52) has meant that skills in the use of typewriters, calculators, telephones, copiers, and computers are still so scarce and sufficiently removed from traditional sex distinctions that rigid sex-typing has not yet developed.[10]

A general distinction in Villa Rosa is that men are more likely to receive a specialized technical or professional education in areas such as engineering, dentistry, agricultural sciences, military sciences, or economics. While training is obviously a factor in men's occupational advancement in Villa Rosa, other factors such as control of capital and admission to administrative and managerial ranks may have greater relevance for sex segregation than the use of complex technology itself.

Occupational change is just one result of modern technology affecting Villa Rosa. The overall organization of urban life and Villa Rosa's place within it may be seen as a product of modern technology. Efficient use of capital and economies of scale related to modern technology have created a separation between domestic life and the formal economy which specializes in capital-intensive production and distribution. The separation of home and workplace, well advanced in Villa Rosa, is made possible by modern transportation. This separation has important implications for women.

The ease of entering the work force outside the home is related to one's transportation. Control over the means of transportation in Villa Rosa is not equally distributed by sex. Out of thirty-one men and thirty-six women, 100 percent of the men know how to drive and 75 percent have access to a car, while only 36 percent of the women know how to drive and only 14 percent have access to a car. Thus, sexual stratification in occupational opportunities is mirrored in transportation. Women tend to rely on inconvenient bus transportation while men drive to work. Few women can earn enough by working outside the home to maintain their own car. The irregularities of public transportation on overcrowded buses whose condition frequently verges on ramshackle may contribute to women's lower rate of participation in the formal economy. It is unclear, however, whether this was ever considered in the choice of residential neighborhood.

In Villa Rosa, those who work at home are isolated from the major productive processes of the urban economy. Within the cash economy, these households are principally units of consumption; they accumulate highly sophisticated consumer technology, largely developed by and acquired from industrial capitalist economies. Some of the new items lighten the work of maintaining the home and health of the work force. Each household tends to acquire its own stove, vacuum cleaner, washing machine, clothes dryer, and any other appliance that may ease the job.

Modern consumer technology increases the ratio of capital to labor in housework, but unlike modern productive technology it does not entail any significant reorganization of the work process. There is little evidence in Villa Rosa that the acquisition of labor-saving technology for housekeeping has yet helped to redistribute the housework between the sexes or to integrate the housekeeper into the modern labor force. In fact, this technology seems to correspond to the development of higher standards for and greater emphasis on housekeeping for women, in part because advertising promotes new household appliances as *aids to women*. However, it may be that Villa Rosa households have yet to reach a threshold which would permit greater transfer of labor to non-domestic contexts.

The expansion of industrial technology is obviously part of a general reorganization of production that has meant greater concentration of capital plus increased social complexity and efficiency in work organization. In contrast, much domestic consumer technology encourages the dispersal of capital, the proliferation of individualized housework, and low emphasis on efficiency. The growing gulf between the production and consumption processes is a significant factor in the economic position of middle-class women. Unlike the men, who can focus their work on public production, women find their housekeeping and child care responsibilities are ever more segregated in the consumer sector, inhibiting their full participation in production.

Economic Strategies

The development of an increasingly formal, institutionalized economic structure in the national capital affects the women of Villa Rosa by furthering a preference for men in positions of responsibility and higher pay. Women's economic strategies are obviously conditioned by the overall pattern of demand for their labor in the modern urban economy, but they are also conditioned by a complex set of domestic considerations. Among these are the economic position of the household, the earning capacity of the male members and their demand for female services, the need for child care, and the class background of household members. In contrast to the formal economy where it seemed appropriate to stress exogenous factors that influence the demand for middle-class female labor, the domestic sphere is one in which endogenous cultural factors assume greater importance. The maintenance or abandonment of a sexual division of labor is in part an expression of the demand for female labor in the home which, in turn, affects women's entry and prospects in the labor force. The economic strategies of Villa Rosa women must be viewed in terms of the interaction of the general demand for their labor in the market economy and the specific demand for their labor in the household.

The cases in this section illustrate the diverse ways in which domestic considerations affect women's economic strategies, most specifically their decision to join, stay in, or remain outside the paid labor force. Although there is considerable variety in domestic conditions, the domestic pressures against labor force participation by married women of Villa Rosa are fairly generalized. These pressures reinforce the modern structure of sexual dichotomization noted within the formal labor sector.

The domestic pressures against paid economic activity by married women are both overt and covert. Overt pressures involve a direct prohibition of or veto on a woman's desire to earn an independent income, while covert pressures are those which indirectly prevent or inhibit her full participation in the market economy. Covert pressures include one-sided domestic burdens and responsibility for child care as well as secondary consideration as when male and female household members' careers conflict. Domestic pressure against female employment is not expressed as pressure against labor force participation by women per se, but as pressure against participation by *married* women. As the cases show, a significant proportion of married women would like to join or expand their role in the market economy, and are dissatisfied with the constraints imposed on them.

Marital pressure against female employment. A common theme in the work histories of Villa Rosa women is the husbands' overt demand that they quit their jobs and stay home once they marry. Many women must anticipate this and try to resign themselves to the situation. As one housekeeper describes it: "On getting married, I stopped working to dedicate myself to the home. When a man can maintain you, this is what a woman is expected to do." Another states, "I never worked because my husband was very responsible; he did not want me in the street. He was against women working. But a man must be responsible" (That is, he must support her). Nonetheless, some women are deeply disillusioned when they are forced to make a choice. Often, they have had a taste of earning their own incomes in formal or informal jobs before marriage, and are reluctant to give it up. Or their higher education and ambitions make them feel they deserve a larger role in society. The following case is not unusual.

1. Amanda is forty-five years old and has been married for twenty-one years. She is currently a housekeeper and looks after four children who attend high school and university. With a teaching degree, she first worked at age eighteen in a provincial school. She stayed there five years and then came to teach in the capital. She worked two more years, and during this time got married. When she began having children, her husband pressured her to quit her work and she did. Until that time, she had worked, was active in local party politics, was "elected by men" as a party secretary, and was considering a university career. Her husband was opposed to this and they argued. He won, and she says: "I withdrew from everything to dedicate myself to him and the children." Her husband is a successful accountant and administrator of a provincial plantation.

For several years the whole family lived together on the plantation and she was the teacher at the plantation school. However, when they moved back to the capital, she was again not permitted to work. She wants to go back to work now but says that her husband "*pone el zapato encima*" (puts his foot down). Describing women's domestic work, she complains, "it is not seen; it is anonymous," and says half-heartedly, "I have loved him a great deal to sacrifice all this."

In cases where the husband overtly opposes the wife's desire to work, she generally submits to his decision although she may harbor hopes of changing his mind. The following unusual case involves a woman who has not resigned herself to complete economic dependence even though she has had to sacrifice her primary career ambition due to her husband's opposition to her work.

2. Berta is forty-seven years old and has been married for twenty-three years. She has three sons at home, all studying in secondary school or

university. One is married, so that her daughter-in-law and grandchild also live with her. Berta's father was a lawyer and Berta has always had an interest in law. When she received her teaching degree, she went to work in a provincial school. She worked there three years, earning Q. 72 per month and living with her parents. Her father valued education. He demanded that his sons study for university careers, and indeed they received university degrees. His six daughters all received teaching degrees, the equivalent of finishing secondary school. Her father wanted the girls to have a general cultural background. Five of them, including Berta, married professionals, but her youngest sister, who never married, became a professional herself.

At age twenty-four Berta married. At that time she had her *plazo fijo* in teaching, essentially a right to permanent work, and she had also begun to study law and economics. She wanted to continue working or studying, but her husband demanded that she renounce her position even before they married. She adds that such positions are very hard to get now. Although she did not really agree, she stopped working to avoid problems. At her marriage, the priest told her, "The wife is not a slave, but she must obey her husband."

In her thirties Berta attempted to resume her education. In a family of lawyers (father, husband, father-in-law), she wanted to study the same profession. She studied law for one year in the university, but she went in secret. She would hide her books and instructed the children not to tell her husband. This was possible because he works in another city during the week and is only home weekends. If he was home, she would skip classes. But he found out. "I was careless, and left my books on the sewing machine. He saw them and asked, 'Who is studying law here?' and I had to confess." He was very angry and rebuked her. He wanted to know why she would do that when she would "'never get a degree, never get a job, and only neglect your home and your children.'" She says, "That is how men are, not all, but many." Her father was the same with her mother and never wanted her to work or study.

For the last three years, Berta has worked at temporary positions as a teacher. She now earns Q. 150 monthly. At first claiming that her husband changed his mind, she admitted that he still would never want her to work. Her job is hidden from him. For her now, it is like an adventure. The children help her hide it, and she helps them buy things. She works both for enjoyment and "for necessity" because what her husband gives her is no longer enough.

This solution is clearly unique because the husband works in another city, which means he has less control over his wife. Although her subterfuge permits her to work against her husband's will and thereby gain greater economic independence, she has had to pay a price. She has never been able to pursue a law career and she risks discovery which could further disrupt her career or her marriage.

Berta's case illustrates some of the different pressures that work to keep women out of the labor force: (1) Her father encouraged his sons to become professionals, while in his opinion his daughters needed only a general cultural background. (2) Her parents provided an example when her father demanded that her mother stay home and her mother acquiesced. (3) Her husband demanded that she choose between him and her career (a choice *he* did not have to make). (4) The priest supported her husband's authority over her. (5) Her husband emphatically discouraged her and demeaned her abilities when she did attempt to continue her education. The cumulative effect of these experiences is strong discouragement of the married woman who wants a career. Accordingly, Berta's younger sister, the only one who did not marry, is the only one to succeed in establishing a career. In view of the multiple opposition she encountered, it is remarkable that Berta persevered. Encouragement from her grown children and the admiration of her friends have helped her. Instilled with ambition by the professional background and educational emphasis of her family, Berta would have preferred to hold her upper middle class economic position directly as a lawyer, and not as a dependent wife or lowly school teacher.

In another unusual case, a woman is pressured to stay home not only by her husband, but by her grown children as well. This family represents more precarious economic circumstances and upward mobility than the preceding cases with land-owning or professional backgrounds.

3. Candida is in her mid-forties, married, and the mother of six. Three children still live at home. One is in private school, and a grown son and daughter both work and study. Her daughter is divorced and has a young son at home as well.

Candida grew up in a rural town, had a sixth grade education, and began to work in stores at age fourteen. From age 15 to 17 she worked as a seamstress for a hospital for Q. 60 per month. At seventeen, she married and stopped working in order to raise children. When in her late twenties, she separated from her husband for four years. This was a difficult time; to support herself she washed clothes and made them. She moved from town to town renting rooms to live in. Her mother taught classes in some of these places and at times she lived with her mother, at other times alone. Later, she reunited with her husband and they came to live in the capital. For a time, she had a small store. Her capital was Q. 300 and at first she earned Q. 40 to 50 per month. But gradually the store lost sales, and six years ago she had to close it.

Her husband earns a modest living as a teacher, at two schools. Neither her husband nor her children want her to work, but she disagrees. She has looked for work as a home seamstress to avoid problems with the family, but there are no orders. There is more work in factories, although the positions are often full. Her husband claims the bosses in factories seduce the women, otherwise she would have been able to work in a factory. "In practical terms, he is jealous," she says, "but why don't they let me work if they don't give me what I need?" She has also tried to work as a travelling merchant selling clothes. She was doing this about six months ago, selling on installment, but people were not paying and she had to stop after two months. In her house, she makes *tamales* to sell on Saturdays, but these do not sell well either. She says there is no field for work here. She was offered work in a neighborhood store but her son and daughter would not let her take it.

"They treat me as if I were a servant in the house, only without a salary. [Indeed, they have no servant.] At times I despair. Closed up in the house, it's greatly depressing. One wants to leave running." She does not want to go around the neighborhood gossiping to ease the boredom. She would just prefer to be working.

Candida is not absolutely prohibited from working. It is all right to earn some extra money, but she must not have *regular* employment outside the home. Her domestic situation suggests several interpretations for the concerted family opposition to her employment. Her husband's opposition allegedly stems from jealously or fear of unseemly contact with other men, while her children seem interested in having her as a housekeeper. Her divorced daughter, in particular, benefits since Candida cares for her seven-year-old grandson while the daughter advances her career. The daughter gives Candida Q. 20 monthly out of her earnings, coincidentally the average amount paid to domestic servants. Candida's son and husband give her money sporadically.

Another interpretation is that the jobs Candida qualifies for (with only a sixth-grade education) are not within the realm of socially acceptable work for middle-class women. Work in a textile factory or as a local store employee may be considered demeaning by Candida's family. As long as Candida works informally or is self-employed, it is relatively invisible and can be interpreted as a hobby, but when her work is directly comparable to that of working-class women, it throws into question the socioeconomic status of the entire household—a status that is newly acquired.

The ability of the husband overtly to restrict the wife's work outside the home is not simply based on informal traditions that persist in some households. The examination of the case studies in isolation gives the appearance that this question is resolved by mutual discussion, combined with traditional tendencies for women to yield eventually to their husband's authority. In fact, the married women's right to work is not only a matter of mutual negotiation between spouses. The Civil Code which deals with civil rights in matrimony states that:

El marido puede oponerse a que la mujer se dedique a actividades fuera del hogar, siempre que suministre lo necesario para el sostenimiento del mismo y su oposición tenga motivos suficientes justificados. El Juez resolverá de plano lo que sea procedente.
(The husband can oppose the wife's dedication to activities outside the home, as long as he supplies what is necessary for the support of the same and his opposition has sufficient justified motives. The Judge will clearly resolve that which is proper.)

The exposition of the motives of the law states:

. . . pero una vez que la procreación comienza con el nacimiento del primero hijo, la mujer debe comprender que su misión está en el hogar y, a no ser por circunstancias muy especiales no debe desatender a sus hijos so pretexto de necesidades personales y del deseo de ayudar al marido.
(. . . but once procreation starts with the birth of the first child, the woman must understand that her mission is in the home, and except for very special circumstances she must not neglect her children under the pretext of personal necessities or the desire to aid her husband.) Código Civil Dto. Ley 106, Articulo 114, quoted in Chavarría 1975:2.

This law and its official interpretation indicates that the women of Villa Rosa cannot expect to use formal legal means to establish their right to work. While this law is theoretically applicable to all marriages in Guatemala, it is particularly in wealthy areas such as Villa Rosa that such legal regulations are most effective. In this colonia, the higher levels of male income are such that it would be relatively easy for men to claim that they "provide what is necessary for the sustenance of the home."

Other deterrents to female employment. In concordance with legal norms, marriage in Villa Rosa entails one-sided domestic burdens, particularly child care, which often draw the middle-class woman away from her career. If at a later time she seeks to resume her career, this period of interruption, her age, and loss of active contacts may become a serious handicap in obtaining a position or reestablishing herself in her former line of work. The two cases which follow illustrate how the disruption of the married woman's career for domestic reasons combined with the conditions of the formal job market leaves experienced educated women underemployed or unemployed.

4. Dora is in her early thirties, married with two young children. She was educated to the level of *perito contador*, or accountant. Her first job was in a provincial bank. She earned Q. 60 monthly and after two years earned Q. 100 monthly. At her next job, she worked at a bank in the capital and earned Q. 250 per month at the end of nine years there. When she

first married she continued to work. At that time her husband was irresponsible and she paid for everything. Later, he began to help with expenses and she finally quit working when she had her second child. Her
mother earlier had cared for her first child while she worked.

Describing the change when she stopped working she says: "At first I
cried a lot. I was used to working. It is difficult to ask my husband for
money for shoes. I would like to have it myself. I want to work to be free,
but jobs are scarce. One needs contacts, good connections. It is harder if
there are children. Many offices hire kids—girls—for their appearance. It
is harder for the middle-aged woman. There is discrimination against older
women." She cites a talented school friend whose income, in her thirties,
has also declined. Dora is currently seeking work. Meanwhile, she knits
and makes flowers and other craft products to sell among friends and to
stores. She earns Q. 40 to 50 per month this way. Her mother lives with
her, has a store in the house, and earns about Q. 70 monthly.

In this case, the husband does not oppose his wife's desire to work.
Indeed, it would help with their debts. Rather, the responsibility for
child care, the interruption of her career, and loss of contacts combine
to diminish her chances of obtaining employment commensurate with
her training and experience. Her allegation that young, attractive women
receive preference over older women does not seem unfounded.[11] Under these circumstances, Dora's strategy is to employ herself in lower-
level work. Although she produces some cash income in this fashion,
hers is clearly a case of underemployment.

5. Elsa was born and raised in another Central American country. She
has been married for five years and has two children and three stepchildren. She had fifteen years of work experience before marriage, starting as
a teacher and moving up to become supervisor of an education project.
She had earned the equivalent of Q. 300 monthly in her own country. Since
arriving here, in five years she has only had work for one year, in an A.I.D.
statistical research project. Since then, she has not found work, although
she has looked. She reads the paper every day for ads. If she goes to apply
for a job at 8 A.M., they say they have already given the job to someone
else. There is high unemployment among teachers and she has lost hopes
of working. Last year she was offered a job that pays well in her own
country, but her husband said she could not take it because of the children.

In this example, there is a fairly straightforward relationship between
the husband's demand for Elsa's domestic labor in child care and her
inability to pursue her career. In Elsa's particular case, the difficulty in
resuming her profession is compounded by her national origin and the
fact that her husband's career in Guatemala receives priority.

275

The next two cases concern an older and a younger woman, each in situations which permit them to participate in the market economy without directly challenging the economic priority of the husband.

6. Fidelia is fifty years old, married with five grown children. She was educated to the secretarial level, but has never formally worked in any job. However, for many years her husband ran a *colegio*. When he gave classes, she also gave classes in such subjects as "education for the home, accounting, and secretarial skills." She worked without a salary for eight years. Now her husband has another business selling household articles and safes. He earns around Q. 200 monthly. But in fact this business is run by both. They both go out in the car as traveling salespeople to sell their products in other people's homes.

7. Gladys is only age twenty, married, with a two-year-old child. She has completed part of secondary school, although she and her husband married while she was still studying. At first, they lived with her mother and she continued to study. Now they live with her husband's widowed mother. Gladys works as a teacher and earns Q. 60 per month. She no longer goes to school although she would like to. Her husband works half-time for the city and earns Q. 125 monthly. He continues to study and is in his fourth year at the university, studying law. Gladys says that he is not opposed to her working or studying, but that *she* has to be responsible for child care. She says that if she were a man, she would have better opportunities to work and would have been able to have more education. She notes that her husband earns twice as much as she does, and that she does more work for her job than he does for his.

For the older woman, petty bourgeois family businesses have benefitted from her particpation. For the younger woman, the costs of her husband's professional education mean their budget is strained without her contribution. Yet this case might eventually parallel that of other women who held jobs only during the early years of marriage, before the husbands' career took off. These cases show that even where women participate in the market economy, at the household level men receive priority in the right to pursue their ambitions, or even the right to recognition for a joint economic effort. When the social obligations to attend to home, husband, and children are stressed, women experience pressure against their employment.

Class background and social mobility. Despite the numerous pressures against women's equal participation in the market economy, a considerable number of women do participate. The following examples give some indication of the diverse ways that class background and the struggle for upward mobility can affect women's economic options. Important here are women's assessments of their own versus their husband's possibilities for upward career mobility, and the best avenues for investment.

8. Henrietta's parents were both provincial teachers. Her father earned more than her mother because he taught middle-school rather than primary, and became an educational director. They separated for a while, and Henrietta lived with her mother in various provincial towns until a reconciliation between her parents brought her to Guatemala City. Henrietta got her teaching degree, entered the School of Social Service, and taught for a year. "When I got married, I couldn't continue, the schedule . . . and my husband wouldn't permit me. For two years I did only housework. Then I went back to teaching. I now have 16 years' seniority. When the other children were born, I was helped by my mother and the maid." Her husband, who owns and manages a small textile factory, was educated as an accountant. Although Henrietta claims that he provided the capital, she mentions that she helped with the purchase of a typewriter, sewing machine, car, display case, and that she has cut and ironed garments for the business as well. She states that he is the owner, but that the law gives her the right to half of the business acquired during the marriage. Henrietta finds her husband unusually permissive, but also knows her rights and makes her own decisions.

Henrietta exhibits the confidence of a woman with job security in a formal occupation, albeit not one with much potential for female upward mobility or capital accumulation. She invested some of her extra money and energy in a family business, and has also struggled to improve her own economic position through the teachers union.

9. Inez was born in a provincial capital where she received a primary education. Her father was a grain merchant and her mother a housewife. At age seventeen, they moved to the city of Antiqua where she started to work at home as a dressmaker. She did this for a number of years, earning Q. 50 to 60 per month. She also went for a year to live with her brother in the United States where she worked in a factory on an assembly line, earning $100 every two weeks. She returned to Guatemala and eventually enrolled in a beauty academy, investing Q. 160 in the ten months' course. She came to Villa Rosa, and set up her own business in her parents' house there. Approaching age thirty, she married in order to have children. Although her parents live elsewhere, she still lives in their Villa Rosa house and runs her beauty salon, earning about Q. 100 per month from her own investment of around Q. 1,200 in sinks, mirrors, hair driers, and other equipment. Her husband, three years into his career as a professional lacks full-time work, and earns slightly more than she does, Q. 112 per month. He attempts to restrict her social life, so that her friends are confined to clients and close relatives. She doesn't appreciate this, but feels economically independent.

277

This example illustrates that a woman's parents can help her stake her claims to economic independence: providing her with a middle-class house and business locale. Although her income combined with her family's assets should give her considerable autonomy, she is vulnerable to social criticism. She not only yields to her husband's restrictions, but has largely stayed in a domestic work context in Guatemala, serving a female clientele. Her right to work in this context, however, is unchallenged, given that her family supports her.

The following example shows how a family business provided scope for a provincial woman's participation in partnership with her husband, and became an avenue for upward mobility in two generations.

10. Jasmine is fifty years old, married, and has grown children living at home. She was born in a small town in a western department where her father was a farmer and her mother a baker. At age eight, after two years of schooling, she began making bread, candles, and sweets to sell with her mother, continuing until she married at age nineteen. Her husband has a sixth-grade education. After marriage, "I continued working with my husband, but in the store." She's been working with him for 30 years. They moved to a provincial capital, had a store there, and moved to Villa Rosa where they opened their store seven years ago. Living with them are a son, daughter, and son-in-law. Both of the young men are professionals and contributing cash to the household. The daughter received a teaching degree, but is not working.

Here, a provincial petty bourgeois couple, by working together, have managed their business well enough to invest in children's education and, combining their income with the young men's, are able to afford middle-class housing. Nonetheless, their pattern is hardly typical of the middle-class, and Jasmine complains of isolation because of her lack of education. She does not participate in community social life, and comments that despite their middle-class clientele, most of the people who come into the store are the servants. Her daughter's education may have been less useful in obtaining a job than in qualifying for a well-educated husband.

Taken together, these cases illustrate some of the great diversity in family backgrounds found in Villa Rosa and in the context of female choice. The discussion would not be complete, however, without considering the economic behavior of at least one of the single mothers who live in the colonia. Even here, it is difficult to generalize due to the variety of family and other assets that women draw on.

11. Kathy was born in Guatemala City. Her father had been a military officer, and her mother sold jewelry. Her parents separated when she was

young, and she spent her early years in an institution while her mother worked. She was educated to be a commercial secretary. After working several years in a bank and for a lawyer (later to become a government minister), she got married, stopped working and had three children. When she and her husband separated five years ago, her sister got her a job in a school as an administrative secretary. Then, she decided to open a secretarial academy. With the help of a good friend, she got a loan from the Bank of the Army. With that Q. 800 loan, she bought used typing machines. She has now paid for nearly Q. 1,000 worth of machines, and will soon add a beauty salon to her home business, hiring an employee. She has already invested another Q. 600 in this. She will also have another employee teaching sewing classes, and has started advertising for classes. In the evenings, she is studying for a bachelor's degree at the university and hopes to continue and become a lawyer. Her house payments are being made by her husband who is now living with another woman, but she is paying all the food and clothing for herself and three teen-agers, plus the wage of a live-in domestic employee.

Kathy's economic status was not devastated by the separation from her husband, but she is clearly a resourceful woman, not just in her entrepreneurial spirit, but also in the family ties she has been able to call upon. Not only is her husband still paying the mortgage, but her job and crucial loan opportunities were obtained through important personal contacts. As a native of Guatemala City's middle class, she has a kinship and wider social network that includes military and government figures as well as relatives in the United States.

In reviewing these examples of women's economic constraints, ambitions, and resources, it is difficult to generalize about women in this "middle class." Some residents, moving up from successful small-town businesses face a drastic change in milieu from being top dog to something less distinguished. Their lack of education is a handicap. Others with partially provincial backgrounds, have merely transformed the wealth and education of a rural aristocracy into that of an urban bourgeoisie but have not really changed levels. Some families have followed the route of educational investment in professionalism or have tried to marry professionals. Where the women come from families that are already well established within the national elite, they have more confidence in pushing into the labor market. Some have managed to get formal-sector jobs in feminine fields, and a few are attempting to push out of those limited dead-end careers into more promising ones.

Husbands' attitudes are clearly an important factor, and are not uniform. While a number of husbands evidently feel that a working wife diminishes the status of the husband and the household, or leads to a reduction in domestic services, others appreciate the financial contribution which makes it easier to support a middle-class lifestyle. The husbands have to weigh the prestige of having a housebound wife versus her job opportunities in society. Attitudes seem to be more favorable if her job has prestige (particularly in cases where it would not directly compete with the husband's prestige), or if it is a domestic enterprise which permits him to claim she is still in the home. Possibly, households with provincial backgrounds are more concerned about the symbolic value of a "nonworking" wife, while others who are more comfortable in their class position may feel it is acceptable for her to seek higher education and commensurate professional employment.

Despite ideological, domestic, and institutional constraints, the women of Villa Rosa display considerable ingenuity in pursuit of their own cash income. They view education as the key to a changing opportunity structure. What remains unclear is how class background and gender will interact as the more highly educated population grows.

Social Organization

Since Villa Rosa is heterogeneous in class and regional backgrounds, education, and occupational specialties, there is little to bind people of the colonia together beyond their proximity in residence and their present middle-class status. In fact, the neighborhood resembles a suburban "bedroom" community for its commuting work force. Thus it is not surprising that social activities seem highly dispersed when viewed from the perspective of the colonia as a location. Relevant social organizations may encompass the street, the metropolitan districts, the department and the nation, or may even have international membership.

Formal Organization

Politics. Villa Rosa is under the larger political jurisdiction of Guatemala City and therefore local interest in politics is directed toward the offices of mayor and the deputy mayors who are responsible for different zones within the city. Yet at the *national* political capital, even city politics pales beside the attention given to the policies of the President and Congress. Formal political organization revolves around allegiance to national and urban political parties; it is not tied to the colonia as a discrete political base. Clearly an analysis of the formal and informal political processes of the city and nation lies beyond the scope of this investigation, but a few preliminary comments regarding the informal side of politics in Guatamala City will shed some light on the nature of the data that could be obtained in Villa Rosa.

Guatemala City is the political center of the nation, and the middle class its most politically active sector (Dombrowski et al. 1970:162). But Guatemalan politics is a dangerous subject. Many Villa Rosa women do not even want to discuss it, saying they avoid politics and only read about it in the newspapers. Some women confide that they cannot talk freely about their political views, and that even with very close friends one has to be careful. An inhibiting factor, of course, is the history of political assassination and violence in Guatemala. In the seven years preceding my fieldwork, there were several political murders of residents of the colonia. One local woman described the assassination of a family member whom she claims was mistakenly targeted by the government. Accounts of political violence continually appear in the news. In this atmosphere, it is difficult to speak openly of either female or male participation.

At another level, a survey of thirty-five households showed that 60 percent of the women vote in elections, while all of the men vote except the military personnel, who are legally prohibited from doing so. The high rate of female electoral participation is related to the high level of literacy and the importance of government jobs, such as teaching, which make voting mandatory.

Explicit political participation by women rarely goes beyond voting. Of the women interviewed, 80 percent claim they are inactive and disinterested in politics. Women who assert political apathy frequently cite the electoral fraud of 1974, and the fear of violence and/or the consistent failure of politicans to fulfill their promises as reasons for their disinterest. One woman explains, "To belong to a political party is dangerous. You make enemies, you might get killed." Another asserts:

There are no political leaders who help the community. When they are in power, they do not worry about the people. I have no goodwill toward any of them. There is great poverty, but they are making their millions. There is no progress because they are robbing the people. I do not like all the violence we have had under the past president.

While about half the women simply asserted they do not understand politics, the remainder keep themselves informed. There is certainly no uniformity of political views; they range from strong anticommunist to strong antigovernment sentiments.

Not all women wish to be detached from political activities, but the exceptions are few. As with the issue of female employment, the husband's opposition to a wife's participation can be an inhibiting factor, as in the case of Amanda (case 1 above). The most active of the women interviewed said:

> Many women do not participate in politics because men will not permit it. My husband is very open-minded and I am very liberal. If he said "no," by all means I would still go. I participated in the movement to improve teachers' salaries. He said, "If you continue to participate, we are going to end the marriage." I said, "That's fine." We triumphed in the movement. I was a representative of my school in the national organization.

Beyond this exceptional case of active participation in the labor movement, several other women participated in a local clerical power struggle that occurred several years ago, but then withdrew, allegedly because of a sexist insult and a fear of communism within the church. Only a few others admit they have attended political meetings ("just to listen") or demonstrations in the past.

Due to the high level of political mistrust, I was unable to obtain detailed information on the level of male or female political participation. However, there is little question but that the men are much more involved than the women. Some of the men have held important government posts, such as Governor or Ambassador, which entail active political roles. Others attend political meetings, usually without their wives. A number of women assert that their husbands are much better informed about politics because it is an area of greater male participation.

Asked to name important female figures in Guatemala, very few women could name female political figures, although they could easily name the leading male politicians. The women politicians that were named included two women in Congress, a woman recently appointed Governor of the department of Guatemala (only the second woman governor in the history of the country), and more frequently, the wives of the various national Presidents who had performed social services. More commonly cited were journalists, women known for charitable works, and women who were outstanding figures in education. By far the most commonly cited figure was Eunice Lima, who is known as a journalist, television personality, Director of Fine Arts, and a politically active personality. Lima herself points out that very few women have become integrated into the power structure:

In spite of the fact that the participation of women has been increasing each time at the polls and in political parties, there has been no decline in the total domination of men in the political direction of our country. The numerical proportion [of women] in governmental tasks that involve executive posts with political decisions is nil. Their influence has been felt only in social welfare or in education, branches of public administration occupied by predominantly female personnel. The percentage of women nominated to slates for the Congress of the Republic or municipal posts is also almost nil. We have had only five women deputies in four different Congresses. At present, in a legislative body comprised of 61 deputies, only two are women (translated; Lima 1975:10).

Formally, then, women are not represented among the political power-holders drawn from the middle class, and do not feel that these channels are normally open to women beyond the act of casting their token ballots. Yet they are not politically naive; their apathy often hides cynicism. They follow political events in the news, and are aware of the ways these affect their family fortunes. Quite often, they express dissatisfaction with male-run politics per se, showing incipient feminist leanings. In the news, many have heard about feminist groups and sympathize with their objectives.

Viewing politics from a wider perspective than official party electoral and military channels, there are various ways that Villa Rosa's middle class attempts to influence the government. One important avenue is through the formation of special interest groups, usually centered around occupational interests. One of the main purposes of these varied groups and associations is to influence government regulations, taxation, and benefits (Adams 1970:322). Villa Rosa males are active in a number of such occupational interest groups. Among them are the Chamber of Commerce and various associations of lawyers, engineers, agricultural export producers (plantation owners), ex-military officers, air force pilots, and journalists. From all the available evidence—newspapers, published research, and discussions with residents—these organizations are overwhelmingly male, with a very few exceptions, such as the Teachers Association. Wives of male members sometimes join ladies auxiliaries, but these groups generally do not articulate with national government or political institutions directly. This is not to say that women lack a behind-the-scenes importance, yet some women scoff at the Wives of Lawyers and Wives of Engineers groups for their lack of creative social contribution.

Religion. In keeping with its character as a new residential development, Villa Rosa does not have its own local houses of worship. Here again participation means dispersal. Those with religious inclinations travel to other areas of the city to join in public services. The population is predominantly Catholic at 88 percent, with roughly 5 percent Protestants, and 7 percent unaffiliated, and with no significant differences by sex.

Although Catholicism represents a powerful ideological orientation in Villa Rosa, it is relatively weak as a focus of formal social organization. Of the Catholic women, 55 percent described themselves as inactive Catholics. Others say they are active, but not "fanatics." Regular attendance at Catholic mass is exceptional. Those who do attend go to a variety of churches. The nearest Catholic church in the zone is unpopular with many of the residents of Villa Rosa because it is located in a lower-class section and organizes around the concerns of the poor. Thus, some residents report that they skip around and attend churches in other parts of the city.

Several years ago, a group of about forty women organized to try to have a Catholic church built within their colonia, but the group was not successful and has been dormant for some time. A few devotees keep a religious icon ("saint") in their home, or make the pilgrimage to Escuipulas, but they are exceptional. The Catholic church continues to provide the context for major life cycle rituals such as baptism and marriage, yet these events seem to hold more significance for the integration of family and status groups than for the integration of residents into the church.

Clearly, the Church represents a potential channel for organizing Villa Rosa women, given that it so often serves this function in other Guatemalan communities. But without an established presence of the Church in the community, Villa Rosa women tend to regard religion as a matter of personal faith and occasional ritual. While religion is not currently significant as an ongoing or integrating basis for sociopolitical organization in Villa Rosa, its potential in terms of ideological leadership and as a focus of loyalty should not be underestimated. Catholic ideology regarding marriage, divorce, birth control, and abortion is widely disseminated in Villa Rosa, if not accepted by all its Catholics. Indeed, many Villa Rosa women have a rather eclectic attitude toward their religion, choosing the portions of doctrine and priests that most suit their lifestyle.

Education. Formal education is a preeminent concern for Villa Rosa men and women. Their upward mobility and their children's ability to remain within the privileged class depend heavily upon educational qualifications. The educational attainments of the adults and the contemporary education of Villa Rosa children are informative regarding past and future gender divisions.

The census-derived data (the sample of 1973) showed that the average educational level for men in Villa Rosa is 11.8 years, while that for women (excluding domestic employees) is 9.2 years. Obviously, both sexes are well educated, and the separation between the educational levels is not enormous, being only about 2.5 years. The difference is nonetheless a critical one, for it is usually after the ninth year that more highly specialized career preparation is undertaken. The first three years of secondary education (grades six through nine) are called "prevocational" and completing these corresponds to the level attained by the average woman of Villa Rosa. This is sufficient to qualify for primary school teaching or secretarial work if one has taken the appropriate courses. Although students who continue their education pursue vocational or university courses after the completion of ninth grade, or secondary school, a few go straight from primary school into vocational training programs. In Table 6–6 which follows (based on my 1975 interview data) I have listed the areas of educational specialization and vocational training that were found among parents and their young adult children of each sex in Villa Rosa. The table shows that women generally receive less specialized academic and professional training than men. While there is not an absolute pattern of exclusion of women from business careers or the physical sciences, women are underrepresented in these fields and concentrated in services and social sciences. Few of the women are educated in fields that have major decision-making potential.

Some of the women of Villa Rosa are returning to school to further their education after interruptions due to marriage and motherhood. A few are taking university night courses in academic subjects, while others feel that domestic responsibilities place professional careers beyond their reach and therefore pursue diverse courses in handicrafts, languages, or interior decorating, which need not take them out of the home. Women frequently stress the relationship between education and employment opportunities. One women believes that the position of women is improving "because there are more women who have studied. Studying frees them. More women work now than before. Education and income are necessary for liberation. Education is the key to success." Although others make similar statements, some feel that occupational opportunities are not developing at the same rate as educational ones and their enthusiasm is somewhat dampened:

The woman must prepare herself to become involved. It is not like it used to be in the home. . . . Woman's place is not at home. She merits the same as the man, but perhaps there is a lack of opportunity for women, in the

Table 6-6. Post-Primary School Education for Academic/Professional and Vocational Occupations by Sex, 1975

Specialization	Women (Number)	Men (Number)
Academic/Professional		
Teaching*	12	6
Accounting	2	9
Psychology	2	–
Sociology	1	–
Plastic arts	1	–
Dietetics	1	–
Architecture	1	1
Engineering	1	2
Economics	1	3
Law	1	6
Literature	–	1
Medicine	–	1
Public Health	–	1
Dentistry	–	1
Veterinary medicine	–	1
Business administration	–	1
Advertising	–	1
Music	–	2
Agronomy	–	2
Military Science	–	2
Vocational		
Secretarial training	11	–
Beauty culture	3	–
Industrial mechanics	–	1
Computer programming	–	1
Total subsample	37	42

* Teaching is a mixed category. Some teachers have special degrees in education, taken after completion of the standard prevocational course work. Others are teachers by virtue of having completed three years of secondary school without any specialization, which is nonetheless sufficient to qualify for primary school training.

jobs that come to women, in executive positions. The preparation of women is improving, but the positions are not.

In recognition of their ongoing domestic burdens, some women maintain that women should study dressmaking or beautician's courses since these lead to occupations that can be practiced at home; others say that teaching is good because a woman can do it part-time whereas office work is more difficult if one's children get sick.

Given the high educational attainments of the parents and the general belief that higher education corresponds to higher socioeconomic status, it is not surprising to find that all children over seven years of age are attending school regularly. The fact that the colonia lacks its own public school is hardly a deterrent. Virtually all households in the 1975 sample with children between the ages of seven and fourteen send their children to private schools (twenty-five out of twenty-six households). The schools are dispersed in various neighborhoods and zones of the city, and cost a minimum of Q. 6 per month per child. I did not encounter evidence of differentiation between the sexes with respect to the willingness of Villa Rosa parents to pay for a private school at either the primary or secondary level. Although some of the private schools are segregated by sex, I lack sufficient information on this aspect of education to comment on its implications.

The effect of universal primary and secondary education on sex roles in Villa Rosa might seem on first sight to reduce sexual differentiation. Yet the observed dichotomies in career specialization and orientation which occur when students approach adulthood clearly illustrate its continued existence. Indeed, my own impression is that Guatemala is about to be flooded with young women trained as bilingual secretaries—an extremely popular career choice among middle-class high school girls. Finally, domestic responsibilities and job opportunities may ultimately bear little relation to women's educational preparation.

Other social organizations. Slightly more than half of thirty-five women questioned report that they do not belong to any formal social organizations. Of those that do belong, the degree of participation and the organizations to which they belong vary greatly. The following list of organizations in which the women are active indicates some of their diverse interests:

Wives of Air Force Pilots*
Feminine Military Fraternity*
Association of Sportswriters*
Women Rotarians*
Lions Club*
School Parents Committees
Girls Guides
Movement for a Christian
  Family
Women's Church Committee
Tuberculosis Charity
(* = women's branch)

National Council of Women
Quiché Ladies Association
Fraternity of Quetzaltenango
Association of Mexican Women
National Federation of
  Gymnastics
Teachers' Association
Ancient Friends of Educational
  Promotion
UNESCO
Red Cross Youth

Participation in these organizations can be divided into two forms: dependent participation, in which the woman's participation is linked to the status or interests of other members of her family, and autonomous participation in which the woman joins an organization that reflects her personal interests. Those in the first five organizations listed are cases of dependent participation. About half of the organizations listed are sex-segregated either as independent women's groups or as branches of male organizations. In a number of the groups, women combine social activities and *obras beneficas* (volunteer work). For example, the women's branch of the Association of Sportswriters holds monthly teas and organizes activities such as bingo, rummage sales, and volunteer work for hospitals; the branch for women is described as "altruistic," while for the male sportswriters it is clearly a professional association.

These organizations serve a variety of purposes for the women who join them. Some, such as the Teachers Association, serve the professional interests of women and men as teachers, while others reflect parental concern about the quality of their children's education. Several associations reflect women's regional origins. These represent an effort to maintain important contacts and status within an urban environment where recent arrivals may feel swamped by the greater concentration of elite groups. The National Council of Women is an organization of upper-middle-class women that meets to promote the interests of women from a middle-class feminist perspective: They sent representatives to the 1975 conference in Mexico for International Women's Year. Some of the charity organizations simply provide a focus for social gathering and a sense of achievement which is otherwise lacking for some women, particularly those who are not employed. The ability to participate in charities is both a symbol and a product of middle-class status for households which have the leisure to devote to organization and the financial means to be charitable.

Although these organizations join people from different zones of the city, they generally do not entail a cross-section of socioeconomic classes. Indeed, a few of the women mentioned that their social organizations are an indication of their class status. That is, they can help to socially define and perpetuate privileged groups. The very heterogeneity of the organizations listed, together with their often national or even international character makes it difficult to generalize about Villa Rosa women as members of public social organizations, except to note that they do indicate a number of wide-ranging and cosmopolitan interests.

Domestic Organization

Household structure. The most common form of household group in Villa Rosa is the nuclear family. The data from my 1975 survey showed that 51 percent of all households are nuclear families; 37 percent include three generations and/or collateral kin in addition to a conjugal pair; 11 percent are families which lack a conjugal pair, although they may include three generations (such as grandmother, mother, and children). In terms of household responsibilities, this means that in a significant number of households other adult women are present to share the work. In the census sample of 1973, the classifications indicate that 16 percent of the households are headed by women or lack responsible adult male members. For women over fifteen years of age, family status is displayed in Table 6–7.

In the census sample of 1973 three-fourths of the women who are both single and childless are age twenty-five or under. Most of them can be expected to join one of the other two family statuses as they grow older.

Marriage and the family. Marriage is an extremely important social institution in Villa Rosa. Not only do most of the women marry at some point in their lives, but roughly 90 percent of the marriages (based on the census sample) are legally contracted. The high rate of legal marriage in Villa Rosa is related to the fact that there is significant property and income at stake in marriage—in contrast to lower-class populations. In Villa Rosa, legal rights and obligations are taken seriously, and women are cognizant of the legal implications of marriage.

The legal rights and duties conferred by marriage differ for men and women. The Civil Code states that the representative of the household will be the husband, although both spouses will have equal authority regarding the home and children (Chavarría 1975:1). Legally, men are obliged to support their wives and children economically, while women are obliged to provide domestic services and child care. In the section on economic organization, we have seen that in marriage the husband

Table 6–7. Family Statuses of Villa Rosa Women (Age 15 and Over), 1973 and 1975

Status	1973 %	1975 %
Childless single women	30	26
"Married" women*	56	58
"Single" women**		
with children	14	16
(Sample Size)	(196)	(60)

* Including women who are married by common law
** Women who are separated, widowed, divorced, or never-married mothers, who do not live with a conjugal partner.

can impose economic dependency, with the support of the Civil Code, by denying his wife the right to work. In keeping with these legal distinctions, marriage and fatherhood generally do not interrupt a man's economic activities or deflect him from his career. In contrast, marriage and motherhood usually do disrupt the previous economic activities or careers of Villa Rosa women.

Another area of legal inequality is adultery. The Criminal Code, on the grounds of protecting paternity rights, is much more lenient toward male extramarital sexual relationships than it is toward female ones. In this regard, Chavarría (1975) has demonstrated that specific provisions and interpretations of Guatemalan law nullify the assertion of sexual equality, particularly for married women.

Marriage is a sign of adulthood and social respectability for both sexes in Villa Rosa. For women especially, it is a social authorization to have sexual relations and bear children under a contract guaranteeing male economic support. Traditionally, a women is expected to postpone sexual relations until she has received a marital commitment that will safeguard both her own class standing and that of her children.

At the same time, marriage establishes a state of social dependency for women, symbolized by the possessive "*de*" (of) form of address that identifies married women in terms of their husband's last name, as in Maria *de Gonzales* (of, or belonging to, husband Gonzales). This possessiveness is not only symbolic. Married women frequently find their social contacts outside the home restricted by marriage in a way that parallels restrictions on economic activity for married women. As with economic restrictions, the extent to which social restrictions occur is variable and open to negotiation between husband and wife. Of twenty-five married women questioned, roughly a quarter claimed they faced no social restrictions imposed by their husbands. Some women emphasized how fortunate they are in this regard, implying that the norm is otherwise. Another quarter of the women felt that their husbands did not restrict their social life, but complained that marital status itself was restrictive in terms of the social expectations for married women. The remaining half described various restrictions on their social contacts and mobility imposed by their husbands. The following remarks reveal a climate of social restriction as well as mixed responses such as resignation, resistance, and gratitude for any "freedom."

290

a. My husband does not want me to have friends. I cannot meet with them. I can only go to visit my parents once a month. I do not like to go out much. There are husbands who want to have a wife like a slave. My husband is a bit like that, but I do not like it. Single life is better because there is more freedom.
b. I do not like to have a social life without the intervention of my husband.
c. The husband commands and gives orders. One has to obey.
d. A single life is a happy life. It is hard to find a man who lets you think. [A long-time widow]
e. I like independence. Only my mother, father, and husband have the power to give me orders. [A widow]
f. I am fine, because my husband is very liberal. He always lets me go out and come in. Here men are terrible; they do not give liberty.
g. If my husband says "*no*," I cannot go somewhere. He is independent. I cannot deny him. . . . In economic matters, he commands and I have to say, "Amen."

Women explain the curtailment of outside activities after marriage by direct references to the husband's jealousy and restrictiveness, unalleviated responsibility for young children, and the fear that neighborhood criticism may arouse a husband's distrust.

The existence of general restrictions on the social life of married women relates to a system of more specific restrictions on female sexual and reproductive activities. Villa Rosa partakes of an archetypical double standard which guides behavior. Premarital and extramarital sexual relations are considered unacceptable for women, while female virginity is emphasized as highly desirable. On this subject, a young woman declares, "I think virginity should not be important, but men do not think so." A mother of four teen-age sons elaborates:

I do not have to watch out for my sons so much. If I had a daughter it would be different. I would not tell her about birth control pills before she got married, only afterward. Virginity is important in our setting, because the men demand it. It is more beautiful. The man has security that it is only for him. Here, women cannot have free sexual relations.

This statement indicates that it is not enough to control female fertility before marriage, but that female premarital sexual activity per se must be prevented.

The control of female sexuality can be contrasted with the overall permissive attitude toward male sexuality. A 21-year-old unmarried woman described the difference:

I have heard that at a certain age men need sexual relations. It is better that they have experiences before marriage. I think sex is more important

for a man. Men want to demonstrate their *hombría* (manliness). A woman
can reserve herself. She must deny sexuality. If she did not do so, she would
be like the prostitutes. In my environment, there are some girls who are
freer for love, but later, it is thrown in their face.

This statement reveals not only a dichotomy between standards for
male and female behavior, but a dichotomy between two "classes" of
women: those whose sexual-reproductive activity is reserved for their
husband, and prostitutes. Obviously, a dichotomy that broadly and
pejoratively compares any woman who engages in nonmarital sex to
prostitutes is intimidating to a broad spectrum of women, including
the middle-class women of Villa Rosa. On the other hand, in speaking
of prostitutes, narrowly defined, as women who specialize in relatively
anonymous, commercial sexual transactions, some Villa Rosa women
feel that they perform a positive function. A married woman explained
that it is not only necessary to protect daughters from premarital sex
and pregnancy, but "one must also protect one's sons from producing
pregnancy, because sons can be forced to marry. In our culture, it is
better that a boy goes to a prostitute."

An indication of the effectiveness of the controls on female sexual
behavior in Villa Rosa is the relative infrequency of unwed motherhood. In contrast to other areas where unwed mothers are not uncommon, such cases are either absent or well-concealed in Villa Rosa. A
few women admit they were pregnant when they married, but virtually
all resident mothers claim to have been married to the father of their
children. In the one exception I encountered, a divorced woman with
children lives with a second man and bore his child outside wedlock.
She is strongly criticized and in fact shunned by most of her peers for
maintaining this illicit relationship. A married friend says of her.

I do not approve of her relationship. It would be better if she married the
second man to form a stable household. Other women criticize her for her
lifestyle and say, "How can you visit her?" They say it is a bad example
for the children.

Although women expect premarital sexual experimentation by males,
they are in favor of mutual monogamy after marriage. Yet some women
candidly admit that this is only an ideal, for in reality they have little
control over their husband's extramarital affairs. A few informants
claimed their divorces were provoked by their husband's philandering,
and one stated she underwent a sterilization operation so that her husband would stop seeing other women. Infidelity is said to be much
more common among men than women, with wives overlooking visits

to prostitutes and protesting mainly when a prolonged affair disrupts family life. Women also have affairs, but assert that they have to be much more discrete.

Divorce is not rare in Villa Rosa (five out of sixty women are currently divorced or separated in the 1975 sample), but it carries a stigma. Normally, the divorced woman with children who can continue to reside in Villa Rosa depends on alimony and child support money. In three cases of divorced women with children, two receive Q. 250 per month and one receives Q. 100 per month from the ex-husband. All of the divorced women encountered also work for a cash income.

There is general uneasiness over the status of divorced and single women in Villa Rosa. Women frequently mention the unfavorable connotations of nonmarried status as well as independent behavior which may be interpreted or criticized as an indication of illegitimate sexual activity. Their statements show concern with their reputations as sexually faithful wives and vulnerability to gossip about their sexual behavior whether married or not. By maintaining an image of exclusive sexual loyalty to her husband, a woman promotes his paternal interest in their children and strengthens her position in the family. To a large extent, the women themselves appear to exercise policing functions of gossip and criticism with regard to the sexual behavior of their sex.

While they frequently comment on marital restrictions, women uniformly stress the positive aspects of motherhood. It is not surprising that motherhood is an extremely important social role for most Villa Rosa women. It is the one social relationship in which they are permitted to assert themselves fully with very little interference. It creates an especially close tie between mother and daughter, remaining strong and mutually supportive after the marriage of the daughter. Mothers and married daughters live together in quite a few households, and even when they don't, visiting is very frequent, along with exchange of services.

Responsibility for child rearing is one of women's central obligations in marriage, but it differs significantly from child raising in poorer communities of Guatemala. Affluence means that good nutrition and clothing are easily provided. Villa Rosa children are not needed as an assistant or apprentice labor force, for productive activity is largely separated from the home. Domestic servants take over much of the burden of providing physical care and babysitting for young children. Finally, with formal education as a universal benefit for Villa Rosa children, mothers are not required to transmit specialized educational or occupational skills.

LAUREL HERBENAR BOSSEN

While the basic concerns of poorer women as mothers are much attenuated in Villa Rosa, mothers there place great emphasis on the careful and lengthy socialization of children into appropriate middle-class culture and behavior patterns. This is one aspect of middle-class mothering that cannot easily be displaced. It is not surprising that Villa Rosa women seize upon just this aspect of motherhood as uniquely important. They are deeply concerned that their children may be set back if the mother decides to work. The following statement expresses this point of view:

> Children cannot be left in the charge of servants. They will not learn well. They will acquire the vocabulary of servants. A woman should not work until her children are well formed. I am opposed to nursery school. Mother's love is indispensable . . . special. It offers security and affection. Others do not care for your child in the same way. Servants will neglect the children to go gossip with other servants.

Anxiety about daycare centers and their possible lack of middle-class standards is also a factor, with some women expressing the fear that the centers may also be attended by poorer children who have lice and other "contagious" problems. Although there are mothers with work outside the home who feel that this is not inconsistent with effective motherhood, they too stress that children's values come from the home and the mother especially, not from their formal education.

Children are a major expense in Villa Rosa. They require care that may keep the mother out of the labor force; they require a costly education; and they are often in their twenties before they begin to earn a cash income. Given the high costs of child raising combined with the low mortality which accompany a middle-class standard of living, the married women of childbearing age in Villa Rosa widely practice family planning and exhibit considerable knowledge of birth control techniques.[12]

The problem of establishing children's legitimacy is one which affects the sexes differently. Since biologically a particular man's paternal contribution is much easier to question, men are able to deny affiliations to children produced with lower-income women. In contrast, women cannot deny maternity. The middle-class woman who produces children without a contract of paternal recognition (legal marriage) from a man of her class jeopardizes her membership in the class. She must be able socially to "prove" the paternity of children in order to maintain class privilege. Social proof generally consists of the absence of any evidence or insinuation of independent interaction with males other

294

than a woman's kin or husband. She must be above suspicion. Hence, virginity for unmarried women and the appearance of absolute sexual monogamy for married women are means by which legally married parents of middle or upper socioeconomic status ensure the right of their children to inherit their class status and privileges. (This value system, which is beginning to weaken, has obvious roots in Spanish colonial legislation, where only children who were legitimately Spanish on both sides were permitted to inherit coveted Spanish privileges and where noble descent was doubly prized.)

An emphasis on the social aspects of mothering can supplement legitimacy as a means of reinforcing women's class position. Given that their economic contribution is generally inadequate to support middle-class aspirations, women inflate their importance as mothers who can offer legitimate children the appropriate cultural orientation and social graces. Compared to women of lower socioeconomic classes, Villa Rosa women conform to more comprehensive social and sexual restrictions. With production and education largely removed from the home, they stress the primacy of motherhood.

These standards for marriage and parenthood are a means of reproducing an ascribed class structure in which new individuals have unambiguously assigned positions that can be assumed with minimal economic instability or competition. In the colonial system, these marriage rules helped to maintain concentrations of wealth and capital within a stratified society. Although the class structure has clearly changed greatly since colonial times, legitimate parentage is still one of the mechanisms used to perpetuate class structure via inheritance. From this perspective, it becomes clearer why some Villa Rosa women contribute to the social enforcement of restrictions on the social and reproductive behavior of their sex even though they may personally resent these controls. Women themselves are anxious to show that their sex is upholding the principle of controlled reproduction of the class, *within* the class.

Informal Networks

Kinship plays a relatively small role in the social integration of Villa Rosa itself. Very few people have kin living in other households within the colonia. This is not only related to the newness of the housing, but also the patterns of neolocality, urban migration, and occupational mobility. The kin ties of people in Villa Rosa are dispersed throughout the various zones of the city and the other urban centers of the departments.

More than a few have kin in the United States or Europe. The United States link is, in fact, a particularly important one, for it includes not just distant cousins but primary kin for a number of households. For example, one informant has two children married to United States citizens, while another has parents living in Florida, and a third has two brothers in the United States. Add to this the various residents who have studied or have children studying in the United States and those who have taken vacations there and it is apparent that the networks of Villa Rosa residents have a very important international dimension. While these networks cannot be observed as a continuous daily, monthly, or even annual interchange as can the more localized networks of poorer communities, they have an enormous practical and prestige value to the middle and upper sectors. Knowledge of the United States or other foreign powers, even on a casual level, is a definite advantage for careers in large corporations and government. For the Villa Rosa women whose families can provide such linkages along with cultural savoir faire or American know-how, as the case may be, their value to their family's economic success may go well beyond any cash contribution they could make in the labor market. Of course, not all the women of Villa Rosa have such backgrounds or connections. While a thorough study of these networks was beyond the scope of this research, the available evidence suggests that women who can act as culture brokers to advanced capitalist societies, whether by speaking two languages or by guiding their children through Disneyland in Florida, make an immeasurable contribution to their family's success.

On a more local level, the neighborhood, small groups, and wider networks operate on an informal basis but seem relatively attenuated or insubstantial compared to the formal institutions that govern the workplace and to the recognized occupational interest groups. Indeed, the very slang names women give to their informal gatherings, roughly equivalent to the American "hag" or "stag" parties, indicate that they view them with considerable levity. Yet one-third of the women interviewed belong to such small neighborhood women's clubs.

The basis of such informal organization is simply proximity and affinity. Women friends from the same street or neighborhood section decide to organize regular weekly or monthly meetings in their homes. The purpose is primarily to provide diversion in a convenient and comfortable setting. Activities include the collection of dues which are distributed to fund monthly dinner and birthday parties for members. These are informal afternoon or evening gatherings where women talk, banter, dine, drink, dance, and play cards or parlor games among themselves. Attending such all-female gatherings revealed that the women relish the chance to be loud, boisterous, and tell sexually risque jokes—behavior which they usually restrain in mixed groups. But they also exchange information and compare opinions on current public events with a shared understanding of the social constraints and challenges they face. Groups range in size from five to fifteen members.

One attraction of these women's groups is that they are unlikely to provoke opposition from jealous husbands since meetings are held in nearby homes for groups of women only. Although some members have jobs, this type of association is especially important to counteract the isolation of house and child-care for those women who are more housebound. One woman whose husband limits her social activities justifies her attendance with the saying, "After all, one does not live by bread alone!" Although women discuss personal problems as women, wives, or mothers at these gatherings, the groups are not designed to systematically challenge sex roles. Far from threatening the sexual status quo, these groups are more akin to a safety valve that permits Villa Rosa women to vent their individual feelings and drop some inhibitions in a social context where such behavior does not create a scandal.

Apart from neighborhood clubs and visiting, the women of the colonia engage in varied entertainment and recreational activities on an irregular basis. These include parties, baby showers, wedding showers (*despedidas de soltera*), cultural programs, handicraft courses, gardening, watching TV soap operas, and listening to radio programs. A number of women mention belonging to a "club" called the "Pot and Pan," which is a radio-organized telephone network that offers support and counselling to troubled housewives. Movies are a popular form of evening entertainment, and women generally attend *with* their husbands to see the latest Hollywood or Mexican productions. Family trips to the country on weekends are also popular, and occasional family vacations to foreign countries are particularly valued. While soccer captivates the men, sporting activities are not very important to married women. As single women, particularly in their school days, team sports had been important to them and are now to some of their daughters. As adults, they occasionally swim, jog, or do calisthenics, but have few opportunities to join any team sports.

In general, the kinds of informal entertainment and recreation sought by Villa Rosa women reflect their privileged but dependent economic position, which grants them considerable leisure but a relatively home-centered existence. The networks that women develop are generally those which do not undermine the traditional socioeconomic structure of the family, nor its class position in society. When networks are international, for women they are family-oriented rather than directly job-related. On a local level, their social activities are channeled through all-female or family-based social groups and adapted to traditional concerns over the reputations of married women.

The Middle-Class Woman's Dilemma

The economic analysis has shown that Villa Rosa women form a significant part of the labor force in the cash sector, but that compared to men, fewer work for cash incomes and they are less well paid and less integrated into the formal employment sector. The incomes women can command for their economic activity are generally inadequate to support Villa Rosa's standard of living without male assistance. At the same time, a modern middle-class lifestyle involves a higher education and growing demand for numerous new consumer goods and luxuries which have become available in the capital through international trade. Women whose husbands earn high incomes nevertheless want employment both because they believe that higher education has made them "capable," and because any additional cash income makes it easier to pay for more education for children and more prestige goods for the household.

In their efforts to earn such income, however, Villa Rosa women are stymied from three directions. First, demand for their labor in the formal sector is limited by the structure of large institutions and corporations linked to advanced capitalist economies; these systematically channel women into lower-paying secretarial, service, and teaching occupations, and bypass them for training and advancement in responsible careers in business, government, and military institutions—the dominant sectors of the economy. Second, even before women have the chance to be rejected, they are improperly prepared for assuming positions of power in these institutions due to pervasive media diffusion of gender stereotypes that orient women toward banal or nonescalating careers. This two-pronged foreign influence, institutional and cultural, combines with a faded Latin tradition to restrict the opportunities for women of elite or upwardly mobile groups to achieve economic autonomy, and encourages them to emphasize marriage and their husbands' career over their own.

Finally, once women marry, their careers are further compromised by domestic and child-rearing responsibilities that are not viewed as economic contributions to the household because they do not directly increase cash income. These responsibilities, labeled "status production" work by Papanek (1977), help the household and the husband maintain status within society, but do not necessarily give the woman much status with her husband. Even with cheap domestic labor available, Villa Rosa women cannot relinquish certain symbolic and social roles in the home without jeopardizing their claims upon their husband's economic resources.

Economically, then, unless they receive a superior endowment from their parents (which is clearly true in a few cases), Villa Rosa women hold a position that is decidedly inferior to their men. Their economic contributions are not viewed as vital to the household and do little to reduce their economic dependence on the income of male members of the family. At the domestic level, women's personal strategies aim at balancing two widely separated objectives: (1) increasing their cash income through personal employment, and (2) bolstering the status of the husband and household by improving their social image, social networks, and socialization of children. In some cases, husbands and wives arrive at a happy compromise between these two objectives, yet frequently there is a tension between the women's desire to pursue the first objective and the men's insistence on the priority of the second. To date, Villa Rosa women show relatively few efforts to address this conflict at the societal level—demanding integration into the core capitalist institutions.

Despite the limited options for women's economic and social action as compared to Villa Rosa men, the position of these women as members of the labor force and as members of the middle class is very enviable for lower-class women. To women who have known poverty, the economic dependence and social restraints must appear to be a small price to pay for the advantages of good food and health, fine clothing, and housing which Villa Rosa women enjoy.

Because Villa Rosa women have more formal education, they currently enjoy an advantage over lower-class women (and men) in acquiring some types of formal employment. Expansion and intensification of capitalist enterprise have increased the formal employment opportunities in Guatemala City, drawing in more women. As a result, the women of Villa Rosa are overwhelmingly optimistic regarding their changing economic horizons. The fact that women now have some access to formal employment outside the home is perceived as a substantial improvement in women's status, despite the fact that a close analysis shows a revitalized division of labor between the sexes, not only in terms of earning power, but in terms of occupational segregation.

Socially, Villa Rosa has a low level of formal social organization or integration within the neighborhood or colonia, but its residents maintain extensive networks and organizations which span the larger metropolitan district, extending to the provincial departments of Guatemala for some, and outward to the international arena for others. Although women are part of these extended networks, their place in them is more often linked to family considerations than to occupational interests. Politically, the women of Villa Rosa claim to be inactive, apart from casting their vote in major elections. This must be qualified by an awareness that no one, male or female, wants to admit to being "political." Yet women's claims to a low profile in politics matches their relative invisibility in major urban and national political positions. Religious institutions are important culturally, but have limited importance for Villa Rosa women as a means for social organization and integration into the modern sectors. In contrast, education is an area of open and sustained interest to women. They are highly educated and concerned about further educational opportunities for themselves and their children. They attend school meetings, compare and evaluate private schools, and emphasize education as an avenue of economic independence and greater social participation for women as well as of upward mobility for their children.

Participation in extradomestic social organizations and activities is generally conditioned by family obligations and husbands' domination in accordance with class interests. Independent social activity by married women in mixed groups is exceptional. One of the most interesting aspects of social life in Villa Rosa is the retention of sexual codes regarding female sexuality and legitimate sexual conduct. Even with widespread knowledge of modern birth control techniques, formal compliance with social prohibitions on female premarital and extramarital sex is upheld at this class level. Indeed, the cultural complex of concern with female virginity, female adultery, the legitimization of offspring, and the stigma of divorce is weakening as educational standards develop into new elements of class recruitment and legitimacy. But evidently Villa Rosa men and women still feel that the class system is not entirely "open" on the basis of educational qualifications alone. While family diplomas are on display, family *escudos* (coats of arms) are not forgotten.

CHAPTER SEVEN

Conclusions: Sexual Stratification and Economic Change

The preceding chapters describe the economic and social position of women in Guatemalan communities. These very different populations are drawn from four major segments of the national society. Each chapter shows how male-female relations are affected by local economic conditions in combination with social and historical factors, as well as by the relation of the community to the complex socioeconomic order of the nation. Position in the national economy, in particular, has been seen to shape the division of labor in each community.

Taken together, the community-level data confirm that the gender division of labor and structure of male-female relations in one small nation, Guatemala, exhibit significant variation according to economic conditions as well as ethnic and class background in each region. We may thus return to the questions posed at the outset of this book:

1. How do changes in the larger world economic system impinge on male-female relations at the local level?
2. Is modern capitalism a liberating force for women, or does it undermine their position relative to men?

Part of the answer to these questions is a consideration of the explanatory power of economic variables with respect to other aspects of male-female relations. This chapter will present at least partial answers after briefly comparing the four communities along three axes: the way in which each community is integrated into the national economy and hence the world capitalist system, the relative economic position of women, and women's relative social position.

Integration into the Modern Capitalist Sectors

Guatemala is part of the world capitalist system, as are all of its communities. Still, communities can be considered as less or more integrated into modern capitalist society. The relative degrees to which the four communities are so integrated can be assessed in various ways. Some of the most typical considerations are the degree of urbanism, the relative dependence on the cash economy, the incidence of formal employment, and the standards of consumption and education.

Using these indices, T'oj Nam is clearly the least integrated into modern capitalist sectors. T'oj Nam is rural and retains a partially subsistence economy that still provides an important share of the food, clothing, and housing. Although increasingly dependent on cash incomes earned through migrant wage labor, as well as small-scale commercial farming and crafts, the community overall has extremely low levels of cash income and formal employment. The people enjoy very few modern consumer goods and have the lowest levels of education of the four communities. Without claiming that capitalist expansion historically has left them undisturbed or unexploited, it should be appreciated that in much of their day-to-day labor they are still their own bosses as peasants and petty commodity producers. No large permanent institutions directly determine their allocation of time and labor; the impositions of the civil-religious bureaucracies and their plantation crew bosses are relatively temporary or intermittent demands.

El Cañaveral and San Lorenzo occupy intermediate positions. Both are heavily dependent on cash incomes and enjoy similar standards of living, with access to a limited range of modern consumer goods. San Lorenzo is an urban neighborhood, but its economic base is largely informal, and even its housing essentially belongs to the informal subsistence sphere, since it was not legitimately acquired through legal purchase. El Cañaveral, although is located in the rural sector, is not isolated from urban centers, due to its essential link to national and foreign sugar markets. El Cañaveral enjoys a higher incidence of formal employment than either T'oj Nam or San Lorenzo, and for its males there is a more thorough proletarianization. El Cañaveral men do not control their time and labor allocation. They must work to the schedule of the sugar mill owners. San Lorenzo's economic integration, despite its centrality, is less well established. Neither its men nor women are highly proletarianized. Looking at the consumer levels, housing facilities in El Cañaveral are closer to modern standards in that they have running water and electricity. Levels of education are comparable in

El Cañaveral and San Lorenzo, and are significantly above those of T'oj Nam.

Villa Rosa is most completely identified with the modern capitalist sector of Guatemalan society. It is urban, enjoys high cash incomes, and has the highest levels of formal employment for men and women of the communities studied. Its residents have become accustomed to a wide range of modern consumer goods that demonstrate their high standard of living, and they have attained higher levels of formal education than the members of the other communities studied. Although there are not many full-fledged large capitalists among them, their high-salaried professional and managerial positions make them close allies of large national and international capitalists. In their allocation of labor, professionals and bureaucrats generally operate within the time framework set by large institutional employers.

Table 7-1 schematically illustrates the extent to which the four communities are formally incorporated into the modern capitalist sectors of Guatemala. The upper segment includes characteristics usually associated with modernism, while the lower segment includes indices of capitalist integration. Two of these indices—formality and association with large-scale capital are unconventional descriptions of capitalist integration. Formality, as used throughout this work, refers to the size and stability of the workforce, denoting more rigid scheduling of work and larger labor groups—conditions associated with large capital investments. Association with large-scale capital refers to the degree to which an occupational structure is strategically placed relative to large concentrations of capital. This indicates capitalist integration even when the individual occupations may be free-lance or may formally bring wages rather than returns to capital. Working with large-scale capital in a capital-scarce world allows the worker some share in these returns. Ownership of capital is, to some extent, diffuse; that is, proximity brings rewards, and less frequently, control. Thus, those doing formal wage work for large capitalist institutions will be better placed than those working for smaller ones.

The indices for capitalist integration differ from those for modernization in that rather than cultural traits they emphasize strategic positions within the productive process. San Lorenzo is thus rather modern, but not very well integrated into capitalism since its work force tends to work for smaller capitalist enterprises than at El Cañaveral. The work force of Villa Rosa is the most closely associated with the largest corporations and the government. Although not capitalists themselves in most cases they are close enough to large-scale capital to exercise considerable control and derive significant rewards.

Table 7-1. Degree of Integration of the Four Communities into Aspects of Modern, Capitalist Society

	Modernity			
Community	Dominant Economic Orientation	Urbanism	Consumer Goods	Education
T'oj Nam	subsistence	rural	very few	very low
El Cañaveral	cash	rural	some	low
San Lorenzo	cash	urban	some	low
Villa Rosa	cash	urban	many	high

	Capitalism		
		Dominant Employment	
Community	Class	Formality	Association with Large-Scale Capital
T'oj Nam	peasant	informal	very distant
El Cañaveral	proletarian	formal	close
San Lorenzo	subproletarian	informal	variable
Villa Rosa	dependent-bourgeois	formal	very close

Women's Economic Position

As in the descriptive chapters, women's economic position will be considered with respect to the sexual division of labor, the distribution of rewards, and the control of strategic resources. Comparison across these variables will allow us to determine the comparative degree of economic stratification by sex which exists in each community.

In T'oj Nam, traditional subsistence production performed by the domestic unit remains an essential economic activity for most households. The traditional subsistence economy reveals a sharp division of labor by sex in many fundamental tasks, but the tasks are complementary ones. The economic partnership of the sexes is still an indispensable condition of traditional production. Cash values and modern technology have not defined the utility of male and female labor in terms of external conditions of supply and demand. Traditional subsistence contributions of each sex are roughly equal with respect to time, effort, and utility.

In this household-based economy the rewards of production do not lend themselves to individual accumulation or unequal distribution by sex. A man without a wife may have corn without tortillas, cotton without clothing, a house without a hearth. A woman who can transform raw materials into usable products needs a male partner to maintain her long-term supplies. The sharing of subsistence goods between men, women, and children ensures the survival of the principal production unit.

In the subsistence economy, the two most strategic resources for any household are land and labor. In T'oj Nam, with patrilineal inheritance of land and housing, men control a major strategic resource. But in the subsistence sector, land has value only with the addition of labor. In a community with little cash, the principle way for most households to expand or diversify production, or to invest in old-age security, is to produce offspring who will contribute to the household. Women's reproductive capacity is thus a strategic resource where alternative means of increasing the labor supply are unavailable. Women also retain a strategic position in the child-rearing process. The children a woman produces and trains expand the future labor supply for the household. Since the household is an informal unit of production, children are able to make substantial contributions to the household economy at an early age without disrupting production or jeopardizing their health.

The overall picture of balanced labor contributions, shared rewards, and balanced access to strategic resources in the domestic mode of production of course can be altered by external relations and constraints that impinge upon the peasant community. We have observed that the seasonal wage labor migrations from T'oj Nam have not seriously upset the economic balance between the sexes.

The growing commercialization of traditional productive activities does alter the balance of sex roles in T'oj Nam. A commercial transformation of the local economy is clearly under way. Although the division of labor in household commodity production is initially the same as for subsistence production, the rewards assigned to the various products are no longer determined by household utility but by the impersonal market mechanism. The money economy is indifferent to local values and household utility. Cash returns are more easily monopolized and manipulated by individuals than are subsistence goods.

In T'oj Nam the impact of the international money economy has been such that the resources which men traditionally control (land) and the products for which they are responsible (corn) have higher commercial values than women's traditional resources and products. Women's reproductive labor has also remained officially outside the commercial economy so that women have not been able to "cash in" on this capacity. In addition, the few formal jobs available to the inhabitants have thus far gone exclusively to men. The traditional balance of dependence between the sexes is beginning to be transformed into a system of female dependence on men.

In contrast to T'oj Nam, El Cañaveral is characterized by a sexual division of labor into two separate economic spheres. Men are selectively recruited for the sphere of formal company employment for a cash income while women remain in the subsistence sphere of domestic production. The large business corporation is the dominant unit of production. Only the men of El Cañaveral currently possess the alternative of formal employment. Women have few ways to contribute to the economic well-being of the household. The productive aspects of their domestic role are attenuated; wives are not needed to haul water, to build fires, nor to weave or sew clothing. Their children are no longer needed as part of the household labor force.

The distribution of rewards in El Cañaveral reflects the division of labor. The major source of income for the community is the individual wage paid to the rancheros who are employed by the company. Other rewards are also attached to employment with the company: housing, health care, and education. The cash incomes that women earn are very small by comparison. The reciprocity of the household is undermined by the loss of productive functions and by the availability of alternative goods and services in the "market place." The devaluation of women's labor in the market economy, combined with their lack of access to formal employment and its rewards, means that they are dependent on the discretion and goodwill of male wage earners (husbands of family members) for their economic support.

The control of economic resources in El Cañaveral is heavily weighted in men's favor. The key resource is a formal job as a unionized ranchero. The women of El Cañaveral do not control any important resources. Their reproductive role is certainly not indispensable, for the national labor market can maintain the supply of wage labor. Their domestic services—cooking, laundering, and sexual recreation—are all available commercially. In sum, the division of labor, rewards, and strategic resources in El Cañaveral all point to a position of economic dependency and marginalization of women relative to men.

In San Lorenzo the sexual division of labor by sex is not as clear as in El Cañaveral. High rates of labor force participation are found for both women and men in the informal economic sector. By and large, both sexes lack the means of subsistence production and access to formal jobs in the modern capitalist sector. Although men experience some advantage in obtaining formal employment, the incidence of formal employment among men is much lower in San Lorenzo than it is in El Cañaveral. Both sexes are predominantly active in informal cash activities. They nonetheless perform distinctive types of work. The general finding is that men experience a much broader range and variety of employment opportunities than women, who are largely confined to the service sector in tasks that require minimal specialization.

The rewards for labor of each sex are mainly individual cash incomes, which are informally allocated to personal and household consumption. The fact that women's incomes are significantly lower than men's places them in a relatively weak position, but women can usually earn enough to achieve a measure of economic independence. A generalized economic insecurity fosters mutual sharing of incomes with the opposite sex and with other family members in order to spread the risks and carry the individuals through periods when income is scarce. Although there is inequality in economic rewards between the sexes, it is not as fully institutionalized as in El Cañaveral. Women in San Lorenzo have the opportunity to earn a cash income in the service sector, while few San Lorenzo men have access to formal jobs which offer high pay and side benefits.

The control of strategic resources in San Lorenzo is extremely limited for either sex. Very few of the women or men work in secure, unionized jobs. One of the most indispensable resources, apart from access to a cash income, is housing. Because of its extralegal status, squatter housing is not clearly controlled by either sex. Ownership claims stem from the original invasion and continuous occupation thereafter. Men who make claims to being "head" of household do not have the legal authority to alienate women from this basic resource.

The division of labor and rewards in San Lorenzo shows that males enjoy definite advantages in obtaining a greater variety of jobs and jobs that are higher paying. However, the availability of even low-paying jobs in the city means that women are not completely dependent economically Moreover, their strong de facto claim to the squatter housing by right of occupation gives them considerable leverage. The economic characteristics of the community of San Lorenzo do not support a well-defined or rigid sexual stratification. Pooling of incomes and control of strategic resources are more balanced between the sexes than in El Cañaveral.

Of the four areas studied, it is most true of Villa Rosa that economic activity means formal employment and that productive activities are structured by large institutions and corporations. The division of labor in Villa Rosa places men in the principal economic role, working most commonly in higher-status professional, business, or military capacities. The percentage of women who work is significantly lower than in San Lorenzo, and comparable to that of women in El Cañaveral. Yet

Villa Rosa women have much greater access to formal employment than either sex in San Lorenzo. Compared to their men, however, Villa Rosa women are more likely to pursue informal self-employment in small businesses such as stores, beauty salons, or other enterprises that can be run from the home. Women are principally responsible for running the household and maintaining middle-class comforts and standards of living for their husbands and children.

Cash incomes in Villa Rosa show the same kind of differential that characterizes male and female earning power in all the communities, except for the seasonal plantation work done by the people of T'oj Nam. It is almost always the male income in Villa Rosa which maintains its middle-class standard of living. Residence in Villa Rosa itself is evidence that men share their incomes with their families and contribute substantially to the joint well-being of the household, but given that the income is their own individual reward, men retain a great deal of discretion in allocating the money to their individual advantage.

The strategic resources of Villa Rosa are in part nonmaterial. They include good breeding (pedigree) and education, as well as formal employment in the most strategic sectors of the modern economy: business, government, and military establishments. For men, it is possible to secure all three types of occupation. In contrast, women, even with proper family background and education, are not admitted into the strategic occupations. Thus Villa Rosa women make a generally marginal economic contribution to the household from a secondary position within the labor force, having low incomes compared to men.

The four communities can be compared with respect to economic equality between the sexes based on the qualitative descriptions above. On this basis, T'oj Nam enjoys the highest measure of sexual equality. While tasks are divided by sex, they are complementary, carried out in the same subsistence sphere, using similar technology and employing similarly limited amounts of capital. Rewards are largely distributed to the productive unit, the household, so that opportunities for individual appropriation are small. Men enjoy some advantage in the control of strategic resources by virtue of their preferential inheritance of land, an advantage only partly offset by women's control over the supply of labor. Increasing commercialization is beginning to erode this relatively egalitarian structure, but the overall cohesion of the subsistence economy still remains.

At the other end of the spectrum, El Cañaveral is marked by the greatest economic inequality of the four communities. Men perform almost all the economically valued labor, women being denied access to formal employment by the only employer. Access to this employment is, in fact, the key strategic resource for residents of the rancheria. Rewards in the form of cash wages are also almost uniquely distributed to men, women being for the most part relegated to sparsely rewarded peripheral activities. While women have some claim on the noncash rewards of employment, such as a stake in the residence, men have much greater overall discretion in disposing of the family income, most of which they earn.

It is more difficult to distinguish between the remaining two communities, both of which are intermediate between T'oj Nam and El Cañaveral. Women of both San Lorenzo and Villa Rosa live and work in the modern city of Guatemala. Both men and women in San Lorenzo are much less likely to work in the formal sector than are those of Villa Rosa. Cash income from work, accruing at least initially to the individual worker rather than the household, is the major form of reward in both communities. In both, this reward is distributed disproportionately to men. In San Lorenzo, control over the family house is a strategic resource. In accord with the community's origin as a squatter settlement, control remains significantly a matter of occupation. Women have an important degree of control over this strategic resource. Partly balancing this, the women of Villa Rosa have some control over the production of a strategic resource, legitimate heirs. Overall, the women of San Lorenzo enjoy a greater measure of economic equality than those of Villa Rosa, but the difference is not vast.

Tables 7-2, 7-3, and 7-4 present some quantitative information bearing on the degree of economic equality between the sexes in the four communities. Data for T'oj Nam have been included, but are not really comparable and will not be discussed further here.

Table 7-2 reports the percent of women and of men who earn cash incomes in each community. Using here and in the following comparisons in this section the highest of the proportions reported for Villa Rosa for both sexes, the relative exclusion of women from cash earnings is greatest in El Cañaveral and least in San Lorenzo, with Villa Rosa occupying an intermediate position. This can be seen by dividing the percent of women who earn cash incomes by that of such men in each community as given in Table 7-2.

When cash income *for those who have any* (as presented in Table 7-3) is compared on a relative basis across these three communities, there is little distinction, women generally having an income about 40 percent that of men in the same community. Taking all adults, whether having a cash income or not, in effect combining Tables 7-2 and 7-3, women in El Cañaveral have a cash income of just 24 percent of that

Table 7-2. Proportion of Each Sex Earning Cash Incomes by Community, 1974–75

Community	Women (%)	Men (%)	Relative Proportions Women to Men (%)
T'oj Nam (Mam)*			
rural	(60)	(100)	(60)
town	(100)	(100)	(100)
El Cañaveral	50	88	57
San Lorenzo	70	86	81
Villa Rosa	57	79	72

* Cash incomes in T'oj Nam are both highly irregular and very low, and are not really comparable to the more regular cash activities reported for the other communities.

Table 7-3. Average Monthly Cash Incomes of Economically Active of Each Sex by Community, 1974–75

Community	Women (Q.)	Men (Q.)
T'oj Nam (Mam)*	–	–
El Cañaveral	25	59
San Lorenzo	21	54
Villa Rosa	136	328

* Monetary incomes in T'oj Nam can be compared in terms of plantation wages, where piece rates are equal, or in terms of local wages for day labor where men earn 1.5 times as much as women. The differential is greater still in the returns to small-scale commodity production.

of their men, while for San Lorenzo the figure is 32 percent and for Villa Rosa it is 30 percent.

This pattern of strong distinction between El Cañaveral and the other two communities is repeated when the relative incidence of formal employment is compared between the sexes, using the data in Table 7-4. In El Cañaveral formal employment is almost exclusively a male matter, while relative equality is nearer the case in both San Lorenzo, where few members of either sex work in the formal sector, and in Villa Rosa, where access to formal employment is common for both. Women of Villa Rosa are about 47 percent as likely to be found in the formal sectors as their men, a figure that falls to 41 percent for San Lorenzo and 4 percent for El Cañaveral, based on the combined data in Tables 7-2 and 7-4.

310

Table 7-4. Formal Employment among Economically Active Members of Each Sex by Community, 1974–75

Community	Women (%)	Men (%)
T'oj Nam (Mam)*	0	12
El Cañaveral	6	76
San Lorenzo	13	26
Villa Rosa	56	86

* The incidence of formal employment among Mam men is greatly exaggerated by the nature of the sample, which overrepresents town dwellers. For the municipal Mam population as whole, formal employment is around 0.1%. T'oj Nam plantation wage labor is *not* formal employment, despite the large size of most migrant work crews, because it is *temporary* work.

Overall, the quantitative data tend to confirm the position of El Cañaveral as the community of greatest economic inequality, and do not particularly distinguish between Villa Rosa and San Lorenzo.

T'oj Nam is distinguished by the virtual absence of formal employment among the Mam for all but a handful of men. The seasonal work crews, although hired by formal plantation establishments that employ other formal workers such as the rancheros at El Cañaveral are not a permanent work force. They are therefore *in*, but not *of*, the formal sector for one or two months per year. Since only about 0.1 percent of the *total* municipal Mam population of nearly 10,000 have anything resembling formal employment, T'oj Nam would appear to be relatively egalitarian on this score. However, the extreme disparity in access to the first few formal opportunities does not bode well for Mam women as formal employment expands.

Women's Social Position

The relative position of the sexes in society can be evaluated in terms of the following social variables, already used to structure the descriptive chapters: formal public organization, informal public organization, and the domestic sphere. In a complex society, these variables do not necessarily share the same order of importance within the social structure of every community.

The heritage of Spanish conquest is evident in sociopolitical relations in T'oj Nam. For the Mam peasantry, social organization is centered on the household and municipality, while external relations re-

311

main largely in the control of resident Ladinos who function as intermediaries.

The participation of Mam women in formal public organizations is extremely low. Women scarcely vote in municipal or national elections, rarely join political parties, and do not hold positions in the largely unpaid civil-religious hierarchy that performs functions for the municipal government and the church.

In general, formal public organizations are weak among the Mam. The organizations present are not simply an outgrowth of peasant society and local conditions, but represent the expanding interest of large national and international institutions in rural areas. The sexual imbalances found in formal public organizations receiving outside organizational and financial support reflect larger systems of economic inequality. These systems override the local economic forces of peasant society. Exclusion of women from public social organizations parallels the exclusion of women from the few formal jobs available on T'oj Nam.

Among the few formal public roles that appear to be more authentically Mam in origin, we find only the roles of shamans and midwives. In some respects, the role of the Mam midwife seems comparable to that of the shaman. In addition, the male shaman often performs with his wife acting as a professional partner or assistant. Beyond these public roles, information is scanty because so many of the public traditions of the Mam have been destroyed by conquest, colonialism, and impoverishment.

In the informal public sphere, women are mobile individuals whose social life grows out of a diverse economic role which takes them from the home to the fields, the marketplace, and the plantations. Women have regular access to informal networks of information and social contact. While most of their work occurs in or near their homes, women are not necessarily more isolated than their men, who work in equally isolated fields. Women's informal social life in T'oj Nam exhibits a degree of flexibility and access that is comparable to men's.

Domestic organization is based on a pattern of patrilineal inheritance of land, patri-virilocal marriage, bride price, and occasional polygyny. While this complex of domestic institutions appears androcentric, a number of factors indicate that male control over female labor and reproductive activity is limited. These include the ease of separation and remarriage for women, the lack of stigma attached to sexually experienced, previously married women or to single mothers, and the nonrefundability of bride price after a limited period of time.

312

In T'oj Nam, the major relationship of dominance appears to be generational, such that parents control their children, including the grown ones. Men and women do not control each other as much as operate in separate but mutually dependent spheres. The women of T'oj Nam do enjoy a large measure of social autonomy and equality with men in the major spheres of Mam social activity.

In El Cañaveral, the rancheros' role in formal public organization is limited by the institutions of the plantation. The chief instrument of local political expression for the ranchero community is the workers' union, which is essentially an all-male organization. The major role of the union in the sphere of formal public organizations means that men and women are not equally represented; women are excluded because they do not work for the company. Men are more active than women in electoral processes, as well. They also participate more in formal organizations such as sports clubs, community clubs, and voluntary organizations, often based on male cohorts from work. Women's participation in formal public organizations occurs mainly in religious groups that promote the maintenance of marriage and family life.

The participation of women in informal public activities in El Cañaveral is also limited when compared to men's. Women have less ease of movement through the community than men. Gossip stalks them if they appear independent. They are less free to attend public entertainments, or to enjoy consumer goods such as bicycles or motorcycles, which imply mobility.

In the domestic sphere, the women encounter a strong double standard. There is social pressure for women to be monogamous to verify paternity, while sexual promiscuity of a commercial or irresponsible nature is a prerogative of men. In El Cañaveral, the growth of the public sphere at the expense of the domestic sphere has been marked by social segregation of the sexes, and increased male domination over the social activities of women.

San Lorenzo lacks the ordered social life of either T'oj Nam or El Cañaveral, for the community is not unified by a common cultural heritage or by common employment. San Lorenzo, as a social subsystem within the city, does not have a long or stable history, but was born out of the shared desperation of a broad spectrum of poor people. Due to its density and the special characteristics of squatter existence, extradomestic social organization is extremely important to the residents in order to regulate competition among themselves and to organize cooperation for the survival of the community.

Women are highly active in the public social organizations of San Lorenzo, including many of those that are formally organized. They were active in organizing the original invasion and continue to mobilize the population in defense of the community. At mass rallies of the colonia, women may outnumber men. In the more official sphere of electoral politics, women are less active than men, but show a significant level of awareness and voter participation.

In informal social relations there is a high degree of heterogeneity and flexibility. Women who have defied the army to maintain their homes are hardly likely to accept many restrictions on their mobility or social interaction. Women experience a wide range of social contacts through their work in city markets, their domestic chores for wealthier homes, and their need to utilize diverse resources within the city. Unlike El Cañaveral, women are able to enjoy public entertainment.

Domestic organization in San Lorenzo is influenced by the same kind of sexual double standard or machismo complex that characterizes El Cañaveral and many other areas of Ladino culture in Guatemala. However, domestic behavior in this colonia shows a low degree of conformity to this broad cultural ideal so predominant in the mass media. For instance, virginity at marriage is stressed, yet few marriages or common-law unions in San Lorenzo seem to conform to this ideal. Common-law unions established after sexual relations have begun appear to be more usual. The ideal that men should work outside to support the family while women remain at home to reproduce children whose paternity is undisputed is a pattern that simply does not accord with the realities of existence in San Lorenzo.

For the people of Villa Rosa, the sphere of formal public organization and activity is not centered on the colonia, but in the capital city itself. Women play an active role in certain forms of formal public life. For example, a higher proportion of women in Villa Rosa vote in the municipal and national elections than women in any of the other communities studied. Despite a relatively high level of involvement in formal groups, however, there is sexual segregation in the public sphere. Women feel particularly excluded from official political organizations, which remain thoroughly male-dominated from the urban to national levels.

In informal social organization, women tend to confine themselves to neighborhood gatherings and to social events and parties which they attend with their husbands or families. A significant segment of the population of married women feels isolated from social life by the domestic role of wife-mother which they are expected to perform.

The domestic role of women in Villa Rosa should be light, given the numerous domestic employees residing in the colonia. However, status considerations regarding the proper socialization of children and suitable maintenance of the home require their presence and attention. In Villa Rosa many women find that marriage is restrictive. More than in other communities, women take seriously the public expectations and values placed on female virginity and the male demands for complete sexual fidelity from their wives. These same women realize that reciprocal controls are not imposed on men. In marriage, women largely accept a condition of secondary social status and sexual rights in return for a rather firm guarantee of economic support and middle-class standing.

In T'oj Nam women are relatively disadvantaged in the sphere of formal public organization, but enjoy a high degree of equality in the informal public and domestic areas. Since formal public organization is less important in this community, women enjoy a high degree of social equality. In El Cañaveral, women are virtually excluded from the one significant public organization, the union. They face restricted options in the sphere of informal organization, with their mobility constrained by community pressure. They are also assigned a clearly subordinate role in the family, as foil to the machismo acted out by their spouses. This community is characterized by a high degree of social inequality.

San Lorenzo and Villa Rosa are again intermediate cases. Women in San Lorenzo do participate in the formal public organizations of the community to a considerable extent, although not equally with their men. The informal public sphere, however, is one in which they predominate. Their role as guardians of the settlement is a major element here, as is the great freedom with which they move through the colonia and the city. While the machismo-madonna ideal exists in San Lorenzo, it is mostly honored in the breach. Overall, women of San Lorenzo enjoy a fairly high degree of social equality.

Women in Villa Rosa enjoy less social equality than those in San Lorenzo. Their presence in the formal public sphere is, relatively, about equal to that found in the shantytown community. In the informal sphere, however, they are substantially restricted relative to the men of their own community, as against the more advantageous position of women in San Lorenzo. The isolation of the suburban home produces this result almost automatically. Finally, the women of Villa Rosa come closest of the women to living up to their half of the machismo-madonna ideal. They accept a clearly subordinate place in the domestic organization of their community, and enjoy a somewhat lower degree of social equality than do the women of San Lorenzo.

As we have seen, the ranking of the communities, in order of decreasing economic equality between the sexes, is

1. T'oj Nam
2a. San Lorenzo*
2b. Villa Rosa*
3. El Cañaveral
    (*Note: these two are nearly indistinguishable)

The same rank order prevails with respect to social equality, with the distinction between San Lorenzo and Villa Rosa much more apparent. An interesting specific instance of the relationship between economic and social equality is the matter of machismo, which deserves special notice because of its place in Guatemalan culture, and its place in the cultural and academic view of Latin America more generally.

Mesoamerican Machismo Reconsidered

The hypothesis that economic factors play an important causal role in female-male relations proves particularly useful in accounting for the commonly observed ethnic differences in the treatment of women by men. In Chapter Two, I referred to the assertions by different anthropologists (Maynard 1963, 1974; Wolf 1959, 1966; Adams 1960) that Maya men are more responsible economically to their families, while Ladino men place a high value on machismo and often abandon their wives and children. This holds even though Ladino men are generally found to have real economic advantages relative to indígenes, and should, therefore, be better able to assume responsible family roles. This paradox has prompted Mesoamerican anthropologists to suggest that sociocultural or social structural differences are responsible for the contrasting strength of male-female dyads in the two ethnic groups. They reasoned that Maya culture places a greater cultural emphasis on the husband-father role than does the Latin culture. The observation that at comparable economic *levels* the two cultures maintain different forms of female-male relations was deemed sufficient to reject economic causality. However, it is necessary to consider the general differences in the economic *forms* or modes of production that characterize the two ethnic groups, as well as their integration into the market economy. A closer examination of the economic differences generally found between the two groups shows that these differences can account for very fundamental contrasts in female-male relations between ethnic groups.

In T'oj Nam, subsistence production by the entire family remains important not only in the realm of agriculture, but also in clothing and food processing. The level of cash used by traditional Mam households is extremely low, and modern technology has not yet replaced many of women's functions. This is not true of the Ladinos in this study, nor of Ladinos generally. Ladinos, even in poor, rural areas, do not often reach the level of self-subsistence production which still persists in certain Mayan areas; Ladinos do not produce their own cloth, and have not generally settled in such isolated communities that they must depend on stone-grinding grain for food. Since the Spanish Conquest, the expansion of Ladino culture has been associated with expanding commercialism rather than with subsistence farming. We have also seen that greater integration into the cash economy is associated with individualized incomes, sharp disparities in the levels of cash income available to each sex, and a diminution of women's economic contribution in traditional domestic tasks due to modern technology.

These differences in the economic position of the two ethnic groups within the national society and the money economy explain why Ladino men should be more likely to abandon their wives than Mayan men. The indigenous Maya women still make essential contributions to production in a low-cash economy such as T'oj Nam. The Ladino women are more likely to be dependent consumers who provide welcome services, but who are also economically burdensome and less indispensable to men who earn most of the cash income as *individuals*. The most basic reason for lower responsibility among Ladino men, then, is not so much the result of a lower value placed upon the husband-father role as it is a result of their greater access to individual incomes and their economic independence of women, which in itself can devalue the husband-father role. The indigenous man, on the other hand, is responsible because, as a poor peasant, he cannot afford to be irresponsible.

Economic Position and Social Standing

As the discussion of machismo makes clear, relative economic position can have an important impact on social standing and even on the cultural valuation of various members of a community. In the four communities described, there is certainly a correlation between the degree of social and of economic equality. If the bourgeois community of Villa Rosa is excluded, the correlation is very strong, moving smoothly from the relatively egalitarian T'oj Nam to the very sexually stratified, proletarianized El Cañaveral. San Lorenzo is clearly intermediate in both economic and social terms. While it is neither more nor less modern than El Cañaveral in any unambiguous sense, the en-

tire shantytown community is subproletarian—less dependent on formal employment than is the rancheria. In this key respect, San Lorenzo
is intermediate between the highlands and the plantation.

Villa Rosa does not fit so neatly along the same axes. As a community, it is as dependent upon formal employment as is El Cañaveral,
but women enjoy a degree of economic equality more nearly like that
found in San Lorenzo. It may be that class is here dominating sex as a
category, a result made more plausible by the small size of the elite
classes in a country like Guatemala. Interestingly, the social position
of women in Villa Rosa is more noticeably inferior to that of their men
than in the other communities and thereby in accord with what would
be expected based on the importance of formal-sector employment to
this community. Overall, then, the importance of large-scale capitalism
and formal-sector employment to a community is strongly related to
the relative economic and social standing of women, with greater formal-sector importance suggesting greater inequality. The actual situation is complex, of course, with economic and social variables far from
perfectly correlated. Nonetheless, the view that links increasing penetration of Western capitalist institutions with increasing sexual equality
can be rejected. The truth, in Guatemala as in many parts of the Third
World, may be closer to the opposite.

Capitalism and the Domestic Mode of (Re)Production

Why is employment in the formal economy, with its larger institutions and large-scale capital, preferentially masculine? Answering this
question will provide the key to understanding the impact of economic
change upon women in Guatemala and in the Third World more generally. Whatever the effect of increasing integration into the world system on Third World societies as a whole, it is clear that those groups
excluded from its institutions find their economic and social standing
devalued.

Indigenous traditions. The rather egalitarian society described in
T'oj Nam stands as a strong counter to one common explanation, that
intruding capitalist enterprise simply accepts or adapts to local biases
concerning the division of labor and relative social value of the two
sexes. This mechanism may well exist in certain places, but it has little
explanatory power in Guatemala. The discussion of machismo above
suggests that the chain of causality may well run in the opposite direction, with economic considerations shaping cultural biases.

318

Capitalist tradition. A mirror image of this first explanation is the view that world capitalist institutions are simply bringing along their cultural baggage when they actively discriminate against various groups in their hiring practices in Third World environments. A certain degree of sexism, a fondness for martinis, and the wearing of three-piece woolen suits in the tropics are all part of the corporate cultural imperialist's repertoire. That one element may be simply comic and another may subvert entire cultures is largely a matter of chance. This is not an intellectually satisfying sort of explanation, forcing the causality back to the capitalist core countries, but it is relevant for those parts of the Third World, particularly dependent elites like Villa Rosa, which are almost consciously attempting to replicate metropolitan conditions.

Divide and rule. Of course, discrimination against important parts of the population is a more fundamental aspect of capitalist institutions than the other characteristics mentioned, in the metropolis as well as in the Third World. Selectively incorporating one section of the population, which then becomes privileged against the rest—whatever the impact of economic changes on the well-being of the whole—creates a potential ally and multiplies the points at which social leverage can be applied. This is a familiar concept in its various guises, including the "privileged unionized sector" and the offsetting "reserve army of the unemployed." The description of El Cañaveral above contains these elements in its rancheros over against other poor segments of the plantation labor force. Dividing the resident population further on sex lines has the effect of extending the divisions in the society which the plantation management seeks to control.

The domestic mode of (re)production. All this is not, of course, a full explanation even for the relatively straightforward situation which prevails in El Cañaveral, much less for the more generalized discrimination against women which exists in the formal sector in Guatemala and the Third World more generally. An overview of the four communities reveals that women's economic position is relatively devalued as men gain access to the formal sector, because the household and reproductive outputs women produce are still, even in the "modern" Villa Rosa, essentially the product of a cottage industry or even preindustrial mode of production. The core of this is reproduction. Because child rearing remains a cottage industry, it is costly for the formal sector to accommodate to its very different rhythms and requirements. At the same time, those who continue to pursue this mode of production will share only indirectly in the greater productivity of enterprises using large-scale capital. They are disadvantaged because it will pay the intruding capitalist sector to recreate the same pattern of sexual inequality which it has shaped in its metropolitan regions.

It is important to understand the complex nature of factors that prevent women from moving toward greater equality of opportunities with men as their division of labor is reformulated under capitalist expansion. The traditions and adaptations of men and women at the community level cannot account for the changing relations between them. Both structurally and culturally, capitalism has brought about a redivision of labor which has relatively penalized women. Understanding the dynamic of this process allows us to perceive a wider range of implications when evaluating economic change in the Third World. It also makes clear the links between sexual discrimination in the metropole and the hinterland. Under dependent capitalism, a more favorable redivision of labor for women may ultimately require changes in the capitalist centers of the world economy.

Historical Background of Guatemala

Guatemala's historical background reveals the political and economic conditions that have shaped and continue to shape its social structure and labor force. Contemporary Guatemala is imbued with a tradition of military domination and ethnic-class conflict that can be traced to the Spanish Conquest and the colonial period. Through four and a half centuries of changing forms of political domination, land and labor control, foreign intervention, and export production, Guatemala has remained a society organized to harness an impoverished, segmented rural labor force for the production of exports that a small landowning elite, in partnership with foreign commercial interests, parlays into profit in world markets. A consistent feature is that the majority of the Maya are still found concentrated among the rural poor, while the ruling elite is a composite of Euro-American and Guatemalan wealthy families. To comprehend the historical depth of Guatemala's social divisions, its present turmoil, and their implications for women, it is useful to review some features of the colonial period as well as the nature of change in Guatemala since independence and into the present period of intense civil-military warfare.

The Conquest and Colonial Period, 1524–1821

Prior to Spanish intervention, Guatemala had a flourishing regional civilization. In 1524, Spanish conquerors defeated the Quiche Maya,

321

the most powerful among the highland Maya states, and initiated their transformation and subordination to the larger world of mercantile capitalism. In the early days of Spanish rule, Maya towns were destroyed, populations were concentrated and resettled, and political and religious leaders were persecuted. Many Maya were enslaved, sold, and exported, or subjected to harsh tribute and labor requirements to enrich their new masters. These drastic changes, combined with new epidemic diseases to which the Indians lacked immunity, had a devastating effect on Maya populations in the sixteenth-century (MacLeod 1973). There was an estimated 75 percent to 90 percent population decline in the central Quiche highlands (Carmack 1981:105), while the lowlands, with less dense populations before their conquest, became essentially depopulated.

By the mid sixteenth-century, the Spaniards, alarmed at the declining numbers of Indian subjects, curbed some of the worst abuses and outlawed Indian slavery in order to preserve the natives for a long future of forced labor. Although harsh exploitation continued, new colonial institutions rationed Indian labor in order to use it more efficiently. New forms of labor control included *encomienda*, which granted Spaniards the right to collect tribute and labor from Indian communities, and the *repartimiento*, systematically rotated labor conscription from Indian communities. Tribute assessments specified goods and cash; goods included cash crops and specific commodities demanded by elite Spaniards, while cash could only be obtained by working for or trading goods to the Spanish. Receiving large land grants from the Crown, Spanish colonists and Catholic missionaries gradually took over lands released by Indian depopulation, by forced resettlement, and by legal and illegal expropriation. Spaniards steadily came to control the best lands near urban centers and on lowland plains were they could practice commercial Spanish-style plow agriculture and ranching. The Indians, on the other hand, were allowed to keep the more marginal highlands for subsistence farming.

Spaniards enriched themselves by exporting cash crops produced by forced Indian labor. Their capacity for capital accumulation depended on their ability to keep labor costs low through military control, and their ability to stabilize socioeconomic inequality with political-religious institutions that would persuade Indians to cooperate rather than resist. Given their small numbers, limited funds and lack of economic infrastructure, they did not reorganize production processes as much as redirect the output by demanding specific commodities as tribute. They introduced new products: wheat, cattle, sheep, and sugar for their own consumption and for commercial purposes as local Spanish and Ladino (mixed) markets grew.

The first major export, cacao, was a pre-Hispanic lowland crop which, after lowland depopulation, required the regular importation of highland Indian labor. This labor was supplied both through formal systems of forced labor and indirectly by tribute demands for cacao from highland Indians who had to work to buy it in the lowlands. When the cacao boom died down in the seventeenth-century, other export crops followed: first indigo (blue dye) and later cochineal (red dye) became important exports to European textile producers up to the mid-nineteenth-century. Spaniards controlled the profits both from agricultural exports and from tribute goods they sold in the regional economy: food and textiles.

How was the sexual division of labor affected by the colonial economic system? Historians have not addressed this question in any systematic way, and have been handicapped by the fact that the colonial record was largely written by Catholic churchmen and male administrators whose biases against women obscured women's economic importance. Native women were a crucial part of the labor force that Spaniards had at their disposal. They were not only sexual and domestic servants to the Spanish, but during the early post-Conquest years, they were enslaved, branded, and sold along with the men; they were drafted for labor in mining regions, required to haul water and wood, to prepare meals, and to transport loads as *tamemes*, or porters. In one report, a gang of Guatemalan slaves working in Honduras was composed of "twenty men and forty women, the indias working in the mines right along with the men" (Sherman 1979:326).

When slavery was outlawed, Indians were made Crown tributaries. Policies toward women and men might appear different, but their real impact was probably indistinguishable. Officially, all male Indians from age eighteen to fifty (excepting *caciques*, or nobles) were required to pay tribute, while single and widowed women paid at a lower rate. Yet men were actually assessed "household" or "conjugal" tributes with women as implicit cotributaries, whereas the women assessed the lower rates did not have such assistance. Single and widowed women were on the tribute lists at least until the end of the eighteenth-century (Martinez 1973:233; Carmack 1973:287, 391).

Beyond the underlying similarity of tribute burdens, the array of tribute goods collected confirms that a substantial portion were drawn from women's domain. For instance, tribute records of the year 1553 from Utatlan, the former Quiche-Maya capital, included one-hundred cotton cloths, fifty chickens, and ten loads (thirty *juiquipiles*) of cacao

323

beans (Carmack 1981:311). While economic historians have underscored the importance of cacao exports, in highland communities the cash values of cloth tribute may have been as high or higher than cacao. Textiles, after all, were important not only for clothing, but for a great variety of transport, packing, and bedding uses in a preindustrial economy. Notably, cloth was needed for sacks to hold export products such as cacao, and probably sugar. Native textiles, while not for overseas export nor for Spanish status symbols, were nonetheless, along with food supplies, an important part of highland-lowland rural-urban regional exchange. Even when the collection of highland tributes was demanded in cash, this may merely have meant that Maya women had to sell their cloth to pay the tribute. The fact that textiles and certain other common items, such as chickens, were collected as tribute indicates that women's traditional economic activities were directly harnessed by the colonial economy.

The *repartimiento*, or labor draft, in its most generalized form was a burden that fell selectively upon Indian men, who formed a pool of labor assigned in rotation to Spanish public works and colonial estates for construction, field work, and other tasks. Men would legally be taken from their homes and village for a number of weeks to work in other regions, while their wives and other family members had to maintain subsistence production in their absence. Unlike tribute, paid in goods or cash by a household production unit, the repartimiento organized male labor differently from female. It placed men on public works, earning a nominal wage. Its intention was to protect the domestic economy and reproduction of the indigenes by exempting women and equalizing the burden among men. Although the Crown imposed legal limits on the removal of indigenous women from their homes, they were nonetheless taken to work in Spanish haciendas on a variety of domestic and nondomestic tasks ranging from wetnursing Spanish babies to working in textile and indigo dye-making workshops (Sherman 1979:324–326, 340).

Even in their homes, Indian women were not overlooked as producers. For three centuries varying forms of forced textile production were imposed on them, until the close of the colonial period. The *repartimiento de hilazos* (the distribution of thread) is an important example of women's forced labor in cottage industries. It recalls medieval European tales of women locked up, expected to spin straw into gold overnight. In this profitable system, Spanish officials distributed raw cotton to women of highland Maya towns four times a year, returning to collect it when it had been cleaned, carded, and spun into thread three months later. Payment was extremely low or nonexistent,

324

and women who did not comply were fined, flogged, or jailed (Martinez 1973:527–530). Whether through tribute or repartimiento, Spanish administrators, including missionaries, accumulated the benefits of this coercive economic structure which granted them control over the labor and products of Indian men and women.

In addition to economic institutions which kept the indigenous communal-domestic economy intact, if heavily burdened, individuals could contract themselves to private Spanish estates where they became resident dependents, typically locked into a system of debt servitude. This practice applied to both sexes, but it involved closer social integration where work assignments were more likely to reproduce Spanish norms regarding the sexual division of labor, and contributed to the growth of the Ladino population.

The colonial government regulated the economy both to guarantee a steady flow of income to the Crown together with large landowners, merchants, and the Church, and to maintain a large stratum of servile indigenous labor. Economically, the Crown licensed Spanish monopolies and funded its administration through a mass of tributes, taxes, fines, and tariffs on economic activities by non-Spaniards. This top-down economic structure, dependent on decisions made abroad, lacked the flexibility to supply the needs of colonial society and gave rise to a vast array of intermediate socioeconomic niches, quasi-legal and illegal. Regulations which envisioned a simple and static division of society into distinct castes of Spanish colonists and indigenous subjects were steadily undermined. Initially, given the small number of Spaniards, former Maya nobles filled some intermediate positions. As the Spanish and Ladino populations increased, however, indigenes met greater competition and were usually edged out by Ladinos. The intermediate status groups—lacking the landholdings and rights of pure-bred Spaniards, and lacking membership in indigenous tributary communities, became a pool of mobile, landless workers who filled varied rural and urban occupations as skilled and unskilled workers, artisans, labor contractors, overseers, traders, black marketeers, cowboys, and militia. Although many were impoverished or trapped into dependent status as debt peons, their lack of clearly ascribed status gave them somewhat greater potential mobility than rural indigenes, who were largely bound by culture and community controls into leading a peasant existence. Moreover, as overseers and militia, they were likely to be enlisted in the exploitation of the indigenes, creating an important cultural division among the dominated populations.

How did the indigenous peoples adjust to the economic burdens and political constraints imposed on them? Although historians once tended to portray them as resigned and passive, they persistently fled, resisted, and revolted against their dominators. Their strategies ranged from individual escape to collective liberation. In the early colonial period, Spanish efforts to Christianize the Maya were aided by some Maya nobles in exchange for individual privileges and exemptions from tribute. Local political authority was granted to former Indian noble men (colonial administrations followed a Latin cultural blueprint that excluded women from political posts) to keep order and collect tribute. This system represented some continuity with the past and was more easily accepted by the indigenes than direct Spanish rule. From the indigenous perspective, this offered limited autonomy in internal affairs, and gave them some representation with Spanish authorities; but for the Spanish, indirect rule economized on scarce Spanish administrative personnel. The indigenous officials were responsible for defending community territorial claims and protesting excessive tributes. They were liable for punishment and jailing if they failed to collect the full tribute quota—a common problem when tribute assessments were not adjusted to population losses. By the end of the colonial period, the burdens of office holding had increased, and Indian noble privileges had largely disappeared. Most of the indigenous population had been compressed into an agrarian peasantry, ever-struggling to defend their lands against Ladino encroachment.

The Maya could escape tributary status by moving (often illegally) to Spanish cities or haciendas where they ultimately merged into the Ladino population. Their disappearance, while aimed at bettering their individual chances, often meant increased tribute difficulties for the communities they left behind (Lutz 1976). Indian women migrants tended to find employment in Spanish homes in the cities, while the men found work in artisan trades, commerce, and agriculture. Many joined other interstitial groups in resisting Spanish economic controls and protective legislation. For instance, Lutz reports that Indian and *mulatta* (of mixed African and European descent) women conducted blackmarket beef sales in the central plaza and barrios of the capital for decades, in defiance of colonial monopolies. Almost an informal guild, the women petitioned officials for the legal right to sell beef, and continued to trade illegally despite the threat of public whippings and jailing (Lutz 1976:574–576).

Individual efforts to escape from Indian caste status and obligations had both cultural and biological dimensions. The cultural option was for Maya to migrate to areas where they could abandon Indian cultural attributes and language and "pass" into the Ladino population. This was often combined with the biological option, which was to have children in formal or informal unions with the free castes or Spaniards, defining a new, higher status for their children due to the complex and ambiguous rules of legitimacy and bilaterally hereditary status. Colonial litigation shows numerous Indian efforts to escape caste status, as when women sought tribute exemptions for their children with free mulatto husbands, or when Ladinoized Indian men claimed exemptions on the basis of service in the militia, normally forbidden to Indian men in the colonial period (Lutz 1976:272–283; Samayoa 1962:156). While such strategies were certainly significant, the vast majority of the indigenous population was still locked into an impoverished, segregated and subordinate position as tribute payers.

Throughout the colonial period, the indigenous communities were sites of resistance and rebellion. Spanish authorities and landowners were ever aware of the threat of revolt, and desired to prevent collaboration between indigenous communities. Maya officials were confined to community jurisdiction, reporting to Spanish officials, and separated from other Maya communities. Maya were forbidden to bear arms or join militias, for fear of rebellion. Maya religious leaders were persecuted lest ancient religion ignite anticolonial sentiments. Catholic missionaries, an integral part of the colonial enterprise, struggled to convert the Maya to the values and work habits of obedient Christians. Yet the remoteness of many Maya communities permitted a resistant substratum of rural Maya culture—attenuated and modified by impoverishment and persecution—to persist. Elements of the native religions would generally resurface as an important cohesive ideology when the Maya revolted against Spanish exactions.

Reports of Maya nativistic rebellions against colonial rule indicate women were active participants. For instance, at the end of the colonial period (1802–1824), when the Quiche Maya of Momostenango rebelled against tribute payments, women were not only included among the mass of rebels (some 600 men and women, or "the entire community"), but were also within the active nucleus (Carmack 1979:226, 238–239). This is suprising since colonial political structures rigidly excluded women from all official participation. It suggests that women's economic concerns as tributaries, and their threshhold of political mobilization, were rather similar to those of Maya men. Given that indigenous men were still largely excluded from organized militias, they did not have a significant head start in armed political struggle at the close of the colonial period.

Independence and a Century of Caudillos, 1821–1944

The achievement of Independence in 1821 was the result of the collapse of the Spanish empire as Spain's position in Europe deteriorated, and of growing dissatisfaction among *criollos* (Guatemalans of Spanish descent) over the privileges of peninsular Spaniards. Independence ushered in a long period of dislocation as factions among the agricultural and merchant elite struggled for hegemony. Liberals were in favor of abolishing the privileges and protective monopolies granted under Spanish colonialism. The rules that guaranteed wealth to some sectors of the colonial elite were too static for others, including indigo producers who found their once dominant export declining in competitive world markets. The Liberals wanted a more dynamic economy permitting the importation of foreign technology and capital investment. They also wanted to attract European immigrants, and to transform the agrarian structure from one of colonial corporate landholdings to private ownership. The vast corporate landholdings of the Church (the nation's largest landowner) and the Indian territories were resources that they could exploit, they argued, more efficiently. Liberals pressed for a national land reform that would seize these lands and sell them to capitalist investors who could develop the country more profitably. The Conservatives, in contrast, allied themselves with the Church to defend a rigidly stratified economic structure based not on risking capital, but on relatively secure incomes they obtained through rents, traditional estates, and monopoly control of foreign trade. They favored a paternalistic state rather than a laissez-faire capitalist one.

As the criollo elites disputed national power, Indians were struggling for greater autonomy and reduction of tributes. The western highlands saw a series of indigenous rebellions from 1802 to 1834. While in a sense these were independence movements, they were not concerned with independence from Spain as much as with independence from local Ladinos and criollos who had been increasing their penetration of Indian areas. Ultimately defeated, these movements were responding to increased pressure against their territorial rights and community self-government.

After Independence, and particularly in the 1830s when Galvez held power, liberal changes were enacted, permitting foreign immigration, import competition from foreign (primarily English) merchant houses, and expropriation of Church and Indian lands. The effect was chaotic in rural areas and was bitterly opposed not only by Conservative and Church interests, but also by Indian communities that had lost lands (Carmack 1981). In 1838, the Liberal government was ousted and a mass of men and women stormed and looted the capital crying "Long live religion" and "Death to foreigners!" (Winter 1909). Liberal programs were then reversed by President Carrera, a twenty-one-year-old indigenous *cacique*, or strongman, who gave Guatemala a Conservative "30-Year Dictatorship," closely allied with the clergy. While the Liberals stewed, corporate protectionism favoring the old elites and clergy was revived. Ironically, this military dictator, so firmly detested by progressive capitalist sectors, was popular with the indigenous populations who at this point were exempt from tribute and labor conscription and were able to cultivate their communal lands with relatively little interference from the land grabbers and aspiring capitalist entrepreneurs who placed priority on export production. As historian Cambranes observed:

> The period of the so-called "30-Year Dictatorship" is the epoch in which Guatemala's indigenous people for the first time in more than three centuries had the possibility of dedicating all their energies to living a stable life, dedicated to agriculture, livestock, and artisan crafts, free from all the tributary exactions and labor obligations that had so oppressed them. Now, independent agricultural activity made possible a florescence of communities formerly in decline (translated, 1976:62).

The picture was not exactly rosy—debt peonage, rents, and land shortages still plagued the peasants—but this may well have been a moderate recovery period between two long eras of more intense political-economic exploitation.

The political changes of the first half of the nineteenth-century were accompanied by changes in the country's export dependency for the ruling class. Indigo, once the dominant export, was in decline, while a similar dye material, cochineal, replaced it from the 1830s to 1850. Although cochineal was produced on large and small plantations, often by Ladinos, it often required loans at high interest from foreign merchants. By 1850, production and export of cochineal was largely concentrated and controlled by one German landowning merchant-financier (Cambranes 1976:195). Soon, this export also began to falter due to bad harvests and cheap competition from the Canary Islands. Finally in the 1870s it was displaced by the invention of cheaper aniline dyes in Europe.

After 1870, foreign investment went increasingly toward coffee production as this became the next export crop to dominate the national economy, increasing rapidly from 1859 to 1880, until by 1884 coffee accounted for 90 percent of exports (Cambranes 1976:29, 113, 196). German capital and immigrants played a major role in developing coffee production. By the end of the 19th century, Germans controlled eighty agricultural enterprises in Alta Verapaz, and ninety in western Guatemala, or some 3.7 percent of Guatemala's total territory (Cambranes 1976:93–95).

In 1871, the Liberals took power again, and this time with their own military strongman, President Barrios, the Liberal program was effectively carried out. Barrios laid the infrastructure for a more dynamic agrarian capitalism that would prove to be a new source of enrichment for the agro-export elite, revitalized with injections of foreign capital and personnel. Yet the reforms would also vigorously undermine the Indian peasant communities.

Under the banner of free trade, corporate lands of the Church and the Indian communities were abolished. Land was expropriated on a large scale, and sold to private owners. The beneficiaries were mainly Ladinos and capitalists entrepreneurs, many of them German. Large private landholdings remained intact, and many small Ladino farmers acquired lands, especially in the east.

These measures favored the development of agrarian capitalism based on the new export, coffee. Unlike indigo and cochineal, coffee required larger capital investments and more hired labor, placing it beyond the capacity of most small producers, unless they had loans—hence the entry of German capital. It also used hilly land at higher altitudes which until then had been left to the indigenous communities. The new coffee entrepreneurs wanted both Indian lands and Indian labor. "Unproductive" subsistence farmers who were dispossessed had to turn to wage labor. In addition, the government system of *mandamientos* (labor conscription) forced them to work to prevent "unemployment." Debt peonage, with full government support, became the dominant form of labor coercion, trapping Indians and poor Ladino peasants into a lifetime of bondage to coffee estates, never able to work off cash advances or debts contracted at plantation stores. Debts were treated as corporate family obligations so that death did not cancel them, but merely passed them to spouses or children.

The Liberal reforms also brought changes in national sociopolitical institutions. The Catholic Church and its clergy lost power not only economically through expropriation of church properties, but also politically through expulsion of the Jesuits and other clergy, the admission of Protestant missionaries, and the secularization of education. Government expenditure on education increased from 6,168 to 399,859 pesos between 1858 and 1883 as education was decreed compulsory (Cambranes 1976:162).

330

The breakdown of Church influence was matched by the increasing concentration of state power, particularly with the creation of a national army as a permanent institution. Barrios established a Military Academy for training officers in 1874, and decreed military service compulsory for all Ladino, or Spanish-speaking, males—including Ladinoized Indians (Cambranes 1976). Although the vast majority of the soldiers were Ladino recruits (Cambranes 1976:86), for the first time Maya men could become official soldiers. Yet indigenous men were largely in the lower ranks, often as unpaid "volunteers," while "regular" soldiers were usually Ladinos. Formerly, under Carrera, some Quiche communities had their own informal militias, complete with patron saints, linked to their local civil-religious service system, but under Barrios, military service became more secular (Carmack 1979). As the military became an instrument of government terror used in support of the Liberal capitalist land and labor reforms, it also developed into a new power sector in its own right. Cambranes asserts that "the constant wars directed by Barrios in the interior of the country and against neighboring Central American states made possible the birth of a military caste, many of whose members later developed into great landowners" (1976:86).

The Liberal reforms—anticlericalism, the promotion of private property and industrial development, and the building of national educational and defense institutions—did not greatly alter the fundamental class divisions. Criollos retained their large landholdings, while the Maya populations were forced to subsidize capitalist enterprise by giving up their lands and labor once again. The changes made possible more efficient capitalist production, while the Maya were pushed into the proletariat. The changes necessitated brute force to carry them out; Barrios' solution to political dissent was often the firing squad. When an indigenous revolt in the western highlands was sparked by Liberal reforms, the response recalls both the Conquest and contemporary demonstrations of military brutality. Barrios ordered troops to burn all the peripheral hamlets suspected of harboring rebels, to concentrate and resettle the population, to imprison any Indians under suspicion, and to execute those who supported the rebels (Carmack 1979:262–269).

The dictatorships which followed Barrios, the most lengthy being those of Cabrera (1898–1920) and Ubico (1931–1944) continued the tradition of strongman rule. They preserved the privileges of the large landowners and foreign capitalists, and guaranteed a supply of cheap peasant labor for the plantations. Under Cabrera, the debt labor system was maintained, with political authorities collaborating in the roundup of workers. When Ubico took power, he instituted a labor reform abolishing debt labor and cancelling the peasants' debts to plantation owners, a measure welcomed by peasants. But this did not in fact alter their obligation to work on the plantations, for he substituted a harsh Vagrancy Law which stipulated that peasants had to work 150 days per year on plantations if they lacked a certain quantity of land. While these obligations, like colonial tribute, appeared to fall specifically on males, often entire families would contract themselves out to help fulfill the obligations, or they would have to assume extra work at home to compensate for the loss of the men's labor. The main effects of Ubico's labor reform were to take recruitment and control of labor out of private hands to have it administered by the state, and to grant peasants greater choice of *where* to work. Possibly this new element of competition for labor produced modest wage increases (Grieb 1979:39), but the continued coercion plus the repression of the labor movement severely limited gains for peasant-workers.

The infusion of German capital into coffee production and exports was soon followed by increasing U.S. penetration at the turn of the century. The American-owned United Fruit Company was building its banana empire, acquiring vast landholdings on both Guatemalan coasts, while two other North American enterprises gained control over electric power and railways. With generous property and tax concessions under Cabrera, American companies gained a major foothold in the Guatemala economy, and exercised corresponding political influence. In the mid-1930s, coffee exports to the United States surpassed those to Germany and most of Guatemala's foreign trade was with the United States (Grieb 1979:147). By World War II, U.S. influence was sufficiently dominant to pressure the Guatemalan government, as its hemispheric ally, to confiscate German properties and intern German Guatemalans. This left the United States in an undisputed position of influence. The principal United States corporation, United Fruit, was like a "nation within a nation," controlling directly or indirectly some 40,000 jobs—the largest landowner and employer in Guatemala (Schlesinger and Kinzer 1982). In general, U.S. business interests were opposed to any social or economic reforms in what they recognized as a very favorable investment climate, with extremely low taxes and labor costs. Yet the preservation of the very lopsided agrarian structure and the coercive labor mechanisms blocked improvements in rural standards of living, literacy, health, and social organization which should have followed the introduction of industrial technology, improved transportation and better commmunications.

As disparities increased, the forces of national repression expanded to maintain the status quo at the expense of the majority. Under Cabrera, the standing army increased to more than 15,000 active men; every male between the ages of twenty and sixty was considered a soldier (Dombrowski et al. 1970:29; Winters 1909). Conscription (in practice more akin to capture) was not evenly imposed, and now the mass of soldiers were indigenous conscripts. Military service was an avenue of upward mobility for a few indigenous men who were able to achieve officer status, but Ladinos were disproportionately concentrated in the officer ranks (Carmack 1979). Breaches of ethnic stratification were, of course, not entirely new but they were significant given the growing importance of the army.

During Ubico's dictatorship, the military was further professionalized. The Military Academy was expanded and modelled on West Point, with an American officer in command, to ensure that American training methods were applied (Grieg 1979:47, 75). In government, there was a "creeping militarization of the administration," for Ubico felt that officers were better qualified. Among the Indians, Ubico saw the army as a device for social integration, and promoted the "educative mission of the barracks" which aimed at "ladinizing" the Indians, changing even their food and clothing habits (Grieb 1979:48). Although rarely recognized, this selective Ladinization and militarization of men acted to create a new social gulf between men and women. It fostered sexual stratification between men as soldiers and women as civilians, as well as stratification between military officers and the majority of peasant men and women who were still forced to labor and forbidden to organize on the plantations and other public projects.

Detailed studies of the changing sexual division of labor during the century of caudillos are lacking, yet it is clear that changes were taking place. Apart from the expansion of the army as an exclusively male branch of government, the establishment of large North American enterprises such as railways, the electric company, and the banana plantations led to the creation of a proletarian segment that was predominantly male. While women were evidently still very active in local markets selling food and agricultural products at any transportation stop or urban center, it is likely that much of their cottage industry employment was in decline due to increasing competiton from foreign industrial products, particularly textile and tobacco goods (Winter 1909; Chinchilla 1976:36). In the public sector, one area that expanded for women was teaching, and teachers, women and men, were a major segment of the emerging middle class which, with the help of dissident army officers, deposed Ubico and established Guatemala's first democratically elected civilian government in 1944.

One Decade of Democratic Reforms, the "Revolution" of 1944–1954

The "revolutionary" period in Guatemala's modern history consists of a brief interlude of two democratically elected presidencies, those of Arevalo and Arbenz, during which a new constitution was established guaranteeing basic democratic freedoms. Inspired by Franklin D. Roosevelt, Arevalo sought to establish a new social order that would legalize political and labor union activity, extend voting rights, establish minimum wages, create a social security system, exclude the military from public office, and extend public education. The Vagrancy Law and forced labor were eliminated, and peasants were free to choose where and how long to work. The 1949 Law of Forced Rental forced large landowners to rent unused land to tenant farmers. Rural and urban workers were encouraged to participate in new forms of organization: political parties, unions, and agrarian reform committees. The new measures, radical as they seemed in the Guatemalan context, were often compromises, as when unionization was permitted but only on large plantations, or when women were granted the right to vote in 1950, but only *literate* women, while the vote was simultaneously extended to both literate and illiterate men.

This break away from authoritarian military rule was viewed with reservations if not consternation by the landed obligarchs and U.S. business interests. During the presidency of Arbenz (1950–1954), the pledge to carry out a land reform to benefit landless peasants by nationalizing some of United Fruit Company's vast unused landholdings raised great alarm in the company, and in the Cold War atmosphere of the 1950s, its charges of communism mobilized the U.S. government against the Arbenz administration. By 1954, United Fruit Company, through careful lobbying and collaboration with the U.S. administration and the C.I.A., was able to engineer an end to Guatemala's experiment in civil democracy and reform by sponsoring a right-wing military coup by Castillo Armas (Schlesinger and Kinzer 1982). The succeeding military governments reversed the land reforms and persecuted labor and political opposition leaders, while adopting a strident anticommunist ideology. U.S. business and government leaders had sponsored a return to a system that provided military guarantees of stability and U.S. investment rights, ignoring the cost to democracy and human rights.

334

Military Governments and Civil War: 1954–1982

After the 1954 coup, the old alliance between the military, the landed oligarchy, and U.S. business interests was restored. They were joined by the Catholic Church, which, as a vocal anticommunist ally, was again permitted to own land and establish social and educational institutions. Land was taken away from peasants and returned to former owners, labor unions were declared illegal, and reformers and progressives were hunted down or forced into exile. Democracy persisted only as a facade of periodic "elections" that shifted leadership among factions of the military and changed faces at the helm of government. Since 1954, electoral absenteeism has roughly doubled, from one-third to two-thirds of the registered voters; (CGS 1981:61). The role of government has been to suppress popular movements for socioeconomic change, and to protect the large plantation owners and new foreign investors. Significantly, U.S. military aid, which had been turned off under Arbenz, increased dramatically after 1954, and supported the professional training and strengthening of the armed forces in exchange for political loyalty and cooperation. Meanwhile, U.S. investments have increased and diversified, accounting for a large part of Guatemala's agro-industrial development and broadening their monopolistic control in a number of areas (Tobis 1974).

The violent suppression of dissent led to the formation of a guerrilla movement to engage in armed struggle against the government and its supporters. In the 1960s, small guerrilla groups were formed by dissident young army officers, who staged an unsuccessful coup attempt and by socialists and progressives drawn mainly from the disenchanted urban and rural petty bourgeoisie. These groups lacked a base in broad popular organizations, and by the end of the 1960s they were largely defeated by military campaigns of indiscriminate terror that killed an estimated 6,000–8,000 people in the eastern part of the nation (CGS 1981:21). After a slight abatement, repression shifted to Guatemala City in 1970, when President Arana initiated a year-long state of siege during which thousands were killed in an effort to quell left-wing activity. Although government repression and political killings decreased briefly in the mid-1970s, it is estimated that about 20,000 people have been victimized between 1966 and 1976 (Amnesty International 1981). After 1976, repression was again on the rise, this time in the northern and western zones, and was sufficiently well publicized that in 1977 the U.S. government suspended direct military aid to the Guatemalan government due to its human rights violations.

The renewed political violence of the late 1970s can be seen as a response to the proliferation of popular organizations that could challenge the traditional political controls and hegemony over rural peasants in isolated communities. With increasing tourism, international development assistance, foreign missionaries, and health and educational personnel in the rural areas, new links were forged between the peasants and the outside world, increasing the levels of social integration and multiplying channels of outside appeal. Organizations dedicated to relieving conditions of poverty—poor farm yields, bad water supplies, illiteracy, malnutrition, and inadequate housing (especially after the tragic 1976 earthquake which killed 25,000 and left more than 75,000 homeless)—were often frustrated by the lack of cooperation, and in fact deep opposition, from government and large landowners to any substantial improvements. The conservative elite generally disapproved of any fundamental social change that would (a) increase the consciousness and political voice of the indigenous peasantry or working class, and (b) improve the economic outlook for peasants enough to undermine their dependence on underpaid seasonal plantation work. This disapproval eventually extended to include the activities of the Church, educational institutions, labor unions, and neighborhood organizations.

The Church, initially welcomed back by conservatives as an ally, became involved in organizing on behalf of indigenous communities, fostering educational and health services as well as agricultural cooperatives and land colonization projects. In *organizing* the indigenous peasants, the Church was overstepping its conservative mandate to provide charity and spiritual guidance, and was increasingly viewed as subversive, if not communistic, by the elite. Increasingly, progressive religious groups—indigenous lay workers, priests, and nuns—were persecuted and murdered.

Labor unions also revived in the 1970s. Industrial, agricultural, and public sector workers found their real wages decreasing with inflation, and became more militant. Teachers, plantation workers, and miners organized major strikes during this period, as workers in a variety of urban industries struggled to unionize in the face of government repression. By the late 1970s, unions had achieved higher levels of organization and collaboration nationally, and were joining other popular organizations in solidarity against government repression. In 1980, the new strength of the union movement was demonstrated (at a time of intense government-sponsored terrorism) by a massive strike of 75,000 permanent and migrant farmworkers, which led to an increase in the official minimum wage from Q. 1.12 (unchanged in 3 decades) to Q. 3.20 per day (CGS 1981).

Urban committees in poor neighborhoods and squatter settlements also became increasingly organized, demanding improved neighborhood services and protesting consumer price increases. In 1978, they launched a city-wide demonstration against a doubling of city bus fares, during which numerous protestors were shot and jailed. In addition to these expanding popular organizations, students, journalists, opposition political parties, and educators all represented vocal sectors that advocated changes in the traditional political-economic system which they held responsible for the nation's underdevelopment and repression.

Since 1954, Guatemala's wealthy, conservative elite had learned that it could continue to prosper without the direct, forced labor institutions of former eras, as long as the peasant's lack of land and alternative economic options channeled them into plantation work. Those who contributed to any disruption of this labor supply, the traditional basis of wealth, were considered dangerous and suppressed by government or paramilitary forces.

During the Lucas Garcia presidency (1978–1982), the extreme fears of the traditional aristocracy were increasingly translated into violent repression and military action against all sectors promoting change—with minimal concern for world public opinion. A massacre of more than 100 peasant men, women, and children in the village of Panzos in 1978, and of 35 indigenous protestors in the Spanish embassy in 1979 signalled willingness to use any measures to crush peasant organizations. The nation experienced a massive military huntingdown of catechists, health care workers, community and union leaders, cooperative members, students and university professors, rural educators, radio broadcasters and journalists—in short, anyone suspected of being capable of peasant-worker mobilization or communication. According to Amnesty International (1981), political "disappearances" and killings by paramilitary groups were planned in secret annexes to the National Palace and reached 5,000 in the first two years of the Lucas presidency.

The escalation of political terrorism directed at a wide spectrum of social organizations increased opposition to the government and drove many middle-sector groups underground and into the guerrilla movement. The growing movement, after suffering setbacks in the 1960s, revived with new strategies of rural organizing, building a more solid popular base in rural areas, and incorporating Maya peasants into their organization for the first time. In the late 1970s, the Guerrilla Army of the Poor (EGP) emerged as a particularly effective clandestine group. In the early 1980s, guerrilla organizations and political opposition groups achieved greater unification as government repression grew more indiscriminate. From a stage of selecting leadership, suspected guerrillas, and organized peasants as targets—a time when adult men were disproportionately victimized—in the early 1980s, the government forces were slaughtering entire villages, concentrating their heaviest attacks on rural indigenous populations. The move from selective to collective repression represents a declaration of full-scale war in the northwest highlands, where women, children, and the aged are all seen as the enemy, or as "guilty" enemy supporters. At this stage, women, who had previously lagged behind in organizational activity due to the modern redivision of labor, have had to take action to survive. They have joined the guerrilla movement in increasing numbers, and have taken their children to hunt for refuge. It is estimated that some 500,000 Guatemalans are now refugees, with as many as 25,000 located in refugee camps in Mexico. (Simons 1982)

The 1982 elections offered little hope for an end to the war; the official candidates merely represented rival factions among the same military-conservative establishment. But a military coup by General Rios Montt, in March 1982, shattered any facade of electoral democracy. Upon seizing power, he imposed a state of siege and reduced urban violence. Yet rural massacres have continued with such brutality that they brought new international denunciations of the "scorched earth" campaign against indigenous peasants, and the "guns and beans" programs that round up hungry peasants into camps and bribe them to join civil militias to hunt down subversives. Amnesty International has charged that 2,600 political killings occurred between March and July 1982, and that the pace continues, (UG: Oct. 18, 28, 1982) Nonetheless, the U.S. government has moved to restore military aid to Guatemala on the grounds that Rios Montt has improved human rights. Shored up by outside economic and military aid, the military forces can continue this long and costly war despite the complete lack of internal popular support for the government.

In this context of prolonged military-civilian warfare, the sexual division of labor seems trivialized by the intensity of life and death struggles. Yet the war itself is conducted in a lopsided fashion between an all-male military establishment defending the status quo, and several million men and women who seek ways to change the course of Guatemalan labor history. For the women involved, their first step must be to end the military occupation of the country.

Research Conditions and Fieldwork

Research conditions in Guatemala were generally positive and co-operative, if one stayed away from politics. Even though political repression in the mid-1970s had not yet reached the level that it has since attained, there was no question that political constraints and fears were on the minds of many people, and often inhibited explicit exploration of certain questions. How hard can an anthropologist push people for information, when such questioning can lead them to fear that the anthropologist may act as an informer against them, and when the anthropologist does not have full assurance of personal safety or the ability to protect confidential information against theft, seizure, or misuse? In some respects, my investigation of the status of women and male-female relations was considered an innocuous question, given that women were (at that time) not viewed as powerful or dangerous enough to have political significance. Even so, I could often sense limits to the security people felt in discussing touchy political and economic issues, and avoiding pursuing them further.

T'oj Nam

Fieldwork in T'oj Nam was conducted primarily from February to May 1975. Brief visits to the town were made both before and after the main research period, and I was fortunate to have visited the town during its important annual fiesta in 1974. Intending to concentrate on the traditional Maya farm economy, I found that it could not be realistically disassociated from town life. It seemed equally unrealistic to ignore Maya women involved in a difficult transition to a more urbanized, commercial way of life in the town. Hence, I collected data on women in both the rural and more "urbanized" town sectors. While the rural and town-dwelling Mam populations overlap and share many cultural and socioeconomic patterns, somewhat different field methods were used, due to their varying degrees of exposure to national society. Generally, it was more difficult to gather information about rural than town women, since town women are often functionally bilingual and bicultural.

As in most highland Maya communities, language is a major research barrier. Outside the town center, women rarely speak Spanish, having little direct contact with strangers. They meet foreigners occasionally as tourists to whom they can sell textiles, but interaction usually ends there. It was difficult to find an interpreter to work with rural monolingual Mam women since few women were fluently bilingual, mobile, and uncommitted to other kinds of work. (A male interpreter was ruled out since men have restricted access to unrelated women, and tend to produce stilted responses on issues concerning women.) It was also important that an interpreter possess a positive orientation both toward the traditional culture and toward foreign research (a rare combination). Fortunately, I found such an individual, who also served as a valuable source of information herself on women and men in both rural and town milieux.

Basic distrust of foreigners and strangers is a more encompassing problem in rural T'oj Nam than in other, less isolated communities. Some rural women simply feared visits by any stranger. On two occasions, women declared that their husbands would not approve of an interview. On other occasions, women were apprehensive that speaking to a stranger could endanger their domestic property when they migrated, or fearful lest an interview entail legal difficulties (land claims, or discovery of illegal alcohol sales, polygyny, or school truancy). Moreover, the use of any type of recording device, even a pencil and notebook, sparked strong anxiety and could not be used in most situations. Even with a skilled interpreter, interviewing was sometimes a delicate procedure. Also, after my interpreter worked very hard to create a congenial atmosphere for interviewing, I found it difficult to keep up with the stream of information and maintain control over the direction of the interview without disrupting the rapport achieved between the women. Such spontaneity had the advantage of providing unexpected insights, but made it difficult to acquire a consistent sample of certain basic variables.

An alternate approach to the rural sector developed when I was not "interviewing" people. By renting a house in an aldea (hamlet), I lived among the very people who would be most distrustful of interviews. Immediately, neighbors began to drop by to interview *me*. Through informal conversations in the context of mutual visits, food exchanges, and other shared activities such as washing clothes, hauling water, planting potatoes, and pasturing sheep, the women revealed their problems and their great sense of humor. As friendships grew, I gradually obtained more information on women's economic and social roles in the area. Communication was mostly in Spanish and did not involve note-taking in their presence. My efforts to learn Mam were more effective as a sign of goodwill than as a means of communication. When women beheld my laughable struggle to speak their language, their inhibitions about speaking dropped, and I was surprised to find that quite a few could communicate successfully in rudimentary Spanish once they knew me. This combination of participation, mutual interviewing, assistance, and language instruction yielded data that could not be obtained solely with an interpreter. I had the opportunity to verify that my neighbors' activities were as they described them. Such informal approaches, however, are more time-consuming than formal interview procedures.

By the time I had sampled my immediate neighborhood, the annual migration of land-poor farmers had begun and most of my neighbors locked up their houses and dispersed to seek land or pasture on the coast and in lowland municipios. At this time, I moved to the town center and continued my research among the more bicultural Mam women. In town, language barriers and distrust were less problematic. With considerably less strain, I gathered a sample of women that was slightly larger than the rural one. Also, the small-town intimacy and links with rural residents made possible cross-checking of much information.

Taken together, the data are based on participant observation and on interviews in households that cluster around both the hamlet and the town center where I resided, supplemented by additional rural households that were randomly selected with my interpreter. With a stratified sample of rural and urban households, I have been careful to specify rural and urban components where they have different characteristics. Indeed, the comparison of rural and urbanizing segments reveals some of the dynamics of women's position. Limited interviews and interaction with the town-dwelling Ladino minority also provided a useful contrast to Mam women, and clarified the nature of their cultural influence.

341

T'oj Nam posed another problem of "translation"—that of translating the complex socioeconomic activities of a largely preindustrial society into the standard categories of modern Western social science (which were designed to describe modern Western societies). The economy of T'oj Nam consists of a mixture of disparate phenomena: cash and subsistence occupations, local and migratory work, seasons of intense work and periods of slack activity. The lack of regularity and standardization in work makes it hazardous to compile statistics on occupations, employment rates, or average income. Severely distorted economic measures can easily follow from rigid adherence to the concepts used in industrialized economies. There are many forms of productive work that are performed by a family group where the income in cash or kind cannot be properly attributed to individuals. In many cases, a calculation of the annual income produced or earned by an individual could only be roughly approximated. With limited time, it proved impossible to compile the kinds of quantitative summaries of women's economic status that could be achieved in other regions.

El Cañaveral

Fieldwork in El Cañaveral ran from the beginning of August to October 1974, with several return visits in 1975. My entree was arranged with the permission and cooperation of the owner and the administrators, who provided me with housing and an initial orientation. My arrival, however, coincided with increasing tensions concerning an imminent strike by resident workers. It was difficult to remain neutral under these conditions, but such a position was essential since either side could have easily terminated my research. During the strike, there were some rumors that I was a spy for management, but the fact that women of the rancheria told me this and defended me was an indication that they had decided the rumors were rather unlikely. Fortunately, my interest in women seemed sufficiently innocuous so that I was able to conduct most of my interviews and observations without major difficulties. The strike also provided a unique opportunity to observe the different positions taken by men and women in a time of crisis.

As elsewhere, I conducted a small survey of households aiming at both quantitative and qualitative data. The households were selected randomly in two barrios of the rancheria. Interviewing procedures were not rigid. Due to the constraints on women's behavior when men are present, I usually tried to arrange my interviews when husbands were at work. Where rapport was good, interviews were extended to include life histories. For selected information on employment, I extended the household survey to include a larger sample of households from other barrios.

During my stay, I became friends with a variety of women and began to participate in their activities and to discuss with them some of their major concerns. Such friendships included daily visits, small favors and exchanges, cooking lessons and shared meals, and the opportunity to stay in their homes as a guest. I also conducted interviews on special aspects of plantation life with administrators, the doctor, the school director, the local alcalde, and the union leader. These people were generally helpful, but frequently statistical information which would have been useful was not readily available. Less systematically, I became acquainted with other members of the plantation society at all levels, from the owner to the cuadrilleros.

San Lorenzo

From October 1974 through January 1975, the squatter settlement of San Lorenzo became the site of my fieldwork. Fortunately, I was able to build on the previous work of social anthropologist Bryan Roberts. His work was an important starting point for my own investigation. To facilitate my entry into the community, I originally made contacts through a local priest who directed me to some of the leading women. These dynamic women helped to orient and introduce me informally to the community. With friendly encouragement, they opened up several social networks through which I gradually was able to branch out into the various neighborhood subsections.

San Lorenzans also showed various degrees of distrust, along with considerable sophistication in dealing with outsiders. The major categories into which residents attempt to fit outside strangers are: census taker, government informer, social worker, or profiteer. At first, people seemed to expect that eventually I would come up with a social welfare project to justify my presence. The census-taking aspects of my role did not seem unusual, but could evoke an impatient reaction that was not conducive to more intimate interviewing. Experienced as subjects of inquiry, people were not surprised if I wrote notes during interviews, or went from house to house soliciting information. For interviews of greater depth, I had most success among the several networks of friends and neighbors who exchanged information among themselves regarding my presence and character. Gradually, some people came to accept me as a friendly acquaintance who broke the routine with visits and an interest in their activities. Of course, a few people undoubtedly believed that as a representative of North American culture, my friendship and approval might somehow be valuable.

During and after the main fieldwork period, I joined in informal activities with various residents which provided a great deal of supplementary information and insight which normally result from participant observation. These activities, which ensured my attachment to and deep respect for the people of San Lorenzo, included shared meals with various families, sporadic lodging with one family, Christmas with another, excursions, marketing, family crises, attendance at miscellaneous meetings of clubs and organizations within the colonia, and joining people in various work, social, and recreational activities carried out within the colonia and in other parts of the city.

The statistical data come from several sources. The sample I collected in 1974–75 was obtained by means of interviews covering seventy-six households in San Lorenzo. It is based on sets of interviews representing three different levels of intensity. Roughly a third were long, open-ended interviews, conducted with one or more of the female residents in a household. Another third of the sample consisted of more restricted interviews which nonetheless included a rather long list of economic and social variables. For the remaining third, I briefly surveyed economic variables with 26 households, and was ably assisted by a young woman resident who was raised and well known in San Lorenzo. Since this variation in technique did not result in any significant differences in the statistical breakdown of the economic data, I have combined the three sets to form the San Lorenzo sample of 1975.

The sample of 1969 is supplementary data compiled from a 1969 survey of Guatemala dealing with urban family incomes and expenses (Orellana and de Léon 1972). It is a random sample of forty-four households from contiguous neighborhoods within the larger shantytown which includes San Lorenzo. Ten of the households are from San Lorenzo itself. In view of the shared history and characteristics of the entire shantytown, I use this sample as a whole. (See Note 4, Chapter Five for more information on this sample.) Another important source of supplementary information is Robert's research (1968a, 1968b, 1970, 1973), conducted between 1966 and 1968, which provides a wealth of background material, and which was an important consideration in my selection of San Lorenzo.

Villa Rosa

Villa Rosa represented the final phase of fieldwork, from mid-May through July 1975. Again I engaged in open-ended interviewing, participant observation, and collection of statistical data on the colonia. Interviewing in Villa Rosa posed distinctive problems, principally, gaining initial access to the residents, for most households are effectively closed to strangers. Fences, gates with buzzers, and servants restrict the opportunities for the uninvited social scientist to make acquaintances informally or to call upon residents for a systematic house-to-house survey. Friendly contacts would not be generated directly by opening conversations with passersby. This impenetrability apparently grows out of a fear of robbery or even a generalized anxiety due to the extreme contrasts in wealth so evident in the city.

My initial contacts derived from chance acquaintance, made elsewhere in the city, with people who either lived in or had relatives in Villa Rosa. Only with the introductions provided by these helpful contacts was I able to begin fruitful interviewing with the residents. Once I was accepted by a few, they helped me to make contact with other neighbors and friends, so that I arranged for interviews in a snowballing fashion. With these introductions, interviews themselves proceeded with ease. In contrast to other areas, neither language nor the purpose of my study posed problems. Generally, women were quite familiar with the types of project which grow out of higher education, and once an interview began they proved cooperative and voluble. As members of the urban middle class, some were interested in both comparing and validating their modern lifestyles with me as an envoy of North American culture, a culture which represents many of their aspirations. In other cases, friendly relations came easily because of shared interests and experiences. In addition to interviews, generally held in the homes of Villa Rosa residents, I participated in a variety of enjoyable social activities with women from different sections of the colonia. These included informal house parties and women's club meetings, sporting activities, watching television with the family, and simply dining together. In an environment where servants do much of the housework, some kinds of participation were ruled out. Yet I was able to visit some of the women at their places of work in other zones of the city, and was invited to attend urban cultural events which they had helped to organize.

Statistical data on economic and social variables in Villa Rosa were obtained from three sources. The 1973 sample is a 16 percent sample of the colonia's population based on data collected for the 1973 national census. It consists of 125 households randomly selected to represent the entire colonia. The sample of 1975 is based on my own interviews and includes thirty-five households. The 1969 sample is a very small sample of just thirteen households drawn from the 1969 mass survey of incomes and expenses of urban families in Guatemala in 1969 (Orellana and de León 1972), and is used simply to verify the other samples.

While most anthropological fieldworkers live for a year or more within a single culture or community, my work involved four short but intensive segments within a single year. This difference requires some comment. Each approach has its own advantages and disadvantages. One gives up something in continuity, rapport, intensity, and evolving comfort by shifting research sites every three months. Each move entailed changes in domestic arrangements, in lifestyles, in work habits and language patterns, and required the development of new contacts and friendships. These changes can be strenuous, and the constraint of trying to cover four communities in the time usually allocated to one, means one cannot afford to gradually "settle in." Yet these difficulties are not insurmountable, and are offset by the considerable advantages of the comparative perspective.

My own solution was to go into the field as an individual, leaving my family to carry on their lives in North America. From previous experience, I knew that a family in the field can be a tremendous comfort and asset (especially children) but that unless they can all be full-time fieldworkers, their needs and the daily opportunity to retreat into one's own language and culture slows down the work. Without family, there was less planning involved in moving, and less concern about disrupting other people's adaptation. I also discovered that by minimizing my domestic concerns and accepting makeshift housing and eating arrangements I could begin work in each locale immediately. Thus I attempted to replicate neither my own culture's domestic arrangements nor those of the host culture, which gave me greater flexibility in joining the activities of other households. Finally, although my stay in each community was relatively short, leaving and returning to visit within the year contributed to the continuity of friendships and my knowledge of the communities.

I have returned to Guatemala at various times since the completion of this fieldwork: in 1976, to assist in community reconstruction after the earthquake, and in 1978 to renew old friendships and leave copies of my research in Guatemala. At that time, political repression had begun to intensify with massacres of peasants and violent repression during an urban bus strike. Since then, Guatemala has become an increasingly dangerous place for foreign researchers and journalists, to say nothing of the dangers to its own people; women and men alike.

T'oj Nam Weekly Food Budgets

Below are two town-dwelling Mam women's expenditures for food for a week (individual consumption only) at March 1975 local prices:

Table A-3-1: Sample Weekly Town Mam Food Budgets, 1975

I.		II.	
Food Item	Cost (Q.)	Food Item	Cost (Q.)
7 lbs. corn	0.56	14 lbs. corn	1.12
2 lbs. beans	0.40	½ lb. beans	0.10
5 lbs. potatoes	0.30	1 lb. potatoes	0.06
1 lb. coffee	0.30	1 lb. coffee	0.35
2 lbs. sugar	0.20	2 lbs. panela (sugar)	0.16
1 lb. meat	0.45	1 lb. meat	0.45
3 eggs	0.21	3 eggs	0.18
chilis, salt, & fruit	0.10	salt, fruit, & nuts	0.15
Weekly total	Q. 2.52	Weekly total	Q. 2.57
Annual total	Q. 131.04	Annual total	Q. 133.64

Notes

Chapter One

1. The concept of dependency (Frank 1967, Cardoso y Faletto 1969) has sparked an extensive debate among scholars concerned with Third World development problems and capitalist growth. There are clearly many variants of this approach, and as many critiques. For the Latin American context, much of this debate appears in the special issues of *Latin American Perspectives* (1974, 1976, 1979, 1981) and also in Bath and James (1976), and concerns the relationship between dependency and Marxist class analysis. C. Smith (1978) has addressed the relationship between dependency and capitalism in western Guatemala. Attempting to bypass the polemics and pitfalls of dependency versus Marxist exegesis, my goal here is simply to present my own interpretation of dependent capitalism, for want of a less controversial label, as it affects gender. Others who have explored the relationship between dependent capitalism and gender are Schmink (1977); J. Nash (1976), Safa and Leacock (1981).

2. These include the works of Adams (1970), Cambranes (1975), Melville and Melville (1971), Jonas and Tobis (1974), Quintana Diaz (1973), C. Smith (1978), Torres-Rivas (1980b), Schlesinger and Kinzer (1982). Whether or not these authors espouse the idiom of dependent capitalism, they present various views of external political-economic influence and meddling in Guatemala.

3. A number of important works on women and development have appeared in the last decade. These include: Nash and Safa (1976), B. Rogers (1981), Etienne and Leacock (1980), Dixon (1978), and special issues of *Signs* (Wellesley Editorial Committee 1977, Safa and Leacock 1981) and *Latin American Perspectives* (1979). Most of them describe worsening conditions for women with the growth of the world economy.

4. Such research would have to include the effects of massive foreign spending and cultural influence through a myriad of institutions, agencies, and their personnel: religious missionaries, military aid and training, corporate development programs, pervasive consumer advertising, international lending policies, the Peace Corps, and a host of development programs.

5. Wolf (1957) introduced the concept of closed corporate peasant communities within a framework of capitalist exploitation and indigenous resistence to that process but his emphasis on community cohesion fostered the impression that external discrimination could not infiltrate or transform community culture. Recent anthropologists have criticized studies that emphasize indigenous cultural traditions to explain the ongoing poverty and marginality of indigenous populations in the larger society (W. Smith 1977). Wasserstrom claims that anthropologists were "seduced by the exoticism of Indian life" which "blinded them to a more general system of social classes throughout the country at large" (1975:472).

6. Among the many interesting descriptive ethnographies of Guatemalan communities are: Bunzel (1952), Wagley (1941, 1949), Tax (1953), Oakes (1951a), Reina (1966), M. Nash (1967) and Colby and van den Berghe (1969).

7. Some recent examples of works where Maya women continue to be overshadowed, invisible, or mute with respect to political, economic, or ideological questions are Brintnall (1979), Cancian (1965, 1972), Gossen (1974), W. Smith (1977), and Warren (1978).

8. Deere and Léon de Leal (1981), Stoler (1977), and other recent works on women in agriculture (see ILO report 1976), expand the understanding of agricultural work to include various necessary tasks ranging from weeding, transporting, and marketing crops to preparing meals for hired field workers.

9. Deere and León de Leal take this approach (1981). However, the emphasis on monetary payment as an indication of capitalist relations is misleading in that it tends to imply degrees of proletarianization and capitalist accumulation that simply do not apply to many small household enterprises, be they farms, workshops, or those hiring domestic help (see also comments in Schmink 1977:173 and Young 1978). While money is clearly a link to the capitalist sectors, its use in production is not always capitalistic. *Formal* wage labor, however, is a more accurate sign of capitalist relations in that it encorporates key factors of size and contract that contribute to accumulation.

10. Chiñas' model divides the social system into four quadrants using the formal/nonformal and public/private dichotomies, but is vague regarding the distinction between formal and nonformal roles in the domestic sphere. Indeed, the distinction is less obvious in the domestic context, so I have chosen to treat domestic organization as a single category. Other research on women emphasizes one or the other of these divisions. Rogers (1975) and Rothstein (1979) describe different dimensions of formal and informal power in peasant society, while Rosaldo (1974) and Reiter (1975) emphasize the distinction between public and private domains.

11. This situation is described by Lamphere (1974) as one in which domestic and political spheres are integrated. Sahlin's analysis (1972) of societies with a domestic mode of production shows that domestic structure and kinship relations encompass most social interaction, while community or more extensive social organizations are relatively weak in such societies.

12. See Lamphere (1974), Harding (1975), Bestor (1977), and Chinas (1973) on women's informal power.

13. For a blatant example of this type of error, see Hart and Pilling's account of Tiwi marriage (1968) and compare with that of Goodale (1971) and Bell (1981). More commonly, there is a tendency to compare wives' to husbands' power without regard to age differences. In a marriage system where husbands

are consistently older than their wives, they may have more power *than their wives*, but at the same time the gap between the social power of women and men *at the same age*, say forty, can be minimal, especially when women develop an important basis for power in the loyalty of their young-adult children.

14. The closest examples, Colby and van den Berghe's (1969) study of three neighboring Ixil villages and W. Smith's comparison of four diverse indigenous communities of the western highlands in terms of economic change and the cargo system (1977), both stay within the indigenous departments, whereas my material includes cross-ethnic, cross-regional comparison.

Chapter Two

1. The conventional regional division of Guatemala emphasizes contrasting ecology and sociocultural organization. C. Smith (1976, 1978) has written extensively on western Guatemala as a regional economy within Guatemala, and divides Guatemala into economic zones based on regional integration. Thus her western region includes two southwestern "plantation" departments that are intimately connected with the western highlands via movements of consumer goods and seasonal labor.

2. Recent descriptions of development projects in the northern region and their relationship to the colonizations of Maya peasants can be found in Brown (1974), Melville and Melville (1971), Morissey (1978), Manz (1977, 1981), and Peckenham (1980).

3. The western region (Chimaltenango, Solola, Totonicapan, Quetzaltenango, San Marcos, Huehuetenango, and Quiche) has 36 percent, the southern region (Retalhuleu, Suchitepequez, and Escuintla) has 11.7 percent, and the Metropolitan area (Guatemala, Sacatepequez) has 23.4 percent, for a total of 71 percent of the national population. (A good part of Alta Verapaz, although geographically north, is often included in the "western" region due to its overall economic similarity.)

4. Guatemalan census data are often criticised for inaccuracy and inconsistency (e.g., Early 1983, C. Smith 1978, 1982). Although the census ministry (Guatemala 1977) shows rural population dropping to 64 percent, other sources show that in 1980, at 68 percent it has scarcely declined since 1950 (IDB:1981:254). Moreover, Smith reports from her 1977–1978 survey of 131 rural hamlets in western Guatemala that agriculture was the major occupation for only 32.5 percent of all males even though "most male respondents reported a secondary or tertiary occupation in agriculture" (1982:32).

5. Statistics on landholding patterns reported by Guatemala (1976), and Wilkie and Haber (1981) are still based on data from the 1964 agricultural census.

6. Early's estimate of 47.3 percent Maya is based on his revision of Guatemalan censuses from 1950 to 1980. The Maya population listed in the last (1973) national census was 48.3 percent compared to Early's estimate of 48.0 percent. Measurement of the Maya population of Guatemala is subject to debate due to ambiguous definitions of "Indian," yet it is commonly estimated that the Maya are undercounted and are more than 50 percent of the popula-

351

tion. It should be recognized that various sources use the terms Maya, Indian, "indigenous" or "native" to designate the same subset of Guatemala's population. Here, the terms will often be used interchangeably.

7. The eight departments with over 60 percent Maya are:

	(%)		(%)
Totonicapan	97.1	Chimaltenango	79.2
Solola	94.4	Huehuetenango	69.0
Alta Verapaz	91.1	Quetzaltenango	62.7
Quiche	85.8	San Marcos	60.6

Of these, only Quetzeltenango is excluded from Fletcher's classification of eight departments of traditional subsistence agriculture—which included one eastern department, Jalapa (Fletcher et al. 1970).

8. Herbert (1970) argues, partly on the basis of unequal control over the means of production by the two ethnic categories, that the Maya constitute an exploited "class" in Guatemala, and Ladinos an exploitative "class." I feel that this position is a misleading oversimplification of the ethnic relationship, even though I do not dispute that as a group the Maya are the most disadvantaged sector of the population.

9. C. Smith suggests that unequal control over land is overemphasized as a factor explaining stratification and the need for Indians to accept low-paying plantation wage work. She points out that location, or center-periphery relations, and the ability to control the exchange system can help to explain why Ladinos who own no land may still be better off than Indians with land, and why Indians residing nearer to central markets may accumulate the wealth to escape agricultural dependence through commerce (1976:116–120).

10. Pansini disagrees with the assumption that indigenes lose their ethnicity by becoming permanent residents on plantations. His study (1977) suggests that ethnicity is persistent and is particularly likely to be preserved, at least in the eyes of the ethnics, when there is a critical mass of people with shared backgrounds, and opportunities to maintain contact with home communities.

11. The 1964 Guatemalan census gave the following economic activity rates by sex, residence, and ethnicity:

12. C. Smith (1978:599) states that census data on the agricultural labor force

Proportion of Each Sex Economically Active in Guatemala by Residence and Ethnic Group

	Male		Female	
Residence	Number	%	Number	%
Rural	805,900	76	49,400	5
Urban	337,300	65	117,300	20
Ethnic group				
Latin	628,400	55	116,700	70
Maya	522,200	45	49,800	30

Source: Guatemala, Censo de la Población, 1964, cited in Monteforte 1972:55, 60.

in Guatemala has been "distorted both over time and space by the fact that women were classified as occupied in an extremely variable and arbitrary fashion." Chinchilla (1977), and Arizpe (1977) also refer to inadequate census data on women's employment, while Boserup (1970) and recently B. Rogers (1981) have launched general attacks on these reporting procedures. Examples of ethnographic methods used to obtain a more accurate picture of the distribution of agricultural labor can be found in Stoler (1977), Deere and León de Leal (1981).

13. Schmid's interviews were apparently conducted only with male migrants, for he provides no data on sex composition of his sample, but gives data for "wives and children," as if all interviewees were male. Since there is evidence that women are hired directly as well as indirectly, this appears to have been an unacknowledged bias in his study of migrant workers.

14. Flores Alvarado (1971:162–176) reports that of some 275,000 migrant workers, 59 percent are adult men, 21 percent are women who are hired individually or accompany their husbands as assistants, and 20 percent are children between seven and fourteen years of age who accompany their parents to assist them or who are individually hired. Pansini (1980) describes how contracts under the names of men may actually be fulfilled by women.

15. The four departments bordering the Pacific Coast (the lowland plantation zone) have the highest indices of masculinity (males per 100 females), in contrast to the departments in the subsistence sector. This is clear from the following census figures (Guatemala 1970, 1974a):

Ratio of Males to Females in Pacific Coast and Subsistence Region in Guatemala by Department, 1964 and 1973

	Index of masculinity		
Department	Total (1964)	Rural (1964)	Total* (1973)
Pacific Coast region			
Escuintla	129.9	138.8	110.4
Santa Rosa	108.5	110.0	109.2
Retalhuleu	116.0	121.5	106.5
Suchitepequez	110.9	115.6	104.4
Subsistence region			
San Marcos‡	106.9	108.2	105.9
Solola	102.3	103.2	102.5
Chimaltenango	103.7	106.4	102.3
Huehuetenango	103.2	104.6	102.3
Quiche	98.3	98.4	101.6
Jalapa	101.1	104.1	100.2
Totonicapan	97.2	98.1	98.3
Alta Verapaz	96.5	98.2	97.1

Sources: Guatemala 1970, 1974b

* Separate figures by rural-urban division were not available due to changes in data reporting.

‡ San Marcos has both subsistence and plantation zones which helps to explain its high male-female ratio.

The imbalanced sex distribtuion seems to have been declining on the south coast during the 1970s—a finding which would weaken my thesis regarding the general lack of jobs for women in capitalist agriculture. However, I suspect that this is probably due less to changes in plantation employment opportunities than to the growth of urban centers serving the southern plantation zone. Urban centers in Guatemala generally have a surplus of women. My own data, discussed in Chapter Four, suggest that formal job opportunities open to women are extremely scarce on plantations.

16. These data are from Bruce Bechtol's study, "Guatemalan Manufacturing 1966: A Preliminary Geographic Analysis," Institute of International Studies, Univ. of Oregon, n.d., Table 1, p. 4., as cited in Adams (1970:172).

17. Chinchilla cites this study as taken from Tobis (1974:133).

18. The option of remaining "formally" unemployed does not exist in a society that lacks unemployment insurance or welfare programs for most of its citizens. For a discussion of government interest in the informal sector, see Arizpe 1977).

19. This outline of class structure and population estimates in each class is based on a paper by Guzman, Herbert, and Quan (1971), summarized in English by Anthony (1974:33). Using their estimates in tabular form, the class distribution is shown below:

Class	Percent
Bourgeoisie	3.8
Ladino: agro-export (.3%)	
dependent (3.4%)	
Indigenous (.06%)	
Petty bourgeoisie	20.2
Ladino (15.7%)	
Indigenous (4.5%)	
Proletariat	20.1
Ladino: rural (11%)	
urban (4.5%)	
Indigenous (4.5%)	
Sub/lumpen proletariat	6.7
Peasants/semi-proletariat	42.5
Ladino (13.5%)	
Indigenous (29.0%)	
Tenant farmers	6.7
Total	100.0%

20. The following works represent a small sample of the extensive social anthropological literature on Maya-Ladino relations in Guatemala: Bunzel (1952), Carmack (1976), Colby and van den Berghe (1969), Gillen (1951), Herbert (1970), Maynard (1963, 1974), Moore (1973), M. Nash (1967), Tax (1952), Tumin (1952), Brintnall (1979), Warren (1978), and Wasserstrom (1975).

21. The machismo concept, described as "hyper-masculinity" by Maynard (1974), entails an extreme stress on individual dominance and autonomy of

men, combined with a double standard of sexual morality which stresses shame and restraint for women as much as it emphasizes ostentatious promiscuity for men.

22. Wolf (1955, 1966) has discussed the concept of peasantry in detail. As in most highland Maya communities, T'oj Nam displays certain classic peasant characteristics. Agrarian producers who retain effective control over local land resources used primarily for subsistence, they belong to a larger stratified social system with urban centers that extract economic surplus from the community in various ways.

23. Mestizo refers to individuals of mixed Ladino and Indian background, usually in transition to the dominant Ladino culture. These individuals usually identify with, but are not fully accepted by, the more established Ladino sectors.

24. Since the community is the same as that studied by Roberts (1973), I have retained the same pseudonym, San Lorenzo, that he used. According to Roberts' survey, 25 percent of the household heads in San Lorenzo were born in Guatemala, while an additional 56 percent had been residents for more than 10 years (1970:488). About 5 percent of the population was Maya, but some 15 percent of the migrants had one or both parents who were of Maya origin (1973:60–62).

Chapter Three

1. This peripheral status can be traced to pre-Columbian times when the more politically centralized Quiché kingdoms achieved intermittent domination over their Mam neighbors (Carmack 1981).

2. Although earlier Ladino occupation has not yet been traced, Carmack's documentary research (1972, 1973) on the Quiché area, and particularly Momostenango, suggests that evidence for earlier Ladino settlement may yet be discovered in the Mam areas such as T'oj Nam.

3. During fieldwork, foreign residents included an American Peace Corps worker, an American missionary pair, a Mexican priest, and several North American and European travelers who rented houses for short periods of time. Until recent years, few tourists came to the town, but now it receives a steady trickle, which may average around ten people per week, and escalates to around 100 during the annual town fiesta.

4. The term peasantry is used despite heavy dependence on rural wage labor because these people continue to identify themselves and to plan in terms of the traditional occupations of cultivator and weaver. Clearly a "truer" label would indicate their composite status as peasant-worker-petty commodity producers, but the advantage of "peasantry" is that it is not cumbersome to use and it is still widely applied for such transitional populations. Some recent writers adamantly reject the term "peasantry" to describe populations like T'oj Nam. Describing a similar population in San Miguel Ixtahuacan, W. Smith writes of a "peasant-to-proletarian devolution" and concludes that "they are no longer peasants: their economic situation exhibits all the classic characteristics of a rural seasonal proletariat" (1977:73, 90). While I agree with the thrust of this distinction, I am not convinced that *seasonal* proletarian identities have

yet supplanted peasant consciousness, and wonder what these people turn to during the nonplantation seasons of their lives, if not peasant pursuits.

5. Stadelman's estimates (1940:103) are based on the yield for "ordinary" land. Yields for good land are higher, but given the increased population pressure in T'oj Nam, it is likely that people are forced to cultivate more of the poorer lands or to reduce their rotation period, which lowers average yields unless fertilizer is applied.

6. Recent research on economic responses to land scarcity in highland Maya communities has been done by W. Smith (1977) for Mam communities in western Guatemala, and by Cancian (1972) and Collier (1975) for Zinacantan, Chiapas. The different responses, whether migrant labor or rental farming, as well as which members of the family become involved, can be affected by local conditions (e.g., transportation improvements, craft alternatives). Unfortunately, these studies are not very attentive to the effects on women's work.

7. The Quetzal (Q.) = 1 U.S. Dollar ($).

8. Waterholes in T'oj Nam have supernatural aspects as they do in other parts of northwest Guatemala (Wagley 1969:57) and in Chiapas (Vogt 1970). While shamans sometimes perform public rituals at waterholes, they are much more a focal point for gatherings of women than for men in everyday life.

9. It has often been mistakenly assumed on the basis of domestic observations that men enjoy more leisure than women because the women work to prepare meals while the men are resting or socializing. This ignores the fact that the periods of peak work for female and male tasks are staggered so that women find time to relax and socialize during the day when the men are away in the fields.

10. Economic activity is used here narrowly to mean activity producing cash income.

11. According to Schmid's report (1973:44), the municipal alcalde estimated that there were 2,500 migrant workers from T'oj Nam in 1965–66. Although Schmid was not certain if this figure includes women and children, the magnitude of the migration is clear in relation to the total municipal population, which in 1965–66 was just under 9,000.

12. These data are not sufficiently broad-based to provide precise percentages for T'oj Nam, but they do show that women's participation is substantial. It is likely that the rate of migration of town women (which equals that of town men) is linked to a higher ratio of separated or widowed women without male partners in the town sample, and possibly in the town population as a whole.

13. Standard contracts were for either one or two months per year. Few people mentioned more extended periods of plantation work. I was unable to quantify the total number of months or years of plantation labor by age-group since informants frequently responded vaguely or inconsistently to such questions. There is no doubt that female migrants worked less total time on plantations over the long run, but the high incidence of plantation labor experience among the female population is an important measure of exposure to this economic alternative.

14. Cotton plantations usually paid more than coffee plantations during the mid 1970s. Some cotton workers cited wages as high as Q. 2 per 100 lbs. Wages on coffee plantations were generally 80 cents to Q. 1 per 100 lbs. Over the last generation, T'oj Nam migrants have gradually shifted from coffee to cotton plantations in response to the wage difference (Schmid 1973: 295, 359).

15. One can crudely attempt to measure the economic value of an infant on the basis of the choices people make. Staying home with an infant can "cost" a household around Q. 60 in foregone cash income. Hence, the infant is worth *at least* Q. 60 as a long-term investment. Those who choose to migrate with an infant may be interpreted as making the choice that an infant is worth less than Q. 60 in the short term, given that the probability that an infant will die as a result of migration is considered higher. The choice is complicated by the fact that in poor households, the risk of infant death may be high even in T'oj Nam.

Similarly, the value of staying home to guard property complicates the decision. Continual migration means that, like nomads, a household cannot afford to accumulate material goods. Established households with more goods to protect would thus tend to be more concerned to leave someone at home. These two factors, risk of infant mortality and property protection, would tend to favor migration by young women who lack material goods and have a high probability of being able to produce more children in the future.

16. The opportunity cost to male labor is considerably less than it is to female labor, for several reasons. December and January, the months of most plantation labor, are months of agricultural inactivity in T'oj Nam. The harvest is over and it is too early for planting. Men lack pressing work and might be considered underemployed during this season. A man's major resource, land, is not likely to be alienated if he migrates. His major concern is to store the harvest in a safe place. If he leaves it in the house, this can be guarded by a trusted person (usually kin). In contrast, a breastfeeding mother is more restricted in the disposition of her child if she wants to migrate and leave it safely cared for in T'oj Nam. Nature dictates that it must be a lactating female who says behind with young children. This is occassionally a grandmother or mother-in-law who stays behind with the children while the young, strong mother goes to work. This caretaker's contribution may be worth more than a cash income, but the wageworker's contribution is measured by an obvious market standard.

17. My data clearly show a much higher rate of labor force participation than the national census data cited at the beginning of this chapter. Despite the differences in sample size, it appears that different data-gathering techniques and/or analytical assumptions result in the exclusion of large numbers of seasonal wage workers from the labor force. The different participation rates probably stem from a bias toward treating only the "head of household" (assumed male) as working in cases where the entire household contributes. Boserup (1970:29–30, 188) has discussed the inconsistencies commonly found in national census classifications and the tendency to understate women's participation in agricultural work.

18. This assumption is based on the requirement for corn as the primary staple, noting that beans are generally cultivated in the same field. As mentioned earlier, the average land holding per household is estimated at 10 cuerdas. If average yields are only 50 pounds per cuerda (which is conceivable if population pressure forces cultivation of exhausted fields), then the average household corn production on its own lands may be less than one-sixth the estimated requirement for an average household (3,650 pounds).

19. This calculation is based on the following data provided by informants regarding coastal production of corn. Coastal land rental is Q. 5 per cuerda with expected yields of 500 pounds per cuerda. The price of corn on the coast

is Q. 5 per hundred pounds, and the labor time per cuerda (assuming family assistance in harvesting) is four to six days. Personal transportation costs are estimated as Q. 20 for the season, while the transport of corn to intermediate markets and to T'oj Nam is estimated at Q. 30 and Q. 100 respectively.

Thus, if 15 cuerdas are rented, they yield 7,500 pounds of corn. On the coast this sells for Q. 375. Deducting Q. 50 for personal and intermediate transport, and Q. 75 for rental, the cash value is Q. 250 for 65–95 days' labor. At the price of Q. 8 for 100 pounds of corn in T'oj Nam, this can purchase 3,125 pounds of corn which, with local subsistence production, is enough to maintain a household. With economies of scale in transport costs, transportation of corn to T'oj Nam can yield higher cash values. Deducting Q. 120 for transportation costs, 3,600 pounds could be brought to T'oj Nam. If 1,000 pounds were surplus, this could be worth Q. 80.

20. This typically occurs first with children's clothing, and includes the men when they desire to change to ladino-style clothing. Women typically change to an intermediate or "generalized" style of indigenous clothing which is mass-produced and cheaper. See Hinshaw (1975) for a discussion of this change in other indigenous communities.

21. It is not possible to say whether single men would have the same difficulty in establishing a profitable business since I discovered only one such man in the town. An old man, his small business did not greatly differ from that of single women.

22. Thus far one Mam woman operates a sewing machine, owned by her brother. The use of sewing machines is more common among Mam men and Ladinos of both sexes.

23. For Middle America in general, see discussions in Wolf (1959), and Cancian (1967). Studies dealing with Guatemala include: Oakes (1951a), Bunzel (1952), Reina (1966), and Moore (1973). Descriptions of the cargo system in Mexico include Foster (1967) and Cancian (1965).

24. Political questions are touchy, and voting information was requested only when it was felt it would not jeopardize the interviews. The consequently reduced sample used here comes from 17 Mam and 12 Ladino households.

25. This statement reflects not only the idea that a woman living alone is abnormal, but that *anyone* who lives alone is deviant or irrational.

26. See Oakes (1951a) and Wagley (1941:48) for the Mam, and Bunzel (1952:83, 93) for the Quiche. Paul and Paul (1975) provide a fascinating synthesis of information on Mayan midwives, comparing their role to that of the shaman.

27. Oakes (1951a:112) mentions a specific role of the chiman's wife. Wagley (1941:33-43) and Stadelman (1940:123) cite instances in which Mam women must accompany their husbands and assist in planting and harvest rituals.

28. People frequently exploit the ambiguity of the term "Catholic" if they do not want missionizing Christians to challenge their beliefs.

29. The training provided by this course is most superficial. The nuns do not reside in the community, but visit to hold classes once a month. The methods and content of the course show almost no comprehension of the educational and cultural background of the women so that even with a Mam interpreter (unfortunately a man is employed for this preeminantly female concern), women can learn very little. A main motive for attending is that upon completing the course, the midwives will receive a certificate entitling them to

continue to practice their speciality. They note that the new equipment they are required to have (white aprons and hats included) makes their practice more expensive.

30. Bride price is discussed in the section on marriage and the family.

31. My findings show literacy rates that are notably higher than the municipal average for all categories except rural Mam women. It is possible that this is a random variation due to the small sample size, or that there is an unconscious bias toward, say, urbanism or youth among my informants compared to the municipio as a whole. Nonetheless, an urban bias is unlikely to affect the relative gap between the sexes in any sector, for they are drawn from the same households.

32. These figures, from the departmental Office of Education in May 1975, report the number officially registered in school. At that time, statistics were also available on the number actually attending classes. These were but slightly lower, with no noticeable difference in the dropout rate by sex.

33. One woman was surprised that, forty years after she had left school, she could still crudely recreate the letters of her name. She had not had a pencil in her hand since she left school!

34. It was observed that committees of schoolboys are sometimes sent out to find out why a boy is not attending school, but this is not done for girls. In the first half of 1974, five men were sentenced to fines or jail terms (two to four weeks) for failing to send their sons to school. The standard defense of the fathers was that their sons were useful in work.

35. Roughly half of these students came from families in which, by chance, the overall boy:girl ratio was 3:1.

36. For a somewhat dated but interesting description of Mam fiesta events and organization, see Oakes (1951a: 209-221).

37. This fieldwork report coincided with the arrival of the Peace Corps worker, when her presence had not yet had any impact. Subsequently, her intense efforts to revitalize the organization met with considerable success: increased sales and membership and the election of one of the weavers as *Presidenta* of the Cooperative.

38. Since I lived alone in T'oj Nam, people would often tell me teasingly that I would be happier if I had a local husband to provide me with corn, beans, and firewood so that I would want for nothing. Such admonishments are not reserved for women. A young Mam bachelor who had no plans to marry was not left in peace on this issue. He was continually questioned and prodded by parents, kin, and neighbors regarding his marriage plans. Old men would stop him in the path and recite to him the advantages of marriage: someone to cook, weave, and wash for him. In their eyes, he would never find happiness without a wife. Both sexes are teased that it must be too cold to sleep at night if they lack a partner. The net effect sounds like "mother's chicken soup cure-all", except that for the Mam the cliche would be, "Marry; it's good for you!"

39. The term bride price has always generated a great deal of controversy because of its connotations of females as objects and as commodities. Although I agree that these connotations are inaccurate and should not be attached to the status of the women involved, I still find the term a useful one both because a form of "payment" is involved which entails monetary values that are the subject of bargaining, and because I wish to maintain continuity with the literature.

40. First-hand reports of extreme parental coercion were not encountered. Susan Miles' notes (1955) indicate that some Mam who accept the bride price system nevertheless condemn as "sales" those marriages in which parents secretly accept marriage payments for girls who are still underage so that when the girl matures, the decision is a *fait accompli*. However, I was unable to verify any cases of prepubescent marriage payments.

41. Miles (1955) reports such a case from this municipio.

42. There are numerous reports of bride service in pre-Columbian and contemporary Mesoamerica. Among Mayan peoples, see Roys (1972:26), Bunzel (1952:26), Hunt and Nash (1967:255), and Davis (1970:111).

43. Events reported after fieldwork indicate that although Anastasio does not approve of brideprice, he is by no means willing to accept purely voluntary marriage. One of his granddaughters ran off to live with a boyfriend, but Anastasio was furious and promptly went after her to "drag" her home.

44. Information on this household is not derived directly from its members, but from Antonia, close neighbors, and confidants of the wives of Pedro. I have reported it since the information is highly consistent despite the sex or personal attachments of the various informants.

45. Women's complaints of illness caused by birth control pills should not be taken lightly. Not only are women who are physically much smaller than North American women given doses that are often stronger than those currently used in North America, but the pills are introduced to women in their thirties and forties who already have enough children. Studies have shown that birth control pills are most dangerous for women precisely in this over-thirty age group.

46. Oakes' interesting description (1951b) of her field experiences reveals the importance of gossip in many facets of Mam life, as well as its impact on her own two-year stay in a Mam community.

47. Wagley's account of the Mam of Chimaltenango asserts that "fear of being left with no one to take care of young children or to do the multitude of female tasks, tempers a man's marital domination" (1941:15).

48. Women suggest that younger men are more prone to violent temper tantrums than older men. It should be remembered that the early years of marriage may be marked by tensions between mother and daughter-in-law. A son may be prodded by his mother to treat his wife badly if the two women do not get along. If a son is pulled into the quarrels of his mother and wife, he can only express his frustration against his wife since anger or violence toward one's mother (and senior) is inadmissable.

49. Since rape is a controversial topic, a few extra comments may help to put it into perspective. (1) Although the judicial treatment of rape seems lax, I lack evidence that municipal authorities are more effective in punishing other forms of violence or crimes among the Mam (local opinions suggest they are not very effective). There is probably a tendency to treat most crimes as minor offenses to avoid yielding jurisdiction to outside departmental authorities who are Ladinos. (2) This type of violence should not be assumed to be more common in T'oj Nam than in other poor communities. However, more modern, urban centers generally have professional prostitutes and special zones noted for alcoholism and violence such that these incidents are segregated or concealed from the community at large. (3) There is no reason to believe that rapes

are a particular reflection of Mam sexual attitudes given their history of inter-action with other cultures, particularly Ladino plantation culture.

Chapter Four

1. In Guatemala, finca is a general term describing a wide variety of farms or estates engaging in commercial agriculture. The term encompasses both the hacienda and plantation as polar types (Wolf and Mintz 1957).

2. In El Cañaveral almost all rancheros live in one of seven barrios. Apart from variations in size and distance from the plantation center, there do not appear to be major socioeconomic differences in their composition.

3. Based on a 20 percent sample of household membership recorded in the administrative files, the average household size was 5.8 persons per household.

4. Although clearly of lower status, a few domestic employees and guardians are paid monthly salaries. Because of their positions of special trust, they are thus distinguished from other wageworkers and do not belong to the union.

5. For instance, some women who are not fully active may be fully occupied within the subsistence household economy producing "use-value" for their families. Others may be less than fully employed in either the market sector or the household economy. Possibly such underemployed women fill in their time with unnecessary tasks or busywork in order to maintain the image of house-wife as a conscientious worker rather than idle dependent. Alternatively, they may choose to invest their extra time in small luxuries or status symbols such as flower gardens, special cooking, or household and personal adornment.

6. The high incidence of informal employment among women is reflected in the finding that 85 percent of the economically active women presented in Table 4-3 are self-employed.

·7. This calculation assumes a monthly rental for equivalent housing would be around Q. 10 to 12 per month, expenditures for the same amount of staple food would be around Q. 8 per month, and education or health care would cost around Q. 2 per month.

8. Characteristically, those residents of the rancheria who are employed in the informal sector do not pay rent, but their housing situation is precarious. Usually they lodge with other residents (spouse or kin) who have housing rights, or they build their own shack on company land allocated to one of the ranchero households. In the latter case, the "squatter" is able to stay only at the tolerance of both management and the ranchero household. In the latter case, housing becomes dependent on the harmony of marital or family relations.

9. In many independent situations in Guatemala, women can be seen car-rying heavy loads of firewood, pottery, babies, and water, and one may see women use machetes to clear brush or cut wood or other plants. In fact, older women of El Cañaveral claim that women used to use machetes on the finca to chapear, or cut down brush. Further, some male cane workers assert that there are some women who cut cane on other neighboring plantations. I have not verified this, but it seems that there is sufficient evidence that women can do the work of cane cutting. The fact that daily scenes directly contradict the logic used to define "male" work seems to have little effect on the tenacity of the belief or the hiring practices of the company.

10. This became one of the important issues in a strike which shall be discussed in a later section.

11. In my sample of forty-eight women, thirty-four currently participated in marital unions: nineteen were "united", thirteen were married, and two unknown. An independent sample of eighty-one marital unions drawn randomly from administrative housing files gave almost the same percentage of de facto or common-law marriages: 58 percent.

12. The behavior of the woman who does not demand economic compensation for sexual favors is so inexplicable that neighbors and relatives account for it by saying she has been bewitched or threatened.

13. Women cite the prices for unprofessional abortionists at Q. 20 to 30, while it costs over Q. 100 for a doctor. They claim that a doctor cannot be persuaded to perform an abortion unless a woman's life is in danger. Because of its illegal nature, it is impossible to estimate the extent to which women of the rancheria seek this service. A midwife who has worked in the community for many years asserts that roughly one-third of the women experience an abortion at some time. Her description of the methods used by the nonprofessionals conforms to the dangerous and unsanitary methods that have been found to prevail in other countries when abortion is illegal. Few of the women of the rancheria would be able to pay a doctor's price.

14. According to the doctor and nurses at the health center, they prescribe pills and injections for birth control, but refer sterilizations to the hospitals in town. They were unable to provide statistics regarding the number of birth control cases they handled.

15. It is at least conceivable that the support of public day care by the plantation combined with the employment of women would favor a stable labor supply with lower costs in terms of housing and social benefits, since rancheros could be married to rancheras and since the employment of women might of itself encourage the kind of more moderate population growth needed to avoid overrepreoduction.

16. A revealing statement was made by a teen-age girl outside the meeting. When asked if she would ever like to speak before a union meeting, she responded, "No!" The reason? "Por qué soy mujer" (Because I am a woman).

17. *Hijos* is ambiguous in Spanish: children or sons.

18. Apart from the formal religious systems, there is some practice of spiritualism within the rancheria, particularly in connection with healing. I was told of women *curanderas* who cure by means of spirits and herbal medicines. Because these women are not formally authorized to practice medicine, they do not want their practice known by outsiders. Due to the short period of research, I was unable to gain their confidence in order to learn more about their beliefs and practices.

19. When ten women and nine men over age fifty are excluded from the sample, 82 percent of the women and 91 percent of the men are literate.

20. There is one case of a rancheria nurse who received training in nursing at company expense and who has continued to work at the health clinic ever since.

21. The consumer cooperative seems to be unpopular since it cannot offer food more cheaply than people can buy it in markets or other stores. Some of its members are disillusioned. One of the factors involved is that the food cooperative competes with one of the few sectors where women attempt to

earn a living—as small storekeepers and vendors. The cooperative pays a relatively high wage to its employees. A ranchera who formerly worked there reports she earned Q. 35 to 40 per month. In contrast, many of the women who engage in small-scale selling settle for a smaller return. In El Canaveral and the nearby town, the food markets are highly competitive so that prices cannot be cut much further and still provide a living for the vendors. The market condition in which a consumer cooperative makes sense as an alternative is one of oligopoly, where the food retailing industry is dominated by a few commercial giants that hold prices high. Other important considerations in El Canaveral are that:

1. The memberships of the co-op seem to come from the husbands who have the cash to invest. If the dividend is returned to the husband who keeps it as *his* saving, then the wife has no incentive to shop there. If she buys for less in the marketplace, the savings are hers to use for other purchases.
2. The consumer co-op is located on a main street of the barrio. If women did most of their purchasing at the co-op, they would lose one of their few opportunities to go to town, which for many is surely an enjoyable occasion and a break from the daily routine.
3. A successful consumer cooperative would put many small-scale storekeepers and vendors out of business. It is not clear that the co-op could distribute revenue in the form of dividends more equitably than the market already does.

22. The prestige of belonging to a team was apparent in the funeral procession of a worker; his coffin was carried by members of the football team wearing their jerseys.

23. The printed program for the 1975 fiesta included three photographs, all of young women: the Queen of the Fiesta, the Girlfriend of Sport, and the Godmother of Culture. In these contexts young women are not honored as *participants* in the organizations that elect them, but they are allowed to participate as *symbols* of organizations of work and sport that are predominantly male. Even if girls participate in some of the athletic events (which I was not able to verify), it is significant that my informants remembered only their roles as candidates for Queen. The dichotomized sex symbols of sports heroes and beauty queens are part of a national cultural complex that appears in town fiestas all over Guatemala.

24. This is based on a sample of twenty-one married women who were interviewed regarding their opportunities to leave the house. As is apparent from earlier discussion, many women do not feel free to leave the house even for the purpose of visiting female friends.

Chapter Five

1. "*Colonia*" is a term commonly used in Guatemala to designate residential districts. It can be used to describe residential districts within shantytowns or in middle-class housing developments. Unlike the *zona*, it is not an administrative unit, but rather an informal territorial unit such as a "neighborhood" in which geographical, historical, or economic criteria may serve to distinguish

one colonia from another. The zona is a municipal division similar to a ward; Guatemala City has nineteen such zones.

2. Some of the residents still sweep the litter-strewn paths in front of their houses each day, as is the custom in the small towns from which some of them have migrated.

3. "Economically active" is used here to describe anyone who devotes ten or more hours per week to income-producing activity. See discussion in Appendix Two for description of different samples.

4. Underreporting of female economic activity is also mentioned in the section dealing with the middle-class colonia, Villa Rosa. Perhaps in the case of San Lorenzo, the response "*officios domesticos*" to the question of a woman's employment has been misinterpreted to mean unpaid family housework when in fact it may frequently have referred to day-work as a domestic employee in middle-class homes.

The data in the 1969 sample, as well as the sample of the same year in Chapter Six, was taken from interview schedules for San Lorenzo and Villa Rosa, respectively. These schedules belong to a larger, computerized sample of 1,736 families taken from Guatemala City as a whole. I am indebted to the authors and personnel at the Instituto de Investigaciones Economicas y Sociales for permission to use their data files to supplement my investigation (see Orellana and de Leon 1972).

5. A study of nineteenth-century prostitution in Ontario finds a strong correlation between domestic service and prostitution (half of the prostitutes had formerly worked as domestics) and notes:

The nature of domestic work in private homes partially explains the entry of domestics into prostitution. When these women were fired or let go by their employer, they suffered greater insecurity than did factory or office workers in similar circumstances. They lost not only their means of earning a livelihood, but also their home and the roof over their heads. Because domestics lived at the place of employment, they were likely to have fewer social connections than other women workers. Thus the insecurity, isolation and loneliness which characterized domestic service made unemployed domestics particularly vulnerable to the recruitment efforts of madames and pimps. (Rotenberg 1974:40)

Arizpe comments on women in Mexico City: "Data on prostitution are virtually nonexistent. . . . Judging from occasional data, it would seem that prostitution is a major informal source of income for women, but it is never taken into account in discussions of female economic participation or survival." (1977:36).

6. Chapter Three (Note 16) shows the high indices of masculinity (males per 100 females) in the plantation regions. In contrast, Guatemala City has a very low index of 88.48, or a surplus of 113 females per 100 males.

7. These figures are estimates since precise information on the nature of the employer was not available in all cases. Roberts (1973:38) made a similar distinction between workers employed in established enterprises (over 10 workers), and others, and found that 19 percent of the male heads of household were employed in this catetory, while only 3 percent of female heads belonged to this group. His classification was somewhat different in two respects. First, by using only heads of household, he eliminated that part of the female population most likely to work in factories: young, single women. Second, his classification

appears to have excluded construction and service workers who are employed by large established companies or institutions. I have included service workers because it seemed that their wages and relative job security made them similar to factory workers.

8. The first aspect is more important than it may appear. It is frequently said in San Lorenzo that one must *occupy* the house in order to keep someone else from taking it over when no one is home. While people do lock up and go out, they do not leave their house regularly unattended for long periods of time, even during the day. Although housing rights are more stable in San Lorenzo now than they were in the years right after the invasion, people still lack titles to the land. It should be taken as a serious economic consideration that households need to designate someone to stay around the house.

9. The unusually high wage for domestic service is related to the fact that this woman worked for foreigners. Experienced domestic workers claim that foreign (European and American) employers generally pay higher wages than Latin Americans for domestic work.

10. For a fuller treatment of politics in San Lorenzo, see Roberts (1968a; 1973:283-331).

11. The percentage of males reported to have voted at least once is 88%. Such figures must always be treated with some skepticism as an index of actual participation, since voting is obligatory for all men and it is likely that some report they have voted when they have not. Roberts reports that 75% of the San Lorenzo male heads of families voted in the presidential elections (1970:501). In contrast, illiterate women are not under legal compulsion to vote. Therefore, the figure for female participation is likely to be more reliable. Clearly, there is considerable abstention from voting since elections in the 1960s are reported to have had only 33% of the population of voting age participating (Amaro 1970:227).

12. MONAP (Movimiento Nacional de Pobladores) is a coalition of urban residents' and squatters' organizations that has affiliations with the Christian Democratic party. Roberts (1973) provides further information on its activities, which include maintaining office space and social workers for community betterment committees, and applying for grants for special projects from international fund-granting agencies, such as A.I.D.

13. Roberts (1968b) refers to this denomination as Pentecostal, which is considered a particular form of Evangelism. I have used the term Evangelists since that is the way these groups are popularly referred to in Guatemala and to maintain continuity with the discussion of similar religious groups in other parts of Guatemala.

14. Hermandad can be translated into English as sisterhood or brotherhood. Roberts called it a brotherhood even though the organization was and is dominated by women. This is one case in which the Spanish term is less sex-biased than any English translation, and for this reason I have chosen to simply keep the Spanish term.

15. See Roberts (1973:229) for additional description of Hermandad activities.

16. Roberts provides an example of local militancy when the women of the Hermandad adamantly opposed the substitution of a different priest for their own in a neighborhood ceremony. As the rival priest attempted to enter the colonia, he was met by the women, armed with sticks and stones, who pre-

vented his entry. Two of the leading women were briefly arrested for an alleged attack, but the charge was later dropped (1973:204). The context for this militancy, which Roberts does not mention, was that the radical priest was under attack from the conservative Church establishment. Failure to preceive or appreciate the political side of the Hermandad led Roberts to find an inconsistency in the alliance between a left-wing political group and the Hermandad: "It is interesting and ironic that it is precisely this group that became identified with the essentially conservative and religious activities of the Hermanidad" (1973:294).

17. This does not prevent her from opening the clubhouse to meetings of the Community Council, which is a rival to the Betterment Committee.

18. Significantly, neither of these women's clubs have made any provisions for daycare for women with small children. The meeting house of the club has a large poster saying: "This hall is only for señoras and señoritas, not children. Please leave your children at home because they are disruptive of the courses."

19. Only the club leaders in both groups claim that they can successfully sell the craft items for a small profit, usually when they are filling a specific order. For example, a set of knitted baby clothes requires Q. 2.90 for the wool and sells for Q. 6.00. One month or at least three weeeks are required to knit them, so that a woman only earns about Q. 1.00 per week. Baby booties are more profitable, but women only make them when they get orders, for there is little demand. The yarn costs 53 cents and they take one day to knit. Bus fare to sell them can be an added cost.

20. Irias and Alfaro (1977) provide a case study of the repression and special problems women have faced in recent attempts to unionize a U.S.-owned textile factory in Guatemala City.

21. This informant reports that market associations are also subject to repression. The association in her market, which includes many women, was banned by one administration and now, under another administration, is gradually reforming. The vendors have collaborated to construct a religious shrine in the market and have made collections to aid needy families with funeral and other expenses. They plan to expand into the defense of marketers against abusive administrators, and to improve market facilities. Some of the improvements sought are improved washrooms, a telephone, a health dispensary, a social aid center, a daycare center, and a library.

22. Studies of San Lorenzo, urban populations of Guatemala, and census surveys employ the concept "head of household" for their inquiries. As discussed elsewhere (Bossen 1976), this procedure has an inherent male bias that conceals important differences in the populations that are compared using this concept. The concept of "head of household" is often ambiguously defined, if defined at all, making it difficult for others to replicate the data. For instance, Roberts never explicitly defined the concept but states in his methodological discussion that second interviews were always conducted with "the head of the family" while the first interview "was occasionally conducted with the wife" (1973:42). Since his sample of heads of households includes women, we are led to conclude that women are defined as household heads only when they lack husbands. In the investigation of Orellana and de León, it was specified in their methodology that: "The person selected as informant must be the head of a family or its principle economic support. The head of family is also taken as the one who is considered as such even if constituting a secondary economic

support" (translated, 1972:4). These studies of Guatemalan urban households use the concept of household head ambiguously, so that it is not clear whether sex, marital status, principle economic contribution, or family recognition are the primary criteria. In terms of principle economic contribution, I estimate that female heads of household are around 18% of the population of San Lorenzo, while in terms of the absence of married males, I find they are 14%, and in terms of family recognition they are about 16%.

23. Roberts reports that "in the accounts of the founding of the shantytown, it is often the wife that takes the initiative in securing a space in the emergent neighborhood. In three of the 10 life histories, it is the woman who negotiated for space in the absence of the husband." (1973:111)

24. The cost of housing in San Lorenzo has clearly increased, but it is not possible to provide an average price. The highest price for a house that I recorded was Q. 1,000 for a house bought in 1973, while a significantly lower-quality house sold for Q. 300 in 1974.

25. Using different categories, Roberts (1973:488) reports that family status in his sample was: 77% nuclear families (husband, wife, child); 17% women and children; 6% single men or single women. His system does not take into account the existence of complex families. My system includes "female-headed" households in both the categories of reduced and complex families.

26. This figure is probably lower than reality. The genealogy of each child was not a prime concern in my interviews. These data were recorded when they emerged informally as part of the overall household data or life histories of my informants.

27. In a small sample of fifteen sexually active women of child-bearing age, nine use modern birth control techniques, three were pregnant or trying to become pregnant, and three were nonusers. The distribution of techniques was:

IUD	4
pills	2
sterilization	2
foam	1

The colonia has been heavily exposed to family planning propaganda by outside agencies so that even nonusers have recently become aware of available techniques.

28. Table 5-6 records some cases of regularly employed minors. Other minors pick up petty, casual income from time to time. In an increasingly formal, modern economy, it is not always easy for a child to find remunerative activities, while the city environment can easily be dangerous for children who work outside the home.

29. In order to maintain trust with people in the colonia, I did not pursue such statements for more specific information on identities of people who were breaking the law in order to interview them. A much longer period of fieldwork would be needed to obtain in mutual safety reliable information on the subject of prostitution and other illegal activities.

30. During this argument, I merely nodded and recorded the words which followed on their own steam. Partly their words were addressed to me as an "impartial outsider," and partly they resumed an ongoing dispute between themselves.

31. Roberts maintains that compadrazo relations are relatively weak in the city and do not serve as an enduring basis for interaction and assistance

(1973:173). My own data and informants' statements are consistent with Roberts' observation.

32. Roberts' data suggest that a possible exception to this may be found among people over fifty and among single mothers. Possibly old women have slightly greater contact with offspring than old men. Roberts notes that single mothers have less kin contact than either married women or men, but does not compare them to single men (who similarly lack affinal kin). For additional discussion of the span of kin relations in San Lorenzo and some quantification of the levels of contact with kin by sex, see Roberts (1973:161).

Chapter Six

1. The statistical data for much of this section is derived from the 1973 census. At the time of fieldwork, published census reports for colonias (as opposed to the larger urban zones) were not available. The Head of the Census kindly made available to me basic population statistics for the colonia, and permitted me to tabulate a 16% sample of the total colonia population for more detailed statistical information. This sample is discussed and labeled as the sample of 1973.

2. Chinchilla's data confirm this distribution within the category of "professionals" for Guatemala as a whole:

Indeed, the large proportion of "professional" women obscures their concentration in three sectors of employment—teaching, nursing, and social work—which require no university degrees and are poorly paid. Three out of every four professional women are actually teachers, the majority in public schools. If nonuniversity teaching were treated separately, professional work would clearly constitute a male sector of employment. (1977:54)

3. For a cross-cultural survey of women's participation in the medical, legal, engineering, and other professions in the Western nations of Europe and North America, see Sullerot (1971:151–167).

4. The data of Table 6–4 can be reduced to a form comparable to the results of an exploratory investigation of 90 families in 1972 in Guatemala City (Alonso 1973:15–36). Although the location of Alonso's sample within Guatemala City is unspecified, it is clear from their income levels that they belong to a "privileged minority even within the capital" (translation). The two samples are compared below:

Middle-Class Monthly Income of Each Sex in Guatemala City, and 1975

Income (Quetzales)	1975 Sample		1972 Sample	
	Women (%)	Men (%)	"Wives" (%)	"Husbands" (%)
Less than 50	11	0	10	2
50–150	44	24	47	23
150–300	41	32	37	50
More than 300	4	44	6	25
Total	100%	100%	100%	100%

Income	1975 Sample		1972 Sample	
	Women (%)	Men (%)	"Wives" (%)	"Husbands" (%)
(Quetzales)				
(Sample size)	(27)	(34)	(90)	(90)

Note: In both samples at least 75% of the men earn Q.150 or more per month, while at least 55% of the women earn Q. 150 or less.

5. Jelin observes that: "The fact that the work of the domestic servant is not part of the production and circulation process in capitalist economies means that no parameters can fix the demand for domestic servants. As students of housework . . . know, there is no end to housework. If there is no end to housework, the demand for paid domestic servants has to be extremely elastic, although the income of the employing household (and secondarily its size) is an important determinant of that demand . . . . The availability of domestic service *may* encourage women to keep or take full-time jobs, but it may also encourage them to conduct a life of leisure and comfort." (1977:139–140)

6. Jelin states that the availability of domestic servants "may mean a delay in the expansion of capitalistic personal-services enterprises, allowing alternative investment in more profitable and productive sectors" (1977:140). This may also explain why there has been relatively little pressure to convert to some forms of labor-saving technology such as washing machines.

7. In fact, room and board may not really be perceived as a "benefit" by the employee, who may prefer to live with her own family, but agrees to live in in order to obtain a job.

8. Curiously, the rapid diffusion of gender stereotypes can be seen in the admission of fashionably uniformed policewomen to work as traffic cops in Guatemala City after my period of fieldwork, and less than a decade after policewomen began to be seen in the United States.

If this represents cultural lag and women will eventually be recruited into the Guatemalan army as in the United States, it is consistent with the general view that the distribution of power in the developed countries has had and continues to have an important effect on the forms of sexual discrimination in the Third World.

9. It is difficult to establish reliable figures on the number of subsidiaries or affiliates of foreign corporations among the employers of the populations sampled in Villa Rosa. Rough estimates based on easily identifiable corporate names suggest that at least half of the large employer institutions for the samples of 1973 and 1975 are linked to foreign corporate interests. Difficulty in compiling more accurate figures stems from the fact that informants sometimes reported the name of the industry, rather than the corporation, or used acronyms that are difficult to identify.

10. At present, the use of office technology remains sexually neutral because of a clash between contradictory systems of gender discrimination. In Guatemala, men are first to acquire the higher education that is a prerequisite to most white-collar jobs. In highly developed Western capitalist societies where secondary education is more generalized, the use of office technology is treated as a low-skilled female domain. In Guatemala, then, the modern sector of clerical work is adjusting to both influences.

11. Other women in Villa Rosa indicate that older or less attractive women have difficulties in obtaining employment or promotions. Both Chinchilla (1977) for Guatemala and Arizpe (1977) for Mexico cite the importance of being attractive for women to gain access to formal employment.

Census statistics on labor force participation of women by age group were not available for Guatemala City. However, if the Mexican experience is comparable, Arizpe's observations are relevant. She finds that in Mexico City, younger women with "good appearance" have an advantage in obtaining formal employment. Regarding the important factors with respect to higher unemployment levels among women than men, she notes that:

Age is an important factor; expanded job opportunities in Mexico have gone to young women between the ages of fifteen and thirty. After thirty, the census indicates, women have more difficulty finding jobs than men. In such a situation, the notion that women should remain at home will tend to be reinforced, even by the women themselves. (Arizpe, 1977:37)

12. I lack figures on infant or child mortality in Villa Rosa, but in marked contrast to women in poorer districts, none of my interviewees mentioned the loss of children born to them, other than a woman whose son was assassinated. Informal questioning regarding birth control in a small sample of seventeen cases revealed that fifteen women are actively practicing birth control techniques while two others who had formerly used them were trying to become pregnant. Out of fifteen users, six women had undergone sterilization operations or hysterectomies after having three to six children.

References Cited

Adams, Richard N.
1956 Ladinizacion en Guatemala. *In* Integracion social en Guatemala. J.L. Arriola, ed. Pp. 213–244. Guatemala: Seminario de Integracion Social Guatemalteca, Publication No. 3.
1960 An Inquiry into the Nature of the Family. *In* Essays in the Science of Culture. Gertrude Dole and Robert Carneiro, eds. Pp. 30–49. New York: Crowell.
1970 Crucifixion by Power: Essays on Guatemalan National Social Structure, 1944–1966. Austin: University of Texas Press.

Alonso, Jose Antonio
1973 La mujer guatemalteca en 1973: de "inferioridad" a "explotacion." Estudios Sociales 10:15–37 (Guatemala).

Amaro, Nelson, ed.
1970 El reto de desarrollo en Guatemala. Guatemala: Instituto para el Desarrollo Economico y Social de América Central.

Anonymous
1973 Memoria de Labores (municipal report of T'oj Nam).

Anthony, Angela
1974 The Minority that is a Majority: Guatemala's Indians. *In* Guatemala. Pp. 28–38. Berkeley: North American Congress on Latin America.

Applebaum, Richard
1967 San Ildefonso Ixtahuacan, Guatemala: Un estudio sobre la migracion temporal, sus causas y consecuencias. Guatemala: Seminario de Integracion Social Guatemalteca, Publication No. 17.

Arizpe, Lourdes
1977 Women in the Informal Labor Sector: The Case of Mexico City. *In* Women and National Development. Wellesley Editorial Committee, eds. Special issue, Signs 3(1):25–38.

371

REFERENCES CITED

Bath, C. R. and D. D. James
1976 Dependency Analysis of Latin America. Latin American Research Review 11(3):3–54.

Bell, Diane
1981 Women's Business Is Hard Work. *In* Development and the Sexual Division of Labor. Helen Safa and Eleanor Leacock, eds. Special issue, Signs 7(2):314–338.

Bestor, Jane
1977 Domestic Politics among Women of an Elite Tribal Group: The Kurds of Iranian Baluchistan. Unpublished manuscript. Author's file.

Boserup, Ester
1970 Women's Role in Economic Development. London: George Allen and Unwin.

Bossen, Laurel Herbenar
1975 Women in Modernizing Societies. American Ethnologist 2(4):587–601.
1976 Household Work Patterns in an Urban Shantytown in Guatemala. Western Canadian Journal of Anthropology 6(3):270–276.
1980 Wives and Servants in Guatemala City. *In* Urban Life. George Gmelch and Walter Zenner, eds. Pp. 190–200. New York: St. Martins Press.
1982 Plantations and Labor Force Discrimination in Guatemala. Current Anthropology 23(3):263–268.

Brain, James
1976 Less than Second-Class: Women in Rural Settlement Schemes in Tanzania. *In* Women in Africa. Nancy Hafkin and Edna Bay, eds. Pp. 265–284. Stanford, CA: Stanford University Press.

Brintnall, Douglas
1979 Revolt against the Dead: the Modernization of a Mayan Community in the Highlands of Guatemala. New York: Gordon and Breach.

Brown, Andrea
1974 CONDECA: Integrating the Big Guns. *In* Guatemala. Suzanne Jonas and David Tobis, eds. Pp. 204–209. Berkeley: North American Congress on Latin America.

Bunzel, Ruth
1952 Chichicastenango. Seattle: University of Washington Press.

Butler, Judith
1981 The Wider War: Guatemala. North American Congress on Latin America 15(3):30–89.

Cambranes, Julio C.
1975 Desarrollo económico y social de Guatemala, a la luz de fuentes históricas alemanas, 1868–1885. Guatemala: Instituto de Investigaciones Económicas y Sociales, Universidad de San Carlos de Guatemala.

Cancian, Frank
1965 Economics and Prestige in a Maya Community. Stanford, CA: Stanford University Press.

1967   Politics and Religious Organizations. *In* Handbook of Middle American Indians, Vol. 6. Robert Wauchope and Manning Nash, eds. Pp. 283–298. Austin: University of Texas Press.
1972   Change and Uncertainty in a Peasant Economy. Stanford, CA: Stanford University Press.

Cardoso, Fernando y Enzo Faletto
1969   Dependencia y desarrollo en America Latina. Mexico City: Siglo Veintiuno.

Carmack, Robert
1972   Barrios y los Indigenas: El caso de Santiago Momostenango. Estudios Sociales 6:52–73 (Guatemala).
1973   Quichean Civilization: The Ethnohistoric, Ethnographic, and Archaeological Sources. Berkeley: University of California Press.
1976   Estratificacion y cambio social en las tierras altas occidentales de Guatemala: el caso de Tecpanaco. America Indigena 36(2):253–301 (Mexico).
1979   Historia social de los Quiches. Guatemala: Seminario de Integracion Social Guatemalteca, Ministerio de Educacion.
1981   The Quiche Mayas of Utatlan: The Evolution of a Highland Guatemala Kingdom. Norman: University of Oklahoma Press.

Cavalla Rojas, Antonio
1981   U.S. Military Strategy in Central America. Contemporary Marxism, No. 3:114–130.

CGS (Concerned Guatemala Scholars)
1981   Guatemala: Dare to Struggle, Dare to Win. Brooklyn.

Chaney, Elsa and Marianne Schmink
1976   Women and Modernization: Access to Tools. *In* Sex and Class in Latin America. June Nash and Helen Safa, eds. Pp. 160–182. New York: Praeger.

Chavarría de Ponce, Carmen Yolanda
1975   Disposiciones discriminatorias para la mujer en Guatemala en sus leyes y reglamentos. Unpublished paper presented at conference of Acción Solidaria de Mujeres, May 21–23, 1975, Guatemala.

Chiñas, Beverly
1973   The Isthmus Zapotecs: Women's Roles in Cultural Context. New York: Holt, Rinehart and Winston.

Chinchilla, Norma S.
1976   Industrialization, Monopoly Capitalism, and "Women's Work" in the United States and Guatemala. Paper presented at conference on "Women and Development," Wellesley College, Wellesley, MA.
1977   Industrialization, Monopoly Capitalism, and Women's Work in Guatemala. Signs 3(1):38–56.

Colby, Benjamin and Pierre van den Berghe
1969   Ixil Country: A Plural Society in Highland Guatemala. Berkeley and Los Angeles: University of California Press.

Collier, George
1975   Fields of the Tzotzil. Austin: University of Texas Press.

REFERENCES CITED

Cuevas, Marco Antonio
1965   Analisis de tres areas marginales de la Ciudad de Guatemala y su inci-
       dencia en una politica urbana nacional. *In* Problemas de la urbanizacion
       en Guatemala. Pp. 47–48. Guatemala: Seminario de Integracion Social
       Guatemalteca, Ministerio de Educacion.

Dauber, Roslyn, and Melinda Cain, eds.
1981   Women, Technology and the Development Process. American Associ-
       ation for the Advancement of Science Selected Symposium, no. 53. Boul-
       der, Colorado: Westview.

Davis, Shelton H.
1970   Land of Our Ancestors: A Study of Land Tenure and Inheritance in the
       Highlands of Guatemala. Ph.D. dissertation, Department of Anthropol-
       ogy, Harvard University.

Deckard, Barbara
1975   The Women's movement. New York: Harper and Row.

Deere, Carmen Diana, and Magdalena Leon de Leal
1981   Peasant Production, Proletarianization, and the Sexual Division of La-
       bor in the Andes. *In* Development and the Sexual Divison of Labor. Helen
       Safa and Eleanor Leacock, eds. Pp. 338–361. Special issue, Signs 7(2).

Dessaint, Alain Y.
1962   Effects of the Hacienda and Plantation Systems on Guatemala's Indi-
       ans. America Indigena 22(4):323–354 (Mexico).

Dixon, Ruth
1978   Rural Women at Work. Baltimore: John Hopkins University Press.

Dombrowski, John, et al.
1970   Area Handbook for Guatemala. Washington: Foreign Areas Studies of
       the American University.

Early, John
1983   A Demographic Survey of Contemporary Guatemalan Maya. Some
       Methodological Implications for Anthropological Research. *In* Heritage of
       Conquest: Thirty Years Later. Carl Kendall, John Hawkins, and Laurel H.
       Bossen, eds. Pp. 73–91. Albuquerque: University of New Mexico Press.

Ehlers, Tracy Bachrach
1980   La Sampedrana: Women and Development in a Guatemalan Town.
       Ph.D. dissertation, Department of Anthropology, University of Colorado.

Etienne, Mona and Eleanor Leacock, eds.
1980   Women and Colonization: Anthropological Perspectives. New York:
       Praeger.

Fletcher, Lehman, B., et al.
1970   Guatemala's Economic Development: The Role of Agriculture. Ames:
       Iowa State University Press.

Flores Alvarado, H.
1971   Proletarizacion del campesino de Guatemala. Quetzaltenango, Guate-
       mala: Editorial Rumbos Nuevos.

Foster, George
1967   Tzintzuntzan. Boston: Little, Brown.

Frank, Andre Gunder
1967   Capitalism and Underdevelopment in Latin America. New York: Monthly Review Press.
1972   Lumpen Bourgeoisie, Lumpendevelopment. New York: Monthly Review Press.
1977   On So-Called Primitive Accumulation. Dialectical Anthropology 2: 87–105.

Gillen, John
1951   The Culture of Security in San Carlos. Middle American Research Institute Publication 16. New Orleans: Tulane University.

Ginsberg, Eli
1977   The Job Problem. Scientific American 237(5):43–51.

GNIB (Guatemala News and Information Bureau)
1975   Guatemala 3(2). Berkeley, CA.

Gonzalez, Lionel
1970   Descripción y diagnósticos de la economía de Guatemala. In El reto de desarrollo en Guatemala. Nelson Amaro, ed. Pp. 83–130. Guatemala: Instituto para el Desarrollo Economico y Social de America Central.

Goodale, Jane
1971   Tiwi Wives: A Study of the Women of Melville Island, North Austrialia. Seattle: University of Washington Press.

Gossen, Gary
1974   Chamulas in the World of the Sun. Cambridge, MA: Harvard University Press.

Grieb, Kenneth
1979   Guatemalan Caudillo: The Regime of Jorge Ubico. Athens: Ohio University Press.

Guatemala. Dirección General de Estadística.
1970   Anuario Estadístico. Guatemala.
1974a   Anuario Estadístico. Guatemala.
1974b   Informador Estadístico, no. 40–51. Guatemala.
1974c   Boletin Informativo, Sept. 30. Guatemala.
1975   Anuario Estadístico. Guatemala.
1976   Anuario Estadístico. Guatemala.
1977   Algunas cifras acerca de Guatemala. Guatemala.
1979   Informador Estadístico, no. 7. Guatemala.

Guatemala. Ministerio de Trabajo y Previsión Social
1969   Población Total y Vivienda de Las Colonias Marginales de La Ciudad de Guatemala, Censo Abril de 1964: Cifras Preliminares, Departamento de Estadísticas del Trabajo.

Guzman Bockler, Carlos, Julio Quan, and Jean-Loup Herbert

1971 Las clases sociales y la lucha de clases en Guatemala. Alero (Suplemento), March. Pp. 7–12. Guatemala: Universidad de San Carlos de Guatemala.

Harding, Susan
1975 Women and Words in a Spanish Village. *In* Toward an Anthropology of Women. Rayna Rapp Reiter, ed. Pp. 282–308. New York: Monthly Review Press.

Hart, C. W., and A. R. Pilling
1968 Tiwi Marriage. *In* Economic Anthropology. Edward LeClair and Harold K. Schneider, eds. Pp. 354–373. New York: Holt, Rinehart and Winston.

Herbert, Jean-Loup
1970 Las clases sociales en Guatemala. *In* Guatemala: una interpretacion historico-social. Carlos Guzman Bockler and Jean-Loup Herbert. Pp. 94–100. Mexico City: Siglo Veintiuno.

Hinshaw, Robert
1975 Panajachel: A Guatemala Town in Thirty-Year Perspective. Pittsburgh: University of Pittsburgh Press.

Hoyt, Elizabeth
1955 The Indian Laborer on Guatemalan Coffee Fincas. Inter-American Economic Affairs 9:33–46.

Hunt, Eva, and June Nash
1967 Local and Territorial Units. *In* Handbook of Middle American Indians, Vol. 6. Robert Wauchope and Manning Nash, eds. Pp. 253–282. Austin: University of Texas Press.

IDB (Inter-American Development Bank)
1981 Economic and Social Progress in Latin America. Washington, D.C.

ILO (International Labor Organization): Office for Women
1981 Women, Technology and the Development Process. *In* Women and Technological Change in Developing Countries. Roslyn Dauber and Melinda Cain, eds. American Association for the Advancement of Science Selected Symposium, no. 53. Boulder, Colorado: Westview.

INVI (Instituto Nacional de Vivienda)
1968 Censo de la Limonada. Guatemala.

Irías de Rivera, M. A. and I. V. Alfaro de Carpio
1977 Guatemalan Working Women in the Labor Movement. Latin American Perspectives 4(1&2):194–202.

Jacobs, Sue Ellen
1982 Women in Development. American Anthropologist 84(2):366–371.

Jelin, Elizabeth
1977 Migration and Labor Force Participation of Latin American Women: The Domestic Servants in the Cities. Signs 3(1):129–141.

Jonas, Suzanne and David Tobis, eds.
1974 Guatemala. Berkeley: North American Congress on Latin America.

Kendall, Carl, John Hawkins, and Laurel Bossen, eds.
1983 Heritage of Conquest: Thirty Years Later. Albuquerque, NM: University of New Mexico Press.

Kuhn, Annette, and AnnMarie Wolpe, eds.
1978 Feminism and Materialism: Women and Modes of Production. Boston: Routledge and Kegan Paul.

Lamphere, Louise
1974 Strategies, Cooperation, and Conflict Among Women in Domestic Groups. *In* Woman, Culture and Society. Michele Rosaldo and Louise Lamphere, eds. Pp. 97–112. Stanford, CA: Stanford University Press.

Latin American Perspectives
1974 Dependency Theory: A Reassessment. 1(1).
1976 Dependency Theory and Dimensions of Imperialism. 3(4).
1977 Views on Dependency. 6(2).
1979 Women in Latin America: An Anthology.
1981 Dependency and Marxism 8(3&4).

Leacock, Eleanor
1977a Women, Development, and Anthropological Facts and Fictions. Latin American Perspectives 4(1&2):8–17.
1977b Reflections: IV. Signs 3(1):320–322.
1981 History, Development, and the Division of Labor by Sex: Implications for Organization. *In* Development and the Sexual Division of Labor. Helen Safa and Eleanor Leacock, eds. Special issue, Signs 7(2):474–491.

Lima, Eunice
1975 La participación de la mujer en la vida civica y política. Unpublished paper presented at conference of Acción Solidaria de Mujeres, May 21–23, 1975, Guatemala.

Loucky, James, and Margo-Lea Hurwicz, eds.
1981 Maya Studies: The Midwestern Highlands of Guatemala. Los Angeles: Department of Anthropology, University of California at Los Angeles.

Lutz, Christopher
1976 Santiago de Guatemala, 1541–1773. Ph.D. dissertation, Department of History, University of Wisconsin Madison.

MacLeod, Murdo
1973 Spanish Central America: A Socioeconomic History, 1520–1720. Berkeley and Los Angeles: University of California Press.

Mangin, William
1970 Similarities and Differences between Two Types of Peruvian Communities. *In* Peasants in Cities. William Mangin, ed. Pp. 20–30. Boston: Houghton Mifflin.

Manz, Beatrice
1977 Santa Cruz del Quiche: A Highland Community and its Relation to Guatemala. Ph.D. dissertation, Department of Anthropology, State University of New York at Buffalo.

1981 Refugees: Guatemalan Troops Clear Peten for Oil Exploration. Cultural Survival Newsletter 5(3):15–17.

Martínez Peláez, Severo
1973 La patria del criollo. San Jose, Costa Rica: Editorial Universitaria Centroamericana.

Maynard, Eileen
1963 The Women of Palin: A Comparative Study of Indian and Ladino Women in a Guatemalan Vilage. Ph.D. dissertation, Anthropology Department, Cornell University.
1974 Guatemalan Women: Life under Two Types of Patriarchy. In Many Sisters. Carolyn Matthiasson, ed. Pp. 77–98. New York: The Free Press.

Melville, Thomas, and Marjorie Melville
1971 Guatemala: The Politics of Land Ownership. New York: The Free Press.

Miles, Susan
1955 Unpublished notes from T'oj Nam. Personal files of Joy Hairs, Guatemala City.

Monteforte Toledo, Mario
1959 Guatemala: monografia sociologica. Mexico City: Instituto de Investigaciones Sociales, Universidad Nacional Autonoma de Mexico.
1972 Centro America: subdesarrollo y dependencia. 2 vols. Mexico City: Universidad Nacional Autonoma de Mexico.

Moore, Alexander
1973 Life Cycles in Atchalan: The Diverse Careers of Certain Guatemalans. New York: Teachers College, Columbia University.

Morrissey, James
1978 A Missionary Directed Resettlement Project Among the Highland Maya of Western Guatemala. Ph.D. dissertation, Department of Anthropology, Stanford University.

Nash, June
1976 A Critique of Social Science Roles in Latin America. In Sex and Class in Latin America. June Nash and Helen Safa, eds. New York: Praeger.
1981a Book reviews. Signs 7(2):492–498.
1981b Ethnographic Aspects of the World Capitalist System. In Annual Review of Anthropology. Vol. 10: 393–424.

Nash, June and Helen Safa, eds.
1976 Sex and Class in Latin America. New York: Praeger.

Nash, Manning
1967 Machine Age Maya. Chicago: University of Chicago Press.

Nelson, Nici
1980 How Women and Men Get By: The Sexual Division of Labor in the Informal Sector of a Nairobi Squatter Settlement. In Casual Work and Poverty in the Third World. Ray Bromley and Chris Gerry, eds. New York: Wiley.

1981   Why Has Development Neglected Rural Women? Toronto: Pergamon Press.

Oakes, Maude
1951a   The Two Crosses of Todos Santos. Princeton: Princeton University Press.
1951b   Beyond the Windy Place. New York: Farrar, Straus and Young.

O'Neale, Lila M.
1965   Tejidos de los altiplanos de Guatemala. Guatemala: Seminario de Integracion Social Guatemalteca, Ministerio de Educacion.

Orellana, René, and Adolfo de León
1972   Ingresos y gastos de familias urbanas de Guatemala. Guatemala: Instituto de Investigaciones Economicas y Sociales, Universidad de San Carlos de Guatemala.

Pansini, Jude
1977   "El Pilar": A Plantation Microcosm of Guatemalan Ethnicity. Ph.D. dissertation, Department of Anthropology, University of Rochester.
1980   Plantation Health-Care in Guatemala: Aspects of the Problem. A Study prepared for the U.S. Agency for International Development Mission in Guatemala by the Patronato Para el Mejoramiento de la Salud de Trabajadores Agricolas (AGROSALUD) under contract No. AID 520–470.
1981   Lake Atitlan: The Seasonal Farm Problem. Anthropology Resource Center Newsletter 5(2):5.

Papanek, Hanna
1977   Development Planning for Women. In Women and National Development. Wellesley Editorial Committee, eds. Pp. 14–21. Special issue, Signs.

Paul, Benjamin, and Lois Paul
1975   The Maya Midwife as Sacred Specialist: A Guatemalan Case. American Ethnologist 2(4):707–726.

Paul, Lois
1974   The Mastery of Work and the Mystery of Sex in a Guatemalan Village. In Woman, Culture, and Society. Michele Rosaldo and Louise Lamphere, eds. Pp. 281–300. Stanford, CA: Stanford University Press.

Peckenham, Nancy
1980   Land Settlement in the Peten. Latin American Perspectives 7(2&3):169–177.

Petras, James and Morris Morley
1981   Economic Expansion, Political Crisis and U.S. policy in Central America. Contemporary Marxism 3:69–88.

Piedra-Santa Arandi, Rafael
1971   Introducción a los problemas economicos de Guatemala. Guatemala: Editorial Universitaria.

REFERENCES CITED

Quintana Diaz, Victor
1973   Inversiones extranjeras en Guatemala. Guatemala: Instituto de Investigaciones Economicas y Sociales, Universidad de San Carlos de Guatemala.

Reina, Ruben
1966   The Law of the Saints: A Pokomam Corporate Community and Its Culture. Indianapolis: Bobbs-Merrill.

Reiter, Rayna Rapp
1975   Men and Women in the South of France: Public and Private Domains. *In* Toward an Anthropology of Women. Rayna R. Reiter, ed. Pp. 252–282. New York: Monthly Review Press.

Remy, Dorothy
1975   Underdevelopment and the Experience of Women. *In* Toward an Anthropology of Women. Rayna R. Reiter, ed. Pp. 358–271. New York: Monthly Review Press.

Richards, Michael
1981   Seasonal Labor Migration and Physiological Risk in Guatemala. Paper presented at the American Anthropology Association annual meeting, Los Angeles.

Roberts, Bryan
1968a   Politics in a Neighborhood of Guatemala City. Sociology 2(2):185–203.
1968b   Protestant Groups and Coping with Urban Life in Guatemala City. American Journal of Sociology 73(6):753–767.
1970   The Social Organization of Low-Income Urban Families. *In* Crucifixion by Power. Richard Adams, ed. Pp. 479–514. Austin: University of Texas Press.
1973   Organizing Strangers: Poor Families in Guatemala City. Austin: University of Texas Press.

Rogers, Barbara
1981   The Domestication of Women: Discrimination in Developing Societies. New York: Tavistock Publications.

Rogers, Susan Co.
1975   Female Forms of Power and the Myth of Male Dominance: A Model of Female/Male Interaction in Peasant Society. American Ethnologist 2(4):727–756.

Rojas, E. R., and Rolando Marroquin
1970   La vivienda marginal en la capital. *In* El reto de desarrollo en Guatemala. Nelson Amaro, ed. Pp. 351–368. Guatemala: Instituto para el Desarrollo Económico y Social de América Central.

Rosaldo, Michele
1974   Woman, Culture, and Society: A Theoretical Overview. *In* Woman, Culture and Society. Michele Rosaldo and Louise Lamphere, eds. Pp. 17–42. Stanford, CA: Stanford University Press.

Rotenberg, Lori
1974   The Wayward Worker: Toronto's Prostitutes at the Turn of the Century. In Women at Work: Ontario, 1850–1930. Janice Acton et al., eds. Pp. 33–70. Toronto: The Women's Press.

Rothstein, Fran
1979   Men and Women in the Family Economy: An Analysis of the Relations between the Sexes in Three Peasant Communities. Paper presented at the American Anthropological Association annual meeting, Cincinnati.

Roys, Ralph
1972   The Indian Background of Colonial Yucatan. Norman: University of Oklahoma Press.

Safa, Helen
1976   Class Consciousness among Working-Class Women in Latin America: Puerto Rico. In Sex and Class in Latin America. June Nash and Helen Safa, eds. Pp. 69–85. New York: Praeger.
1977   The Changing Class Composition of the Female Labor Force in Latin America. Latin American Perspectives 4(4):126–136.

Safa, Helen and Eleanor Leacock, eds.
1981   Development and the Sexual Division of Labor. Special issue, Signs 7(2).

Sahlins, Marshall
1972   Stone Age Economics. Chicago: Aldine.

Samayoa Guevara, H. H.
1962   Los gremios de artesanos en la Ciudad de Guatemala, 1524–1821. Guatemala: Editorial Universitaria.

Schlegel, Alice, ed.
1977   Sexual Stratification. New York: Columbia University Press.

Schlesinger, Stephen, and Stephen Kinzer
1982   Bitter Fruit: The Untold Story of the American Coup in Guatemala. Garden City, New York: Doubleday.

Schmid, Lester
1973   El papel de la mano de obra migratoria en el desarrollo economico de Guatemala. Guatemala: Instituto de Investigaciones Economicas y Sociales, Universidad de San Carlos de Guatemala.

Schmink, Marianne
1977   Dependent Development and the Division of Labor by Sex: Venezuela. In Women and Class Struggle. Special issue, Latin American Perspectives. 4(1&2):153–179.

Schwartz, Norman
1977   A Milpero of Peten, Guatemala: Autobiography and Cultural Analysis. Newark, Delaware: University of Delaware.

Sexton, James, ed.
1981   Son of Tecun Umam: A Maya Indian Tells His Life Story. Tucson: University of Arizona Press.

REFERENCES CITED

Sharckman, Howard
1974 The Vietnamization of Guatemala: U.S. Counter Insurgency Programs. *In* Guatemala. Suzanne Jonas and David Tobis, eds. Pp. 193–203. Berkeley: North American Congress on Latin America.

Sherman, William
1979 Forced Native Labor in Sixteenth-Century Central America. Lincoln: University of Nebraska Press.

SIECA (Secretariat Permanente del Tratado General de Integracion Economica Centroamericana)
1975 Compendio Estadistico Centroamericano. Guatemala City: SIECA.

Simons, Marlise
1982 For 500,000 Guatemalans, the War Comes Home. *New York Times,* Oct. 6.

Smith, Carol
1975 Examining Stratification Systems through Peasant Marketing Arrangements: An Application of Some Models from Economic Geography. Man: 95–122.
1976 Production in Western Guatemala. *In* Formal Methods in Economic Anthropology. Stuart Plattner, ed. American Association for the Advancement of Science, No. 4.
1978 Beyond Dependency Theory: National and Regional Patterns of Underdevelopment in Guatemala. American Ethnologist 5(3):574–617.
1981 Does a Commodity Economy Enrich the Few While Ruining the Masses? Unpublished ms., Author's files.
1982 Local Response to Global Process: Social and Economic Transitions in Western Guatemala. Paper presented at the American Anthropological Association annual meeting, Los Angeles.

Smith, Waldemar
1977 The Fiesta System and Economic Change. New York: Columbia University Press.

Stadelman, Raymond
1940 Maize Cultivation in Northwestern Guatemala. Carnegie Institution of Washington, Contributions of American Anthropology and History 6(33):83–265. Washington, D.C.

Stavenhagen, Rodolfo
1975 Social Classes in Agrarian Societies. Garden City, New York: Anchor.

Stoler, Ann
1977 Class Structure and Female Autonomy in Rural Java. *In* Women and National Development. Wellesley Editorial Committee, eds. Pp. 74–89. Special issue, Signs.

Sullerot, Evelyne
1971 Woman, Society, and Change. Toronto: McGraw-Hill.

Tax, Sol
1937 The Municipios of the Midwestern Highlands of Guatemala. American Anthropologist 43:27–42.

1953   Penny Capitalism: A Guatemalan Indian Economy. Smithsonian Institution, Institute for Social Anthropology, Publication 16. Washington, D.C.

Tax, Sol, ed.
1952   Heritage of Conquest: The Ethnology of Middle America. Glencoe, Ill.: The Free Press.

Tedlock, Barbara
1982   Time and the Highland Maya. Albuquerque: University of New Mexico Press.

Tobis, David
1974   The U.S. Investment Bubble in Guatemala. *In* Guatemala. Pp. 132–142. Berkeley: North American Congress on Latin America.

Torres-Rivas, Edelberto
1980a   Guatemala: Crisis and Political Violence. NACLA 14(1):16–27.
1980b   The Central American Model of Growth: Crisis for Whom? Latin American Perspectives 7(2&3):49–61.
1981   Seven Keys to Understanding the Central American Crisis. Contemporary Marxism 3:49–61.

Tumin, Melvin
1952   Caste in a Peasant Society. Princeton, NJ: Princeton University Press.

UG (Update on Guatemala)
1982   Weekly newsletter of the Committee in Solidarity with the People of Guatemala, Brooklyn, New York.

Vogt, Evon
1970   The Zinacantecos of Mexico. New York: Holt, Rinehart and Winston.

Wagley, Charles
1941   Economics of a Guatemalan Village. American Anthropological Association Memoir, No. 58.
1949   The Social and Religious Life of a Guatemalan Village. American Anthropological Association Memoir, No. 71.
1969   The Maya of Northwestern Guatemala. *In* The Handbook of Middle American Indians. Vol. 7. Evon Vogt, ed. Austin: University of Texas Press.

Warren, Kay
1978   The Symbolism of Subordination: Indian Identity in a Guatemalan Town. Austin: University of Texas Press.

Wasserstrom, Robert
1975   Revolution in Guatemala: Peasants and Politics under the Arbenz Government. Comparative Studies in Society and History 17(4):443–478.

Wellesley Editorial Committee, eds.
1977   Women and National Development. Special issue, Signs.

Whetten, Nathan L.
1961   Guatemala: The Land and the People. New Haven: Yale University Press.

REFERENCES CITED

Wilkie James and Stephen Haber, eds.
1981 Statistical Abstract of Latin America. Vol. 21. Los Angeles: University of California.

Winter, N. O.
1909 Guatemala and her People of Today. Boston: Page.

Wellesley Editorial Committee, eds.
1977 Women and National Development. Special issue, Signs.

Wolf, Eric
1957 Closed Corporate Peasant Communities in Mesoamerica and Central Java. Southwest Journal of Anthropology 13(1).
1959 Sons of the Shaking Earth. Chicago: University of Chicago Press.
1966 Peasants. Englewood Cliffs, New Jersey: Prentice-Hall.

Wolf, Eric and Sidney Mintz
1957 Haciendas and Plantations in Middle America and the Antilles. Social and Economic Studies 6:380–412.

Young, Kate
1978 Modes of Appropriation and the Sexual Division of Labour: A Case Study from Oaxaca, Mexico. In Feminism and Materialism. Annette Kuhn and AnnMarie Wolpe, eds. Boston: Routledge and Kegan Paul.

Index

Administration. *See* Management
Adultery, in Criminal Code, 290
Affluence, in Villa Rosa, 246–248, 293, 299; and housework, 255
Agrarian capitalism, historical development of, 330
Agricultural labor force: Maya, 26–28; permanent, 30–31, 33; seasonal, 28–29; statistics, 31–32; women, 31–32. *See also* Migrants; Peasants; Rancheros
Agricultural work, definitional problems, 350
Agriculture, national: importance of exports, 26, 29–30; systems of production, 25–26; regional differences in, 23. *See also* Commercial agriculture; Crops; Landholding; Subsistence economy
Agriculture of El Cañaveral, 133–134
Agriculture of T'oj Nam: commercial, 72–76; corn yields, 72, on rented land, 73, 76, 357–358; subsistence, 59–60, 63; supplemented by plantation labor, 66–70. *See also* Subsistence economy; T'oj Nam
A.I.D. (Agency for International Development), 101, 365
Alcalde, 54, 171
Alcalde auxiliar, 171
Alcalde rezador, 98
Alcoholism: and domestic problems, 152–157, 212; and Evangelical prohibitions, 175, 184, 224–225; and male economic support, 234–236; and

male peer groups, 154–155; and T'oj Nam fiestas, 127–128; and violence, 127, 152–155, 157
Aldea, 53, 112
Almorzero, 145
Amiga de confianza, 181, 191
Amnesty International, 337–338
Arbenz, Jacobo, 334
Armed forces. *See* Military service
Ayudante, 148

Barrio de los empleados, 133
Barrio marginal, 205. See also Squatter settlements
Barrios, Justo Rufino, 331
Beauty queens, 363
Beneficio, coffee, 134, 210
Betterment Committee: meeting of, 220–221; and neighborhood factions, 230; women's participation in, 220
Birth control: abortion, 165, 362; company policy of, 165–166; El Cañaveral, 132, 164–166; San Lorenzo, 231, 235, 367; T'oj Nam, 124, 360; Villa Rosa, 291–292, 294, 370; and sex prohibitions, 300. *See also* Reproduction
Bourgeoisie, 42–44, 354. *See also* Class structure; Villa Rosa
Boy Scouts, 135, 179–180
Bride price: connotations of, 359; examples of, 115–124; inflation in, 115–116; and Mam marriage legitimacy, 117; refundability and marital separation, 117–118. *See also*

Factory work, 192–196, 198–202; attitudes toward, 213, 273; in El Cañaveral, 149–150; in San Lorenzo, 205, 207–208

Family: extended, 87–90; nuclear, 90–91, 160, 233, 288; religious support for, 174–176. *See also* Childcare; Child support; Fathers; Household structure; Marriage; Mothers

Farm size. *See* Landholdings

Fathers: and career continuity, 290; and jobs for sons, 62, 169–170; status of, and machismo, 46, 316–317. *See also* Child support, male; Household budgets; Legitimacy

Female-headed households. *See* Mothers, single

Feminism, 47, 283

Fieldwork, described by community, 339–347

Fiesta: organizations of, in T'oj Nam 110; Queen of, in El Cañaveral, 363

Finca, 97, 361

Food budgets: Ladino, 80; Mam, 65, 348

Food preparation, commercial: in El Cañaveral, 138, 140–141; in San Lorenzo, 192, 197; in T'oj Nam, 71, 78; in Villa Rosa, 273

Food preparation, household: in El Cañaveral, 163; in San Lorenzo, 203; in T'oj Nam, 62–64; in Villa Rosa, 258, 260

Forced labor, under colonialism, 28, 322–326

Forced resettlement of Mayas, 332

Foregin investment, 329, 332, 369

Formal employment: compared by community, 302–304, 306–311 *passim;* defined, 16–17; in El Cañaveral, 139, 151; in San Lorenzo, 192, 205; in T'oj Nam, 129–130; in Villa Rosa, 260–267, 279, 298

Formal social organization: in El Cañaveral, 168–180 *passim;* in San Lorenzo, 218–232 *passim;* in T'oj Nam, 98–112 *passim,* 132; in Villa Rosa, 280–288 *passim. See also* Education; Politics; Religion

Galeras, 134, 145

Gastos, 90, 97

Government: employment by, 72, 79, 84–85, 261, 264; as male domain, 219, 223; and squatter housing, 212,

218. *See also* Military service; Teaching profession

Government repression. *See* Political conditions; Violence, political

GDP (Gross Domestic Product), 35

Guatemala City: domestic employment in, 39; growth rate of, 33–34; industry in, 35; labor force of, 35–41; migration to, 204; populaton of, 33–34, squatter settlements in, 188; surplus of women, 204; and urban working class, 205, 217–218, 225; and Villa Rosa, 246–247, 268, 280–281. *See also* San Lorenzo; Villa Rosa

Guerilla movements, 171, 335, 338

Guerilla Army of the Poor, 337–338

Heads, of households. *See* Household heads

Health care: as company benefit, 136, 141, 151, 165; professions, 102, 104, 146–147, 249–251, 286, 362

Health conditions, 69–70, 92–96, 145–146, 189, 299, 357

Hermandad: El Cañaveral, 173; San Lorenzo, 226–227, 365

Hijo/hija de casa, 119, 215

Hijos de rancheros, 169–170

History: conquest and colonial period, 321–327; independence, 328–334; reform period, 334–335; since 1954 coup, 335–338

House, protection of: in San Lorenzo, 209–210, 221, 242–243; in T'oj Nam, 70; in Villa Rosa, 246, 345

Household budgets: in El Cañaveral, 143; in San Lorenzo, 208–210, 212–217; in T'oj Nam, 65–66, 87–98 *passim;* in Villa Rosa, 255–257

Household economy of T'oj Nam: economic strategies, 85–86; traditional rural households, 86–94; transitional urban households, 94–98

Household heads: and male bias in data, 8, 10, 41, 196, 364, 366; as members of aldea committee, 100. *See also* Mothers, single

Household structure, 112–114, 160–161, 188, 232–234, 288–289. *See also* Marriage

Households, as units in class structure, 43

Housework: ambiguity of concept, 137, 139, 191, 364; distribution of, 191, 203–204, 254–260; in empleado housesholds, 145; individualized,

Related Titles from SUNY Press

FOR WE ARE SOLD, I AND MY PEOPLE: Women and Industry in Mexico's Frontier. María Patricia Fernández-Kelly.

WOMEN, MEN, AND THE INTERNATIONAL DIVISION OF LABOR. June Nash and María Patricia Fernández-Kelly, editors.

WORK IN NON-MARKET AND TRANSITIONAL SOCIETIES. Herbert Applebaum.

WORK AND LIFECOURSE IN JAPAN. David W. Plath, editor.

CLASSIFICATION IN SOCIAL RESEARCH. Ramakrishna Mukherjee.

METHODOLOGY FOR THE HUMAN SCIENCES: Systems of Inquiry. Donald Polkinghorne.

UNDERSTANDING HUMAN ACTION: Social Explanation of the Vision of Social Science. Michael A. Simon.

WOMEN'S EDUCATION IN THE THIRD WORLD: Comparative Perspectives. Gail P. Kelly and Carolyn M. Elliot, editors.